Memorial (Yizkor) Book for
The Jewish Community of Ciechanow

Translation of
Yisker-bukh fun der Tshekhanover yidisher kehile
Edited by: A.Wolf Yassini

**This translation is dedicated to the blessed memory of
Mordko (Marcos) Hersz Myssior and Lonya (Lea) Szrenskier**

Published Originally in Hebrew and Yiddish in Tel Aviv, 1962

By the Former Residents of Ciechanow in Israel and in the Diaspora

Published by JewishGen

**An Affiliate of the Museum of Jewish Heritage
A Living Memorial to the Holocaust
New York**

Memorial Book for Ciechanow, Poland

Memorial (Yizkor) Book for the Jewish Community of Ciechanow
Translation of *Yisker-bukh fun der Tshekhanover yidisher kehile*

Copyright © 2013 by Samy Katz
All rights reserved.
First Printing: July 2013, Av 5773
Second Printing: August 2019, Av 5779

Project Coordinator: Stan Zeidenberg
Translated by Miriam Dashkin Beckerman
Layout Editors: Janice Sellers and Joel Alpert
Image Scanning by Joe Canter
Image Editor: Errol Ford Genet and Jan R. Fine
Cover Design: Jan R. Fine
Publicity: Sandra Hirschhorn
Indexing: Bena Shklyanoy

Published by JewishGen, Inc.
An Affiliate of the Museum of Jewish Heritage
A Living Memorial to the Holocaust
36 Battery Place, New York, NY 10280

Printed in the United States of America by Lightning Source, Inc.

Library of Congress Control Number (LCCN): 2013909832
ISBN: 978-1-939561-09-1 (hard cover: 514 pages, alk. paper)

JewishGen and the Yizkor Books in Print Project

This book has been published by the **Yizkor Books in Print Project,** as part of the **Yizkor Book Project** of **JewishGen, Inc.**

JewishGen, Inc. is a non-profit organization founded in 1987 as a resource for Jewish genealogy. Its website [www.jewishgen.org] serves as an international clearinghouse and resource center to assist individuals who are researching the history of their Jewish families and the places where they lived. JewishGen provides databases, facilitates discussion groups, and coordinates projects relating to Jewish genealogy and the history of the Jewish people. In 2003, JewishGen became an affiliate of the **Museum of Jewish Heritage - A Living Memorial to the Holocaust** in New York.

The **JewishGen Yizkor Book Project** was organized to make more widely known the existence of Yizkor (Memorial) Books written by survivors and former residents of various Jewish communities throughout the world. Later, volunteers connected to the different destroyed communities began cooperating to have these books translated from the original language— usually Hebrew or Yiddish—into English, thus enabling a wider audience to have access to the valuable information contained within them. As each chapter of these books was translated, it was posted on the JewishGen website and made available to the general public.

The **Yizkor Books in Print Project** began in 2011 as an initiative to print and publish Yizkor Books that had been fully translated, so that hard copies would be available for purchase by the descendants of these communities and also by scholars, universities, synagogues, libraries, and museums.

These Yizkor books have been produced almost entirely through the volunteer effort of researchers from around the world, assisted by donations from private individuals. The books are printed and sold at near cost, so as to make them as affordable as possible. Our goal is to make this important genre of Jewish literature and history available in English in book form, so that people can have the personal histories of their ancestral towns on their bookshelves for themselves and for their children and grandchildren.

A list of all published translated Yizkor Books can be found at:
http://www.jewishgen.org/Yizkor/ybip.html

Lance Ackerfeld, Yizkor Book Project Manager

Joel Alpert, Yizkor Book in Print Project Coordinator

JewishGen
Yizkor Book Project

This book is presented by the
Yizkor Books in Print Project
Project Coordinator: Joel Alpert

Part of the
Yizkor Books Project of JewishGen, Inc.
Project Manager: Lance Ackerfeld

These books have been produced solely through volunteer effort
of individuals from around the world. The books are printed and
sold at near cost, so as to make them as affordable as possible.

Our goal is to make this history and important genre of Jewish
literature available in English in book form so that people can have
the near-personal histories of their ancestral towns on their bookshelves for themselves and for their children and grandchildren.

Any donations to the Yizkor Books Project are appreciated.

Please send donations to:
Yizkor Book Project
JewishGen
36 Battery Place
New York, NY 10280

JewishGen, Inc. is an affiliate of the
Museum of Jewish Heritage
A Living Memorial to the Holocaust

Yiddish Title Page of Original Yiddish and Hebrew Yizkor Book

יזכור-בוך

פון דער טשעכאנאווער יידישער קהילה

ספר-יזכור לקהילת צ'חנוב

רעדאקטאר:

א. וואלף יאסני

רעדאקציע ראט:

זאלה אפעל, יעקב ברונרוט, יהושע גראסבארט, ריבה גונסקי, נח זאבלודאוויטש, משה
פוקס, משה קולקא, יעקב רובינשטיין; חברים פון אויסלאנד — בנימין אפעל, משה
לעסער (דעטראיט), יוסף מאנדזשאק (פאריז).

אַרויסגעגעבן פון

ארגון יוצאי צ'חנוב בישראל און די לאנדסמאנשאפטן אין חוץ-לארץ.

תל-אביב, תשרי תשכ"ג, 1962

Translation of the Title Page of Original Yiddish Book

MEMORIAL BOOK

OF THE CIECHANOW JEWISH COMMUNITY

Editor:
A.Wolf Yasni

Editorial Committee:
Zola Apel, Yaacov Bronrot, Yehoshua Grossbard,
Riva Gonska, Noach Zabludowicz, Moishe Fuchs,
Moishe Kolka, Yaacov Rubinstein:
Chaverim from abroad - Binyamin Apel,
Moishe Leser (Detroit), Yosef Mundzak (Paris)

Published by:
Association of Ciechanow and the
Landsmanschaften abroad:
Tel-Aviv 1962
(Arzi Printers, Ayelet Hashachar 4, Tel-Aviv 34294)

Dedication

**This translation is dedicated to the blessed memory of
Mordko (Marcos) Hersz Myssior and Lonya (Lea) Szrenskier**

Acknowledgements

The publication of this memorial book started with Stan Zeidenberg, who undertook to coordinate the translation project within the Yizkor Book Project of JewishGen. Without this beginning, this publication would never have happened.

We wish to acknowledge the translation provided by Miriam Beckerman, who provided a high caliber and sensitive translation, taking into account the subtleties of the Yiddish language.

We would also like to acknowledge the contribution made by Diana Mingail, who provided the word processing of Miriam's work. Diana remarked how deeply she was moved as she worked through the material. We expect that the reader of this translation will be similarly moved.

Acknowledgements also to Janice Sellers and Joel Alpert for text and image layout; to Joe Canter for image scanning; to Errol Ford Genet and Jan R. Fine for image editing; to Jan R. Fine for the cover design; and to Sandra Hirschhorn for publicity.

BALTIC SEA

LITHUANIA

Vilnius ●

RUSSIA

POLAND

● CIECHANOW

BELARUS

GERMANY

● Poznan

Warsaw ●

● Lodz

● Prague

CZECH REPUBLIC

● Krakow

UKRAINE

SLOVAKIA

250 miles
0

0   250 Km   500 Km

POLAND - Current Borders

Map of Poland with Ciechanow

A SHORT HISTORY OF CIECHANOW POLAND

Jews were living in Ciechanow by the year 1569. In 1656 during the Polish-Swedish war most of the Jews were killed by the troops of Stephan Czarniecki. In 1765, 1,670 Jews were living in the town; in 1856 Jews comprised 2,226 of the 3300 residents; in 1897 4,223 of 10,000 residents; in 1921 4,403 out of 11,977, and about 5,500 in 1925. During this period a rich Jewish culture developed. Before the outbreak of World War II, the Jewish population had decreased to 1,500 to 2,000.

It all came to an end when he Nazis entered the town on Sept. 3 and 4, 1939. Deportations began on December 1941 and ended in November 1942, when 1,800 Jews were sent to other ghettos and Auschwitz.

About 200 Jews from the town survived the war, including 120 who had sought refuge in the U.S.S.R. The Jewish community ceased to exist after World War II.

The town is known as Ciechanow [Polish], Tshekhanov [Yiddish], Tsekhanuv [Russian], and Chechinov, Chekhanov, Chekhanove, Zichenau [German, 1939-45]

Ciechanow, Poland is located at 52°53' North Latitude and 20°37' East Longitude, and is 47 miles NNW of Warsaw.

Notes to the Reader:

Within the text the reader will note "34" standing ahead of a paragraph. This indicates that the material translated below was on page 34 of the original Yizkor book. However, when a paragraph was split between two pages in the original book, the marker is placed in this book after the end of the paragraph for ease of reading.

Table of Contents

Family Notes

5

Introduction

One's heart trembles when writing these lines that must serve to introduce the reader to the *Yizkor Book* of our tortured community – Ciechanów. With this book we want to immortalize the establishment, growth, spiritual rise, struggle, suffering and destruction of a large and important Jewish community that, for several hundred years, had its home in the Polish *shtetl*. Have we, in full measure, fulfilled our debt to the previous generations of Ciechanów Jews and the last destroyed generation? Have we, as necessary, brought into this *Yizkor Book* the types and characters of simple Jews, of community leaders, leaders of the generation, idealists and fighters for national and human freedom with which our small Jewish community was so rich?

We know that five hundred pages do not complete all the historical happenings of past generations of Ciechanów Jewry. By no means has the full extent of the painful experience and tragic destruction of the thousands of Jews in the *shtetl* been described. But is it possible to express our mourning and sorrow for those who suffered/perished? And since we know how bottomless is the ocean of blood and tears of the tortured ones, we beg for forgiveness and pardon from the martyrs whose lifes and murders did not receive the proper reflection in our *Yizkor Book*.

With deep respect, we, the survivors, the by-chance rescued ones, have done everything possible to bring into the Ciechanów community: historical displays, memoirs, descriptions, biographies, description of the period of destruction—written by people from our home town. We have also assembled a large number of photographs that shed light on the communal and spiritual life in the "peaceful" period between the two world wars and in the period of the destruction. We spared no effort to make this book as large and as beautiful as possible.

In carrying out this most worthy work we were consumed with the great desire to eternally remember the destroyed Ciechanów community; not to allow the flame to be extinguished of our lasting hatred of the German murderers that brought such a catastrophe to our people.

Our heartfelt thanks to all those who participated, people from Ciechanów, who with their devotion and action helped in the publication of this *Yizkor Book*. We particularly mention with thanks: our *landsleit* in Detroit with Moishe Lesser and Benjamin Appel at the head, whose tireless work gave the material possibility for the publication of this *Yizkor Book*; the *landsleit* from Paris and Montreal

(Canada) who responded warmly to our call and sent material and money for our book

A blessing to the writer and literary critic, A. Wolf Yasni, editor of our *Yizkor Book*, for his efforts to make this book appear more beautiful and better, and to Moishe Tzinovich for supplying historical material re the establishment and development of the Yiddish community life in Ciechanów.

And finally we want to mention with thanks the editorial committee in Israel who, with their tireless work, each *chaver* according to his abilities, helped so much to bring this book into existence.

(signed) Moishe Fuchs

9

Overall History of the Jews of Ciechanów

The Jews of Ciechanów: Their History, Way of Life, Struggles and the Holocaust They Endured

The descriptive and commemorative passages in this *Yizkor Book*, written originally in Yiddish, were meant to commemorate in the Holocaust literature the rich spiritual life of the community of Ciechanów, its struggle for a humanitarian Jewish existence in Poland and its eventual tragic end.

The most important legacy of that community is ourselves, the survivors, who set a stake in the Land of Israel. We want our offspring to know what happened to their parents in this community in the Diaspora. And so, this is an abridged Hebrew version of the events described in the book.

The Rabbis of Ciechanów and Its Leaders

The name of Ciechanów appears in the annals of history, together with the formation of the Polish monarchy. It was in the 11th century that a settlement began to form in the place where the Ladinia River flows into the Naarev River. The Jews arrived in the 16th century and the names of Jews are connected with Ciechanów from the year 1569 onwards, at which time their tribulations also began. In 1656, when Sweden attacked Poland, battles raged around Ciechanów. Already at that time fifty Jewish families were killed by soldiers of Haatman Chierniachki, under the pretense that the Jews were sympathetic to the Swedish forces who conquered the region. In the 18th century Ciechanów was an organized Jewish community which had a central role in the "Committee of Four Countries" in addition to its standing as a town in the Polish administration proper. Ciechanów at that time had 1,670 persons, a sizable population for those days and Ciechanów was one of fifteen regional communities which enjoyed autonomy within the "Community of Four Countries." Jews of the towns such as Makow, Mlawa, Neustadt and Plonsk paid their royal and ethnic taxes to Ciechanów, which in turn cared to supply them with their religious functionaries and materials.

In the 19th century, with the general development of the town, the Jewish population increased in numbers as well as in importance so that in the second half of that century, the Jews accounted for the majority of the population of Ciechanów. The first notation regarding the first Rabbi of Ciechanów, Rabbi Yitzhak Kahane, appears in 1786. This Rabbi had an honorable place amongst the famous Polish Rabbis.

Following Rabbi Kahane was Rabbi Laibish Charif Chiniech, who was appointed Head Rabbi in 1820.

10

The rabbis had great influence in the community and due to this the Jewish community of Ciechanów developed and a series of religious and educational institutions were established which strengthened the spiritual and social life of the Jews.

The Economic and Social Life of the Jews of Ciechanów in the 1880's

According to a report from 1887, the Jewish population of Ciechanów divided itself among the following occupations:

Merchants of various guilds	12
Merchant assistants	8
Shopkeepers	195
Store-worker helpers	38
Brewers	17
Inns	2
Distillers	3
Exporters	3
Wheat Merchants	55
Brickwork Owners	1
Soda Factory Owners	3
Innkeepers	4
Lumberyards	4
Hay Cutting Machine Owners	10
Artisans/Craftsmen - Tailors and related occupations	300
Shoemakers	360
Hatters	18
Woodworkers	9
Locksmiths	10
Tallit Weavers	3

Tinsmiths	11
Jewelers	2
Watchmakers	4
Rope makers	9
Builders	4
Candle makers	2
Bookbinders	2
Comb makers	1
Painters	2
Bakers	19
Furriers	9
Butchers	38
Confectioners	4
Porters	28
Stonecutters	2
Musicians	4
Barber-surgeons and doctors	4
Teachers	3
Print shop owners	1
Public Writers	3
Leather merchants	8
Tutors	21
Ritual Slaughterers	3
Rabbis	2
Synagogue Beadles	5
Brokers	4
Village Peddlers	28
Market Peddlers	78

| Chicken and Egg Merchants | 25 |
| Miscellaneous | 55 |

(According to the newspaper *Hatzfira* No. 204, 1887)

In the above period, Ciechanów numbered 3,500 Jews. Of those, 1,600 (45.7%) were involved in productive work. (At that time, trade too was considered productive work in that it involved "building bridges" between the village and the city).

In 1887 Jewish Ciechanów had the following institutions: *Talmud Torah, Bikur Cholim, Ein Yaakov, Tiferet Bchurim, Ba'alai Malacha, Chevrat Tehilim* and *Chevrat Kadishah.*

In 1889, a Zionist Committee was formed in the town and it included 80 persons.

The spiritual leaders of the Jewish community of Ciechanów in the 19th century were great Torah scholars and Rabbis. The renowned Rabbi Landau, known as *Rov* Avraham of Ciechanów, was considered one of the great rabbis of Poland. He was known for his sharp wit, steadfastness, as well as his expertise. He was good-hearted and pious and his name went before him for his careful and thought-out words.

The last Rabbi of Ciechanów prior to its destruction was *Rov* Chaim Mordechai Bronrot, who became Head Rabbi in 1916 in the midst of World War I. Rabbi Bronrot successfully mixed his religious leadership with extensive and fruitful social and public activities. He was active in the *Mizrachi* movement in Poland and was amongst its founders and was a member of its board. He initiated the establishment of *Knesset Rabbanai Mizrachi Polan* (The Knesset of Mizrachi Rabbis of Poland).

11

Rabbi Bronrot did much for the *Keren Kayemet l'Yisroel* (J.N.F.), the *Keren HeChalutz Hamizrach* and other Zionist institutions within and outside of Ciechanów, as well as participating in a number of Zionist Congresses.

In 1918, with the withdrawal of Germany from Poland, and the establishment of the Polish government, Rabbi Bronrot and 40 other rabbis had a secret meeting which took a positive stand regarding the Balfour Declaration. They put out an announcement in support of the declaration signed by all the participants at the meeting. This announcement made a great impression on the orthodox and *Hasidic* elements in Poland.

For years, Rabbi Bronrot was a member of the board of the *Agudat HaRabanim in Poland* (The Federation of Polish Rabbis). He led his community until 1939, two months before the outbreak of World War II. He was then sent on a mission to England where he remained until 1943, at which time he made his way to Israel. He served as Chief Rabbi of the *Beit HaDin* of Tel-Aviv-Jaffo until his death.

Hasidim and Mitnagdim

In Ciechanów as in all Jewish towns in Eastern Europe, the Jewish community was divided into two movements, the *Hasidim* and the *Mitnagdim*. The former belonged to the followers of *Rov* Raphael Moshe Zazbend, the in-law of *Rov* Avraham. This following consisted mainly of the more established Jews from Ciechanów and the surroundings who spent *Shabbat* and holidays in Ciechanów, so that in the town *shtiblech* were formed (or centers of the *Hasidic* movement) connected to the rabbis of Gur and Alexander. These centers had a rich religious and social life.

Until the 19th century there was even a *Yeshiva* in Ciechanów to which youth came from different areas to study Torah and who lived as dependents of the townsfolk. For financial reasons the *Yeshiva* was closed. A number of locals continued their studies in the religious higher-learning school (*Beit HaMidrash*) after completing elementary education (*Cheder*), and the sound of these students would fill the air of the surrounding streets from early morning to nightfall.

Three religious judges (*Dayanim*) served in Ciechanów: amongst them was Rabbi Yosele, one who would sit and study day and night and whom everyone respected. On Friday evenings Rabbi Yosele would put on his *shtreimel* (the *Hasidic* head-wear) and his special clothes, and would go out to the streets to plead, "Jews, light candles, close your stores, *Shabbat* is upon us." His face wore the signs of great concern lest the holiness of the *Shabbat* be desecrated. Around Rabbi Yosele in his great study would be those who chanted the psalms, and the elders who respected and liked him. When he died, many rabbis from the whole area came to his funeral and eulogized him. The whole town dressed in mourning.

His place was taken by his son, Ephraim, who served until his death by the murderous Germans, who abused him and screamed out: "Let us see now how your G-d shall help you." Rabbi Ephraim did not heed them and rather walked his last walk deep in thought as to the holiness of G-d. His wife begged before his execution by the Gestapo that she be allowed to die together with her husband. Her request was granted and both were executed together.

12

Jewish Social and Cultural Life in Ciechanów

At the end of the 19th century and the beginning of the 20th century, Jewish social and cultural secular life was being created in Ciechanów as in many other Jewish communities in Poland. In 1897 there arose two freedom movements, the " National Socialist Zionist Movement" and the *Bund,* which left their deep imprint at the Jewish roots level. Amongst the youth there was an increase in books in Yiddish and Hebrew. Older students *(Beit HaMidrash),* who "peeked" in the newspaper *Hatzfira,* were affected. A library for borrowing books in Hebrew was established. Wealthier students left their well-to-do homes to work for artisan workshops in order to free themselves from the strong hold of their extremist Orthodox parents, who believed that reading secular books, even those in Hebrew or Yiddish, was an act of agnosticism.

The social life of Ciechanów began with the establishment of the *Histadrut Hatzionit* and two socialist organizations. *Poale Tsion* (Workers of Zion) and the *Bund,* which operated underground. They organized strikes and demanded increased wages to the existing meager ones as well as a shortened work day to the existing 12 hour work day.

Already by 1910 there existed in Ciechanów a developed Jewish social life. The leadership of the community (Franks), chosen by the established taxpayers, ran the religious affairs of the settlement, which numbered about three thousand. They were also in control of the different charity sources. At the same time secular organizations existed. The above-mentioned library, which was annexed to the "Society for the Distribution of Education" in Petersburg, the capital of Czarist Russia (today called Leningrad), served as the legal branch in Ciechanów as well as the sport organization *Maccabee.* To those institutions were added at the outbreak of World War I modern Jewish schools instead of the traditional *cheder* and *yeshiva.*

In all those institutions and organizations intense ideological differences were expressed between the Zionists, the *Bundists* and the *Poale Tsion* movements. The most intense falling-out was within the families themselves, between the secular youth and their Orthodox parents, who considered the actions of their children as Epicurean heresy. At the same time, anti-Semitism was on the rise in Ciechanów. A townsman, Isaac Kesler, described the situation in his memoirs: "The Poles set up cooperative stores and called upon the Poles to buy only at these places. They imposed a boycott on Jewish stores. In the park at Girko, a fight broke out between Jews and Poles."

Life in Ciechanów became difficult for most of the Jewish youth. It was difficult with regard to Jewish secular life, not to mention the pressure imposed by the Czarist regime, which disenfranchised the Jews of their basic rights. That, in addition to the terror of the pogroms and the Polish chauvinism, badly hurt the economic base of the Jewish population of Ciechanów. The feeling of having no future weighed heavily upon the Jewish youth.

13

The youth felt it. was not possible to build a future life in such an atmosphere. Most decided to go abroad to various countries. Some went to *Eretz Yisroel.*

World War I and Its Influence on the Jews of Ciechanów

The war changed the Jewish life of Ciechanów drastically. The town, which was close to the German-Russian border, fell to the ravages of war. The Russian soldiers had open hatred for the Jews and abused them. Nevertheless, the Jewish population did not hesitate to take in their brethren from the adjacent town of Proshnitz, who had been evacuated from their homes by the Russians.

At the end of summer 1915, the Germans broke through the front of Poland and the Russians evacuated Ciechanów. The town was now under German occupation. Despite their cruelty, it was still a far cry from the German monster yet to come under Hitler. Germany at this time used the pretense of being " the savior of Poland and freedom." Therefore, they allowed relative cultural and social freedom beyond anything that had been allowed by the Russians.

Tankhum Makaver gives a description of the German rule of this period. In this book he writes:

"The economic situation of the Jews of Ciechanów was very bad. The occupation forces requisitioned everything that came to hand: food, money, merchandise etc. Trade was virtually paralyzed. The Germans levied heavy war taxes on the Jewish population as if the Jews had been fighting them and had won...

Nevertheless, at that time a Hebrew kindergarten was established and Jewish youth got involved in cultural and public affairs. An amateur [drama] group was started up which presented performances such as "Kreutzer Sonata" by Yaacov Gordin and "Shema Israel" by Osip Dimov and others. Though the Zionist *Histadrut* did not discontinue its activities during the Czarist era, the *Bund* and *Poale Tsion* renewed their activities at this time. In 1917 the Histadrut of Young Zionists joined the other groups and had a wide range of activities including the establishment of their own library, with evening lectures and readings on national and literary subjects."

At that time there were elections for the local administration. The election was over the ideology of the *Bund*, which stood for a solution to the Jewish problem through the establishment of a democratic rule which would strive for a socialistic society with equal rights for all ethnic groups, and the Zionists who saw the solution in the establishment of a Jewish national home in Israel. The Zionists won by a majority in the local administration. The new leadership re-established the traditional *Cheder* and *Talmud Torah*, as well as establishing secular schools, the *Linat Tzedek*, which attended to the sick, and a public kitchen which gave out some 300 meals a day to the poor of Ciechanów.

14

At the same time, in 1917, the "Zamir Co." was set up in Ciechanów which had a major influence on the Jewish youth. It established a lending library for Yiddish, Hebrew and Polish books and had literary events, readings and performances which drew many people.

In this context, a steep ideological battle was carried on which Yehoshua Grosbard describes in the book as follows: " The arguments between members of "Zamir" brought in its wake a political party/state differentiation. On the one hand were the Zionist youth and the *Poale Tsion* and on the other, the working youth and the less fortunate who supported the *Bund* movement.

15

Jewish Life between the Two World Wars

With the end of World War I, the Jews of Ciechanów once again began to regain their economic standing in independent Poland. The merchants returned to their trade and the storekeepers to the stores - so that the social activity was restored and even widened.

The "Zamir Co." became the National Library and the arguments between the Zionists and the non-Zionists became so embittered, to the point where the Zionists left. This establishment then became a purely *Bundist* one and took on the name " Grosser Club" (on the name of Grosser, a *Bundist* leader who died in his youth). Many youth gravitated towards this club, which included a large auditorium with stage, library, reading room, a club room, etc. This group presented the following presentations, amongst others: "The Snow" by Pshivishovski, "The Father" by Strindberg, "The Thieves" by Bimko, "Dialogues" by Sholem Aleichem, and "The Moon Tells" by Y.L. Peretz. The group's activities spread to the adjacent towns as well.

The liberation of Poland and the Russian Revolution in Russia brought new life into Jewish Ciechanów. In the town, political and economic strikes and protests were held. The police intervened and carried out searches and arrests. Grosbard, who took an active part in the events, recounts:

"The war between the working classes and the upper classes in the Jewish sector became worse on the evening of the elections for the City Council of Ciechanów. We decided not to allow the synagogue to be used for election propaganda purposes. We, as an organized group, arrived there [the synagogue] and didn't allow the speech-makers to speak during the reading of the Torah. At a later date, the police came looking for me in my home and I had to hide in the attic for a week.

The election was a difficult one and the *Bund* managed to enter two representatives to the City Council – Yidel Bronstein and Malink. There was a strike of tailors also at this time and the youth spared no effort in helping the strikers and the election campaign with all the means at their disposal."

The Jewish workers participated in the elections for the Workers' Council in the year 1919. The difficult economic situation in Poland and the consequent terrible unemployment and the effects of the socialist revolution on neighboring Russia, all influenced the election outcome. The election was very tense due to the difference of opinions regarding the form the newly-chosen Council was to take. The arguments amongst the Jewish workers went on night and day while the election was exploited for anti-Semitic propaganda. Amongst the Polish workers the local priest and his allies openly called for pogroms. However, to the credit of the Polish workers, it must be said that they didn't abide by the priest's words and in that year no anti-Semitic incidents were carried out during the election for the Workers' Council.

16

However, what the workers didn't do in 1919 was done by the Polish soldiers who arrived in Ciechanów due to the war between Poland and Soviet Russia in 1920. Their first move was to enter the Grosser Club, causing a pogrom. They broke the furniture, tore the pictures and the books, hit all those present in the building, and arrested some of those who were hurt so badly that they needed medical attention.

There was still ongoing unemployment in Poland, and the persecutions of the reactionary government which didn't end despite the frequent changes in the government itself, created communist strivings amongst the Jewish youth and workers in Ciechanów which increased to the point where even some *Bund* members left their party and formed a secret communist organization.

At the same time, the Zionist movement grew and strengthened in all its forms - *Poale Tsion*- both the rightists and leftists, the *Shomeir Hatzair* and the Revisionists and their youth groups. Encompassing them all was a network of cultural and educational organizations for the learning of Hebrew and for the research of subjects specific to *Eretz Yisroel*. There arose committees in Ciechanów devoted to the *Keren Kayemet* and to the *Keren Hayesod*, which collected money for settling in *Eretz Yisroel*. Zionist youth went to Kibbutz Gronov for *Hachshara* (training) and Zionist businessmen from Ciechanów were among the members of the "Committee for Kibbutz Gronov." The religious Jews also formed a political organization of their own *Agudat Isroel*, whose offshoot were *Agudat Israel - Youth* and *Poale Agudat Israel* and developed as well their cultural and educational religious institutions (i.e., *Beit Yaakov* etc.).

As in other cities, in Ciechanów as well, a social-political match existed between the different political Jewish parties and organizations. Each one strove for power through its professional unions/committees and organizations and in its educational and cultural institutions and in the mutual aid which the Jewish community had established for its very existence. This political struggle reached its peak during the elections for the Polish parliament, the City Council or the Jewish administration. Most of the Jews of Ciechanów were non-political and the rival parties went to great lengths to win over the non-committed.

The Jews of Ciechanów: Their Livelihood and Way of Life

The socialist structure of the Jewish population of Ciechanów changed little after 1887. Moshe Fuchs gives a description of the socialist way of life in the 1930's prior to World War II.

"In Ciechanów, there were very few rich. There were weaving merchants, food retailers and some flour-mill owners and lumberyards. They composed the upper crust of Jewish Ciechanów. Most of the population were craftsmen and peddlers, called in the local lingo, "Strogniazis."

17

Worst of all was the fate of the peddlers, who would go to fairs to make a living. They were on the road all week, in the cold of winter and in the heat of summer, in rain and shine, and would push on to get to their destinations on time. This was their schedule: Sunday – searching out benefactors, Monday -- going to Golomin, Tuesday – to Preshitz, Wednesday -- to Makow, Thursday – to Churzel. Those were the towns around Ciechanów from which the Jews eked out a living, a meager one at best.

The work-trade life cycle continued for many years and wore one down. The peddlers held out due to the old Jewish adage -- "G-d will not forsake me" – from which they got strength and encouragement.

In the late afternoon, the Jews would go to the prayer/study hall in order to 'catch' an afternoon or evening prayer, or to listen to a sermon, or to snooze when the tiredness was too much After the sermon, they would surround Rabbi Yehuda Moshaks and hear from him a tantalizing tale about the wonders of the righteous *Reb Avramele*.

On the 5th of *Adar,* the day of the latter's death, the *Yeshiva* boys would be in a spirited mood. On this day they would complete the tractate, hear tunes by the Rabbis Shlomo Zalman and Ziskind, eat well, drink *L'chaim* and wish each other with a traditional blessing.

The next morning, the Jews of Ciechanów would receive guests from the nearby towns and even from Warsaw, who would be coming to the grave of the fathers and to the *Ohel* (monument) of the *Tzadik* [*Hasidic* Rabbi]. Amongst those who came was the grandson of *Reb* Avramele -- the Rabbi of Strikov. They would go to the *Ohel*, knocking on his door three times with a key and enter in a set order: *Rov* Strikov and the *Hasidim*, the representatives of *Chevra Kadisha*, with *Rov* Yosele at their head, etc. All day people of all ages would pass through the *Ohel*. Some would be content with leaving a small request note and some would let out all their hearts' bitterness on the grave of the *Tzadik*. They would return home with a feeling of relief that the *Tzadik* would care for their own and others' needs.

On *Shabbat* and holidays, Jewish Ciechanów would take on a different appearance. Reb Yosele would go out to the streets pleading, "Jews, *Shabbat* is upon us, light *Shabbat* candles." The Jews would send their shop clients on their way and hurried themselves to the prayer hall or to one of the different *Shtiblech*. The Jewish streets would quickly fill with the different *Shabbat* tunes and prayers that the worshippers continued to chant on their way home. From the prayer hall early on *Shabbat* morning, one could hear the sound of psalms recited by *Chevrat Tehilim*.

18

The joy in Ciechanów was complete, especially when the *Chazan,* Rabbi Lazar Borochovitz from Novidvor, accompanied by his choir of 30 choristers, would arrive. On those *Shabbats* and holidays the synagogue would be too narrow to contain all those who came to hear the singing. Even the *Hasidim* would hurry and pray at their *shtiblech* in order to get to the synagogue, which would fill up to capacity very quickly. The listeners would have true enjoyment from the tunes and sounds of the *Chazan* and his singers. The *Rov* would invite the visitors to *Kiddush* in his house and the Jews of Ciechanów would stand outside savoring the sounds coming from the house.

On *Simchat Torah, Chevra Kadisha* would have a big feast. On this day the Torah scroll would be brought from the home of Rabbi Israel Itzchak Rimrash to the synagogue. The women would light candles and put them in the windows along the way of the procession. Men and small ones would crowd and dance around the Torah which the Rabbi held, with everyone trying to get close enough to touch and kiss the Torah cover. The excitement, the singing and dancing would increase until arriving at the synagogue, and would continue once inside, with the *Chazan* doing the rounds and the participants tired and sweaty, continuing to sing and dance. They would forget all their worries and put themselves heart and soul into the celebration of the ending of the reading of the Torah.

On *Lag B'Omer* the youth of *Shomeir Hatzair* would march in the streets of Ciechanów to the synagogue with flags in their hands and singing songs. The sound of drums and horns would fill the area and announce the coming of the 'troop'. Yaacov Kahane and Yaacov Misher would give speeches to the crowds about *Eretz Yisroel*, the homeland of the Jews, and the freedom and happenings there. A similar procession was held by the *Shomeir Hatzair* on 11 *Tamuz*, the day of Herzl's death.

Such was the life of the Jews of Ciechanów for more than 300 years. Initially, according to the strict religious laws and in the last decades until the Nazi occupation, a life in which religion and secularism were intermingled. In this long period, the Jewish settlement fought for its existence. Their hard work and economic standing caused jealousy and hate towards the Jews by the Poles. These feelings increased, especially in liberated Poland. Whoever could, emigrated from Poland. The Zionist youth went to *Eretz Yisroel*; however, most of Jewish Ciechanów stayed in place, and suffered the persecutions of the reactionary government and the hate of the Polish masses. Such was the situation of the Jews of Ciechanów at the outbreak of the Holocaust.

19

The Destruction of the Jews of Ciechanów by the Germans

Already in the first months of 1939, before the outbreak of the war, the Jews of Ciechanów felt the increasingly ominous atmosphere. They knew what Hitler's Germany was and there was no doubt in their hearts that no good was to be expected from this regime. Nevertheless, no one could imagine the dimensions of the disaster to befall the Jews and no one expected murder and genocide to be so widespread. The Polish army was more or less prepared for defense against the Germans, and there was hope that the democratic powers would be supportive in the case of a German attack on Poland. At the same time, the situation of the Jews of Ciechanów, as of those in the rest of Poland, was a 'dead end." Even if they could and would leave Poland, they had nowhere to go. England, which then had the mandate in *Eretz Yisroel*, closed its gates in the face of the Jewish refugees. The secret emigration to Israel was of course minimal. There was no choice for the Jews of Ciechanów and the rest of Poland than to sit and wait, helpless, for the bitter end.

On the first of September, a Friday, at the beginning of the German invasion into Poland, Ciechanów was the first to be hit. Amongst the Jews a panic arose, and some fled, particularly to Warsaw. Binyamin Apel recounted:

"On the main street leading to the capital, my eyes beheld the cruelest sights of war. The roads were full of refugees, Jews and non-Jews, old and young, and the German planes would soar just above their heads. They would shoot down quiet, unarmed civilians, with no defense or shelter. Thousands of bodies covered the roadsd.

Already on the fourth day of the war the Germans arrived in Ciechanów. On the same day four local Jews were murdered by them. The occupying forces held on to Ciechanów and quickly their cruelty to the Jews was made evident. They were told by a German officer to leave the town. When they refused, they waited anxiously for the inevitable, which came quickly enough.

The Germans entered the synagogues and desecrated them. They removed the Torahs and rolled them along the sidewalks. Prayer halls became garages for fixing German transport vehicles. The occupying soldiers caught Jews in the road and sent them to all kinds of hard and degrading labor. They were hit or brutalized." Binyamin Apel goes on to detail those days:

"The situation got worse and worse. Anyone left with any strength wanted to flee. However, even escaping had its dangers because it was forbidden to leave the town without a license and a listing was made of all the citizens. Despite this, many tried to flee. They would get as far as Austrolanko, cross the border and enter Russia."

20

No one thought to resist the German acts. First of all because they lacked the means to do so, and secondly, there was no centralized 'think tank.' The Jewish political parties and organizations fell apart when the population began to flee, following the first German shelling.

This was followed immediately by the Nazi terror which put an end to any effort at organized resistance.

*

In the next weeks, the German acts of cruelty, which included confiscating Jewish property, torture and murder, became 'legal.' The Jews were ordered to wear the yellow patch on their sleeve, they had to walk on the sidewalks only in a particular direction, and they were at the mercy of any German who might hit, abuse or even murder them.

The German authority ordered the Jews to stay concentrated in an area of some two roads in the town. This place was the Jewish ghetto, though it was without a wall since all of Ciechanów was in essence a ghetto. Jewish homes outside the two mentioned roads were abolished by Jews themselves under the cruel orders of the Germans. In the ghetto at times five families would share one room.

According to a German order, a Jewish council (*Judenrat*) was established in the ghetto for the purpose of carrying out any ordinances set by the occupation forces. Beside the council there was also an employment office which supplied the Germans with Jewish labor.

Binyamin Apel describes the situation in the ghetto as follows: "The Jewish population would receive their food rations by cards, which would give each person 5 decco of bread per day and 10 decco meat per week. Obviously the meat was not kosher because there were no active Jewish *Shochets*.

Trade came to a standstill. Artisan and workshop owners could not continue their work without a special license. Poverty took over. People were hungry for bread and sold their furniture and private belongings to the Poles for a bit of food. The Poles got richer through this trade.

The crowded and dirty conditions in the ghetto bred disease. There was hunger and cold and the situation was catastrophic. The Jewish area in Ciechanów in the time of the Germans was like a graveyard of living dead."

Where Jewish homes once stood, new buildings were erected for the Germans. The Poles too were evacuated from Ciechanów, with no resistance on their part, and so the Polish town became a German one with the name Chechno.

21

The Jews continued to live in the ghetto under the constant threat of death. The Germans worked them as slaves and even the most experienced artisans worked for starvation wages. On December 11th 1941, 1,200 Jews were brought together, men, women and children and were beaten or shot to death. Those that survived were sent off to a new ghetto in Nowe Miasto (Nuestadt).

The expulsion was a planned stage in the German extermination policy. They would centralize the Jews and then transport them from one place to another for no reason other than to 'break' and demoralize them and then send them to "work" -- in actuality, the death camps. This was the fate of the Jews of Ciechanów. From one expulsion to the next the Germans would increase their murderous activities. They would shoot the evaders of the expulsion or abuse them in the eyes of all who would be ordered to observe. Binyamin Apel recounts in his memoirs the terrible sights:

"Chills take hold of me when I remember the horrible event. Children stood and observed the hanging of their fathers, and were forbidden to cry. The hangmen would look into their eyes to make sure there were no tears. The five victims hung from six until nine at night."

In another incident, five Jews were hung for hiding a Torah in a graveyard in order to protect it from harm by the vandals. As if it wasn't enough, prior to the final expulsion of the Jews from Ciechanów, they were threatened and tortured to destroy the gravestones in the graveyard and to plow it over.

On November 6th 1942 the Jewish community of Ciechanów was wiped out. On this bitter day the Germans centralized, through terror and shooting, some 1,800 Jews, and divided them into two camps -- those able to work and those not capable. The elders were killed on the spot and the rest were put into closed train cars. Ciechanów was "purified" of Jews. The blood-tainted Nazis, or the "superior German race" had completed its terrible murder and had uprooted its victims from one of the towns of Poland.

The Heroic Resistance of the Jews of Ciechanów in Auschwitz

The Jews who were expelled from Ciechanów were brought by the Germans to the concentration camps. The stronger ones passed through some other ghettos where the Nazis needed more human labor. They too were eventually sent to concentration camps. Totally overworked and exhausted, many died. Those that survived recount their memories in this book. We will suffice here with the description of the life of the Jews in Auschwitz. In Auschwitz, as in other camps, Jews made every effort to be together with those from their town and to give mutual support. It was a tragic caricature of *landsmanschaft* through awaiting death in the gas chambers.

22

The Jews of Ciechanów tried to stay together in order to help each other with a slice of bread or some soup, etc. Not everyone got to live there a long time, because the fate of most who were brought to this terrible camp was to be killed, some by shooting, some by suffocation and some by some other form of torture. Nevertheless, the German businessmen didn't hesitate to exploit the inmates' last source of strength in the factories within the concentration camps. The inmates were under terrible conditions. Besides this, the liquidation machine was in need of services which the victims themselves provided.

Amongst them were a number of Ciechanów Jews who were the strongest and healthiest. Their work gave them hope that, through it, they would be saved from the gas chamber. Their vain hopes did not advance the organization of a resistance. An inmate from Auschwitz, Moshe Kolka, gives here an answer to the question many posed: Why did the many inmates not simply fall upon their German guards, whose numbers were much smaller?

"The answer to this tiresome question lies in the precise murder orders [methods] that the Germans organized in Auschwitz – searchlights would light every corner at night time; there were shooting towers, the high voltage fences around the camp and the terrible dogs who were trained together to follow the prisoners. All put fear into the whole camp. In addition to that were the mechanical and scientific means available to the camp officers against the inmates. The liquidation machine suppressed the inmates in the camps and wiped out their physical and spiritual selves. The fear of the predator animal as personified in the German human image was rooted in the inmates' senses. As well, the national hate, especially towards the Jews in the form of anti-Semitism which the Germans encouraged, caused demoralization amongst the inmates and weakened their will.

Despite the above, there arose in Auschwitz an underground which prepared to counter the Germans. Jews from Ciechanów were attracted to this movement. These were the ones who had managed to survive selection and extermination. They were for the most part men and women who had worked in the arms factory "Union" established by German entrepreneurs within the camp. Noah Zabludovich, an inmate from Auschwitz, brings forth his memories of those persons and their role in the resistance organization in Auschwitz.

"Only Jews worked in the "Union" factory -- men and women separately in three shifts. The Germans made sure they had no contact between them. They were inmates in Birkenau. Organizers of the underground movement gave instructions to contact the persons worthy of trust who could be useful in obtaining ammunition and arms. For a short while, I managed to contact a home girl -- Rosa

Robota, who worked in the clothes section in Birkenau camp. She organized a group of women who worked in the explosives shop. About twenty women, with great danger to their lives, hid packages full of explosive powder in their bras. Rosa would then get the "merchandise" from them and pass it on to our people who worked in the Sonderkommando, a special department for passing corpses to the ovens. The Sonderkommando persons would then hide the packages in their carts and put them in a hiding-place close to the ovens. This continued for a year plus. With time, we acquired some ammunition from the Poles with the money and gold which we still had in our possession. It was in this way that we prepared for the resistance in the worst concentration camp set up by the Germans – Auschwitz."

24

Rosa Robota: The Holy Heroine from Ciechanów

In the annals of the brave resistance of Auschwitz against the murderous Germans, Rosa Robota from Ciechanów wrote by her suffering a wonderful chapter of heroism, bravery and moral standing. In the Jewish martyrdom literature the word "holy" is only used in reference to her, due to her deeds in Auschwitz. Rosa Robota is worthy of being numbered amongst the saints.

She was born in Ciechanów to a family of good standing and had a sister and brother. Rosa completed elementary school with excellence and was attracted to public work through the *Hashomeir Hatzair* movement from a young age. She was still young when the Germans entered Ciechanów and took her and her sister to do cleaning in the home of the ex-Polish head of Government. Both sisters were badly mistreated in this work. In the meantime, their home was destroyed and their family went to live with relatives in the ghetto, until its destruction in November of 1942 and the deportation of most of its residents to Auschwitz. Rosa was amongst those sent. In the camp, she went through the awful selection process in which each one's fate was sealed – who to slave labor and who to the gas chambers.

Noah Zabludovich, who was in contact with her, tells (in the *Ciechanów Community and its Destruction, and Death of Hero Rosa Robota* in Yiddish, edited by Moshe Fuchs, Tel-Aviv 1952 by the Committee for the Memory in honor of Rosa Robota; contributors: Yechiel Israeli, Noah Zabludovich and Moshe Kolko; material collected by Noah Zabludovich and Moshe Kolko) with what enthusiasm young Rosa gave herself to the efforts of the underground. Her eyes would light up with revenge when she had the possibility of operating against the enemy. She was well-loved by her friends in the camp and would supply them with bread when hungry. In a short while she was able to organize around her tens of youths like herself who would bring her gunpowder for explosives. Rosa would keep this gunpowder until it was handed over to the *Sonderkommando.* This important and dangerous task she fulfilled with unusual speed and great care.

In mid-1944, the heads of the underground movement in Auschwitz called for a revolt to include all the camps simultaneously. They hoped for the help of A.K. – (*Armaia Kraeebo* in Polish -- the land army; a military Polish government in London). The uprising was set for the first Sunday of November of 1944. The organizers of the uprising hung great hopes on the *Sonderkommando* who worked, as said, beside the ovens. About six hundred men were occupied in this most terrible of jobs, knowing full well that the time would come when the Germans would liquidate them as they did the others. Therefore they decided to fight their murderers to the last man.

The Sonderkommando uprising broke out surprisingly and at an unexpected time for the heads of the underground. Moshe Kolko tells of this in his memoirs:

25

At the same time the rumor was spread about a transport of the men and the *Sonderkommando*. Hardly a few minutes went by and six hundred *kommando* workers rose up. Oven number 2 went up in fire and the German *kapo*, who was known for his cruelty, was thrown into the burning oven. In a face-to-face fight, four S.S. were killed and a number were injured. The area around the ovens turned into a war-zone. The barriers around the area were destroyed and the rioters escaped from there.

All the S.S. in the area were alerted to the camp. The work units stopped work and were returned to their bunkers. A head count was carried out and the S.S. ran around the camp like poisoned mice. It hadn't occurred to them that they may have to defend themselves against the Jews.

Unfortunately, the hoped-for aid was not given to the *Sonderkommando* by the rest of the inmates in the camp. The Germans got the situation under control, killed all the participants of the uprising except for a few from Ciechanów, and carried out a thorough investigation using terrible torture.

The investigation uncovered, of course, that the explosives which the rioters used came to them from the ammunition plant. Suspicion fell on a number of women who worked in the department for explosive powder. They were arrested and taken to Block 11, where they were badly tortured. Amongst them was Rosa Robota.

The failure of the uprising, together with the torture and killings, put fear into the inmates of Auschwitz. Each one thought that their end was near. A particular depression was upon those few inmates from Ciechanów who had been connected with Rosa Robota and knew of her great suffering and the cruel tortures she was subjected to. Their desire was to meet with her before her death.

With the help of a Jewish *kapo*, an S.S. guard who watched over Block 11 got drunk and Noah Zabludovich stole inside...

"I managed to see Rosa for the last time a few days before her death," tells Zabludovich in his memoirs. " At night when all the inmates were asleep, during curfew time when any movement was strictly forbidden in the camp, I went to the "bunker" (Basement) of Block 11 through the passageways and dark rooms. I heard the sighs of those who were convicted and a horrible feeling rose within me. I went down the stairs, led by the *kapo*, until we got to Rosa's cell. Yaakov (the *kapo*), opened the door, admitted me into the cell and disappeared. When my eyes got used to the dark I noticed a figure wrapped in shreds on the cold cement floor. The figure turned her head to me. I barely recognized her. On her face were etched endless suffering and pain. After a few minutes of silence, Rosa began to tell of the sadistic means used by the Germans against her in the investigation and said she took full responsibility, without naming any other names.

26

I tried to comfort her, but she wouldn't hear. "I knew what I did and what I could expect." Furthermore, she requested of the friends to continue in their work: "It is easier to die, when you know that your work is to be continued," she said. I heard a sound at the door. Yaakov called me to leave. I parted from Rosa. It was the last time I was to see her.

A few days later, the Germans collected all the women who worked at "Union" in the explosives factory to witness the hanging of four of their friends. Amongst the condemned was Rosa. The women spoke of how quietly, and with bravery and pride, their heroine from Ciechanów walked to the gallows. This was at the end of November 1944."

At the same time there were no more Jews remaining in the Polish town of Ciechanów. The Jewish offspring of those who had established a community in the Polish settlement on the banks of the Ladinia a few hundred years ago were murdered by the Germans in different ways. Only a small number of Ciechanów Jews survived, scattered in different countries, with a sizable number living in Israel, rebuilding a Jewish life in their national homeland.

27

Ciechanów and Its Jewish Kehillah
Historical Notes

Ciechanów, the *shtetl* where, during World War II, the German mass-murderer ruled limitlessly, the *Gauleiter* Robert Koch, belonged to the oldest *yishuvim* in Poland. Proof of this are the remains of the ancient *kloiz* (small synagogue) that is found beside the Lydinya River and the ancient church on the hillock, rising high above the city.

The beginning of Ciechanów is rooted in the beginning of the Polish state. In the eleventh century, the *yishuv* started to be built, bordering on the River Lydinya.

In a document from the year 1065, this *yishuv* is mentioned as having paid taxes, at the command of King Bolesov Shmiali, to the Benedictines. In 1207, after the inner partitioning of the Polish state, during the period of Leshek Biyali, the city belonged to his brother Conrad – the squire of Mazovich.

In the above-mentioned century, when the Lithuanian and Prussian invasion of Poland increases, Ciechanów and the surrounding area becomes an arena of constant wars that Poland carried on to protect their soil. Because of this, Ciechanów is wiped off the face of the earth several times, and each time it gets rebuilt. In the year 1267, the Prussians and Lithuanians destroyed the city. Seventy years later in 1337, when the city was already properly rebuilt, and led a normal life, an invasion of Lithuanians once again destroyed Ciechanów.

After the *khurban* (destruction) of Ciechanów, it is restarted under the rule of the Mazovich fiefdom/rule. Yanush, the Mazovich nobleman, rebuilt the *yishuv* and moved it to a more comfortable location. In the year 1400, Ciechanów received city privileges, and sixty-three years later, a great battle with the Crusaders once more took place in Ciechanów, and the Mazovich rulers once more suffered a defeat.

In the sixteenth century a revival of Ciechanów begins and it comes under the crown's possession. And so the city develops and grows. The clay soil around the city helps to develop brick-making there.

The wars ceased in Ciechanów region, and the *yishuv* carried on its normal life until 1657, when the Swedes attacked the city, plundered it and burned it. Since that year, continual misfortunes befell the *yishuv*.

In 1662, when the *yishuv* was already built up, a fire brought a new *khurban*. When the city revived after the fire, an epidemic broke out amongst the Ciechanów residents. The government officials who took over, after the epidemic was over, asserted that Ciechanów was left without inhabitants. Since then a hillock remains beneath the *shtetl* and it is called *Famrak*. There, supposedly, is the grave of those who died during the epidemic. Every year, at the time of the Green Holiday (*Zieloneh Shvionski*) the Christians of Ciechanów march in a procession to *Famrak*.

After the aforementioned misfortunes, Ciechanów no longer reached its previous status. The small *yishuv* found itself under the control of local government, and only the ruins of the former castle beside the Ladinya River remained, which told of the former great days of the city on whose behalf great battles were fought – days when noblemen and kings visited the castle.

The remainder of an ancient destroyed castle in Ciechanów.

Of the four churches that Ciechanów once had, only two remain. One church, the oldest, that stands on the hillock, is for the whole region, and for hundreds of years maintained the Gothic crusader style.

In the eighteenth and nineteenth century Ciechanów lived through all the historical storms that occurred in Poland: division of Poland, Polish uprising, occupation of Napoleonic army that turned the famous old church into a military warehouse.

After all the divisions of Poland, revolutions and uprisings, Ciechanów, in the second half of the nineteenth century, remained a typical Polish-Yiddish *shtetl* in the province of Plotz, with its own train station, ninety kilometers from Warsaw and thirty-five kilometers from the *shtetl* Mlova.

The local government building

Jews of Ciechanów and Their First Rov

Until the sixteenth century there were no Jews in Ciechanów. It is only by the year 1569 that Jewish names are first mentioned in Ciechanów. In 1656, while the Swedes attacked Poland, and the battles took place around Ciechanów, fifty Jewish families perished at the hands of Hetman Charnetski's army. A false accusation was made against the Jews of Ciechanów, that they were on friendly terms with the Swedish army that had occupied the city. In general, the Jews suffered greatly from the Polish-Swedish wars.

In the eighteenth century we once again encounter an organized *Kehillah* in Ciechanów that builds a center for all the small communities in its surroundings. It had a population of 1,670 that was quite a large number for that time. The *shtetl* that built a center, under the Polish administration also had a prominent role in the Jewish *Kehillah* management called (in Hebrew) *Vaad Arba Artzot*. The Ciechanów *Kehillah* was one of the fifteen regional *Kehillas* in Poland that had their own autonomy in the *Vaad Arba Artzot*. The Jewish residents of the *shtetlech* Mlova, Reishtat and Plonsk, paid *Kehillah* and governmental taxes which also provided the above-named *shtetlech* with religious functionaries and sacred objects.

At the plenary meeting of the *Vaad Arba Artzot* that took place in Yaraslov in 1753, a struggle took place between the representative of Ciechanów, Avram ben Eliezer and the representative of the smaller communities in the region who fought for their independence. They not only tore themselves away from the Ciechanów Regional *Kehillah*, but they also took upon themselves the leadership regarding every act for the smaller communities that were connected with Ciechanów.

The representative of the Polish Finance Ministry, Kazinyes Grachovsky, who was present at the meeting of the *Vaad Arba Artzot*, in Yaraslov, brought reasons to the *rabbonim* and leaders of the Ciechanów region to concern themselves with this struggle between Ciechanów and the smaller communities.

In the archive material there is no proof of results of this struggle between the *Kehillahs*. It is known, though, that the Ciechanów *Kehillah* lost its hegemony of the *Kehillahs* in its region, that grew larger in number of their membership and became independent in their activities and in the collection of general and local taxes. In the nineteenth century, when the *shtetl* Ciechanów reached a higher level of development, the Yiddish *Kehillah* also grew, both in number and in appearance.

31

In the beginning of the twentieth century, Jews become a majority in Ciechanów and remain so until the '80's of that century. In future years the number of Jews grows even larger when the Polish population greatly increases because of an influx of peasants from the surrounding villages, as can be seen from the table below:

Percentage	Jews	General Population	Year
85.9	1194	1395	1808
62.42	1644	2640	1827
67.0	2394	3575	1860
68.70	3761	5469	1880
42.23	4223	10,000	1897
36.70	4403	11,977	1321
32.8	4562	13,930	1931

According to the survivors of Ciechanów in the year 1939, before the outbreak of war, there were 2,000 Jewish families in Ciechanów.

*

As already shown, Ciechanów had a significant *Kehillah* already in the second half of the eighteenth century. It is therefore clear that such a *Kehillah* could already afford its own *Rov*.

Information about the first *Rov* in Ciechanów exists from the year 1786. The name of the first *Rov* was *Rov* Yitzhak Kahane. In the aforementioned year he gave his endorsement of the *sefer* (book) *P'nai Aryeh*, whose author was *Rov* Aryeh-Leib Brebi Moshe Katz, the in-law of *Rov* Yitzhak Kahane. He signed his endorsement to the book with the title "The Rav of Ciechanów." His endorsement appears together with other great rabbis of that time, such as: *Rov* Yosef Katzenelenboign – *Rov* of Brisk in Litn; *Rebbe* Tzvi Hersh – *Rov* of Herandeh and *Rebbe* Klunumees Kalman Lichtenstein – *Rov* of Bialystok.* It must therefore be accepted that the first *Rov* of Ciechanów occupied an important position amongst the *Rebbes* of Poland at that time. It is not known exactly when he died. His replacement was *Reb* Laibish Kharif Tzinty, who took the Ciechanów rabbinic position in the year 1820.

*The *sefer, Pnai Aryeh* of Rav Aryeh-Leib Brebi Moshe Katz of Tallin appeared in Navidvar and contains new Talmud explanations on the portion *Moed*.

32

The first *Rov* of the Ciechanów *Kehillah* had a great influence on his congregants. Under his leadership the Ciechanów *Kehillah* developed very much and there were established a number of religious and educational institutions that spiritually uplifted and strengthened the Jews in this Polish *shtetl*.

Economic and Social Conditions in the '80's of the Nineteenth Century

We did not succeed in finding any information on the life of the Jews in Ciechanów during the stormy years of the multiple divisions of Poland, and later, during the Polish rebellions at the end of the eighteenth and nineteenth centuries. It was only when the Hebrew newspapers started to appear, in the '80s of the aforementioned century, that the life of the smaller *Kehillahs* is reflected.

According to the *Hatzfira*, there was no Jewish hospital in Ciechanów in 1884, nor was there an orphanage or guest house for the poor. Because of this the *Bais Hamidrash* (House of Study) became a place for the poor and sick and elderly. They slept on the floor together with children – orphans who did not have a home. In the year 1886 a *Bikur Cholim Society* (Society for visiting the sick) was established. The communal leaders drew up a list of 140 Jews who distinguished themselves with their willingness to help and care for the poor sick. They slept over with the sick ones and helped them with medicine and money.

Regarding the relationships of Jews in that region, the *Hatzfira* reports in No.15 of the year 1885: The peasants from the neighboring area have suddenly started to show hatred to the Jews, who had always lived in peace with the peasant population; they attacked and struck at Jews and thereby warned them: "If they will not leave their places there will be a sh*chita* (slaughter*).*"

"The Jews of the village came to the *Rov* and poured out to him their bitter hearts. The *Rov* immediately called a meeting of the heads of the community and consulted with them. A plea-letter was sent to the local council, who immediately dispatched police and officials to prevent a pogrom. The local council warned the hooligans that they would have a bitter end. An inquest was conducted to determine where the source of this event originated amongst the peasants."

*

33

The *Hatzfira* No. 204, of the year 1887, brings the following information about the professional figures of the Jewish population in Ciechanów:

Merchants of various guilds - 12; their assistants - 8; shopkeepers of various merchandise - 195; their helpers - 38; brewers - 17; inns (taverns) - 2; distillers - 3; exporters - 3; wheat merchants - 55; brick-makers - 1; soda-water plants - 3; innkeepers - 4; forest merchants - 4; owners of equipment for cutting hay - 10.

Tradesmen: tailors, craftsmen and journeymen of all kinds - 306; cobblers - 300; hatters - 18; woodcarvers - 9; locksmiths - 10; weavers of *tallises* -3; tinsmiths - 11; goldsmiths - 2; clock-makers - 4; rope weavers - 19; painters - 4; candle-makers - 2; bookbinders - 2; comb makers - 1; house painters - 2; bakers - 19; furriers - 9; butchers and their helpers - 38; manufacturers of candies - 4; carriers - 28; stonecutters - 2; *klezmorim* (musicians) - 4; barber-surgeons and doctors - 4; teachers - 3; printers - 1; letter-writers - 3; dealers in hides - 8; Hebrew teachers - 21; *shoichtim* (ritual slaughterers) - 3; *rabbonim* - 2; synagogue beadles (*shamashim)* - 5; brokers - 4; village peddlers - 28; market dealers - 78; egg and poultry dealers - 25; miscellaneous - 55.

Of the 3500 souls who were in Ciechanów at that time, 1600 were economically active. That is, 45.7 % of the Jewish population were occupied in productive activities. Because actually the trade of that period - that actually created the business handling between village and city – also belonged to the productive field.

In the aforementioned year, 1887, Jewish Ciechanów had the following societies: *Talmud Torah, Bikur Cholim, Eyin Yaacov, Tiferet Bchorim, Baalei Mlochets, Chevra T'hillim and Chevra Kadisha.*

The *Bikur Cholim* Society was supported by the wealthy townsman, I. Lakh, who lent the *Chevra Kadisha* 50 rubles (a large sum at that time). In the *Chevra Eyin Yaacov*, that was founded in the year 1850 approximately, there assembled - nearly every evening - around fifty people to hear words of Torah. Winter time – every day, and summer time only on *Shabbat*, tradesmen gathered, members of the *Chevra Tiferet Bchorim*, and studied with a *rebbe*.

The Cholera Epidemic in the Shtetl in 1894

In the year 1894, a cholera epidemic broke out in Ciechanów, from which the Jewish population suffered greatly. In the first three months ninety people died and a large number lay sick in the hospital.

Because of the epidemic the Jewish population in Ciechanów was impoverished.

34

The more prosperous Jews ran away from the city. Those who remained had to support the sick in the hospital and feed more than one hundred families who were driven out of their homes that were overcome with the epidemic. Trade also ceased. The stores were closed. A false accusation was spread that the Jews were responsible for the outbreak of the epidemic, because the Jews are the most sick. Because of this the peasants did not come to the city, and all business ceased.

The local governor of Plotsk denounced the accusation against the Jews. He gave a speech to the meeting of the Ciechanów inhabitants that the epidemic is a general one and that the rumor is false when it says that Jews are responsible for the plague. In one city there are a large number of Jews amongst the sick while in another there are a large number of Christians who are sick with this contagious illness. The local government called upon everyone to contribute and help people, then the plague will end. This speech encouraged the Jews and calmed the Jews.

The Beginning of the Zionist Movement in Ciechanów

After the cholera epidemic ended, the Jewish life of Ciechanów returned to normal.

In the year 1899 a Zionist Committee was established in the *shtetl*, consisting of approximately eighty members. The number grew daily. At the head of the committee was Waxman and Nathan Tzeitag.

In the year 1900, Ciechanów men joined the fire brigade that had been in existence for eighteen years. The Christian members of the fire brigade did not warmly welcome the Jews, and only when it was absolutely necessary they called the Jews to help.

Sources

Slownik Geograficzny Krolestwa Polskiego i innych Krajow Slowianskich, Warszawa 1880.

Dr. Ignacy Schiper: Dzieje Handlu Zydowskiego na Ziemiach Polski Str. 25g.

Hatzfira - 1884, No.5, 46; 1885, No.15; 1886, No. 190; 1887, No. 204. The correspondents who contributed the articles in *Hatzfira* were: S. Alishever and Moishe Kirshenbaum. The material from the named newspapers was gathered by M. Tzinovich. The complete article was composed by the editor, A. Wolf Yasni.

35

The Rabbonim and Religious Leaders

Sh. Rotstein

The Gaon and Tzadik Rabbi Avraham Landau

The *Gaon* and holy man, *Rebbe* Avraham Landau, of blessed memory, known as "The Ciechanów *Rebbe*", was one of the most notable great leaders that Polish Jewry produced. *Rebbe* Avraml was not a *Hasidic* rebbe, as is commonly understood by the term *Rebbe*. Externally, he was far from *hasidut* and he devoted himself fully to Torah. He even *davened* according to the Ashkenazi way, though everyone was amazed at him. In all his conduct there was a synthesis of the style of the Vilna *Gaon* and the style of the *Baal Shem Tov.*

He was descended of a long line of great men and traditions: his father, *Rebbe* Raphael, was a hidden *tzadik*. He operated a tavern in the townlet and dealt with the gentry, but he was a great servant of God. *Hasidim* told that this innkeeper was a truly holy man. *Rebbe* Raphael – so *hasidic* tales tell - once traveled all alone with his wagon on the road. Suddenly several armed robbers sprang out of the forest, with outstretched swords. The robbers did not want to satisfy themselves only with the money that *Rebbe* Raphael offered them. They wanted to kill him also. At that moment a horseman came along, in the form of a military man. As soon as the robbers saw him, they quickly ran away. But at the same time the rider also vanished. *Rebbe* Raphael was sure that this horseman who saved his life was *Eliyahu Hanavi* (Elijah the Prophet).

Rebbe Avraml's mother became an orphan at a young age and she was raised in the home of her grandfather, the *Rebbe* of Lenchitz, *Rebbe* Zev Wolf Auerbach Z"L. She was already a grown young woman without a suitor. The orphan cried her eyes out, but her grandfather gave her hope, saying that when the right time came, she will be helped.

Once, a peasant-Jew came to the Lenchitzer *Rebbe*, to arrange for the burial of his deceased wife. After the *Rebbe* explained all the rites to him, he said to him: "Be so kind as to come in to me after the *shiva*. I have to discuss an important matter with you."

36

When the peasant Jew came to the *rebbe* after the *shiva*, he proposed to him that he marry his granddaughter, the orphan, Rhoda. Obviously the *rebbe* knew the "peasant-Jew" very well, but the orphan girl was shocked – to marry a widower, of all things – someone who is much older than her, and besides, a peasant-Jew, a lesee – is this supposed to be her destined one?

But the grandfather calmed her and assured her that with this widower she will have children who will light the Jewish world. It was only then that she agreed to the *shiduch* (marriage).

It was this couple who later gave birth to the famous *Gaon* and *Tzadik*, *Rebbe* Avraham of Ciechanów *Z"L*.

Since he was a very talented child, his parents did not want to keep him in the townlet so they sent him to Plotsk, that was at that time a city full of learned men and scribes/writers. There he was turned over to a *melamed* (teacher), a very observant Jew, to study.

It did not take long before the whole city was ringing about this young boy who distinguished himself with his keen mind, diligence and astonishing erudition. In addition, he was very kindhearted, feared God, full of modesty and humility. He was also very exact. Every word he uttered was measured and considered. Besides, he was subdued. His *davening* and learning was done quietly, almost for himself alone. He attempted not to draw anyone's attention. Still, it did not help. Soon he was "discovered." The teachers of his city were full of wonder at his learning and from his observance and as is the custom, the prosperous of the city began to put forth proposals, draw a net, to get him as a son-in-law.

At that time there was a famous teacher and important man, *Rebbe* Itchele Plotzker. He kept his eyes on this wonder-boy, in order to try to get him as a son-in-law. So he sent his son-in-law, Dan Landau, who was renowned for his learning, to the townlet of Avraml's parents, to ask them to allow their son-in-law to live in their house until he will grow up.

37

Reb Dan, though, had a different objective: since he already had a grown daughter, he represented himself as the interested future in-law, and *Reb* Raphael and his wife agreed to the *shiduch*.

Reb Dan did a lot for his talented son-in-law. He made it possible for him to reach what he reached. In thanks, the

Ciechanówer changed his family name to "Landau" - as his father-in-law was called.

Rebbe Avraham was *Rebbe* in Ciechanów more than fifty years and he was one of the most recognized great ones of his time. Nothing in Jewish public life was done without his advice and approval. From all over the world people came to him with complicated matters, and though he was not a *Hasidic rebbe,* he behaved like a *Hasid* and lived a life of holiness and purity. It was only at the end of his life, after the death of *Baal Khidusha Hari'm,* that he finally agreed to become leader of the community.

He started to *praveh tish* (have gatherings at his home), accept written prayers (*kvitlech),* as the *Hasidic rebbes* do, and the contributions that were given he distributed for needy purposes. At that time thousands of Jews, including great scholars and *tzadikim,* through the *talmidim* (students) of the Kolzker and Gerer *Rebbes,* came to him in Ciechanów, he did not change his style of behavior. He still *davened* in the Ashkenazi style, and generally felt more at home with the style of the Vilna *Gaon Z"L.*

Rebbe Chaim Tanzer said about him that since the days of the *Baal Shem Tov, Rebbe* Avraham Ciechanówer was the first *tzadik* who reached that level without anyone's help. His children were already famous *tzadikim*; his eldest son, *Reb* Zev Wolf of Strikov, was one of the great *Hasidim,* a *talmid* of the old Kolzker. Still he chose a different system. Besides, he was a person with a poetic soul, with a great command of language and song. His poems, full of the love of God, love of Torah, love of the people, Israel, served as a source of inspiration for Jews. The second son was *Rebbe* Berish Biyaler – a Vorker *Hasid.* The third son was the Ciechanówer *Reb* Raphael – and the fourth, *Rebbe* Yaacov Yezover, who later took up the position of head of the *Rabbanut* in Ciechanów.

38

Harav Reb Yaacov Landau of Yezev

Reb Yaacov Landau of Yezev (Yedzov), the son of *Rebbe* Avraham Landau who, for fifteen years, from 1875-1890, occupied the position of chair of *Rebbe* of Ciechanów, was born in the year 1844 approximately. Already as a youth he displayed a great faculty for learning. He grew gentle and refined, and distinguished himself with good qualities and simple yet deep thoughts. The young *Reb* Yaacov was locked in his studies of Torah. Already in his youth he was recognized as a great prodigy.

When he received his rabbinic degree, *Reb* Yaacov became the *Rebbe* in Nashelsk. Later he came to Ciechanów in order to give honor to his father, as is the commandment. His father, *Rebbe* Avraham, was already an old man and needed his help. When *Rebbe* Avraham Landau died, his son Yaacov filled his position in the rabbinate of Ciechanów.

Rabbi Yaacov Landau had a great love for the Land of Israel. Twice he made *aliyah* there: In the years 5650 and 5663. Both times he was forced to leave the Land and return to Poland because his wife could not endure the climate of the Land of Israel.

Since the year 5663, *Rebbe* Yaacov Landau gave up his position of *Rebbe* in Ciechanów, and after the death of his brother, Harav Wolf Strikow, ZT'L, Rabbi Yaacov Landau took over the position of *Rebbe* of Strikov and settled in Yezev, near Łodz. There he got the name of *Reb* Yekeleh of Yezev.

Reb Yaacov occupied the position of *Rebbe* in Yeznev for only a short time. He soon became ill. He was brought to Warsaw and there he died. A huge crowd attended his funeral.

Reb Yaacov Landau did not publish any books during his lifetime. His Torah new insights remained in manuscript form.

Harav Zeidenfeld

After *Rebbe* Yaacov Landau of Yezev gave up his position as *Rebbe* of Ciechanów, *Rov* Zeidenfeld took over his place. Unfortunately, no particulars of his life have been found, nor of his rabbinic activities in Ciechanów. We only know that he lived in the *tzadik's* house.

Rov Zeidenfeld was the father of several sons and a daughter. They emigrated abroad. According to unconfirmed information, one son lives in England. In Ciechanów we knew the *Rov's* son-in-law -- Avraham Pafa, a respected man in the *shtetl*.

39

The *Rov* Mordecai Motl was the third son of *Rov* Zev Wolf of Strikov. After the death of his father, he was the Strikover *Rebbe* and a while later he moved to Ciechanów, where he died in the year 5677.

The Rav Yitzhak Yehuda Trunk

Rov Yitzhak Yehuda Trunk, a grandson of the famous *Rebbe*, *Reb* Yehoshualeh Kutner, accepted the position of Ciechanów rabbi for another five years, from 1907-1912; he was still very young when he arrived as *Rebbe* in Ciechanów. A total of thirty years.

40

Before *Rov* Trunk came to Ciechanów he was *Rov* in Lubranetz.

With his knowledge of Torah, learning and wisdom and love of mankind, *Rov* Trunk made many friends. His house in Ciechanów was open to everyone, especially for good-learning boys. He had an unusual influence on every Jew who came in contact with him.

During his tenure as *Rov* in Ciechanów, he did many good things for the community there. Through his initiative a fine *shul* was built there. The *Rov* also made sure that around the cemetery there should be built a cement wall so that the cattle should not be able to enter there.

Harav Yitzhak Yehuda Trunk), *rebbe* in Ciechanów from 1907–1912

In the year 1912, when his father died in Kutner, *Rov* Yitzhak Yehuda was called by the Kutner *Kehilla* to fill his place. The Ciechanów Yiddish *Kehilla* found it very difficult to part with its dear *Rov*, but they understood that this is how it must be: the *Rov* Yitzhak Yehuda Trunk must occupy the position of *Rebbe* in Kutner, the place of his great ancestors.

The *Rov* Yitzhak Yehuda Trunk died in Kutner in the year 1939, before the outbreak of World War II. During his lifetime he published a book called *Mikreh M'furash*, a commentary on the Torah that distinguished itself with a particularly beautiful and lively style.

Harav Shmuel Yitzhak Landau

In the year 1913 (after *Rov* Yitzhak Yehuda left for Kutneh, the position of *rebbe* in Kutneh was taken over, in Ciechanów, by Harav Shmuel Yitzhak Landau, a great-grandson of the one-time Ciechanów *Rov, Reb* Avraham Landau.

The new Ciechanów *Rebbe* was born in Proshnitz, in the year 1875. He was the son of *Rov* Yechiel Michael and a grandson of *Reb* Zev Wolf of Strikov.

At the age of three years, Shmuel Yitzhak lost his father and was raised by his grandfather in Strikov. From his early years *Reb* Shmuel Yitzhak excelled in learning and in good traits. When he reached a ripe age, he married a daughter of a Strikov learned man and once more busied himself in Torah and *hasidut*.

In the year 1895, *Reb* Shmuel Yitzhak, at the age of twenty, became *Rebbe* in a small townlet in the Warsaw area, and six years later he took up the position of *Rebbe* in Sakhachev, in the year 1913.

41

Drawing of the old House of Study. Above can be seen the windows of the *shul*
Drawing by Yehoshua Grossbard

42

After two years, *Rov* Shmuel Yitzhak led the Ciechanów *Kehillah*. In the year 1914, World War I erupted. In the brief time the *Rov* managed to do much for the *Kehillah* in religious matters he was very strict, not departing from the precepts by even a hair. Still, he was a very friendly person and attempted to lighten people's lives. He set aside certain hours of the day when he accepted callers, straightened out disputes, carried out rabbinic judgments, and settled arguments between people. He devoted much time to the needs of his community.

There was no (*Gmilat Khesedim Fund*) fund for loans, so the *Rov* himself carried out the *mitzvah* of lending money without interest to those in need and also to market people who needed a few rubles on market-day.

43

Twice a week the *Rov* went to the slaughter-house to watch the slaughtering and examination. He also took an interest in education and started a *yeshiva* that he conducted for the Ciechanów boys. From the surrounding *shtetlech*, *yeshiva* boys started to arrive in Ciechanów in order to study Torah there.

Rov Shmuel Yitzhak Landau was a strong opponent of reforming the education. He did not allow the establishment of *Cheder M'tukan*, where *yiddishkeit* and Hebrew would be taught in a more modern manner and secular enlightenment subjects would be introduced. Regarding this there was quite a controversy between the *Rov* and the Enlightened of Ciechanów, but the *Rov* with his principles prevailed, and in Ciechanów, at that time, a modern school was not established. In general, this strictly-religious *Rov* tried to have a moral influence on the youth and did not allow the dancing of mixed couples.

As in that time, *Rov* Landau, who was the official *Rebbe* of Ciechanów for the Czarist government, also had some influence with the local police. With his influence he prevented the allowing of Yiddish Theater to be performed.

At the outbreak of World War I, the strictly religious activity of the Ciechanów *Rebbe* was interrupted. But even with the tragic outbreak of war for the Ciechanów Jews, *Rov* Shmuel Yitzhak Landau continued his faithful devotion to his Ciechanów *Kehillah*.

Ciechanów, as a city on the border of what was Germany at that time, was, like other townlets of that region, amongst the first to be caught in the fire of the War. Many Jews who suffered from the Czarist anti-semitic military escaped from Ciechanów, leaving everything helter-skelter. The *Rov, Reb* Shmuel Yitzhak Landau, did not want to leave his community, basing his decision on the words of the *chazal*, that the leader of a community does not abandon his people in an hour of need. And so it is told that the pious *Rov* saved the rest of his *Kehillah*, through a miracle, from a terrible decree. This is what happened:

44

The leaders of the Czarist military issued an order to the Ciechanów Jews to supply a thousand men to do difficult work for the army. The *Kehillah* had no choice. The military order had to be carried out.

At the appointed place the thousand Jews appeared, amongst them many elderly, weak people, and at their head was *Rov* Shmuel Yitzhak, who did not want to leave his flock, though the law allowed the *Rov* to be free from being taken to work.

While the thousand Jews were waiting thus to be sent to work, important people asked the *Rov* to go to the grave of his great-grandfather, *Rov* Avramele ZT"L, to plead for mercy for the Almighty to abolish the decree.

The *Rov* obeyed the flock and, with the elders of the group, went to the grave of the *Tzadik*. The cries and wailing at the gravesite split the heavens. The decree was abolished. The Jews were freed from the hard war work.

These life events had a bad effect on the *Rov* and destroyed his health. After the decree was abolished, the *Rov* went to the *mikveh* and from there to the *Bais Medresh* to *daven Shacharit*, together with others. No sooner did he remove from himself *Rebainu Tam's t'fillin*, he felt ill. Those present at the prayer service removed the *tallis* from the *Rov*. It was damp with tears. His soul departed in purity and in holiness on Tuesday, *Parasha Pinkhas* 1915. He died of a heart attack.

The *Rov* had a large funeral and was buried in the new Ciechanów cemetery where the saintly ones of Ciechanów are buried.

45

The above was written according to the description of *Rov* Zev Wolf Yechiel Landau of Tel-Aviv, a son of Harav Shmuel Yitzhak Landau. The son of the Ciechanów *Rov* published a book called *Chidushei Sh "I in Halakha and Agadah* by Harav Shmuel Yitzhak Landau of Suvuta, Sukhchiv, Ciechanów.

In the year 1916, *Rov* M. Bronrot was appointed as *Rov* in Ciechanów. For twenty-three years he was the religious authority of the Ciechanów *Kehillah*.

Rov Mordecai Bronrot was born in the year 5641 in Astrolenka, a *shtetl* in the Lomyer region. His father, *Reb* Nachman Tzvi, a bookseller, brought up his son with a love of Torah and Talmud. In his young years Chaim Mordecai learned Torah in Sakachev in the *yeshiva* of the famous *Gaon, Rebbe Reb* Avraham Bornstein.

The beloved last *Rov, Rov* Chaim Mordecai Bronrot, who occupied the position of *Rebbe* until the outbreak of World War II. More about him in his biography.

46

He absorbed the *Hasidic* spirit from the well-known *Tzadik*, Rabbi Yirachmiel, Yisroel Yitzhak Danziger, the famous *Alexandrian Rebbe*, the *Baal Yismakh Yisrael*. The young genius got his rabbinical motivation from the *rebbes, Reb* Malkiel Tanenbaum – Lamzer *Rov*; *Rov* Moishe Nachum Yerushalimski – Astralenke *Rov; Rov* Shimon David Anilik – Shedletz *Rov*.

After being ordained, the young *rebbe* got married to Faigl Matl, the daughter of the *Hasid* and great scholar, *Reb* Shmuel Cohen from Sterdin, Stredletz region. *Reb* Shmuel Cohen was the son of *Rov* Yaacov Yehudah Cohen – *Rov* in Cabrava, a *shtetl* near Astralenka.

Before Chaim Mordecai Bronrot took up his rabbinic position in Ciechanów, he was *Rov* in the *shtetl* Cherbin, by Astralenka. Then he transferred to a larger city, Khurzel, close to the Russo-German border of that time.

During this time, when *Rov* Bronrot led his *Kehillah*, World War II broke out. The Russian military command chased the Jews out of the *shtetl* and *Rov* Bronrot arrived in Warsaw as a refugee with his family. He was there for two years and occupied himself with organizing help for the thousands of Jewish refugees who were chased out of their homes by the Russian commanders. *Rav* Bronrot was, in Warsaw, a member of the committee to bring help to the refugees, a committee that was under the jurisdiction of the Central Refugee Committee in Petersberg (Leningrad at the time this was written). From this committee he took up the position of *Rov* in Ciechanów.

Already in the year 1918, immediately after the Germans left Poland, the Polish state was established. *Rov* Bronrot participated in a secret conference with forty *rabbonim*. The conference adopted a positive position toward the Balfour Declaration and decided, in this spirit, to let out an appeal that was signed by the *rabbonim* and made an unusual impression on the religious, *Hasidic* world.

47

Rov Bronrot was also a long-time member in *Vaad Hapoel* of *Agudat Harabbonim*. In 1922 *Rov* Bronrot, together with the former Chiechanow *Rov*, Harav Yitzhak Yehuda Trunk, went on a rabbinic mission to America. On this trip there was the expression of the great love that the Ciechanów Jews had for their spiritual and religious leader. All the *shtetl* came to say farewell to their *Rov* and to wish him a safe journey. The surrounding streets and the area in front of his house was full of Jews who awaited him as he came out of his house. Many of his relatives accompanied him, and parted from him with the words: "Go in peace and come in peace."

Community workers and Rabbonim, present at the Museum in Tel-Aviv, at the announcement of the declaration of the establishment of the State of Israel. Among them, seen from right: *Rov* Chaim Mordecai Bronrot of Blessed Memory

48

Rov Bronrot was in America for two years and worked there on behalf of the religious Jewish community. Though in many places, including Chicago, he acted as Rabbi, he did not want to remain there and did not bring the members of his family there because the life of the Jews there was not religious enough for him. In particular, the desecration of the *Shabbat* bothered him.

During the complete two years, the Ciechanów *Kehillah* kept his rabbinic position open for him and awaited the return of their leader. Upon his return, *Rov* Bronrot again led his *Kehillah* until the tragic year 1939. During all those years he was active in the Zionist movement (*Mizrachi*) and did much both in the Ciechanów *Kehillah* and elsewhere on behalf of the Jewish National fund, the Hechalutz Mizrachi Fund, and other Zionist funds. He also participated in several Zionist Congresses.

In the year 1939, two months prior to the outbreak of World War II, *Rov* Bronrot went on a rabbinical mission to England. He was trapped there because of the war and remained there for several years until he had the possibility, in 1943, to make *aliyah* to the land of Israel. Here he was appointed Rabbi of Tel-Aviv and Jaffa. He served in this rabbinic capacity until the last day of his life, and was present in the

Tel-Aviv Museum when Ben-Gurion proclaimed the establishment of the State of Israel.

49

In Tel-Aviv also the *Rov* was active in the community. He was the chairman of the Talmudic Education Net. He was also at the head of the *Yeshiva Hayishuv Hakdashah* that was created by Harav Emiel. Generally, *Rov* Bronrot did much to establish Torah learning in Tel-Aviv.

Rov Chaim Mordecai Bronrot was also the author of several books on Torah matters. He wrote publicity articles in various Zionist and *Mizrachi* publications. In 1950 he died and finished his spiritually creative work on earth.

The biographical particulars about *Rov* Chaim Mordecai Bronrot's life and activities were collected by Moishe Tzinovich.

Rav Mordecai Bronrot, The Folk Leader
Portraits of His Personality

50

Avraham Dov

The city of Ciechanów distinguished itself with its great rabbinic personalities. The most outstanding personality was the last Ciechanów *Rov*, *Rov* Chaim Mordecai Bronrot ZT"L. The title *Manhig HaEda* (leader of the flock) suited him very much. *Rov* Bronrot knew his flock very well. The Jews of Ciechanów, their feelings, thoughts, their good acts were very close to his heart and the bad deeds he tried to cast aside, according to the line: "you cast the evil aside from you", in order to clean out the evil from your surroundings.

Rov Bronrot had a deep understanding of the newly-rising Jewish cultural life of the young people. When he felt the new winds that started to blow in Jewish circles he ruled the winds and led them in the direction that he felt appropriate for the normal development of Jewish folk-life.

The leader of the Ciechanów Jews saw how the Jewish youth is drawn to a new lifestyle, so he did not cast them aside. Just the opposite; he drew them closer and showed them the way of revival of the nation in the Torah spirit. With his beautiful talks, held in a modern style, spread throughout with Talmudic words of wisdom, he won over the Orthodox youth for Zionism, and had an extraordinary influence also on the so-called "freethinkers."

With his words that "Words that come from the heart..." *Rov* Bronrot lit up the hearts and won them over to the idea of settling in *Eretz Yisroel*, tied with loyalty to the Jewish tradition.

Rov Chaim Mordecai Bronrot united in his person the ideal, honest, pure communal worker, and the great *Talmid khokhem* (learned scholar). He was a great learner/teacher, well versed in all aspects of Torah, in their laws and so on. His books were highly praised in the scholarly world. Many of his Torah commentaries, however, did not reach the public. They were drowned in the ocean together with part of the *Rov's* baggage during his trip to the Land of Israel: It was only in Israel that he published an important book about the observance of *Shabbat*. This book has special significance for the agriculture that is going on in Israel, on their own soil, where there is no *Shabbes-goy* to perform work such as milking the cows on Shabbat, for example.

51

Rov Bronrot reached a great depth with his knowledge of Torah and Talmud. An example:

To what is this comparable?
To a bee that sucks the pollen from many flowers.

That's how the *Rov* and wise men found the deep meaning of every word of every bit of writing in the Torah. His knowledge of human conflict solution was very great.

During a rabbinical court case the *Rov* would calmly, and weighing all the facts, quickly grasp which side is telling the truth and has a just complaint. He almost never made a mistake. For this reason, he was considered the best arbitrator in Ciechanów and in all the surrounding area. People came to the *Rov* with the most difficult, complicated matters, both in business matters and in family relationships.

People from other cities also came to the *Rov* with matters and questions in *kashruth,* and whatever he judged to be right, that's what was the law.

In addition to all these good qualities of the *Rov* – leader of the flock, wise man, *Mizrachi* activist, of a high caliber, a good-hearted person – his journalistic talent must also be mentioned. His journalistic articles always stood out with their humor, clarity and logical approach in communal matters.

A great religious and worldly personality was the leader of the flock in the not-large Ciechanów *Kehillah* --- *Rov Reb* Mordecai Chaim Bronrot.

52

Religious Functionaries, Religious Institutions, and Tzedakah Societies

Isaac Kesler

Hasidim, Misnagdim, and Religious Chevras/Societies

When *Reb* Avramele Ciechanówer was a *Rov* in the town, he had a great influence on all the inhabitants of Ciechanów. He influenced the religious and social life in town.

The R*ov* organized the following societies: *Hakhnasat Kallah* (assistance to poor brides), *Pidyon Sh'viim* (rescuing prisoners) and also a *Chevra Bikur Cholim* (society for visiting the sick). From the thousands of Jews who came from the surrounding cities for *Shabbes* and *Yom Tov* to his table, *Reb* Avramele took money for poor brides for *naden* (dowry), to rescue Jews from military service, as well as for hospitals for the poor.

Rov Shlomo Zeidenfeld, a very learned man, who was head of the *Rabbanut* in Ciechanów, in 1890, had little influence on the social life of the Jews there. He just devoted his time to answering religious matters and religious judgments but interfered very little in the communal life. He took over the living quarters in the *Bet Din* that was together with the *Bais Medresh*.

The *Kehillah* leadership was divided, at that time, into three branches/sections, elected by a vote of the Jewish. But the only ones who had a right to vote were those who paid taxes to the Jewish *Kehillah*. One of those, without whose agreement nothing could be done, was Lakh. The other two – Yosl Kahane and Yishakar Chechanover, who were wealthier people. After 1905, when the tradesmen managed to exert some influence in the *Kehillah*, one of the three most important people was Leib Kanarick, a tailor.

The religious leader, *Reb* Henekh Perlmutter, belonged to an extensive family in Ciechanów, intelligent people, but not leaders of religious life. One of his sons was Ephraim Perlmutter, who was very learned in Yiddish and worldly knowledge. He did not attempt, however, to take his father's place. When *Reb* Henekh died, his place was taken by Reb Yosele, a fanatically religious Jew but not very scholarly.

*

53

Nearly the complete population of Ciechanów was divided amongst *Hasidim* and *Mitnagdim*. The *Rov, Reb* Raphael Moishe Zazenband, the son-in-law of *Rebbe Reb* Avramele, carried on with a table with *Hasidim*. The wealthier Jews of Ciechanów as well as those from surrounding cities grouped themselves around the *Rebbe.* They spent their *Shabbosim* and *Yomtovim* with the *Rebbe.* There were also *shtiblech* in the *shtetl*: Gerer, Alexander and Atvosker.

In the *shtiblech* the *Hasidim* lived out their lives both religiously and socially. In every *shtetl* there was a spiritual leader. In the Gerer – Mashkers; in the Alexander one – Dovche Ciechanówer. The majority of those who *davened* in the *shtibl* knew very little about *Hasidim*. They considered themselves as people of a higher standing and instead of living out their lives in the *Bais Hamedresh* or in the *shul* amongst the working people, the merchants preferred to go to the *Hasidim* who were not workers.

In Ciechanów there was a cobbler who knew how to learn – Shilem Strepliak. He was not admitted to the community of learners, though, because he was a cobbler, so he took revenge on the learned ones through letting them have it in a stinging and humorous manner.

Once a *Magid* came to Ciechanów. After his *drash* in the *Bais Hamedresh,* he stood with a cup at the door so that when people left the *Bais Hamedresh* they should pay him. So Shilem Strepliak approached him and asked: "And how goes it with *parnoseh?*" The *Magid* replied: "Not good." Shilem said to him: "Our *parnoses* also are no good. So the *Magid* asked him: "So who are you?" So Shilem replied: "I am also a cobbler" -- with such biting jokes he would tease the *Magid's* learners.

There was also a *yeshiva* in town where boys from various cities came to learn and ate "days" by the local population. At the end of the nineteenth century the *yeshiva,* for economic reasons, closed. A certain number of the local children, after they left the *cheder,* learned in the *Bais Hamedresh* from pre-dawn until late at night. In the evenings, when everything was quiet, one could hear the singing of learners in the streets around the *Bais Hamedresh.*

54

The *Bais Hamedresh* boys used to split up into three groups. The older ones used to decide what sort of books to buy and what to learn. The younger ones helped teach the newcomers, and the youngest ones used to go around to the houses every Thursday to collect money to repair books.

It was a custom to invite boys to perform before a wedding for the groom, *Shabbes* before the wedding, and also before the *badekn* of the bride. For this purpose the wealthy of the town used to invite the *Bais Hamedresh* boys to their *simchas*.

Reb Yosele Dayan and His Son the Kadosh, Reb Ephraim
Moishe Fuchs

Ciechanów had three *dayanim*. The eldest was *Reb* Nachman Perlmutter. He was already *dayan* in the time of *Reb* Avramele Ciechanówer Z"L. There is very little information about him. He did not live in my generation. I remember only his son and grandson. He was called *Reb* Yosele. He had a strict. earnest face. I do not remember ever seeing him smile. He was a man, very strict in *Halacha*. So he was very careful with what he said. He did not look at the person, only at the *din* (religious judgment).

Butchers were deathly afraid of him. When there was a question concerning a cow, people already knew that the reply to a *sh'ailah* would always receive a *treif* judgment, and when he would sometimes find by a poor woman a question regarding a *pipik* of a fowl, and he knew that if he will consider it *treif* the woman would have to go hungry, he would plead with her to go with the question to the *Rov*. Characteristically, nobody was angry with him. It was known that he was the last of the *tzadikim cheder* and that he is very afraid of making a mistake in *halacha*.

Many hours in the day *Reb* Yosele used to sit in the *Bais Hamedresh*, deep in study of a difficult problem. Everyone treated him with much respect. He always prayed on time according to the *Tzadik's* Ashkenazi way.

Still, people said that from time to time he would go in to the Sfat Emet Z"L, but his behavior was an Ashkenazi one. In community matters also he stuck to the *halacha*. He strongly objected to all the Parties that arose in his time. He had a positive attitude only to the *Agudat Yisroel*. But even in this religious party he was not active. He was always occupied with Torah study.

55

On Friday, an hour before candle-lighting, *Reb* Yosele Dayan used to go around in the streets, dressed in a *shtreimel* and *Shabbes* clothes and plead: "Jews, light candles. Close your stores. *Shabbes* is approaching "One could note the worry on his face at this time, lest someone desecrate the *Shabbes*. The storekeepers started to rush out the customers with the shout: "*Reb* Yosele is coming. *Reb* Yosele is coming." The stores got closed and the *shtetl* assumed a true attitude of *Shabbat* rest.

Fathers and their children rushed to *shul, Bais Hamedresh*, and to *shtiblech* in order to greet the holy *Shabbat*.

In the *Bais Hamedresh*, where *Reb* Yosele *davened*, the members of the Psalm Readers group assembled, older tradesmen who strongly respected *Reb* Yosele. Nachman, the *shamesh*, gave a knock at the *shul* and announced that *Shabbat* is being greeted. It was still daylight outside.

Reb Yosele lived to a deep old age. I do not remember the exact date of his death, but I remember the funeral. *Rabbonim* gathered, from the whole area, to eulogize him, and the city deeply mourned the passing of this great Jew, *Reb* Yosele.

After his death his son *Reb* Ephraim took over by us as the *dayan*. He was decidedly different from his father: He was a passionate Gerer *Hasid*, very esteemed by the *Rebbe* and in the Gerer courtyard. *Reb* Ephraim's face always had a sweet smile for every Jew. He felt everyone's pain and rejoiced at everyone's joy. A quiet, gentle Jew, *Reb* Ephraim was almost always sitting and studying, but one could feel that in his heart there was a burning love for every Jew. He put his heart into every aspect of *Halacha*. He saw the Torah as a Torah of Life. He served the Almighty with joy and had a purpose in his life on earth.

Reb Ephraim drew close to himself boys who studied Torah. He considered human beings as a part of Godliness, and because of this he was greatly loved by all, both *Hasidim* and *Misnagdim*.

56

In the midst of his spiritual, highly acclaimed activity, the war broke out with its tragic consequences. The pious *dayan* saw the destruction of his *Kehillah*. His heart was torn apart with pain for the suffering of the Jews. He prepared himself to fulfill the *mitzvah* of *Kiddush Hashem*. He took strict care of his beard, so as not to let the Nazi murderers cut it off. He went around with his face wrapped in a kerchief.

Benjamin Apel, who presently lives in Detroit, told me that his father, one of the fiery followers of *Reb* Ephraim Z"L, had once seen him as he looked, so he started to cry bitterly and asked: "This is Torah and this is its reward?"

The *dayan*, *Reb* Ephraim, consoled his *Hasid*, that it is not the time to mourn. It is necessary to prepare for the act of giving up ones soul. "The One on high wants me to fulfill the sacred text words: 'With your whole soul even to the death.' -- was the way *Reb* Ephraim interpreted the words.

The Hitlerite murderers captured *Reb* Ephraim and issued the decree – to be shot in the castle. The beasts teased him: "*Nu*, let's see how your God can help you."

Proudly, with his head held high, the pious *dayan* made his last way, deep in thought about *Kiddush Hashem*.

The tortured Jews had to witness how their *Rov* was being led to the execution. His wife pleaded with the Gestapo murderers to let her die together with her great husband.

The Germans showed their generosity and allowed the *dayan, Reb* Ephraim Z"L, to be shot together with his wife.

57

The Ciechanów Hazzanim (Cantors)

M. Fuchs

There were very few modern *Hazzanim* in Ciechanów. Until recently, the *shtetl* only had prayer leaders. One of them was *Reb* Yaacov Hillel. When I got to know him, he was already an elderly Jew, tall, with a yellowish beard. He had a fine voice. He *davened* the *Musafim* in the *shul* and in the *Bais Hamedresh*. *Shachrisim* others *davened*, as in the *shtiblech*. He was also *shoichet* and *mohel*.

His heartfelt prayers penetrated the hearts of the men. Until World War I he was recognized as a good prayer leader.

In the *Bais Hamedresh*, Mendl Shokhet also *davened*. He was a pious Jew, respected by all.

When the *shtetl* started to modernize and the youth were no longer drawn to *shul*, the *gabbayim* decided that it was necessary to bring a modern *chazzan* who will influence the youth. The first one was *Reb* Elimelech Gotheimer, a young man from Łodz, an Alexander *Hasid*. He had a fine tenor voice, and was also a good *Shochet*. I was privileged to be amongst his first choir-boys. Understandably, he could not read notes very well, but for Ciechanów it was a novelty to hear *Mikalkel Chaim* in four voices. His brilliant tenor was also heard outside of the *shul*, that was always packed with people. When the cultural life of the town developed further, choirs and musical groups were organized so the regular *shul* goers wanted to benefit from a modern *chazzan*.

So *Chazzanim* started to apply. Every *Shabbes* a *Chazzan* visited our town. Lovers of religious music filled the *shul*. It was difficult to find a suitable candidate because he had to be both a *Chazzan* and a *Shoichet*.

After much searching, the right expert was found in all respects, *Reb* Laizer Baruchovich from Novidvor. *Reb* Laizer was the teacher of Eisenshtadt, the famous director of the Tlomatzker Synagogue in Warsaw.

It was a festive occasion when *Reb* Laizer came from Novidvor with a choir that numbered thirty people. When I recall his praying, I feel to this day the elevation of the spirit from *Reb* Laizer's choir from his cantorial musical tricks. People forgot about food and drink, and stood with bated breath to catch a fresh melody and to be enthralled by the beautiful singing. *Reb* Laizer became the darling of the town.

I was one of his first choir-boys and sang solo. *Reb* Laizer organized a good choir of all voices that are necessary, and started to teach the choir-boys how to read notes. In time, the choir developed into an important musical institution that concerned itself with religious music.

Laizer's son -- Yechiel -- was the main tenor and director. Now he is a *chazzan* in America. *Reb* Laizer perished with his family in Neishteter ghetto.

58

Shoichtim, Shamesim, and Religious Institutions
Simcha Fuchs

The *Kehillah* in Ciechanów, just as in every Jewish *shtetl* in Poland, attended to its religious needs in these ways:
1. Talmud Torah
2. *Shuls* for *davening*
3. *Mikvehs*
4. *Chevra Kadisha* and cemetery
5. Pay for *Rabbonim/Shoichtim, Shamesim* etc.

Under the pressure of the worldly members, the activities broadened. Subsidies were given for learning institutions and libraries, understandably under condition that the upper hand should still be with the religious and philanthropic institutions. The religious functionaries that the *Kehillah* supported consisted of : *Rov*, religious head, and the *shoichtim* such as *Reb* Eliezer Baruchovich – *Chazzan* and *Shoichet*, *Reb* Elimelach and *Reb* Menachem.

The majority of the town's *shoichtim* also had the authority to be the prayer leaders during the High Holidays. Ciechanów Jews considered themselves fortunate to have as *Chazzan* the great prayer leader, Eliezer Baruchovich. This was a Jew of great stature, a learned man. He composed several compositions and had quite a choir group. Every year, for the High Holidays, he would prepare new compositions.

Jews who liked choral music came, for this reason, to *daven* in the great *shul* during the High Holidays.

59

Amongst the religious functionaries we must also include the two *Shamesim*: *Reb Pinhas* from the *shul*, and the *shames* of the *Bais Hamedresh*.

Beside the *shtot-shul* and *Bais Hamedresh* there were also many *shtiblech*. There were also a few *minyanim* of tradesmen: tailors, cobblers, and the night-shelter for the needy also had a *minyan*.

The Religious Educational Institutions and the Philanthropic Institutions

The *cheder* of Trallin, as it was called, had a resounding name. Who did not learn in Trallin? This *cheder* was on the Yiddishe Street. The teachers of Reb Mordecai Trinamon *Reb* Shlomo Zalman Levcovitch and Ziskind learned in the Talmud Torah. Also active was a *Yeshiva K'tana* named after *Reb* Avramele Ciechanówer *Z"L*. It was called *Yeshiva Bais Avraham*. Its leader was *Reb* Avraham.

The Bais Yaacov School was the beloved institution of the *Agudah* of *Reb* Yoel Dovid Weingarten. In the *Yavna* School, children of Zionist parents studied.

Kindergarten of the Bais-Yaacov School with the teacher, Freedman

60

There were also some philanthropic institutions in the *shtetl* whose job it was to help the needy with loans. For example: the *G'milat Chesedim*, established by Moishe Klinger and others established by Shmuel Fuchs.

The *chevra Linat Hatzedek* supported the sick. The Burial Society was also an important institution. It provided for a Jewish burial. The *gabbayim* were *Reb* Yisroel Yaacov Student, *Reb* Avraham Freedman. The *Chevra Kadisha* was an old institution and had a list of rules that every member had to observe. For instance, they had a custom that for *Shmini Atzeret* they must all *daven* in *shul* with the *Rov,* and all the *gabbayim* received an aliyah.

61

Community Activities in the Years before World War I

Isaac Kesler

From Bais Hamedresh Religiosity to Secular Enlightenment Judaism

At the beginning of the twentieth century, a change of thought entered the minds of the *Bais Hamedresh* youth.

The Russo-Japanese War elicited great interest amongst the young men and they started to read *Hatzfira,* that reported news of the war.

The *Hatzfira* was brought into the *Bais Hamedresh* by the boys, Yehoshua and Eli Klinger and the *Rov's* son Alter. Through the newspaper we discovered what was happening in the world and were influenced by new ideas. The articles about world news and secular enlightenment Judaism gave the young men new ideas. The struggle awakened within them, between *Yiddishkeit* and universalism and traditionalism. Together with the sacred texts, we started to read secular enlightened books, and the more we read, the more we wanted to change the stagnant Jewish life for a worldly one.

We developed a strong desire to read Hebrew books and journals and since individually we did not have funds to buy them, it was decided to form a library. With the help of the *Rov's* son, Alter, we got a room above the *Bais Hamedresh*, in the living quarters of his sister and brother-in-law -- Avraham Pafa.

At night when the Jews left the *Bais Hamedresh*, the organizational meeting took place for the Hebrew Library. The majority of the *Bais Hamedresh* fellows, especially the younger ones, were represented there. The older ones were engaged to be married, and were somewhat afraid lest it interfere with their prospective marriages.

The following names remain in my memory as being present at the founding meeting: the *Rov's* son, Alter, Mendl Krimko, Yosef Yacubovich, Izak Lieberman, Yehoshua Kleinetz, Avraham Kleinetz, Avraham Trombka, Yaacov Milyard, Yechiel Maier Naman, Yosef Rosenblum, Moishe Rosenblum, Moishe Misher, Hershel Misher, Gershon Milovsky, Shmuel Yaacov Cohen, Moishe Chaim Kostsheva, Avraham Izak Kostsheva, Yehoshua Munshtig, Dovid Fuchs.

62

Besides those who participated in the meeting, others lent their support in favor of the library: Tzaduck Burstein, Mechel Shon, Avraham Bontzke, Yehoshua Klinger and Elyeh Klinger.

Krimko, Gershon Milovsky and Moishe Misher. The library was sustained mainly by weekly dues of its members. But an important source of income was from a group of boys who were invited to perform for a wedding. The groom had to make a contribution to the library.

In a few years we collected close to four hundred Hebrew books. We kept the books at Moishe Rosenblum's mother's place. His father was in America. His mother did not know that the Czarist government forbade a library, nor that it is not *kosher* in the eyes of the religious Jews.

Only a small number of readers came directly to the library. The main exchange of books took place in the *Bais Hamedresh*, beneath the *capote*. Reading was done in hiding so that the parents should not see. But it did not take long and word of our library became known – that instead of learning *Gemara*, we are reading secular enlightenment books by Achad Ha'am, and that we are reading *Haskaloach*.

The struggle started. A certain number of our members feared public opinion. They wanted to remain good children of their parents and in general, so as not to jeopardize their chances of marriage.

They immediately distanced themselves from us but the majority remained convinced that Jewish nationalism and universalism is the solution for the Jewish people.

63

The thirst for secular enlightenment knowledge to reconstruct Jewish life on a new basis, spiritually founded, sharpened the struggle between parents and children, and when our parents argued that they feed and clothe us and we cause them disgrace in town, we decided to go to work so as not to rely on our parents.

Henekh Dubnow, the only one from the "pearl" button factory in our town, who came from Sachatchin, near Plonsk, where Zionism was widely prevalent – was happy to employ us when he found out about our decision to become independent.

With one of our boys this is what happened: Ephraim Meyer Tchurek was younger than us and his father was very protective of him lest he become a good friend of ours. Nothing helped, though, and he became an avid follower of our ideas of the new period. True, at *davening* time he kept his distance from us. After he had already read a few books of history, Enlightenment journals, he went off the "right track" and started to read secular enlightenment books one after the other.

The *Maskilim* in Ciechanów

He chose for himself "the last time" to read pre-dawn when his father was still asleep.

Once he brought home Fierberg's book *Le'an (Whereto)*. Ephraim, as was his custom, was ready pre-dawn, and he dozed off. It happened to be *Tisha B'Av*; his father happened to get up early as usual, and went to awaken him to *daven* and thereby found this forbidden book on his bed. Ephraim Maier was asleep and did not hear, so his father took the book and ripped out the first page, with Fierberg's picture with his uncovered head. He smeared the picture with chimney ash and hung it up on the wall opposite Ephraim Maier's bed. When Ephraim awakened and saw what had been done to the book, he jumped up, grabbed a *Zohar* and wanted to tear it up. His father beat him up and threw him out of the house.

Tisha B'Av, going from the new cemetery, where *chevreh* were throwing thistles at one another, Ephraim Maier appeared, in tears, because his father had torn up his book and driven him out of the house.

Since, by that time, we had our library near the property of Lichtenstein in a loft, we put a bed there, bought a primus machine for cooking, and Ephraim Maier was put in charge of the library. Every Friday his mother would bring cooked fish, meat, *challah* – so that his father would not know.

*

By this time there were already a few prominent Jews in town amongst the older ones, who came to the conclusion that secular enlightenment *yiddishkeit* is necessary. They were: Shlomo Rubinstein, Dovid Weis, Vinditsky, Fishl Lachover, and a few others whose names I cannot recall. They wanted to give their children a modern education; did not want to send them to the old-fashioned *cheder*, so Ephraim Maier took it upon himself to teach their children, according to Krinsky's program of modern schools in Warsaw. These were the first steps of modern Jewish education in Ciechanów. Afterwards came Divan from Sachatchin, a relative of Shmuel Rosen, and officially opened a modern school.

64

The desire to study spread very much amongst our youth. Yechiel Maier Gomen, Yenkl Milyard and Moishe Misher decided to study for an academic profession such as: doctor, pharmacist, or lawyer. For this it was necessary to first complete a *gymnasia,* but the Czarist government decreed that there would be a quota for Jews in the *gymnasia* and it was almost impossible for Jews to enter the learning institutions, so they had to study privately in order to prepare for the examinations.

65

That's what our boys did. Their teacher was a graduate student by the name of Chiginolov. They studied day and night, as much as their minds could absorb, and several times failed the examinations because of the special difficulties that were posed for Jews. It did not take long before our students became ill. Yechiel Maier Gomen and Yenkl Milyard died in Ciechanów. Moishe Misher emigrated to America. Daytime he worked in a factory and in the evenings he studied dentistry. After being in New York for nine years he married, and later died of tuberculosis in a hospital.

*

The library directors arranged cultural evenings, lectures, readings, discussions and a choir that was led by Shmuel Makaver, the carpenter's son. The evenings used to be conducted in Hebrew by Moishe Rosenblum, the teacher at school. There was also a drama group that performed "Hafni and Pinchas" – which was performed in the firemen's hall near the magistrature. The performance took place on the twentieth of the Hebrew month of *Tamuz,* at the time of the memorial day of Herzl.

The Polish youth also started cultural activities at that time and a culture-house was established. We were invited to attend their programs at the culture-house. Dovid Klezmer used to play at all their functions. Dinched Razikeh, a girl who had a beautiful voice, sang there. But it did not take long before the Polish chauvinism started to rule in the culture-house. They no longer invited Jewish musicians, singers, and fully cut off all contact with Jews.

The Poles organized the co-op *Spoolka* with the slogan: "Poles buy only from Poles!" This boycott against Jewish businesses started also on the *Gurka* and in the stroll-gardens there began a fight between the Jewish and Polish visitors.

For the majority of us young Jews, life in Ciechanów became very difficult. The struggle for secular enlightened Judaism became very difficult. The discrimination against the Jews in the Czarist laws took away their rights. The pogroms, the chauvinism of the Polish population that was expressed against the Jewish economic existence -- all this together proved to us that there is no future for us. We cannot build our future in such a difficult atmosphere.

The majority of us decided to move elsewhere in the world to various countries.

That's how I remember life in Ciechanów. Moishe Klainyud took over direction of the library at that time. Vovak Berstein became active. The Cohens came to Ciechanów. Their house became the cultural center of the Zionist organization.

The Start of the Jewish Socialist Movement
Yisroel Borenstein

In the year 1899, when my father died, I was eleven years old. My mother sent me away to an uncle in a village, three miles from the *shtetl*. There, at my uncle's, I started to learn a trade (cobbler).

66

A few years later I returned to Ciechanów, where I worked a short time and then went to Mlava. In Mlava, the *Poele Zion* Organization had just been founded. I was one of its founders and already at that time took an active part in the work of the Party. I learned a lot and returned to our *shtetl* a full socialist. The youth in Ciechanów was very far from knowing anything about socialism at that time, so I became the organizer of the tradesmen: cobblers and tailors and others.

In the Hebrew month of *Elul*, in the year 1908, in the month when shop-owners demanded of their workers that they work longer hours at night, I started to organize the workers against night-work and at the same time demanded a "normal" work-day, from 8:00 a.m. in the morning until 8:00 p.m. in the evening.

The workers elected a committee, and right at the first *S'lichot*, when the night work was supposed to start, I and one other of the committee went out to control whether the workers were carrying out our decision.

67

The first place where we went to check was at Shmuel Khumeles. He lived in the market by Laketch. Two apprentices and a young boy worked for him. The main apprentices were Yochanan, nicknamed Burmisch: (in the *shtetl* everyone had a nickname). His father was a carrier.

Shmuel Khumeles found out that a committee is coming to check the work at night so he stood at the entrance to await us. When he saw us approach, he called out loudly: "Socialists! Murderers!" From his screams a crowed gathered from nearby. Realizing what was happening, we tried to avoid a scandal and we went away. A few days later the same Shmuel Khumelis, with another few business operators from the *shtetl*: Laibl Kanarick, Yishakhar Ciechanówer, Ephraim Khumeles, went to the local governor and told him that a "Socialist" society had been formed and gave him the names.

The very next day, police came to the given addresses and arrested whoever they found and put them in the Ciechanów prison. They were looking for me also. When I went up to my boss where I worked, two soldiers with guns were already waiting for me. They led me through the market. I was proud of the fact because, after all, I was not a criminal. I was arrested with another twelve people. I remember some of them. The little Yehezkl who lives presently in Philadelphia and calls himself Charley Boilner; Avramche Shuster, son of Shmuel Glezer, a tailor.

The arrest took place between *Rosh Hashana* and *Yom Kippur*. Parents, sisters and brothers of the arrested ones went to the business owners and also the *Rov* and warned that they, the families of the arrested ones, will not allow *Kol Nidre* to be said, and will knock out the windows if the boys will not be led out of prison. The business owners saw that the situation was bad, so they went to the local governor and at the cost of several hundred rubles we were freed.

Besides this episode of my young years, I also remember: the *Bais Hamedresh* where the sound of Torah was always heard; the Bet Din House where the *Rov* lived with the Spanish wall that kept the *Rov's* bed out of sight. On the bed there always rested the *shtreimel* and the cane.

68

I remember the fire at the *shul.* Jews raced to put out the fire. Moshe-Leib (nicknamed "sand-handler") harnessed the horse to a wagon on two wheels and with a container, ran to the river to get water in order to put out the fire in the *shul.* But the *shul* burned down.

When I left my *shtetl* they started to build a new *shul.* At that time it was decided that in the new *shul* there should not *daven* an official *chazzan,* only a prayer-leader. This was all written down and put into a glass container that was cemented

into the foundation. The *Kehillah* accepted this decision because it was felt that because of the dispute about a *chazzan-shoichet* the *shul* burned down.

That same year I enlisted in the army and I was accepted. I stole out of the barracks, however, and that same cold winter night I went through the Proshnitz Way to the market and went to Yanover and smuggled across the border to Germany. With a ship from Hamburg I sailed to New York and from there to Detroit, where I live to the present day with my dear wife (Vita), two daughters, one son and five grandchildren.

My one-time birthplace, Ciechanów, I have never forgotten.

The Ideological Struggle between Children and Parents
Rivka Kahane

It is difficult to recall when this struggle started. There was a search, a desire that took root in our souls and brought us together. To this day I do not know how I found myself encircled by young people (I myself was young), thirsty for spiritual sustenance in life; a youth that strove for something better, higher, and does not allow itself to be satisfied with the status quo.

In our house the young people found some ground under their feet, a place where they could express their longing for another life and freely express themselves about various problems that plagued their minds.

69

At that time there developed, in Jewish homes, the great struggle between parents and the younger generation. In Ciechanów also the parents felt that their children have been "turned upside down" and are sliding out from their up-to-now watch. Nearly the same struggle went at an engagement party. Naturally everyone had to be prepared in advance, should a sudden "guest" appear. For that everyone had to have an excuse ready.

70

In the years 1913-1914, the organization *M'fitzai Haskala* in Petersburg (Leningrad at the time this was written) got permission from the Czarist government to open branches throughout the land. "Statutes" also arrived in our name, and we organized a sort of "Cultural Society." We used to receive from the central office in Petersburg letters in Yiddish which we had to translate into Russian and hand over to the powers there to okay. They used to send their representative to every such gathering. In 1914, when World War I broke out, all the cultural work came to a halt.

Maccabee Organization and Dramatic Group
Maier Gotliber

In the year 1908 there used to come to our house, to my brother Yechezkiel, a group of friends to play cards. Amongst them was one who did not play cards. He was a complete stranger in town. He often carried on discussions with my brother's friends.

I was a boy of twelve years then. The talk of that stranger had a profound effect on me. He spoke about revolution, about overthrowing the Czar. His revolutionary talk so captured my imagination that it influenced my future path in life. In the city there was a rumor that he had been sent by the "Socialist

Revolutionaries" (a revolutionary party in Czarist Russia that depended for its support mainly from the peasants and applied terror against the Czarist ruler).

70

In a very short time afterwards a group of young people was organized that gave themselves the name "Maccabeans" The group consisted of Zionists, well-off young people, and of course some workers. The main purpose of the organization was supposed to be to give the young people physical training.

Sport organizations in Ciechanów above and below *Hapoel*

"Maccabee" (sport) and the Hebrew language.
A rich library that was not a Party one was established at the sport club

73

Party groups started to be formed. It got a little "crowded" to work together. Friction arose that grew in intensity. It came to a split in the

Maccabi organization. And so a few members created a workers' dramatic group that got organizational help from Mlava *chaverim*. Greenberg was at the head of this group. It carried through several theatrical works with much success.

74

The Beginning of a Yiddish School Presence in Ciechanów
B. Fuchs

Before World War I, during the Czarist rule in Poland, there was no compulsory government school, only private ones. One such school belonged to Moishe Lerer. In a room of his own living quarters, he installed some school desks and a table and that was the whole school. There boys and girls learned together for two hours daily, Russian and Yiddish. Naturally, persons with a higher education could not come out of such a school.

Teacher Flam's school, its pupils with the teacher in the middle

A better type of school was by the teacher Flam. His school consisted of two rooms. On the wall hung a large portrait of Czar Nicholaas the Second and smaller pictures of his family members. Beneath the Czar's picture, mounted on a step, there stood the teacher's table covered with a green tablecloth. On the table – a globe and writing material. On both sides of the table – two blackboards. On one of them one of the pupils would write the date each day and on the other there hung a large Russian map.

75

In Flam's school, classes took place from eight in the morning until twelve noon. Subjects were: Arithmetic, History of Russia, and other subjects. The primary language was Russian. Boys and girls were taught together but they sat on separate benches. The separate rows of benches also served as "dividers" according to the level of the students. In each division one studied for a year. If the students made progress they were moved forward one division.

Those, though, who "sinned", i.e., did not do their homework or disturbed, the teacher seated closer to him. That was the worst punishment for the students. If such punishment made a small impression on the student, the teacher would use a rod that he held in his hand always. Between seventy to eighty children of various ages attended this school.

In 1914, when war broke out, the schools closed. During the German occupation three Jews: Rabinovich, Divan and Tchurek, opened private schools where Hebrew was taught, but unfortunately they did not have much success. At the same time, a woman arrived from Warsaw by the name of Indik, and opened a girls' school ("philological pension"). Beside the fact that tuition there was very expensive, she did have success. To start there were two departments, but in time the school expanded and had five departments.

There were very good pedagogues in the school. Subjects taught were: German, Polish, French, Latin and Hebrew – the same subjects as in the Polish men's *gymnasia*. *Frau* Indik's school did not have official sanction. At a later term, evening classes were organized there for older youth.

The *Bund* organization brought down teachers from Warsaw and opened a school with Yiddish as the language of instruction.

76

World War I and Its Effect on Ciechanów Jews

Tankhum Makaver

Memories of the Years 1914–1918

The outbreak of World War I, on the ninth day of the Hebrew month of *Av*, greatly worried the Jews of Ciechanów. It was approximately forty kilometers from the *shtetl* to the German village; therefore a great fear fell upon the Jewish population in Ciechanów. Suitable Jews and non-Jews were conscripted. They were immediately sent to Modliner Fortress. The fear and panic increased even more when a great explosion was heard. On the horizon, in the direction of Mlava, clouds of smoke were seen. This was the result of the Russians blowing up the bridge. Jews started to pack their household belongings and wanted to run away and many became apathetic because of fear and did not know what to do.

The confusion grew even worse when two German planes appeared in the sky above Ciechanów.

Soon all coin money disappeared. The Poles went to the Jewish stores to shop – some for bread, some for butter and sugar and they paid three or five rubles in coin in order to get the rest in small change. But the storekeepers did not have that much small change. There were scandals, shouts and threats.

A meeting was called in the magistrature of the Jewish and Polish bosses. The meeting made the following suggestions:

To issue coupons in place of small change.

Everyone who will want to exchange will get coupons with the same worth as the change.

To take charge of the security in town.

The security was put in the hands of the voluntary fire brigade, Jews and Poles.

A committee was elected consisting of four people, three Poles and one Jew – Moishe Yaacov Rakovsky.

People calmed down somewhat but the normal daily life did not resume.

77

The trades-people did not work. Children did not attend school. This situation continued for several weeks, until General Sasonov arrived with his army from Russia and went to conquer Germany.

The Russian army brought a slight revival in the economy. Besides the merchants, others also started to earn. But this calm did not last long.

In Ciechanów some *cherkasn* were found at that time who went wild over the Jews. They grabbed twenty-one Jews in the streets of Ciechanów, took them to the prison and beat them. The tortured ones came home in great pain. Jews were afraid to be seen in the street. Still, before dawn people went to *S'lichot*. Here one could see the same *cherkasn* who were the heroes of yesterday over the defenseless unprotected Jews, now escaped, two on each horse, barefoot.

It did not take long before several divisions of German soldiers arrived. They brought along a Jewish male, Bainish Kansky-Volsky, from the village of Niestem, where he lived with his family. The Germans tied him to a post in the middle of the market. Jews wanted to speak with him but the Germans guarded him and would not allow this. Immediately a rumor spread that they will hang the young man, or shoot him.

Moshe Rosenberg, whom religious Jews in Ciechanów called Moishe "Apikores" because of his education and knowledge of languages, went to the temporary German commander, who was billeted at Mendl Klainyud, and explained to him that the young fellow who was tied to the pole in the market is an idiot who does not understand the German language. He did not understand what he was being asked.

The German occupiers of World War I, who were not yet poisoned with Hitler's poison, still took such arguments into consideration. The commandant said to call the *Rov* of the *shtetl*. The *Rov, Reb* Landau Z"L, was not in Ciechanów at that time. The religious prayer leader, the *dayan Reb* Yosef Perlmutter Z"L, an honest and trustworthy person, one who sat day and night studying Torah and in prayer, who had never looked at the face of a non-Jew and did not know the language of the non-Jews, represented him. Moishe Rosenberg went to the *dayan* and told him what was going on. The *dayan* asked for the *gabai* (sexton) of the *Bais Hamedresh, Reb* Moishe Strashiner, and the three Jews to be called: Yosef Dayan, Moishe Rosenberg, and Moishe Strashiner went to the commandant.

The commandant demanded from *Reb* Yosef Perlmutter to tell him whether it is true that the young man is an idiot, that he did not understand what was said to him. The *dayan* assured the commandant that this is true; the fellow did not understand what he was asked, so he was freed.

78

Two hours after he was freed the German division left Ciechanów.

The Anti-Semitism of the Czarist Soldiers and Officers

In October, November 1914, Russian military divisions arrived in Ciechanów from Siberia, peaceful people who were not yet contaminated with anti-Semitism, but in the area of Ciechanów there were also Don Cossacks, true murderers. Some of the officers of the Cossack brigade lived in a Polish hotel. Opposite the hotel there lived the Ciechanów *Rov* Landau. One night, when the officers got drunk and went wild, the hotel owner indicated that across from the hotel there lived the Ciechanów *Rov*. At two o'clock in the morning they dragged the *Rov* out of his bed, took him to the hotel, and there amused themselves with the old *frum Rov*. At daybreak they released him. It is easy to imagine the fear and the suffering of *Rov* Landau Z"L, a great-grandson of the Ciechanów *Tzadik, Reb* Avraham Z"L.

At the same time the Cossacks took out two Jews from the village Sammierz near Ciechanów, and shot them. In the year 1915, after the German army occupied Ciechanów, the occupying forces allowed the two bodies to be exhumed and brought to Ciechanów. They were given a Jewish burial.

December 1914 the powers in Ciechanów demanded from the Jewish *Kehillah* that a Jewish delegation, headed by the *Rov*, should present themselves to the nobleman Michael, a brother of Czar Nicholaas II. The delegation was to be picked up at the Ciechanów train station.

Rov Landau was not in Ciechanów. After the night when the Cossack officers dragged him out of bed, he went away for some time The *dayan Reb* Yosef could not appear in the *Rov's* place in the delegation because he did not understand the Russian language. So it was decided that *Reb* Moishe Shlifkeh should be the *"Rov"* . He was a military tailor, understood Russian, and had a wide beard. He greeted the nobleman in the name of the Ciechanów Jews. The nobleman gave him his hand. The very same month the Ciechanów Russian front was visited by a delegation of the Russian Jews with the well-known advocate, A. A. Gruzburg, at its head. The delegation distributed gifts to the Russian soldiers. It did not come in contact with the Ciechanów Jews.

79

Winter 1915, the Russian authorities arrested three Jews: Yaacov Kalflus, Mendl Burstein and Mendl Klainyud as hostages for the Jewish population in Ciechanów and sent them to Siberia. When the Russian revolution broke out, they returned to Ciechanów.

Spring of 1915 arrived. The cannon shots from the front were heard more often, but the Jews of Ciechanów were used to this. From Turkestan a new military division arrived. It settled outside of the town. A town commandant was appointed. Power was transferred from civilians to the military.

The *dayan, Reb* Yosef Perlmutter Z"L, was arrested as a hostage for the Jewish population of Ciechanów. He was given a room at the magistrature and he was allowed to bring in bedding, food and books for learning. Shimshon Perlmutter attended to this. He was a carpenter by trade. Three times a day Perlmutter went to the *dayan* at the magistrature in order to bring him something, or simply to ask him what he needs. The *dayan* lived this way for days, in great fear and distress. All the Ciechanów Jews suffered the *dayan's* pain along with him. Finally he was freed.

The military local commandant was not an anti-Semite. During a consultation of high-ranking officers, when it dealt with sending out all the Jews of Ciechanów, the commandant was against this. He proved that the Russian soldiers would suffer thereby; he won't have where to buy his needs. In fact, during the time that he was commandant, not one Jew was accused in any transgression. Eight Poles were hung at that time as spies.

The Expulsion of Proshnitz Jewry and the Help of the Ciechanów Jews

A few days before Pesach 1915, Nicholaas Nicolevich, the father of Czar Nicholaas II, issued an order that in the course of twenty-four hours all Jews in Proshnitz must leave there. Proshnitz was twelve kilometers from Ciechanów. This date was Friday *erev Shabbat Hagadol.* The news spread like lightning regarding the expulsion of the Jews of Proshnitz. Quickly, not in an organized manner. Jewish Ciechanów wagons set out for Proshnitz in order to rescue the poor Jews with their scanty belongings. The wealthier ones had already long before left for Warsaw.

80

In Proshnitz they also found Jews from the *shtetlech,* Khurzil Yanov, who had left their homes months before. Impatiently the return of the wagons was awaited in Ciechanów. The sun set as usual in the west. Shlomo Shames knocked with his wooden hammer as usual and called out: "To *Shul*" The stores closed for *Shabbat* and through the windows of Jewish homes Sabbath candles were seen. *Reb* Yosef Perlmutter Z'L, with his *shames* Yaacov Dantos, as usual were going to the *Bais Hamedresh* to welcome in the Sabbath (*Kabbalat Shabbat)* and at the same time he takes a walk through the nearby streets calling out: "Light candles. It's late. Light candles."

It was only in the quiet of the night that the clatter of the returning wagons could be heard. Without delay the wagons rode up to the *Hasidic shtiblech* and brought in the Proshnitz Jews with their few possessions. Food was not lacking because every Jewish woman brought from the *Shabbat* cooked food: fish, meat, *challahs* for the homeless. The wagons returned to Proshnitz. The arrival of the homeless continued until the following night.

A group of Ciechanów youth was organized to help the homeless. Meanwhile, after the holy Sabbath, the homeless were arranged in private homes. A committee was founded, consisting of Zionists and non-party youth: Esther Milner, Avraham Rembom, Baruch Mordecai and Hershel Malina, Dvora Kviat, Wolf Levine, Chaya Rivka Robota, Tova Klinger, Yosef Trabker, Yaacov Misher, Yosef Farma, Laib (a baker), Moishe Parakh (Kviat), Moshe Sokolover, Michael Kirshenbaum, Nachum Rosen (a *feldsher),* Natan Berman, Faleh Dresner, Raigl Shutzka, Shlomo Klinger, Shaineh Faigl and Tankhum Makover.

The committee started to energetically gather products for *Pesach* for the homeless because only two days remained until Passover. The work was divided into groups. Every group had its job: Yentzeh (Yaacov) and his wife Chana Chava Robota gave permission to have the *matzah* baked in their oven. Yekhezkl Trombka fired and *koshered* the oven. That took a whole night. Those who owned the mill gave flour for *matzah.* The wood dealers provided wood. The members of the committee gathered everything. The baking of the *matzah* lasted from very early until late at night. But in addition to the *matzah* there was also a need for fish, meat, potatoes..

Tankhum Makover undertook to look after all this. He contacted Chaim Laizer, the butcher, regarding meat. Mendl Greenbaum gave wine and Bainish Kanskavolsky – potatoes.

81

Notes were distributed so that every family could receive products according to the number of its members. Money was collected in a very unusual manner: The *b'chorim* boys who learned in the *Bais Hamedresh* prepared some money for their redemption so that they would not have to fast on the eve of *Pesach* as is the custom. The payment for the *b'chorim* went for the refugees.

The *gabais* (sextons) of the *shuls* and *Bais Hamedreshim* gave the money for their *aliyahs* to the Torah for the refugees. Other contributions were gathered by members of the committee. Tea and sugar were donated by the colonial merchants. That's how Ciechanów Jews supplied the homeless Jews of Proshnittz at that time when, because of the brutal Czar Nicholaas Nicholevich they were driven out of their homes.

On the second day of Pesach the local authorities sent an order to *Rov* Landau, to bring the boy who picked up a package that a German plane had dropped. A Pole construed this libel. The *Rov* Landau went to the local commandant and explained to him that this is no more than a false accusation, and with that the matter was closed.

Amongst the homeless there were old folk and sick people. There were no doctors in Ciechanów. They were all mobilized as soon as war broke out. Only one Jewish *feldsher* remained in Ciechanów by the name of Nachum Rosen. He constantly helped the committee and provided medical help, both day and night, without charge. That's how all the members of the committee worked also. In the case of severely ill cases a doctor was brought. In such a case a military doctor was used, one who someone came upon in the street. They willingly visited the sick and prescribed medication that the committee bought in the pharmacy.

One day two members of the committee - Tankhum Makover and Yosef Trombka, went to seek a doctor for someone who was seriously sick. They came across two military doctors and asked that one of them visit a sick person.

The doctors said: "A hospital has been opened for the civilian sick so that the military doctors will not be called upon."

Tankhum Makover and Yosef Trombka visited the hospital that was outside of the *shtetl* en route to Plonsk. There, there stood several houses that belonged to a German master builder called Weizner. The Russian authorities had sent him and his whole family to Siberia. The hospital was set up in these houses. The committee was informed about this. Two members, Dvora Kviat and Tankhum Makover, were immediately delegated to get to know the personnel of the hospital.

82 contd.

Two female doctors worked in this hospital. One was Jewish, by the name of Kazeri Anovska from Zhitomer. The second one was a Russian, a very liberal one. These two doctors helped the committee very much, that is to say, with the sick.

Those seriously ill were brought to the hospital and the other sick got their medication there.

One day there came to Ciechanów the famous writer and journalist of the Jewish newspaper (*Der Freyndt*), "The Friend" -- Sh. An-ski. He stayed at the hotel of Noach Misher. The purpose of his visit was to help the homeless. He had been sent by the "Moscow Jewish Gezelschaft for Aid to the War Victims". Sh. An-ski visited a row of *shtetls* and *shtiblech*, where he organized local committees to help the homeless. According to his supervision he assigned certain sums of money for help.

In Ciechanów he found an active organized committee. He assembled them and listened to the reports for the time of the existence of the committee; examined the books and the registration of the homeless that consisted of eight hundred people. At his recommendation it was decided that, instead of money, produce should be given to each family according to the number of its members. He decided on 650 rubles per month. In addition, at the recommendation of Dvora Kviat, a one-time sum of 500 rubles was given to the weak ones to improve their health.

The homeless gradually established themselves. They started to earn money. A Talmud Torah was established for the children in the women's portion (*Ezrat Nashim*) of the big *shul*.

The German planes bombed Ciechanów from time to time. The following Jews were victims of the bombing: Yosef Mandchok, Yudl Treger and his wife; wounded ones – Henia Mandchok, Melekh Treger and Laib Treger.

83

The People's Kitchen in Ciechanów during World War I

84

A warplane struck the *shul*. The bomb made a hole in the roof. The ceiling remained stuck on the floor of the *Ezrat Nashim* where the children of the Talmud Torah learned. The bomb did not explode. A military man removed it and in this incident religious Jews saw a miracle from heaven.

85

The Cholera Epidemic during World War I

Epidemics arose and started to spread – cholera included. Ciechanów was not spared this terrible sickness. The hospital let out an appeal for people to come to the hospital to get vaccinated against cholera. The young people did so, but the older folks were afraid to go to the hospital for the needle. The hospital accepted many people, but many never came out of there. The Ciechanów *Rov* Landau also died of this illness.

The situation became very serious. Those who fell ill begged not to be taken to the hospital. The young people who wanted to help did not know what to do.

86

The kitchen for the Jewish poor was established. The cook, every day on her way to work, took along meat from the Jewish butcher that was selected by the manager of the kitchen. A few days before *Rosh Chodesh Av* the question arose about eating meals during the period of the nine days. A representative of the committee came to an understanding with the representatives of the *Zemski-Saiyuz* regarding the substitution of dairy means instead of meat meals, but for this it was also necessary to change the dishes that was associated with a sizable cost.

A delegation consisting of Moishe Rosenberg, Tankhum Makover and Yosef Trombka met with the religious leader,

Reb Yosef Perlmutter and with a few more Jews in the *Bais Hamedresh* and conferred about what should be done. It was decided that the religious leader should call out that it is permissible for those who eat in the kitchen for the poor to eat meat during the nine-day period. He promised us to do this and kept his word.

The third day in the month of *Av* 1915 -- a panic: Jews were being seized in the street. Great turmoil erupted. Everyone hid wherever they could. In lofts, in cellars. Men were taken from their homes, except for those who were tradesmen. Thosse seized were taken to forced labor.

The German Occupation during World War I

A few days later, the German army occupied Ciechanów. Two Ciechanów Jews whom the Russian soldiers had taken with them, later came back. The hospital of *Zemski-Saiyuz* was taken over by the German forces. One nurse and one medic of the former personnel remained on staff. The care in the hospital was far from what it was previously. No longer were the sick sent to convalescent institutions. The Germans buried the dead in an open field, Jews and Christians together. That is how (Yaacov) Yekl Fiever was buried also.

The Jews of Ciechanów could not forgive such acts, and one night some members of the burial society: Benjamin Malina, Yisroel Yaacov Student and Avraham Freedman went out to the field and took out the casket with the dead body of Yaacov Fiever and replaced the whole with an empty casket. The burial society members carried the dead man to a Jewish cemetery and gave him a Jewish burial.

The *shtetl* Ciechanów became closed off – no exit nor entry. The German commandant selected a Jewish mayor, the above-mentioned Moishe Rosenberg, and also a Polish mayor for the Poles. The secretary of the Jewish mayor was Michael Kirshenbaum, and his helper – Wolf Levine.

The first address of the German forces to the civilian population was in three languages: Yiddish, German and Polish. The address made quite an impression on the national youth because it was the first time that an official force addressed the Jews in their own language.

The epidemic ceased. The city reopened. The homeless returned to their homes, each one to the place from whence they had come. The little money that remained in the committee's hands was divided up amongst the homeless. The group of medics also disbanded.

87

As already mentioned, the Ciechanów *Rov* Landau had already died. Ciechanów needed a *Rov*. There were several candidates, amongst them also the *Rov, Reb* Mordecai Bronrot Z"L. He was beloved as a community worker and was also a member of the central committee of *Mizrachi* in Poland. From *Mizrachi* he was delegated to the Twelfth Zionist Congress in Carlsbad. With a large majority of votes, *Rov* Bronrot was elected as *Rov in Ciechanów.*

The economic situation of the Ciechanów Jews became very difficult. The German forces requisitioned everything: food, leather, manufactured goods, etc. Trade nearly came to a standstill. The German powers put a demand for a contribution on the community, as though the Ciechanów Jews had conducted a war against the Germans and they were defeated.

Young people during World War I wearing wooden shoes.

From right, <u>top row</u>: M. Tenenbaum, Liba Grosbard, P. Kostsheva, I. Mantzkeh, M. Gotliber. <u>Bottom row</u>: Zeloner, S. Kostsheva, S. Laznik, S. Grosbard, G. Gotliber.

Some of those who worked along with the committee for the homeless started a kitchen for the poor of Ciechanów. The kitchen was open every day from 12:00 - 2:00 o'clock in the afternoon and in the evening it became a club for Jews who wanted to meet over a cup of tea. The tea covered part of the expenses for the kitchen for the poor. The mayor, Moishe Rosenberg, sent a gift for the kitchen – a music box. One only had to put in five *kopeks* to make it play. The kitchen was maintained by the donations of wealthy Ciechanów Jews.

At the same time, through the initiative of *Frau* Kahane, a children's home was established. In the organization of the educational institution and in its later activities, those who participated were: Chaya Rivka Robota, Fola Drezner, Raizl Shtutskeh, Dvora Kviat, Bronya Kviat, Esther Milner, and Tankhum Makover. The kindergarten was conducted in Hebrew by the teachers Khinich and Gips. The financial situation of the children's home was a difficult one. Tankhum Makover appealed to Warsaw to Dr. Klimel and advocate Altshvanger, who were members of the central committee of the Zionist organization in Poland at that time. Makover informed them about the condition of the children's home in which the poorest children attend, and they agreed upon 70 rubles per month.

Levine-Epstein from America visited the children's home. He noted the addresses of the children whose parents are in the United States.

89

The Ciechanów youth began to devote itself more to cultural and political activities. An amateur group was formed that gave performances from time to time such as the "Kreutzer Sonata" of Yaacov Gordin, Osip Dimov's *"Shma Yisroel"* and others. Besides the Zionist party that had already existed for a long time, the *Poele Zion* and *Bund* parties started to be organized.

End of the German Occupation; Start of the Polish State

When the German occupation ended and the Polish state was established, a regiment by the name of Ullaner became established. In this regiment Jews also served. The Jewish soldiers came to *shul* to greet the Sabbath and also *Shabbat* morning to *daven*, so the people at prayer invited the soldiers to come home with them for the noontime meal, but it seems that Jewish soldiers did not want to eat at the table of strangers.

The *Kehillah* could not stand the fact, though, that Jewish soldiers should not eat a *Shabbes* meal on the *Shabbat*. They therefore came to the conclusion the *Shabbat* meals should be organized for Jewish soldiers. The woman, Chana Raizl Makover, and some other women, took it upon themselves to prepare the *Shabbat* meals. Tables were set up near the *Bais Hamedresh*. Every *Shabbat*, after *davening*, the Jewish soldiers were welcomed and served by the Jewish women. Chana Raizl Makover, Soreh Elevnick, Soreh Gotliber, and others who participated in this important work.

With the establishment of the Polish state, a new epoch started for the Jews in Ciechanów just as it did all over Poland.

90

The Tragic Events on Yom Kippur of 1914

Yaacov Kahane

On that tragic day on the eve of *Yom Kippur* 1914, a rumor spread quickly throughout Ciechanów that the Russian state authorities and its administration are evacuating; a sign that the Germans are entering. This was no joking matter. Meanwhile, the Jewish population remained unprotected, thanks to the dark Christian elements who are on the lookout for such an opportunity.

In the afternoon all the Jewish shops were closed. No Jew was to be found in the street. Through the window one could see the suspected hooligans. With cynical smiles they wandered around as though they were preparing to cause trouble. After a while we saw some officers in Russian uniforms (later it turned out that they were Poles who served in the Russian army). They were chummy with the hooligans and in a short while voices could be heard shouting: "Jews, save us."

Eight half-naked Jews were being dragged to the center of the marketplace, where they were beaten. This wild scene lasted approximately half an hour. The writer of these lines called together a group of householders and also boys from Ciechanów, and it was decided that on the night of *Kol Nidre* the *davening* would not take place in the *Bais Hamedresh* or in the *shul,* but that *minyanim* should be arranged in private houses so as not to put the Jews in danger. The youth were to stand on guard during the *davening.*

The officers, after that shameful act, assembled in the city hall and carried on there in drunkenness and wild orgies all night, and in this way celebrated their victory over the Jews, and their voices could be heard throughout Ciechanów. The Jews spent that night in fear and in prayer.

At the break of dawn on *Yom Kippur,* the noise of a clamor was heard that was caused by the bombardment of the town around the sugar factory. At the same time the officers could be seen running half-naked, to the train. At the bridge they fell into the hands of the German guards who immediately shot them. This was payment from Heaven for the shame and pain that they caused us.

It seemed that we could be at ease for a while, but meanwhile the German soldiers arrived. Some started to saw the telegraph poles and others set off to do "shopping" -- gave instructions to pack up certain merchandise, courteously gave thanks and...did not pay.

The Jewish merchants wanted to go with a complaint to the commandant, but fresh trouble started, a general one, and a very serious one.

91

Suddenly, we saw the Germans leading a chained Jewish boy from a nearby village, called Konskawalsky, whom nearly all the Ciechanów Jews knew. He was tied up to a telegraph pole in the middle of the marketplace and a gallows was erected immediately to hang him. It was bitter for us. Yesterday the Poles beat us, and today, *Yom Kippur*, the Germans are going to hang a Jew. It was painful for us and a shame for the non-Jewish population.*

*The same event of that time Tankhum Makover writes about in his memoirs. We are, however, also bringing Kahana's memoirs; they give more particulars of those tragic events of the Jews. I. Kahana mentions additional names of people who were included in the delegation to the German commandant.

The unfortunate parents did not know what to do, so they ran to the supporters of Ciechanów asking for mercy, asking that they do something to save their son. They told what had happened.

The family Konsawalsky lived not far from Ciechanów on Freishnitzer way. The same day a German guard group arrived and asked the way to Ciechanów. They also asked if there are Russians in the area. The boy went out to show them the way and replied that the Russians had left the previous evening. No sooner had they gone off part of the way when they heard shots, and two Germans fell down dead from their horses. The rest of the soldiers immediately threw themselves down on the ground and dragged the boy to protect him so that he would not be shot also. At the sound of the shooting, more German soldiers arrived, and immediately liquidated the four soldiers that had hidden in a barn and from there had opened fire on the Germans, and because the boy had said that the Russian soldiers had already left yesterday, he was kept as a informer and sentenced to be hung on *Yom Kippur*. As 12:00 noon the order was to be carried out.

Very little time remained to do anything for the condemned one, but something had to be done. The writer of these lines, Shlomo Brenner, and Moshe Rosenberg (who later was the mayor during the German occupation), went to the military commandant and assured him that the whole matter is an error and we guaranteed his innocence.

Gradually the commandant let himself be convinced, but also required the signature of the "rabbi". Since there was no *Rov* in Ciechanów at that time, we ran to the *dayan, Reb* Yosele Z"L. Whoever knew *Reb* Yosele will understand that he did not want to give his signature so easily. We, the delegates, understood *Reb* Yosele very well. He was very strict with the Law and in general was very far from worldly matters, and here was a matter of signing for the "authorities". He pleaded that he had never had anything to do with such matters, so he begged not to have to give his signature now.

Understandably, we could not give up this time, and finally he signed the paper with his quill pen.

92

The boy was rescued, and the Jews started to prepare for *Succot* calmly.

The Zionist Movement and the First Hebrew Schools

Eliyahu Khinich

Thirst for Learning among the Jewish Youth

During World War I, I was destined to be in Ciechanów that was, at that time, under German occupation. The youth of the *shtetl* founded a school for poor children, and I, as a teacher, had to direct the school. At the first acquaintance with the *shtetl* two things drew my attention: It was the first time in my life that I saw young boys dressed in long *capotes* and in *Hasidish* hats. By us in Lita (Lithuania) and in White Russia, I never saw this. Not only amongst the youth -- even the older men did not wear such clothing.

93

Hebrew evening class with the teacher, Khinich, in the middle

I noticed, though, that regarding *frumkeit* the boys were not such angels. Just the opposite. Regardless of their *frumeh* clothing, they allowed themselves a lot of freedom and did not so easily observe all the *Mitzvot*: the *davening*, and were not afraid to "carry" on *Shabbat*. Boys flirted with girls, just as in our *shtetlech*, there were young people who were not even afraid to eat on *Yom Kippur*.

94

The second thing that surprised me was the strong desire to learn Hebrew. Both boys and girls and even young married women were anxious to study Hebrew. In addition to the school, I started evening classes for Hebrew. I was amazed at the enthusiasm, love and devotion that the students showed in their studies.

After I became more familiar with life in the *shtetl*, I noticed some specific characteristics of the Ciechanów Jews (I attributed this to the Polish Jews), that distinguishes them from the "Litvaks", namely: it seemed to me that they were more energetic with business/trade; they are warmer and more devoted to each other. They are much warmer than our Jews in Litn.

When I left Ciechanów, my students presented me with a book: *All of Bialik's Songs (Kol Shirei Bialik),* with a dedication in their handwriting.

In front of my eyes I still picture them, the dear and loving boys and girls of Ciechanów, and my heart pains me when I recall that they all perished at the murderous hands of the Germans.

The First Hebrew Schools in Ciechanów
Rivka Kahane

95

In the year 1915, we started the first Hebrew School, called "Akhranka." The idea of starting this school came about at a meeting of *shul.* Our distinguished *Rov Reb* Kh. M. Bronrot was speaking, but his talk was constantly interrupted by poor children without education, who were behaving wildly, jumping over tables and chairs, and made it impossible to carry on with the meeting. We, a group of women, tried to keep them quiet, but none of our efforts helped. We were ashamed, and felt guilty for this uncultured behavior of the children, and on the spot decided that we must do something in this connection.

After the meeting, we gathered in my house for a consultation in which the cultural activists participated. They were: Hencheh Mundzak, Taube Klinger, Dvora Kviat, Faigele Klainyud, Frumeh Rizikah, Roshkah Rakowsky and others. It was decided to found a Hebrew School. When the Germans entered, the school was closed.

The civic administration that the Germans established after they captured Ciechanów had not yet opened any other school. They did not hinder the population from doing so, though.

Once more we started to organize a school. In the discussion about the character of the school, one of those present, a daughter of the teacher (Blumstein), suggested a school where the main language would be Polish. Their argument was that Poland will become independent and we must be citizens of the country. They also did not feel that anything cultural could be established in Yiddish. This suggestion was rejected.

A Hebrew School was established, but just for girls. We understood that the boys would not be entrusted to us. The students were from the poorer classes. The wealthier ones sent their children to the Polish *gymnasium*. The wealthier women were altogether against such a school and did everything to hinder us.

The youth devoted themselves heart and soul to the school: recruited members who made monthly payments. The drama section worked constantly, gave performances, arranged literary evenings for the benefit of the school.

The Zionist idea grew stronger. The ranks started to grow. Boys from important Jewish families came forward from families for whom Zionism was out of the question. One of those boys was partially independent at that time. Amongst them: Shlomo Klinger, Avraham Hendl, Nachman Mundchuk, who contributed money from their earnings and already helped to rent a place and also be able to make the necessary installations for the school.

96

The school was opened. At our request, the Organization of the Lovers of Hebrew (*Agudat Khovavai Sfat Ha-Ivri*) of Warsaw sent a Hebrew teacher, Khinich -- he was a quiet small-town man -- and for the second year a young man by the name of Gifs. He was ambitious, knew *Tanach* well, and taught the children in an interesting manner, thus elevating their cultural and spiritual condition. He also influenced their homes ... and we were proud of our accomplishments.

The undertakings of the school grew. We also maintained a teacher for the Polish language, and the committee that consisted of the most active members of our organization did everything, availed themselves of all means, such as a "Flower Day", Lotteries, Literary and Dance Evenings, anything, just so that the school should have all its necessities. The students were even supplied with uniforms that were initiated in all Polish schools and got free books and writing materials.

Later, we also received a monthly subsidy from the Warsaw *Curatorium*.

Our school and educational activities encountered difficulties on the part of the fanatically religious Jews. We did not want any "wars" nor brotherly hatred because of the Zionism to which we were totally devoted. At that time the school was our primary effort and we poured much heart into it, even relinquishing our private lives ...

We also had wonderful moments in our school activities such as : *Chanukah, Chamisha-Oser B'Shvat, Purim, Lag B'Omer,* when the children, dressed in their uniforms with the white collars, marched through Ciechanów in rows, accompanied by the teachers and directors. Jews came out of their houses and stores and looked on, some with satisfaction and others with a scornful word at our expense.

The last and best teacher in our school was Plutzer, who gave his heart and soul to the school until it closed in 1921, when Poland itself opened up public schools and also included us in the school network, and turned it into a school with the same program as all the other schools.

97

Parallel to the establishment of the school and its existence, that in time became the spiritual center of the national youth in Ciechanów, the cultural institutions were also established, that were, through the Zionist activists, established before the war with the help of the organization *Mfitzai Haskala* (Spreaders of Enlightenment);but at that time the *Bund* appeared and took over the above-mentioned cultural institutions.

The Party Struggle for Hegemony in the Life of the Community

Both political groups often sponsored lectures: the Zionists and the *Bund.* The struggle for the hegemony in the established institutions was great. But we Zionists managed to gain leadership in a number of institutions, for example: when the "Joint," in the time of the German occupation, opened the free kitchen for children, our people became the management. When a transport of shoes arrived for poor children, we were given the responsibility of distributing them, and soon.

When in the year 1917 England made the Balfour Declaration, the Zionist presence grew anyhow. A Zionist Women's Organization was also established in which a large number of our prominent women became members. Until that time they had not participated in the public national-cultural life. Among them: *Frau* Wise, Hanegman, Lakh, Rubinstein, Sarah and others.

At that time the Indik family came to Ciechanów and wanted to open a private high school. Through us they wanted to influence the wealthy parents to send their children to this school and not to the Polish *gymnasium.* We demanded that the school be a Hebrew High School. The initiators could not agree to this and a compromise was reached: Hebrew would also be taught. The school was opened with the participation of the Hebrew teacher, Saffron, who helped let in our Zionist work.

Activities of the Zionist Organization
Moishe Porakh

98

It was during the years of the Russian Revolution 1905. I was a twelve-year-old youngster and learned in a *shtibl*. In the same *shtibl* there were boys who were not satisfied to learn only *Gemara*. In my memory, I recall Shmuel Yaacov Cohen, to whom I first confided that I wanted to learn *Ivrit*. He pointed out to me another group of boys who are also of the same mind. Amongst that group were: *Rov* Zeidenfeld's son, Alter Avraham Moishe, Yaacov Misher, Shlomo Fuchs, Natan Yosef Mundzak, Vaveh Burstein, Mendl Krimko, Natan Garfinkle, Yechiel Maier, Gershon Melovsky and others.

From amongst the older householders, the ones who showed understanding towards us were: Avraham Perlmutter, Dovid Wise, Moshe Rosenberg, Skurnik, Shlomo Rubinstein, Avraham Zilberstein.

The youth organized themselves and the first covert library was established in the private home of *chaver* Tchurek. Not all readers were of one mind. Some seized upon world literature and some the Yiddish. The reading was kept secret so anyone who was caught with a book by Achad Ha'am or Mapu in his hand – was immediately thrown out of the *shtibl*.

In spite of all the difficulties, our group grew and we decided to meet once a week in order to deal with various issues. This Enlightenment Group became the foundation of the Zionist movement in Ciechanów.

An executive was elected. Shmuel Yaacov Cohen was president. In addition to the above-mentioned active ones, others were very active: Kirshenbaum, Wolf Levine, Chaim Berman, Avraham Rembom, Eliezer Templeholtz, Reuven Stufien, Dovid Gogol, etc. *Shekalim* were sold, *pushkes* were distributed, collections were made at every *simcha*. Hebrew press, such as *Hatzfira, Hashaloach,* were distributed. The Ciechanów *Rov* Trunk related sympathetically to the Hebrew press. The executive truly worked tirelessly.

99

With the growth of the organization and the work, the question of promises arose. All our activities were illegal, so with the agreement of our mother we started to use our home with the home of Rivka Robota, and it was in her house that we had our covert library.

In the year 1909 I, together with my friend Yechezkl Trombka, took over the leadership of the *Keren Kayemet* (National Fund). How we worked can be illustrated by the fact that Ciechanów was declared first by the Central Committee. A cultural commission was established under the leadership of Shmuel Yaacov Cohen. With the move of the Kahana family to our *shtibl*, a new energy arrived. Through their initiative, the first Yiddish Theater came into existence in Ciechanów. With their arrival the Zionist organization revived. Their home became a warm home for all our friends, boys and girls.

After long efforts, we received legalization for the library. We called it *Shaarei Tzion*, and from that time on our open communal work began. From a cultural group we became a group of practical political Zionist workers. We enlarged our library, arranged public meetings; opened a Hebrew School, evening courses. Our influence in Ciechanów grew to such an extent that we were able to send our own delegate to the Zionist Congress in the year 1913, the female friend Ad Vinchitsky. In the *Kehillah* we had, as representatives, Moishe Parach and Yaacov Misher.

World War I

World War I broke out, and together with it came epidemics and hunger. Homeless filled Ciechanów. We especially suffered from the epidemics and hunger. *Rov* Landau Z"L was also one of the victims.

Our group immediately joined the (blank) committee. With much devotion the following worked: Shlomo Klinger, Tankhum Makover, Dvora Kviat and the *Hasidic* Jew, *Reb* Binyamin Malina.

The work went on night and day. With the self-sacrifice and work of these people, the epidemic stopped.

Besides the Zionists, all communal groups in Ciechanów did everything possible to help in the work.

The great need forced us to open a people's kitchen.

100

It was started and at its helm were: Natan Garfinkle, Natan Berman and Shlomo Brenner.

When the Germans entered Ciechanów -- they were not so wild yet at that time -- cultural work increased. The following parties were formed: *Poele Zion, Bund,* and folk parties, as well as hand-workers groups, that arranged readings. We spread the Zionist idea amongst the people. Our speakers, Vaveh Burstein and Flutzer were outstanding.

Peace in the non-partisan culture house did not last long. The Zionist Youth left and founded the *Tzirei-Tzion* movement.

We also organized a sport club called "Maccabee" and a special instructor carried out exercises with our members. *Hechalutz* was also organized. It occupied itself with *Hachshara* (agricultural training) and with *aliyah* to the land of Israel. An agricultural school was opened at Berl Agradnik.

Kibbutz Hachshara at Berl Agradnik's

The *Hechalutz* was led by: Appelboim and Sh. Shvirer . A break in our activity happened when Poland got its independence. We started to feel that the ground is burning beneath our feet and many of our *chaverim* did indeed start to prepare for *aliyah.*

101

The Zionist members of Ciechanów. The committee of the Zionist Organization.

Executive Committee of Keren Hayesod

102   blank

103

A tag-day for Keren Kayemet (JNF) in Ciechanów

104   blank

106   blank

105

**Members of the Zionist Organization. <u>Bottom:</u> Executive of Keren Kayemet.
President, Yichezkl Trombka]**

Executive of Keren Kayemet. President, Yichezkl Trombka

107

Cultural Revival in the Epoch between the Two World Wars

Brina Botchka

Hebrew Courses and Renewed Zionist Activities

A very small number of people could have a realization, fifty years ago, that our people must think, speak and live out its life culturally in its own national tongue, Hebrew. Some reckoned that this is simply impossible. Others that we must speak in the language that our diaspora gave us, Yiddish. There were only a few fanatics who fought all these opinions and agitated for the teaching of Hebrew.

The first one in Ciechanów was Shmuel Yaacov Cohen. One who was learned in Torah and with enlightenment ideas. He organized the first group who were also Zionistically inclined. In the group were: Gershon Mlovsky, Tankhum Makover, Vaveh Burstein, Chaya Milner, Rivka Robota, Dvora Kviat, Bryna Kviat, Moishe Kviat, and others.

The first problem was – a location. Our group was greatly pursued, particularly by the *Hasidic* circles, and it was therefore difficult to get premises, so we met in our house. My mother Z"L, showed great sympathy for our need.

In the beginning the group was satisfied to work on itself. We organized discussions about Strindberg, Max Nordau, Peretz and Bialik. Dvora Kviat brought much life into our group. She had come at that time from Łodz and for a time was under the personal influence of the great writer, I. L. Peretz, but Shmuel Yaacov Cohen could not make peace with the idea that the only aim of our group should be its limited work, and he pressed for the opening of Hebrew courses on a large scale.

108

A struggle started between him and Milner, who leaned towards the *Bundists*, but the majority of our group agreed with Yaacov's suggestion.

Various difficulties did not allow the plan to materialize. Since the Hebrew classes had trouble getting started, some of our members started to study privately, some by Gershon Mlovsky, some by Shmuel Yaacov Cohen himself. He had to resign from his teaching because he did not have the pedagogical ability.

Studying together drew us even closer together toward the Hebrew language, so that we used it at every opportunity. Shmuel Yaacov

Cohen went even further in this thinking and tried to present our group as the first flag-bearers of the Zionist thought. It was decided to organize readings for the youth regarding Zionism. But how was this to be done? And once more we helped ourselves.

Our dear member, Chaya Rivka Robota, put her place at our disposal. At that time this was considered very dangerous because every gathering was forbidden by the Russian authorities. The readings attracted new members. There came: Fela Drezner, Raizl Shtutzke, Ita and Sorah Lala, Chaya Trombka, Finkelstein, Dorkeh Rosen, and others.

The main lecturers were Milner and Vaveh Burstein. The entire group was led by Shmuel Yaacov Cohen. Discussions took place as to what themes the readings should be on. Milner for general themes and Cohen for specifically Yiddish ones. And once more the majority supported Cohen.

With the outbreak of World War I, new needs arose for work in the community. Provision for homeless, protecting the population from epidemic illnesses, arrange food-kitchens, etc. Our group played an active part in this communal endeavor.

Soon a Hebrew school was organized. The Zionist Organization started it. The old dream of Shmuel Yaacov Cohen was realized. We immediately took advantage of the opportunity and started evening courses under the auspices of the teacher Khinich. The evenings when we were learning were the best of our lives. Yehudit Butche distinguished herself in these classes.

109

In the courses, the teacher told us about the achievements of the Jews in the Land of Israel, starting with the *Biluim*, until the present *yishuv*. We studied Jewish history and this made ripe for us the idea that we must be the new pioneers of the *yishuv* in the Land of Israel. We decided to join the General Zionists as a separate body.

At the first meeting I gave the opening speech in broken Hebrew. I was not surprised at the poor impression my unpolished language made, because every Hebrew word that I uttered filled me with joy. We proclaimed the program of *B'not Tzion* (Daughters of Zion) that stated:

"Our aim is to prepare the Jews of the diaspora for the building of the Land of Israel and providing the pioneering core for this.""

Our work bore fruit. Let some names of the older generation be mentioned here, those who helped us with the first Zionist activities: *Reb* Ephraim Perlmutter, a learned Jew. He was already quite old but he showed much understanding of the youth. His room was always full of "enlightened ones" (*maskilim*) who wanted to hear a new word from him.

A group of his *medresh* boys approached us with a request that we admit them to our circle, with the condition that we change our name to *Hafkhiya*. There were: Asher Mantzki, Wolf Butzka, Yaacov Tziekhanover, and Yechiel Trombka. The group brought a new energy to our activities. Soon we acquired books and set up a library.

Our influence in Ciechanów started to be felt.

The Mizrachi Organization

At the end of World War I, when the Balfour Declaration was announced, the Jewish masses in Poland became strong supporters of Zionism. The religious Jews also started to get closer to Zionism. That's when the *Mizrachi* was organized in Ciechanów.

Rov Bronrot, who was the *Rov* in Ciechanów at that time, was one of the four founders of *Mizrachi* in Poland. It was through *Rov* Bronrot that the *Mizrachi* was established in Ciechanów.

Religious Jews of Ciechanów grouped themselves around the *Mizrachi*. The first of the religious Zionists were: A.D.Vinditsky, Shlomo Rubinstein, Dovid Lakh, Skurnik, Shlomo Gotfried, Shlomo Brenner, Aharon, Shmuel Burko, Henekh Sokolover, Avraham Laib Berk, Avraham Gotfried, Henekh Goldman, Shimshon Noymark, Binyamin Bronrot, Moishe Makover, Herschel Misher and Yekhiel Friedenberg.

110

The first meeting place was by Noach Grub. When the party grew, the organization went over to the home of Shlomo Rubinstein. There the party grew in all its activities; its own *bais hatfilla* (house of prayer) was established; evening classes were started, lectures on serious subjects, money was collected for J.N.F.

At the first conference of the *Mizrachi* in Poland two delegates attended from Ciechanów: Shlomo Rubinstein and A.D. Vinditsky.

Besides the general activities of the *Mizrach* in Ciechanów, special care was given to religious education that had to be adjusted and brought up to date. The *Mizrachi* leaders wanted to have such a school that would educate the children in Torah with respect. Worldly/secular enlightenment education that should not lead to a break-away from religious Judaism, love of Israel and knowledge of the Hebrew language.

The *Mizrachi* people themselves did not yet have a clear educational program, but the desire was to educate a religious youth, suited to the modern time, and that they should be able to be *chalutzim* in the historical land of our people. With this program there was established in Ciechanów a *Cheder Mizrachi* (a *Mizrachi* School). Moishe Kirshenbaum was the director. He was a wise, learned man, knew the Hebrew language; and the executive of the *Cheder* were: Herschel Misher, Shlomo Rubinstein, Natan Skurnik, Yekhiel Friedberg. A special teacher was brought from Warsaw. His name was Shore.

Unfortunately, this *cheder* lasted only two years. The *Mizrachi*, still a young organization at that time, did not yet have a sufficiently intelligent pedagogic force. The teachers who taught in the *cheder* came from the personnel of the Povzekhners.

Rov Bronrot, who saw that it was too early to conduct their own school, used all his energy to reorganize the Talmud Torah. He brought in *melamdim* (teachers) who had pedagogical abilities and were able to suit the teaching to the times in which we were then living. The *melamdim* who began to teach at that time were: Zachs from Warsaw, Shultz from Makov, and the famous Rabbi Shlomo Zalman. The already-mentioned *cheder* school was changed into a place of Hebrew courses and Judaism learning for children of the *povshekhneh* schools.

111

In the year 1926, the *Mizrachi* went for the first time to the *Kehillah* elections, in a block together with the General Zionists. At that time the first democratic *Kehillah* election took place. The main strife was between the *Agudah* and the Zionist block. From the *Mizrachi* there were elected at that time: Natan Tzeitog, Dovid Lakh, Shlomo Gotfried, Brenner and Henekh Goldman. During the election for the *Kehillah* executive the Zionist block got in touch with the artisans (hand-workers). The *Mizrachi* candidate, Natan Tzeitog, became the *Kehillah* president.

In 1930 the *Mizrachi* already went to the *Kehillah* elections with their own list. At that time the *Agudah* won. The *Mizrachi* only got one mandate at that time, Dovid Lakh.

One of the most important activities of the *Mizrach* in Ciechanów was the spreading of the idea of buying land in the Land of Israel. *Rov* Bronrot, together with a group of *Mizrachi* entrepreneurs, led in management of three purchases in Ciechanów, and many Jews paid down hundreds of dollars for this purpose. Yoel Weingarten, the well-known *Agudah* active member also participated in purchasing at that time.

Those concerned placed much hope on these purchases. Unfortunately, they could not raise a sufficient sum and the purchase could not be made in what is today the city of Rehovot.

After the defeat in the elections of 1930, the *Tzirei Mizrach* (young people of *Mizrachi*), started to organize. The leader was Michael Shaft, a young man with much Jewish knowledge, a refined man and a respected householder. He had an influence on the religious youth. He brought together the first group of *Tzirei Mizrach*, including: Pinhas Friedman, Natan Bronrot, Yaacov Bronrot, Simcha Fuchs, Dovid Blumstein, Moshe Trombka, Leib Gotfried and others.

They rented premises on Warsaw Street. There a club was opened, with a reading room, chess, etc. Every Friday evening there was an *Oneg Shabbat*. The *Rov* would give *shiurim* (lessons on holy scripture). Michael Shaft also gave lectures on Talmud, Tanach etc., for a long time.

Then a new initiative started for the construction of a new *Mizrachi School* called *Yavneh*. The *Tzirei Mizrachi* brought teachers from other cities. From Pietrkov came Levinovich, a founder of *Kfar Etzion* (he died in Israel's War of Independence). A *shul* was established in the *Yavneh* school, for the parents of the children. The *Yavneh* school did not develop on a grand scale, but it existed until the outbreak of war.

Thanks to the teachers in the *Yavneh* school, the group of the *Mizrachi* was strengthened. The young people organized a group conference in Ciechanów, sent delegates to conferences and participated in all Zionist work. The *Tzirei Mizrachi*, with Michael Shaft at its head, created additional institutions such as *Bait-lekhem*, a soldiers' kitchen, and others. The organization had a broadsheet that contained very interesting material. In 1936, *Mizrachi* won at the *Kehillah* elections and had two mandates. The *Kehillah* then went over to Zionist hands.

Reb Shlomo Rubinstein and his wife occupied an important position in the *Mizrachi* movement. He devoted his free time to the movement as well as money and energy. Every national religious Jew found, in his home, a warm home and an open heart.

Activities of the Right Poele Tzion
Zisha Berko

112 contd.

After the split in the *Poele Tzion* movement into right and left, that took place in the year 1921 at the Vienna conference, nobody believed that it would be possible to create a party of the Right *Poele Tzion* in Ciechanów. The *Bund* had an influence on the workers. There was a *Hashomeir Hatzair* organization in Ciechanów at that time, but children from middle-class homes belonged to it, and the organization concerned itself mainly with sport. In spite of this we started to organize a party of Right *Poele Tzion.*

113

Group of Right Poele Tzion.

Hechalutz Hatzair's first group]

114   blank

115

Picture: Second group of Hechalutz Hatzair

The organizers of this movement were: Yishakar Berko, Dovid Gogol, Laibl Srebnagura, Chaim Lala and the writer of these lines. The first location of the *Poele Tzion* was in the house of Yishayahu Robota, on the Yiddishe Street. We started Hebrew courses that were led by Isaachar Berka. A large Zionist Socialist education program was carried on through lectures, special evenings, and readings.

I made *aliyah* to Israel in 1929. The activities of the Right *Poele Tzion* carried on. According to the news that I received, the movement grew a lot. The organization of the young *Poele Tzion* was founded, *Freiheit (Dror)*. The *Poele Tzion* party went independently to the elections of the *Kehillah* and brought in its representatives. In various community institutions *Poele Tzion chaverim* were active. Through their initiative a *Hachshara* was established in Ciechanów.

Amongst the last active members of the party of the Right *Poele Tzion*, I remember: Nachum Melman and Yaacov Borokhovich. Other *chaverim* were also active but their names are not known to me. They did not live to see the day of the realization of their Zionist socialist ideal and perished during the German destruction of the Jews.

116

The Hashomer Hatzair Organization
I. Apel, Kfar Menachem

Founders of Hashomeir Hatzair

At the beginning of the '20s when, under the influence of the Balfour Declaration, the Zionist movement in Ciechanów was strengthened, a *Hashomeir Hatzair* group, as well as other groups, was formed. It carried the name: *Gdud Hashomeir Hatzair Yehuda HaMaccabi*. The group later enlisted in the *Hashomeir Hatzair* Party in Poland.

The attraction and outer appeal of the movement, the impressive aims and desires to raise a healthy Jewish generation that was filled with the lofty goal of redemption in the Land, drew a great number of Ciechanów girls and boys to the *Hashomeir Hatzair Kvutzot.*

In the *Izba*, the place of the *Hashomeir Hatzair* in Ciechanów, there was great youthful enthusiasm: *Kvutzot Kfarim, Tzofim* and *Bogrim* (as different age groups were called), a colorful picture of flags and pennants, ties on uniforms, a rich program of activities that expressed itself in sport, games, song and dance.

117

One of the first groups of Hashomeir Hatzair, many of whom live in Israel.

Dvora Neuman with her group of Hashomeir Hatzair]

118   blank

119

One of the last groups of Hashomeir Hatzair before the outbreak of World War II

All this was just the outer adornment for the earnest discussions and lectures about Jew and humanity, Jewish people and redemption, what is right and just, wrong and unjust, freedom and slavery. In these discussions a knowledge of *Eretz Yisroel* was primary: the borders of the Jordan, the peaks of the Carmel Mountains, the plains of the *Eretz Yisroel* valleys over which the blue *Eretz Yisroel* sky spreads.

The activities and discussions, the lessons and events, all turned the *Inba* into a second home for the Ciechanów youth.

There was not always peace, though, between this home and the home of mother and father.

The *Hashomeir Hatzair* organization did not know of any compromises. It demanded the total youth and showed her/him another way of life, other than the perception of mother and father. *Hashomeir Hatzair* tried, and mostly with success, to tear the young people out of the small town atmosphere and introduce them to a new way of thinking that was oft times in contrast to the outlook of the parents.

But in the end the parents understood us and changed their attitude to the *Hashomeir Hatzair* movement.

120

Together with the worry over the future of their children, mother and father also wanted their children to receive an education. The parents appreciated the tremendous educational significance of *Hashomeir Hatzair*. They observed the spiritual development of their children that went hand in hand with their character growth.

It is also worthwhile to mention the attitude of the school teachers to *Hashomeir Hatzair*, The Polish state school for Jewish children did not think about, nor could they recognize, any youth organization. The teachers, almost all Jewish, tried to be loyal state employees, but they shut their eyes to our youth movement. Other than small incidents, we did not suffer any wrong from our Jewish teachers.

With the growth of the *Hashomeir Hatzair* movement, the Zionist activities of its members also grew. The "birds" left their nests, grew up and started to be active in the Zionist activities of the Zionist structures. The older *chaverim* worked along with and also led in various community institutions, J.N.F., *Hechalutz*, League for Israel Workers, and were active in *Tarbut* and in organizing various other activities.

Unfortunately, the *chaverim* of Ciechanów's *Hashomeir Hatzair* did little to fulfill their ideal of joining the kibbutz net of *Eretz Yisroel*. With sorrow and pain we recall all those dear and precious *chaverim* who did not realize their goal. They went through terrible suffering and treachery.

Beitar, Hatzhar-Hatzakh, Beit Hakhayal
Yaacov Warshavsky

121

The cradle of Beitar was the *Hashomeir Hatzair* movement that in 1925 was founded by the Ciechanówers: Sh. Fried, the twin brothers Mundzak, M. Kanarik, the Novogrodsk brothers, the brothers and M. Lifsky. A short time after the establishment of *Hashomeir*, the whole organization with its membership joined the ranks of *Beitar* that was one of the first founded in Poland.

In Beitar there was a woodwind orchestra whose founder and director was Sh. Frid. He devoted much time and energy to the movement, especially for the children with whom Beitar dealt.

In the early years *Beitar* met in the same place as *Hashomeir Hatzair*. The site was in the empty building of the Menshtik brothers. When the movement grew, we got a permanent place on Pultusker Street.

Chaverim of the Beitar Organization

122

The main activities of the organization were Hebrew lessons, History, Zionist lectures, sport and exercise, and the woodwind orchestra. I particularly remember the *Lag B'omer* activities which meant going out to the nearby forest, accompanied by the woodwind orchestra. The march through Ciechanów with the orchestra was reason for the Ciechanów population to look upon us with honor.

The bloody events in the Land of Israel in the year 1929, when the Arabs made pogroms on the Jews there, strengthened the *Beitar* movement. The youth and the older people streamed to the *Beitar* organization. At that time the *Hatzair* organization was founded that took into its membership the older members of *Beitar*.

The first *Beitar* members who went to the *Hachshara* were: N. Kanarik, I. Skurnik, and E. Fizner. They were on *Hachshara* in Klosov and in Ivadavitz. A. Zilberstain was sent to Agricultural School in Vienna. Those who completed *Hachshara* had a right to get certificates, but only E. Fizner got a certificate. The others had to use illegal means of *Hatzair* to enter the Land. Their motto was *"Af Al Pi"* which means: in spite of all difficulties, stumbling blocks and disturbances of the British Mandate. The movement brought many Jews to the Land of Israel to spite the angry British.

Many of the Jewish emigrants from Ciechanów reached the Land of Israel in this way, not knowing that the illegal immigration is organized by *Hatzh"r*. I. Skurnik was one of the founding members of the Ciechanów *Beitar* who arrived in the Land of Israel through this illegal means.

We also spread our educational work through organizing frequent meetings, readings and lectures, to which a large crowd came. From the Warsaw *Beitar* headquarters we got a permanent instructor, H. Furluck who, in addition to his organizational work, also gave Hebrew lessons for *Chaverim* of the movement.

The number of members grew and we rented larger premises. On Friday evenings we organized discussions that attracted a large number of young people. I. Zabludowicz, after completing an instruction course, became the head instructor of *Beitar* in Ciechanów. Since many new members joined, such as : I. Tchurek, the teacher, Isadore Mansheim, Elimelech Treicher, B. Lubintzki and many others -- we conducted elections in *Hatsh"r* and so chairman I. Tchurek was elected, a good speaker and lecturer.

123

The Committee of Beitar

Nearly at the same time, there came to Ciechanów Dr. Strikovsky, a member of the Warsaw center. He influenced the growth of the movement very much in Ciechanów. A large crowd always attended his lectures at the local cinema.

In the year 1932, I Zabludowicz and the writer of these lines went to a *Hachshara* at Hantzevich, where we worked as a woodchopper in the nearby Polesher forests. A few months later we, together with I. Oistriak and Krivanofsky, transferred to the *Hachshara* at Proshnitz, closer to Ciechanów.

We organized frequent outings in the area, such as to: Plonsk, Pultusk, Proshnitz. Our outings, accompanied by the woodwind orchestra, made a great impression everywhere. Once, after such a visit in Proshnitz, when we organized a parade in the *shtetl*, the local Jewish communities tried to attack the train. The instructor, I. Zabludowicz, the leaders of the communists who participated in that attack, I happened to meet during the war in Soviet Russia. He was arrested there and sent to Siberia.

In 1933 we, together with the orchestra, participated in the World Conference of *Beitar* that took place in Warsaw. We marched through the streets of Warsaw in the grand parade. A large number of participants were armed with guns, which made a strong impression on the Poles.

124

After the second congress of 5695, the movement took on the same *Hatz"kh* and the leaders of the movement in Poland started to organize the "illegal" aliyah that brought thousands of Jews of the Land of Israel, which saved them from the later Holocaust brought about by the Germans.

When news arrived that the British Mandate-power closed the gates of the Land of Israel for Jews, we organized a public meeting in the Ciechanów *shul*. The Beitar members came in their full uniforms. After the meeting communists aattacked us. A fight erupted. Police intervened and the Beitar *chaverim* who were seized got two days of imprisonment. These were the first Zionist prisoners in Ciechanów.

Organizations of Religious Institutions of Orthodox Jews in Ciechanów

Moishe Fuchs

125

Community of Cultural Activities of Religious Jews

Up to the time of World War I, the Jewish Ciechanów led a small-town life, without major conflict or aspirations. Modern Jewish life started to develop only during World War I. At that time splits arose in nearly every Jewish family. The parents were *frum* and conservative and the children started to look for a new spiritual life, connected with a different way of life.

Great tragedies played themselves out in the Jewish homes. Parents did not feel that because of the new culture their children were being distanced from them. It was a time of social upheaval, and this brought about a modern life. On the one hand there was the influence of the enlightenment-Zionist youth that had a strong influence on the life of the Jewish community at that time; on the other hand the *Bund* carried on activities caught up in the stream of the revolutions after World War I.

There was no lack of work for the youth then. Ciechanów was one of the few cities that had suffered very little from World War I and therefore refugees were attracted to it with the stream of refugees, epidemics began. The spirit of volunteers was great, not stopping their work, and in the face of all danger they gave the greatest help for the unfortunate. It was in the work that we found the organized Zionist youth.

126

Thanks to the important community work the youth felt like an independent factor, and did not want to go in the steps of the older generation. This brought great strife in every Jewish home in Ciechanów. There was another reason that brought to a halt the religious life. Namely: the neglected *Bais Medreshim*, packed with the homeless. The *Bais Medresh* ceased to have an influence.

At that time we found an original Jew in Ciechanów whom not everyone understood -- *Reb* Avraham Aaron Kalman, the later *Kadosh*, the first Jew to be a victim of the Germans in Ciechanów. *Reb* Avraham Aaron could not make peace, at that time, with the idea that the religious education is coming to an end at that time, so he organized a committee together with *Reb* Chaim Mordecai Bronrot at its head, that undertook to shake up the religious education and established a modern Talmud Torah school.

The very active *Reb* Avraham Aaron Kalman

127

Without financial means, simply with great energy, he undertook to save the soul of the Jewish child. He understood that with the old ways it was no longer possible to educate the Jewish children. He could not make peace with the idea that, in order to bring *Yiddishkeit* into the lives of the children, physical strength must be used. *Reb* Avraham Aaron sought ways in which to reach the soul of the child.

One day a Jew from Łodz appeared in the *shtetl*, one whom the Jews of Ciechanów remember. This was the *Rebbe Reb* Shlomo Zalman, who did much to update the religious education. He introduced the system of discussions with the students. With these discussions he attracted the students to himself with great love. Learning there then became a pleasant educational experience where the student lived out his young life.

Rebbe Shlomo Zalman

128

Rebbe Shlomo Zalman organized committees of the students. An inner discipline was established, not because of fear of the *Rebbe*, but out of respect.

The *Rebbe* used to teach the students hearty *Hasidic nigunim* melodies (songs), tell them *Hasidic* tales, and above all, used every pedagogical means to win the soul of the child.

In his private life *Rebbe* Shlomo Zalman suffered a lot. His whole consolation he got from his students. Understandably, such education bore fruit. His students did indeed grow up to be a creative force in religious life in Ciechanów.

Reb Laibish Borenstein: The Rebbe, Teacher, and Spiritual Leader

With the arrival of *Reb* Laibish in Ciechanów, the religious education in the Talmud Torah was expanded and strengthened. The influence of his personality can still be felt to the present day through his students and admirers who were privileged to survive the great tragedy of our people.

Reb Laibish was a quiet man, calm, always deep in thought. He lived in a higher world and strove to create a better, loftier world, and in this spirit he influenced his students.

Reb Laibish was not simply a teacher. He was a spiritual leader who lived together with his students. Nothing in the Talmud was hidden for him. He instigated a new method of learning that made the student independent and put him on the path of thinking. The *Rebbe* organized a separate House of Prayer (*Beth T'fillah*) for his students, conducted *Shalos Seudas* with them, talked Torah at the table, danced, sang, with one word – filled the whole life of the students with content.

He did his educational work with much love so that the children grew very attached to him. They felt a high respect for him. When a student was weak in this studies, *Reb* Laibish had much sorrow, and the medicine he found in the soul of the child. He used various means to light the fire of the soul, the spark, with which he generally had success. Mainly his success showed *Shabbes* and *Yomtov* when he had his students at his table.

130   blank
131

They studied Torah, ate together, sang *zmirot,* danced with much *hasidic* fervor.

In particular there remained in our mind the last *Shavuos* before his death. For a whole 48 hours he did not take leave of his *talmidim.* The children ran home for a few minutes to grab something to eat and returned to the *Rebbe.* His whole conduct that last *Shavuos* was different from previously, all, with so much fervor. He danced, sang, taught Torah, hurried, as though he felt that time is short. He still has something to say before it will be too late. And the students, wrapped in an enormous religious ecstasy, seemed to soak his words in, seized every thought. They felt that something great is about to happen, that every minute is precious, because who knows if there will still be the privilege to hear the holy words.

Reb Laibish left a spiritual inheritance for his students as to how to live as a Jew, how to be a Jew. This inheritance his students cherished faithfully. Generally, he used to go home to his family for *Yomtov*. That last *Shavuos* he postponed the trip, saying that he wants to make the trip in the Hebrew month of *Sivan* on the twenty-sixth day, for his father's *yahrzeit*.

129

The Talmud Torah building, the teachers and the principal: L to R: Wolf Greenbaum, Herschel Nirenberg, Yosef Chaim Stempion, Reb Avraham Aaron Kalman, Mordecai Tzinamon, Mendl Gotliber. Second row top: Yehoshua Bromson and executive member, Isaachar Ciechanówer

He traveled home for the *yahrzeit* Friday evening for the *davening*, said *Kadish*, went to sleep and never awakened. This wonderful person passed away on his father's *yahrzeit*. He left orphaned students who mourn him to the present day. His death came totally unexpectedly.

The students sat in class and learned with interest, as they waited for the *Rebbe's* return. But, like a thunderclap, the news reached them that their saintly *rebbe* will not return to them. A cry from the heart broke out and all the students sat down on the floor – *Shiva*, and mourned their spiritual leader. Like faithful children the students observed the *Kadish* (prayer) and the study of *Mishnot* on the day of his *yahrzeit*.

Years passed, the struggle for life and existence spread the students in all parts of the world. In order that the memory of the *Rebbe* should not be forgotten, at the initiative of some of his pupils, with his beloved student Shmuel Fuchs at the head, a committee was formed to perpetuate his name by writing a *Sefer Torah*.

132

The completion of a Sefer Torah in memory of the honored Rebbe. From R to L, standing: Shlomo Loketch, Yisroel Beckerman, Dovid Bromson, Yechiel Lefkowitz, Shmuel Fuchs, Yudl Kronenberg, Tzadik Stopien. Seated: Shlomo Fuchs, Isaachar Berko, Moishe Malina, Simcha Ciechanówer, Shlomo Slurl and Zelig Ostry

The day of the beginning of the writing of the *Sefer Torah* was a sad one for our family. Our beloved father died on that date. Naturally we could not participate in the joyful occasion. My brother did manage to mention my father before the crowd, but unfortunately he was destined from above to be torn away from us on that day.

In the celebration there participated our *Rov*. He spoke about the great personage, *Reb* Laibish, who was a great Torah leader. The beginning of the *Sefer Torah* writing was very successful, and just at the *yahrzeit* the end of the writing was celebrated. In a great parade, through illuminated streets, a folk-march took place. Ciechanów had never seen such a celebration up to that time. Men, women and drums participated and from everyone's lips a blessing was heard for *Reb* Laibish's holy memory.

133

At the great catastrophe of our people, most of the *talmidim* of *Reb* Laibish perished. Very few remained alive. Their names are: the *Rov*

Chaim Dovid Shevel, *Rov* Simcha Laib Dzedzitz (*Rov* in California), Maier Pshiskha, Shmuel Yosef Tzitrin, Yisroel Beckerman. His most beloved and best *talmid* was *Rov* Chaim Ber Shevel, the son-in-law of *Reb* Binyamin Krainer, *Rov* in Chicago.

Reb Shimon Srebnik

The next outstanding personage who played a role in religious education in Ciechanów was *Reb* Shimon Srebnik. If, according to tradition, there are thirty-six Jewish *tzadikim*, he was definitely amongst them at that time. His service to God was in total devotion, the love of the people Israel boundless. His system of instruction in the *yeshiva* was: every day the *talmidim* had to learn a portion of the *Tanach* from the *Chumash, Nevi'im* and *Ktuvim* and Mishna, so that in the course of a year the students would learn all of these completely. the Five Books of Moses, book of the Prophets and Chronicles and Mishna

Reb Shimon endured the most severe trial in the Soviet Union in exile. He was put in prison because for *Yom Kippur* he organized a service in the Arkhhongelester Forest. There he got sick and died, greatly honored by the whole Jewish population that was found there. I had the privilege of being in the surroundings of *Reb* Shimon until his soul departed from him.

Let us, in our *Yizkor Book*, also remember the others who helped in religious education: *Reb* Moishe, the father-in-law of *Reb* Shimon who knew *Shas* and *p'sukim* and more, off by heart; *Reb* Yirachmiel, who was already head of the *Ger Yeshiva* in the time of *S'fat Emet* Z"L; *Reb* Avraham Yonatan and fine young man, Reb Mordecai Tzimerman, Reb Ziskind Knoble, a great pedagogue.

It is understandable that to maintain such a learning institution, with such educators, was not an easy task, and it all existed because of the tireless work of Avraham Aaron Kalman. Let today's generation, and particularly the youth, take an example from such people as *Reb* Avraham Z"L and let the young people follow in their way.

Activities of the "Agudah" and Its Institutions

134

With the establishment of the *Agudat Yisroel* in Ciechanów, the *frum* spirit in the *shtetl* was strengthened. The *bais medrashim* that were, until then, empty and neglected, suddenly were full every evening with students of Torah. At one table in the *bais hamedresh Reb* Chaim Mrock sat and learned with a group of tradesmen, *Ein Yaacov*, and at a second table a group are studying *mishna*. *Reb* Yisroel Student is teaching the *Daf Yomi*. Psalm reader groups were also organized at that time, as well as other *frum* groups.

At the first *Agudat* meeting in the Talmud Torah there gathered: *Reb* Mordecai Liar, *Reb* Yoel Dovid Weingarten, *Reb* Yisroel Yaacov Student, to give reports from the *Knissiah G'dola*. Great excitement overtook the *frum* public. The religious power was felt, the organizers, who fight to sustain the uniqueness of Jewish life.

With the establishment of the organized religious Jews to proclaim the *Daf Yomi* at that time, the voice of Torah was heard in all *bais medreshim* and *shtiblech*. All Jews, *shomrei Torahs*, learned communally at the same time *masekhta*. Festive *Siyumai Shas Masekhot* were organized. The festivals turned into great Torah manifestations. The *grosh yomi* that was organized helped in the development of a large Torah center in Lublin -- *Yeshiva Chochmai Lublin*, founded by *Rov* Shapiro Z"L. All this had an influence on the religious youth in Ciechanów.

Later the *Tzirei Agudat Yisroel* was founded, the organization of religious youth. It tried to win over the youth that found themselves under the influence of Zionism. The *Tzirim* conducted a strong cultural life in many respects: lectures, readings, parties, establishing libraries, and were also active in the political parties.

The Free Loan Society

One of the most important institutions that the *Tzirim* founded was the Free Loan Society that developed into a large benefit institution for all Ciechanów Jews. The founders were: Moshe Klinger, Yudl Kronenberg (now in America). Moshe Klinger was an especially interesting type. There was a time when he was already far from a religious life. He had already tasted the life of the modern youth movement, but he was quickly disappointed in it and once more joined the ranks of the *Tzirei Agudat Yisroel* and threw themselves with all their energy and stubbornness into all the *Agudah* work, and especially to found the Free Loan Society that was the nicest institution in the whole area. It operated with large financial means and was supported by the "Joint."

In the committee of the Free Loan Society, people of all levels were represented, such as: Avraham Shmuel Lichtenstein, Yoel Dovid Weingarten, Isaachar Ciechanówer, Baruch Mordecai Malina, Wolf Henekh Zilbershtram, Gedalia Nagur, Binyamin Kirshenbaum, Moshe Rosenberg, Shlomo Slud, Isaachar Berko, and the two founders – Moishe Klinger and Yudl Kronenberg.

135

The committee of Tzirei Agudat Yisroel in Ciechanów

The Leaders and Activities of the Agudah Movement

The young people of the *Agudat Yisroel* were active and creative. Unfortunately, the majority perished. Those who distinguished themselves in the movement were: Avraham Hersh Rot, Menachem Shockett's son Chaim Kronenberg (both in Israel), Moshe Klinger, Isaachar Berko, Shlomo Slud, Zelig Ostry, and later we also meet the *chaverim*: Shmuel Dovid Bzshezshinsky, Laibl Fish (now in America), Tzaduk Ostry and others.

Two prominent Jews played the main part in the:*Reb* Mordecai Nior and *Reb* Yoel Dov Weingarten. *Reb* Mordecai Nior was very smart. He greeted everyone with a smile. He had a witticism for every conversation. He gave all his energy to the *Agudat Yisroel* and its institutions. He was the president of the *Agudah* for many years, was at the head of the *Bais Yaacov School* that educated hundreds of girls in the religious spirit. From the *talmidos* (girl students) there was founded the group *B'not Agudat Yisroel* -- a religious girls association. The *Bais Yaacov* teachers conducted there.

136

Torah and Culture Group

137

Bais Yaacov School in Ciechanów

138　　　　blank
140　　　　blank
139

Organization of *B'not Agudat Yisroel*

141

**A farewell party of Tzirei Agudat Yisroel. Shmuel Leventhal (fourth from right)
leaves for the Land of Israel.**

Tzaduck Ostry (fourth from right), leaves for the Land of Israel

142   blank

143

The Activities of Reb Yoel Dovid Weingarten

Reb Yoel Dovid Weingarten was a hearty Jew. He had a good word for everyone. He was a very good speaker and very energetic. With his arrival in Ciechanów he took over all the institutions that were established through *Agudat Yisroel*, such as: *Talmud Torah, Bais Yaacov, Gmilat Hesed*. He gave lectures for the young workers and *B'not Agudat Yisroel*. He also gave a lesson to the Psalm Readers Group. For many years he was the leader in the community. I do not recall any point in the religious community life in which he did not take part. Whoever knew him had to love him because of his sincerity and warmth that he showed for everyone.

I recall when *Reb* Yoel Dovid was hospitalized in Warsaw, severely ill, people of all Parties telephoned there to find out about the condition of their beloved leader.

Everything that he did for the benefit of the community was with heart and soul. The community work and his private life were as one. Unfortunately, we were not privileged to have this great personality with us for very long. In his blossoming young

Reb Yoel Dovid was torn away from us. His death aroused great sorrow in all of the Orthodox world. To learn more about *Reb* Yoel Dovid, see "Types And Characters."

There was another segment of the Jewish population that did not have a place in the existing Parties in Ciechanów – the religious workers and folk-masses. They always had to seek protection, in economic questions, from the secular enlightened workers' organizations, and in the religious domain they were not at all involved.

With the establishment of *Poale Agudat Yisroel* the situation changed.

Poelei Agudat Yisroel in Ciechanów

Between Shmuel Fuchs and the *Bundist*, Yitzhak Yagada, there was once a chance discussion about socialism and social justice in our Torah. Shmuel Fuchs explained to his opponent the moral, social and just laws of our Torah. The powerful talk of our prophets opposing subjugation and slavery. Yagada then asked: " If this is true, why isn't there a Party that renews the prophetic talk in our generation?" The reply was there is such a Party – the *Poale Agudat Yisroel*. Yitzhak Yagada explained that he is ready to devote all his energy for such a Party. From the conversation the foundation was laid for the *Poale Agudat Yisroel* in Ciechanów in the year 1925.

Quick as lightning, the idea spread about the foundation of this organization. At the first meeting there were fifteen *chaverim*. Yoel Dovid Weingarten lectured for them as did Shmuel Fuchs and Yitzhak Yagada. They also later took part in the organizational work. The group grew continually. After one month the founding meeting took place, with the participation of our *Rov,* and more than one hundred *chaverim.*

145

The first executive consisted of: Shmuel Fuchs, President; Shmuel Nair, secretary; Yitzhak Yagada, Nachum Melman, Shmuel Gotfried, Chanan Livsky. Some of them had already been far from a religious life. The movement once more awakened in them the religious feelings.

As soon as this organization was established, lessons in various studies started, taught by *Rov Reb* Chaim Mordecai Bronrot, *Reb* Yoel Dovid Weingarten, *Reb* Mordecai Avraham Albeck, Menachem Shub's son-in-law, *Reb* Mordecai Tzinamon and others. Our *Rov* was very impressed to see sixty young men spending their free time in Torah study.

The first Orthodox library was organized. There was a reading room and other cultural corners.

144

Yitzhak Yagada – one of the leaders of Poale Agudat Yisroel in Ciechanów

The *chaverim* did not satisfy themselves just with their own learning, but took upon themselves to learn with the broad masses, to relive the situation of the poor classes of our *shtetl*. Evening courses were organized for the working youth as well as for children of workers. In these courses more than three children participated in religious studies as well as secular enlightenment studies through the teaching personnel of the folk school. The evening courses received the recognition of all levels of the population without difference of Party affiliation

The Party paid special attention to the so-called *Amei Haaretzim* – grown adults who did not even know how to *daven*. These people were received with much love and this brought them closer to the movement. After some time they became prominent members of the community.

The results if this activity showed immediately. In all the institutions of the *shtetl* there were *chaverim*, representatives of the *Poale Agudat Yisroel*. They took an active part in creating the religious and other institutions and later the organization was able to have their own leader in the *Kehillah* in the person of Avigdor Caplan.

Amongst the most important workers of *Poale Agudat Yisroel* there were: the *Gmilat Hesed* that helped the *chaverim* with loans for constructive purposes, coal-fund, to help the poor with heating; *Pesach Actzich* to help the poor folk make *Pesach*; active help in the soldiers' kitchen and other institutions.

Through the initiative of the *Poale Agudat*, public mass meetings were organized with the participation of the best speakers of the religious workers' movement such as: I. L. Arleon, Laib Frum.

146

Branch of the Poale Agudat Yisroel. R to L:. <u>Top</u>: Nachum Melman, Sh. B. Rosenberg, I. Yagada, Sh. Fuchs, Sh. Gotfried, M. Kostsheva. <u>Second row</u>: Ch. L. Lipski, H. Vina, Sh. Lipsky, I. Kan; the last two names are not known. <u>Third row</u>: D. Bromson, I. Lefkowitz, A. Caplan, I. D. Weingarten, M. Tzinamon, V. Mlover, Chanan Lipsky. <u>Fourth row</u>: A Berstein, M. Fuchs, Simcha Fuchs and others. In the central headquarters, great respect to the workers of the Ciechanów branch of the *Poale Agudat Yisroel*.

Through the initiative of this movement, there took place, in our home in Ciechanów, the first Land of Israel Conference of the Warsaw Central Committee, with the participation of members Dovid Rosenfeld (Cracow), Student Grafil, Lerner and others. The first *Agudat Hachshara* was established in Poland, which gave an impetus to work for the Land of Israel amongst the religious masses in Poland.

My mother Z"L took an active part in all their activities with advice and action and her participation became well known amongst the Ciechanów *chaverim* as well as amongst the central leadership.

147

We established a summer camp in Makuv-Mazovyetz. There was nobody to head it, so *Frau* Fuchs was called and the problem was solved immediately.

She took over management of the summer camp.

The *chaverim* who were active in the *Poale Agudah* movement were: Shmuel Fuchs, as president for many years; Dovid Bromson. Yitzhak Yagada was active until he perished through the hands of the Germans; Sh. B. Rosenberg, *Reb* Avigdor Caplan; the first head of the organization, *Reb* Mordecai Avraham Albick; Shmuel Gotfried – secretary for many years; Chaim Livsky (now in America); Shlomo Fuchs; Yekhezkl Sudjevsky; and finally there was the guiding spirit of the organization -- Levy Fuchs.

My hand trembles when I recall his name. The words of his speeches came from his heart. He had a gentle appearance, dreaming eyes, full of enthusiasm for noble ideas. He was always ready to make sacrifices, both of himself and others. He was just like his mother, together with whom he perished, not wanting to separate from her.

The Ciechanów Kehillah and Its Activities
Yaacov Bronrot

After World War I, in independent Poland, the organization and activities of the Jewish *Kehillah* was regulated by a special law. According to this law, the Ciechanów leadership consisted of a council and an executive. The council consisted of twelve members, elected by the male adult population that paid *Kehillah* taxes. The *Kehillah* executive, consisting of eight members, was elected by the council. This organizational form of the Ciechanów *Kehillah* was established in the year 1926.

Before 1926, the *Kehillah* leadership consisted of four so-called heads. These were: Dovid Wise, Yaacov Misher, Moishe Rakovsky and Avraham Natan Skurnik. As chairman at that time was Dovid Wise.

In the first democratic election in the year 1926, the following three parties participated: Block of General Zionists and *Mizrachi; Agudat Yisroel* and hand-workers. Of the 12 mandates the following received representation: 148

General Zionists and *Mizrachi* – 4, in the persons of Natan Tzeitog, Dovid Lakh, Aaron Kirshenbaum and Shlomo Gotfried. *Agudat Yisroel* – Binyamin Malina, Avraham Friedman, Isaachar Ciechanów, Avraham Klinger; Handworkers: Avraham Yaacov Bilzshiner, Avraham Yosef Alievnik, Mordecai Laib Zazshnitsa and Yaacov Altus.

Natan Tzeitog was elected as president of the council. Vice-President was Binyamin Malina. The elected executive consisted of three Zionists and *Mizrachi*: Shlomo Brenner, Henekh Goldman, Avraham Dovid Vinditsky. Hand-workers: Herschel Kirshenzweig; Vice-President: Henekh Goldman; Treasure: Aaron Gelbart.

In the year 1930 the term of the first elected *Kehillah* leadership ended and as a result of the new election the following Parties received representation in the council: *Agudat Yisroel* – M. I. Rakovsky, I. M. Sokoloff, I. D. Ciechanówer and Mendl Leventhal. *Poale Agudat Yisroel* -- Avigdor Caplan; butchers -- L. Gurni; hand-workers: I. L. Altans, Shtifenholtx, Sh. Shuster; *Mizrachi* – Dovid Lakh; General Zionists: Dovid Wise and Yaacov Misher; as president of the council, M. I. Rakovsky were elected; vice-president -- H. Shtifenholtz.

The executive: *Agudat Yisroel* -- A. Sh. Lichtenstein, J. D. Weingarten, I. Greenbaum; hand-workers: -- A. Alyevnick, B. Tz. Ehrlikh, A. Margolit; Zionists and *Mizrachi* -- Shlomo Brenner, Aaron Kirshenbaum. President of the executive – A. Sh. Lichtenstein. Vice-President – I. D. Weingarten. Treasurer – A. I. Alevnik.

The elections to the *Kehillah* executive that took place in the year 1936: To the executive -- *Agudat Yisroel*: M. I. Rakovsky, Mordecai Noyar, A. Sh. Lichtenstein; *Mizrachi* – Avraham Natan Skurnik, Michael Shaft; Zionists: Dr. Tov; *Poale Tzion* -- V. Gotliber; Revisionists -- Mandshain; hand-workers -- F. Mundzak and B. Tz. Ehrlikh; *Bund* -- Kostsheva. President of the council -- Avraham Natan Skurnik; vice-president -- Dr. N. Tov.

Executive: *Mizrachi* -- Shlomo Brenner; Zionists -- Shabtai Fuerstenberg; hand-workers -- Hersh Kirshenzweig. *Poale Tzion* -- Yaacov Korn; *Agudat Yisroel* -- Ch. I. Greenbaum, Isaachar Ciechanówer, Moishe Klinger. President of the *Kehillah* -- Hirsch Kirshenzweig; Vice-president -- Shlomo Brenner; Treasurer -- Shabtai Fuerstenberg.
149

The Kehillah budget included the following income. Payment for schita direct taxes, and income from cemetery. Expenses were: Maintenance of the Kehillah council, subsidies ongoing support for: Talmud Torah, Bais Yaacov School,

Bais Sefer Yavneh, Religious Evening Courses, Free Loan Society, Linat-Hatzedek, Bais Lekhem, Hakhnasat Orchim, soldiers' kitchen, J.N.F. and Keren Hayesod; assistance for needy individuals in cases such as housing, illness, or recovery after an illness.

The Rebbe Rov Hagaon Rebbe Chaim Mordecai Bronrot and the Kehillah Activities

From the year 1915 until the Holocaust, the *Kehillah Rov* and *Av Bet Din* (head of the religious court) was *Rov Hagaon Rebbe* Chaim Mordecai Bronrot, *Shlita*. His position gave him top religious standing in the *shtetl*, but in his activities he did not limit himself to religious matters only. *Rov* Bronrot was active in a broad range of communal life of the Ciechanów Jews and also took an interest in every individual.

There was practically no meeting or gathering of any institution at which he was not present; or any commission whose activities did not engage him if they dealt with any aspect of Jewish *parnoseh*. He participated with advice and action. He also helped individuals in time of need or in an argument about money or a family dispute. People always found his door open for such cases. In him they found a warm heart to confide in and seek advice. The *Rov* tried to help everyone; used his influence of relatives or interceders in the government organs. Oft-times he would set out in the *shtetl* to call on the wealthy ones in order to gather a proper sum to assist a fallen family.

The Ciechanów Jewish population knew very well how to value this relationship of the *Rov* to the *Kehillah*. When Jews came with their problems, and this wonderful man could not, because of certain reasons, fill their requests, the appealer would say: "To whom can I appeal, then, if not to you? You are, after all, the head of the *Kehillah*." Or some others expressed themselves -- "the father of the *shtetl*".

In the *Kehillah* the *Rov* was always the honorary president and an equally authorized member of the *Kehillah* management, no matter how it was constituted, and in every term of office. The *Rov* was also represented in all the various community and government instances that were active in Ciechanów and in the area. Quite often he was the only Jewish representative present.

The Kehillah President, Chaver Kirshenzweig

150

The *Kehillah* president, *chaver* Kirshenzweig, occupied this important position for ten years. He was one of the leaders who conducted business not according to Party lines, but did what was best in general for all. That was *chaver* Kirshenzweig. He worked on everyone's behalf with the whole fire of his young soul. He particularly busied himself with workers, with craftsmen.

Chaver Kirshenzweig was not born in Ciechanów. He wedded himself to Ciechanów in the year 1924 and immediately threw himself into the work of organizing the hand-workers' movement -- with all his youthful energy.

The workers always found a friend in him, one with an open heart for their painful problems. He was the first one in the *shtetl* to stress the importance of the workers to get organized.

Kirshenzweig had his first victory in 1926 during the first democratic *Kehillah* election when the hand-workers appeared as an organized group and got a third of all the mandates in the *Kehillah* council. At that time, Kirshenzweig was elected as the *Kehillah* president. With him at the helm, the Jewish population felt that it has a devoted representative who is ready, at any moment, to suit every Jew.

The Kehillah secretary and Director of the Folk Bank, *Chaver* Binyamin Kirshenbaum was devoted to his *Kehillah* activities. He was the one who actually carried out the *Kehillah* decisions. R *Chaver* Kirshenbaum remained in his position in all the terms of the elections. Everything that was said or decided was expressed in his precise recordings that he wrote in *Yiddish* and in Polish. If there had been anything left, after the German destruction, of the *Kehillah* archives, the history of the Ciechanów Jewish Kehillah would be able to be reconstructed about the period between the two world wars.

Kehillah Disputes in Ciechanów

151

Approximately in the year 1925, a dispute broke out in the *Kehillah* about the *shoichtim* (ritual slaughterers). Up until that time they were *Reb* Yaacov Hillel and Mendl Shockett. They were already old, and no longer capable to do this work. So many candidates started to arrive to fill the part of *shoichtim*. Every one of them tried to get supporters and followers. The candidates for *shoichtim were: Reb* Chaim Isaachar Fish, supported by the *Aguda* executive; his father-in-law, *Reb* Binyamin

Malina, was then vice-president of the *Kehillah* council. The second candidate was Reb Matityahu Chaim Calberg, a grandson of Tzadik and Alter Zukerman.

The battle regarding the *schita* took on a very sharp form. *Reb* Matityahu Chaim was supported by the older Ciechanów Jews because of the sentiment toward the *Tzadik*.

Rov Bronrot disallowed all the candidates with the motive that their ideas related to *schita* are not perfect The *Rov* immediately sought new candidates from elsewhere who would know the "trade" of *schita* and also be *Chazanim* (cantors), he decided. As *shoichtim* there were hired: *Reb* Melekh Gutheimer, and the famous *Chazan-* S*hoichet, Reb* Laizer Barakhovich.

Everyone saw the great talent o these two *chazanim* and made peace with them. Everyone was convinced that the *Rov* had been proved right and the dispute ended.

It is worthwhile to mention an episode of the *Kehillah* activities. When the *Kehillah* started to organize, the initiation of the *shoichet*, it met with a strong objection at first on the part of the *shoichtim* and especially on the part of Menachim Shockett. He did not want to be an employee of the *Kehillah*.

The dispute went so far that *Rov* Bronrot had to disallow the *schita* of Menachim Shockett. For a long time the *Gerer* people supported him and did not pay attention to the disqualification, but finally the *shoichtim* had to make peace with the idea that the *schita* no longer belongs to them, and the dispute ended.

Jewish Financial Institutions

Yaacov Bronrot

152

Folk Bank and Co-op Bank

After World War I, when the *Kehillah* life started to organize itself on a new basis, two banks were immediately founded: a Folk's Bank and a Co-Op Bank. The banks developed very well in the beginning. Around the merchant bank clung mainly the upper class, large-scale merchants. The president was Avraham Gurney. In the executive: Shlomo Brenner, Yechiel Maier Sokoloff, Natan Skurnik, Dovid Wise and Shlomo Rubinstein.

Merchants and recently prosperous people deposited large sums in the banks and the financial institutions gave sizable loans in the time when the Polish Finance Minister, Stanislaw Grotsky, conducted the economic fight against the Jews.

Parnoses became weaker and a wave of bankruptcies swept over the Jewish businesses and merchants. Jewish Ciechanów fell victim to the economic boycott against Jews, and many merchants went bankrupt. The bank started to feel a lack of capital, a crisis approached. The trust in the financial institutions disintegrated. The wealthy men, Avraham Margolit, Moishe Alters and others, because of the bank's difficulties, started to demand payment with interest, they introduced interest against the bank and it was put under suspicion. Advocate Alshevski was appointed guardian and liquidated the bank. The advocate lived from this until nearly the outbreak of the war. All the attempts of the Ciechanów community activists to save the bank from sinking did not succeed.

The Folk's Bank was, as it was called, a financial institution for the folk. Every craftsman and small merchant was a member there. The capital consisted of "payments" and the institutions got large credit from the central co-op bank in Warsaw.

153

The majority of Ciechanów Jews were members in the bank. Its main bookkeeper was the businessman Binyamin Kirshenbaum. The bank had a right of existence and would have developed well, but the trouble was the inner Party conflict. The Folk's Bank was the center of the political struggle for hegemony in the institution.

At the head of the bank were the craftsmen: Yekhezkl Shtifsholtz, Avraham Yosef Alevnick, Shulem Shuster, Aaron Slivkeh, Velvel Galetzer, Avraham Yaacov Biezuner and others.

The annual meeting always took place in the firemen's hall and the shouts of the assembly when an election of the executive took place for the Folks Bank carried throughout the street.. The ones whom the loudest shouters wanted were elected. At each meeting there was a representative of the headquarters in Warsaw.

At the elections of the *Kehillah,* the Folk's Bank put forth its hand-workers' candidates.

153 contd

The fights and the scarcity in leadership led to the losing of the bank. In its place stood the Free Loan Society.

Wolf Henekh Zilbershtrom
Tel-Aviv

The Free Loan Society

The by far largest group of Ciechanów Jews, at the beginning of the 20's was greatly impoverished. The tradesmen: tailors, shoemakers and others did not have any work; merchants, storekeepers did not have money to carry on their business. The Polish banks that were conducted by anti-Semites did not issue any credit to Jews. There were some Jews, so-called war-speculators, who accumulated money and after the war they lent out money on interest. Normally, interest for 5% monthly on every borrowed sum, but soon these took "daily interest."

155

The war speculators lent out money on a daily basis, only for very high interest. The terms of payment were arranged for only a few days that were long enough to go to Warsaw, shop for goods, bring this to Ciechanów to market day or to the fair, and immediately after the fair the money had to be paid back. If, though, because of bad weather or for some other reason the fair was not profitable, a new series of loans for the debts arose.

These loan payments ate up the profits after the loans were repaid. Things were very bad for the small merchant or shopkeeper. This bad situation brought about the idea of forming a Free Loan Society to loan money without interest. A group of merchants got together. A consultation took place in which there participated: Yudl Kronenberg,

Moshe Klinger, Shlomo Slud, the writer of these lines. It was decided to form a Free Loan Society. Everyone present contributed one hundred *zlotys*. With this capital, free from interest loans started to be given.

154

From R standing: M. Rosenberg, B. Kirshenbaum, BM. Malina, Sh. Ciechanówer, G. Nagar, I..D. Weingarten, Shlomo Slud. Seated: M. Klinger, V.H. Zilbershtrom, A. Sh. Lichtenstein, .I. Kronenberg.

After receiving permission to carry on legal activities, it was announced in the *bais medresh* that a founding meeting will take place for the Free Loan Society. To this meeting came Jews from all levels. And since, at that time, Parties were already active in Ciechanów, a competition around the voting for the president began.

Finally, all the Parties united to elect as president a non-Party man, Wolf Henekh Zilbershtrom. I invited a member of the Zionists to the executive -- Binyamin Kershenbaum, and a representative of the workers whose name I unfortunately do not remember.

At my appeal to the meeting, everyone agreed that the Free Loan Society must be non-partisan and work for the benefit of all. The executive of the Society was elected, consisting of the following: president – Wolf Henekh Zilbershtrom; president of the executive committee -- Avraham Shmuel Lichtenstein; members of the executive and management: Moishe Klinger, Yudl Kronenberg, Shlomo Slud, Gedalya Nagar, Yoel Dovid Weingarten, Binyamin Kershenbaum, Baruch Mordecai Malina, and Moshe Rosenberg.

For the activities of the Society I gave my counter where I had my mill, in order to economize on expenses. The executive made an announcement that whatever needs a loan should request same at the Free Loan Society. The limit of the loan was fifty *zlotys* , to be repaid at the rate of five *zlotys* per week.

The Society helped people in the following cases: a carrier who was evicted from his dwelling, a wagon whose horse had died, a handler who sells goods at a stall in the marketplace, a shoemaker who needed to buy some material for his workshop, etc. Such needy ones got loans.

The "Joint" came to the aid of the Society. It changed its procedure of general support and gave money only for constructive purposes. In reply to our first appeal we received a "Joint" loan of five hundred *zlotys* and later another five hundred *zlotys* that we repaid in various terms.

156

The central management of "Joint" in Warsaw called a conference, at the end of each year, of the Loan Society in Poland, whose representatives had to undergo an audit of their books. From our Society the following were the representatives: Zilbershtrom and Kronenberg. Our bookkeeping and accounting made a good impression on the "Joint" directors and we received a credit of one hundred *zlotys* per person.

After our great success, when the Society had established firm roots in Ciechanów amongst the Jews, we decided to establish our own financial means through collecting voluntary contributions. Members of the executive went from door to door and Jews undertook to contribute fifty *zlotys* per week to the Society. In the beginning, we ourselves made the contribution. Later we appointed Berl "Speculant" as collector, and for a specified fee, he made the weekly collections.

The Free Loan Society developed very well. It moved to its own premises. The "Joint" continually increased the credit and we already issued loans of three hundred *zlotys* per person. This enabled more than one merchant to get established.

In the course of time the executive changed. In place of the president, A. Sh. Lichtenstein, there came Gedalya Nagar. I also resigned from my position and in my place came Yehoshua Greenbaum.

When I went on *aliyah* to Israel, I bade a friendly farewell to my *chaverim* of the Free Loan Society and left them, as a souvenir, my metal box from my counter.

Rivka Kahane

The Elections to the First Polish Siyum

At the time of the elections for the first Polish *Siyum* a united front was formed through the initiative of Yitzhak Greenbaum, together with all the Polish minorities (except for the "Folks Party" of Noach Prilitzky and the *Bund*). Ciechanów was a main locality for a larger circle, and with this work, once again, the leaders were the Zionist activists.

I remember that our house had the appearance of a packing house, full of large show cases, full of election material for the whole area. There came to us, for a special meeting, in the Gemina, three of the later *Siyum* deputies: *chaver* Farbshtein, *chaver* Klumel, and advocate Alshvanger, leader of the Zionist movement in Poland, and we were proud of them.

157

I also remember a request to us from the Warsaw Central Committee that Ciechanów should send, to Pultusk, electioneers to the *Siyum* elections, and the following were sent: Yaacov Kahane -- a Zionist, presently living in Israel; Yisroel Yaacov Student -- an *Agudist*.

Much time and effort was devoted to the J.N.F., where Moishe Kviat was the *Mursha* until he left for the Land of Israel, and he was replaced by Yekhzkl Trombka.

A *Hechalutz* group was also formed, led by Berl Agradnik, the only Jewish member in the *shtetl*. They prepared for work on the land, and part of them did go on *aliyah* in 1920. From that time on the *aliyah* to Israel did not cease. Our ranks began to be depleted.

In March 1925, I, with my three children, left Ciechanów for the Land of Israel.

Moishe Perakh

Accused of Spying

In 1920 Jewish youth started to leave the *shtetl*. They went to America and some to the Land of Israel. I was also amongst those who prepared to go on *aliyah*. But meanwhile the Polish-Soviet war broke out and the Polish powers accused us of spying.

I, and Voveh Burshtein, tried to smuggle across the border into Germany. At the Polish border we were arrested and taken to Warsaw jail and we were in danger of getting the death sentence. When the Bolsheviks neared Warsaw we were given the opportunity to gain our freedom by going as the first ones into the line of fire. We accepted the suggestion, not having a choice. Thanks to the intervention of my wife's sister to the mayor of Ciechanów, *chaver* Yanetsky, our innocence was proved and we were freed. V. Burshtein left for America, I for the Land of Israel.

The Jewish Workers Party in Ciechanów

Yehoshua Grosbard (Vyelkabrodeh) Haifa

158

Home and Surroundings in My Formative Years

In the years 1909-10 my family moved from Sorotz to Ciechanów. I was still a *cheder* boy at that time. My father's occupation was bindery and I read the books that my father bound. Amongst the youths who gave books to bind there was a group of boys whose books I carried over to the illegal library at that time. I was (in a room) in the loft in the home of the Lichtensteins on Proshnitzer Way where the teacher Tchurek lived. I was told to watch out for "Bekerl" and make sure that he does not see the destination to which I am carrying the books.

I had the feeling at that time that I was doing something secret and dangerous. I tried to acquaint myself with the boys who were coming in to us. They were: the brothers Yosef and Yekhezkl Trombka, the Berman brothers, Moishe Kviat, Moishe Kleinyud, and others. Adjoining us lived the Perlmutter family. There were several grown daughters: Shaindl, Faigeh, Manya and a brother Hershel and his bride, Nebkeh Ciechanówer. I often saw them, always with a book in hand.

I was particularly interested in a young boy with a round *kapelush* (hat) on his head and a book under his arm. When I discovered that he works as a printer, I imagined that he was a striker or a revolutionary – since I had heard stories since I was five years old. From this young boy there later emerged the Worker Party's worker -- Yosef Maier Perlmutter.

The teacher, Yehuda Eliezer Divan, who gave Hebrew lessons, also interested me. He taught two girls who were our neighbors, and I listened in on his lessons that had a very strong influence on me.

159As the seamstress -- Chaya Rivka Robota -- where I used to bring meals for my older sister, Libah, who worked there -- I got to know Paula and her younger sister -- Tauba Dresner, Faigeh Listopoel and her brother, the seamstress Milner, Tchurek, Pshisusky and others. In their book discussions I used to hear the names of writers that I recognized from the title pages of the books that my father bound. All those boys and girls I considered as members of the loft room in Proshnitzer Way.

The older I got the more broadened became my acquaintance with young people such as: with the Mundzak's, Garfinkls, Vovo Burshtein, Finkelsteins, Remboims, Beresh Mlovsky. I also heard about Laznick, Isaac Kostsheva, who left for America. They were all, at that time, the "Enlightened" ones of Ciechanów.

Just before the outbreak of World War I, we lived at Aaron (Gelbard) Kovel on Ploinsker Way. The Divan family were our neighbors. The Rosens came to them from the district on the "Glinkes" there was a large military medical division. There, there were many Jewish soldiers. In the evenings they used to come to the Jewish homes where there were young people. They used to enjoy themselves and talk about politics, literature and communal matters, enjoy themselves with young ladies -- played lotto, made *latkes*. Amongst the soldiers there were cultured and educated ones. This I understood later when I recalled their talk and discussions.

Winter time, the soldiers were billeted in private homes. They made sure the houses had fuel for heating. Where food was lacking, they also brought food, and books to read. In our house there were billeted: a medic, a Jew Shenigson, and an older Russian. Shenigson liked to tell folk tales and sing Jewish national songs and workers' songs. His listeners were: my sister and I myself. From time to time the soldiers would arrange other entertainment in the home of Berl Agradnik or at the Divans'.

159 contd.

During wartime, when binding no longer supplied one with an income, we opened a tea-house in *Rebbe* Yitzhak Dovid's house. In the evenings many officers and soldiers came to us from the "Volunteer Ullaner Regiment.

160

In one of our rooms there was billeted an officer whom his colleagues nicknamed "Kniaz." The Russian military men discussed, far into the night, important (blank) and cultural matters. I am sure that these people played a role in the future developments. Particularly one who when he had conversations with my father, would ask him questions about work, earnings, about a school for the children, about relations with the Polish neighbors, etc. This atmosphere had a great influence on my educational development.

160 contd.

The Cultural Society "Hazamir" and Its Library

After the Germans, during World War I, conquered Poland, and the Jewish communal life was revived after being completely suppressed, during Czarist times, the library *Hazamir* opened in Ciechanów. When my father decorated the library and the reading room, and I helped him in this work, I asked for membership in the *Hazamir* instead of the tip money. The executive of the library were: Yosef Trombka, Yoel Garfinkl and Yosef Maier Perlmutter. They tested me, asking me why I want to become a member of *Hazamir*, what books I had read. Finally, they decided to grant me membership in the library as a reader only. Because of my young age, they did not want to grant me regular membership.

160 contd.

At *Hazamir* I met a lot of new people. With many of them I am still in contact to the present day in close friendship. My friends from that time are: Shifra Laznik, Shaiyeh Kostsheva, Soreh Faigeh Kostsheva, Gita and Maier Gotliber, Chaya Zieloner, Montchke, Yudl and Laib Bronshtein, Noske Apel, Rodzinek and others.

In Ciechanów there were also war refugees, amongst them some interesting young people from Warsaw such as: brothers Maier and Shamai Tenenbaum, Shamai Rapoport. In the evenings after work, we decided to organize reading groups in *Hazamir*. We met twice a week. One person would read and then we would have a discussion about it. We evaluated the work from an ethical-moral standpoint. We were inspired by *Ven Keiten Klingn* (When Chains Ring) by Olgin, from the poetry of Morris Rosenfeld, Bashevis and Edlshtat. We also discussed I. L. Peretz, Multatuli, and enjoyed Sholem Aleichem's humor.

161

Literary evenings also took place in *Hazamir* with recitations and performances, to which a large crowd came. The registrar, Binyamin Eisenberg, was also a good reciter. Zak Levy often came from Warsaw. He was, at that time, considered one of the best Jewish artists. Under Eisenberg's direction, Chirikov's *Di Yidos* (The Jews) was performed. The performers were : I. M. Perlmutter, M. Gotliber, Sh. Kostsheva, Shifra Loznik, my elder sisters and I myself.

161 contd.

For me and for my sister it was quite a revolution to act on stage. We guarded ourselves lest our father find out about this. But it turned out that our fear was unfounded. A few days after the performance, my father asked me if I would like to participate in a performance for the benefit of the Free Loan Society, because he heard that I had acted very well. Wiselitz, the well-known actor, also performed in several plays and did recitations. He used to come to Ciechanów to his friend Gips, a Hebrew teacher, a talented reciter and cultural activist. Gips gave lectures on Zionist themes. There was another teacher in *Hazamir*, Plutzer, a capable cultural activist and a Zionist.

At that time political groups started to form within *Hazamir*, with different orientations: Zionist youth mainly from middle class homes; Poele Zion, Party workers, whose leaders were: Naftali Sarek, Boruch Mordecai Malina. The majority of young people from working parents' homes started to organize the *Bund*. From the reading circles in *Hazamir*, there was a group who concerned themselves with establishing a workers' paper in Ciechanów. Very active in this respect were the members: Kostsheva, Bitterband Chaya Zeliner (who was later called the "*Bubbe* of the *Bund*." From Warsaw came *chaver* Yevetz, and though not everyone understood his political terminology, we nevertheless felt that this connects us with all the poor throughout the world, who strive for a better, nicer life. Afterwards we met more often, read together, discussed, and became like a family. During Party strife in *Hazamir* we consulted in advance and dealt according to certain principles.

162

The first Bundist group in 1916. R. standing: I.M. Perlmutter, Riterband, Galke, M. Tenenbaum, Sh. Grossbard. Seated: A. Greenberg, M. Gotliber, Shifra Loznik, N. Apel and I. Fried

The Split in Hazamir Folk Library and Grosser-Club

The war ended. From *Hazamir* there becomes Folk-Library. The Party struggle grew even stronger. The majority of the members were with is because we demanded that the Folk-Library should be the central place for organizing help for the poor and needy. These were harsh postwar years. Hunger and epidemics were prevalent. Our *chavera* showed superhuman devotion when the cholera epidemic swept over Ciechanów. The youth, after a hard workday be on duty all night to give help to the sick.

The Party discussions between Zionists and non-Zionists grew even stronger in the Folk-Library. Conflicts arose, and finally the Zionists left the cultural institution.

The library developed further in spite of the conflicts and disturbances that sometimes even took the form of fights. Finally, the influence of the *Bund* grew. *Bundist* speakers started to come more often from Warsaw. Professional societies started to be organized of leather workers, servant maids, etc.

163

Bundist group with Bunim Warshavsky

164   blank

165

Clarification work was also conducted. The *Bund* gained intellectuals. The teacher, Isaac Greenberg from Mlava, a fiery speaker, a deeply cultured man, an artist and director, had a great influence on many young people from middle-class homes, such as : Mala Pafa, Chaya Burshtein, the two Vashnievsky sisters, May Aigengold, Zilbershtrom Formes and others. Greenberg was active in all respects -- gave lectures, established self-learning groups, conducted them, directed theater performances and performed himself. Also active were : the teacher, Mlinek and Vovo Burshtein.

165 contd.

The Folk Library got a *Bundist* name: "Grauser Club," named after the *Bund* leader who died young, Branislav Grauser. The club, that consisted mainly of the greater part of working youth, had a large hall with a stage, a library, a reading room, a drama group that performed, at that time, Pshivishevsky's *"Shmai"* (Snow), Strindberg's "Father"; Bimko's *"Ganovim"* (Ships), Hirshbein's "Uncle Boyle". We also read monologues of Sholem Aleichem, Peretz's *"Di Lvoneh Dertzailt"* (The Moon Tells), and others. The drama group sometimes performed in the surrounding *shtetlech*. We used to exchange performers or borrow people from a similar drama group in Mlava.

Activists in the Bund organization. R. <u>Standing:</u> **T. Remboim, Sh. Grosbard, V. Kostsheva, L. Bronshtein, Nashelsker, L. Tchurek.** <u>Seated</u>**: Rachel Zilbershtrom, Mala Pafa, N. Apel, G. Rosenshtein.** <u>Last row</u>**: V. Kostsheva, Sh. Kostsheva, I. Bronshtein, Shifra Loznick**

Political Activity and New Splits

The liberation of Poland and the aftermath of the Russian Revolution brought in a lot of impulsiveness in Ciechanów Jewish and non-Jewish life. Political and economic strikes began. I recall the large agrarian strike with its gigantic demonstrations throughout the land. When the demonstration was to take place in Ciechanów, the joint

Polish-Jewish committee sent out some *chaverim,* who called upon people to close the stores at the time of the demonstration. The *chaverim* got arrested. At the beginning of the demonstration the police demanded to disband and they shot into the air. The demonstration continued to grow and stood firmly in the marketplace not far from the magistrature. In spite of the fact that a Military group on horses chased with swords, and demanded that they scatter, nobody moved from the spot until the release of the arrested *chaverim* was promised.

That day perhaps the majority of precious working youth formed the uprising for the future battle. I recall the tears of joy when the *chaverim* met afterwards and told what they had lived through that day of struggle.

166

A new wave of strikes erupted. The elections for the municipality were approaching. In the Jewish street the fight grew stronger between the working class and the others. We decided not to allow the *shul* to be used for an election meeting that the *Rov* wanted to have at the reading of the Torah. A group of us went and demanded to have a word and did not allow any election talk in *shul.* Later, police came looking for me at home. I had to hide for a whole week in a loft at the home of the Pravdes on the Jewish Street.

The election campaign was a tough one, but we succeeded in electing two of our people: Yidl Bronshtein and Mlinek. I want to take this opportunity to state that many religious tradesmen voted for our people since they had more trust in us. The strikes of the tailors and other tradesmen that we conducted cost us much effort and our youth spared no energy and helped in any way they could.

We also took part in the elections for the Workers Council that was established in 1919. I remember the large mass meeting in "Paraflyonem House" to elect delegates to the Workers' Council, in which many peasant workers participated and some not so wealthy farmers as well. It was a stormy meeting because of the differences of opinion regarding the nature of the council. It did not come to any excesses against the Jews in spite of the fact that the priest and his assistants nearly openly called for a pogrom.

*

The difficult economic situation in Poland, the great unemployment, the October Revolution in Russia – affected the Jewish workers in Ciechanów as well. Once again sharp discussions took place. Stormy meetings took place. Discussions went on all night. New ideas started to crystallize. Some members of the *Bund*: M.Gotliber, M.

Rozen and others were stirred up because of the communist agitation, and started to bring material and appeals on very thin paper, that we used to take home and read in secret, hidden from the eyes of the *Bund* leaders.

167

Tag Day to raise money for the victims of the Ukrainian pogrom

168   blank

169

The entry of Poland into the war with the Bolsheviks, the terror throughout the land, did not escape us either. At the beginning of the winter of 1920, one evening, an officer with a regiment of soldiers attacked the "Graus Club", broke the furniture, tore the pictures and books, beat many of those present and arrested a few people, amongst them Bronshtein and Aigengold. The soldiers beat up the arrested ones so badly that they were sick in bed for a long time afterwards.

In a few days we put everything back in order. We went on working, arranged readings and performances and also carried out political action.

One evening, when we were preparing for the May 1st celebration and for a performances, police once again attacked the club and chased everyone out. I hid beneath the stairs. They dragged me out of there even though I was serving in the Military, they took me to the

P.K.O. (recruiting office). I remained working there a few days. I remember the devotion of the *chaverim* who came to say farewell to me and brought me good things. With particular warmth, Kostsheva and Lazniks behaved towards me. I was living with them since my parents lived in Warsaw at the time. With great respect I recall the mother, Nekhe Laznik, as one of the fine persons, a type of woman like Sara Bas Tovim.

Yugnt (Youth) "Tzukunft" and Comtzukunft

On August 16, 1920, I was wounded at the front and after being in the Military hospital for nine months, I came to Ciechanów in March 1921 on sick leave. The situation in the land was a difficult one. The Workers' Organization in the *shtetlech* was weakened because of the police terror that was prevalent during the war. The communist mood increased amongst the workers and the poor folk that also influenced the Jewish working people in Ciechanów. At the front, and afterwards in Bialystok, where I was serving with the Forty-Second Regiment, I often used to come to meetings where I met with true factory proletariats. I began to see events in a different light.

170

In Ciechanów area I started to organize the youth, but no longer in the *Bundist* spirit. A strong fight was held against the *Bund*, that stubbornly defended its position. Finally, a large portion of the *Bund "Tzukunft"* joined the *"Comtzukunft"* organization that slowly started to set up a regular organizational educational work program. The active members were: Margolis, Kersh, N. Laznik, I. Mlotzker, T. Remboim, Misher, Sasskover, Plate, M. Zieloner, I. Gallek, Z. Apel (Khlevak) and others. Our meetings used to take place in the forest near the sugar factory as well as in private homes. At the end of 1921 I, while still in the army, was sent as a delegate for the Ciechanów region to the congress of *"Comtzukunft"* that took place in Danzig.

The election campaign to the Polish *Siyum* in 1922 we carried on under difficult half-legal conditions. The police terror demanded from our *chaverim* much self-sacrifice and devotion. The *chaverim* used to sit whole nights, wrote placards and appeals. They also contributed their last *groshns* for election work A few nights before the elections the police attacked our election office, arrested those present and held them for a few days until after the election in order to hinder our work in that way. In spite of this we had a large number of votes in Ciechanów region.

At the same time we carried on cultural activities through readings and lectures on various communal matters and library themes. With the participation of progressive people, we organized a lecture by the well-known progressive journalist at that time and activist, Vienyava

Dlugoshevsky, about: *"Erev Friling"* (Before Spring) by Djiromsky, that attracted a large crowd of Jewish and Polish workers and intellectuals. Academics such as I. Mushinsky lectured on "New Forms in Modern Literature" and others. We influenced a circle of intellectuals and teachers and used to meet in the homes of the teachers Hoifnagl and Fuchs and there we had discussions about cultural and political issues.

We organized a non-Party inter-*shtetl* initiative group of representatives from Mlava and Ciechanów. the group organized lectures about the new Jewish literature and brought the writers Melekh Ravitch and Peretz Markish, who were warmly received, particularly in Mlava, but an honorary committee consisting of Kuba Kleinetz, Greenberg, Alter, Kanarik and others.

175

The leaders of the Revolutionary Workers Youth in the year 1919.
From R: Noshelsker, Sh. Grosbard, N. Loznik, N. Apel, Shifra Loznik, H. Crystal

172   blank

173

In Ciechanów, at that time, the great Jewish writer, Yisroel Shtern, spent an extended period, after he came out of hospital. His mother, brother and sister lived in our *shtetl*. We tried to arrange for him to lecture on literature and organize his lecture in Ciechanów as well as in other cities. I myself tried to arrange for the writer to stay with my friends -- Vielgalaski and Schgave, where Shtern spent a long time.

Marxist Self-learning Group]

In 1927, the Ciechanów elections took place for the city administration. The influence of the communists was great. We went to the election at that time under the name *Arbeiter Ainheit* (United Workers). We suffered much from police terror yet we came out of the election victorious. We got four representatives: Nieshkovsky -- a shoemaker, and Kaminsky -- a handler in the marketplace. The *Bund* got one representative -- Yudl Bronshtein; P.P.S. representative -- a *feldsher* (medic) from the Sick Society – Uguschak. After the election we approached the *Bund* and the P.P.S. (Polish Socialist Party) about forming a united representation of the workers. The dealing with the *Bund* and the P.P.S., which took place in the course of a few weeks in the *Bund's* premises, did not yield results in this respect.

In the year 1928, we sent delegates to the parliamentary Freethinkers Congress that took place during *Pesach* in Łodz. From Ciechanów the delegates were: Balbinsky, Z. Apel and Sh. Grosbard. The congress lasted a few days. In the end it was declared illegal and the majority of the delegates were arrested. When our delegates returned to Ciechanów they gave reports of the congress to small groups. Discussions were held and decisions were made for the future work.

We also organized a cultural institution called *An-ski Biblioteque*, where lectures were continually given on political, social and literary themes. In the executive and in the commissions those active were:

Binyamin Apel, Melovsky, Yudl Galek, Singer, Zigmunt, Rikl Misher, N. Loznik, Chayche, Yosl Grossbard, Gutmakher and others.

It is worthwhile to mention a friendship outing.

174

Workers' Cultural Activists - In the middle: Binyamin Apel

that the *Anski Biblioteque* arranged together with the *Peretz Biblioteque* of Mlava, legally organized in the forests in the Mlava region. We went to Mlava Friday evening. On *Shabbat* morning, when we started to gather in the Mlava Gardens and in closed rows marched in the forest, police came and chased us away, in spite of the permission that we had.

Our youth was devoted with all their heart and suited themselves to work under the most difficult conditions. In later years, when I was in Warsaw, I was amazed at the news I heard about how our youth conducted themselves during the grand trial of arrested communists in the Mlava court house, where the main witness was the stool-pigeon Con. A sentence of nearly a hundred years in prison for those charges was given.

The youthful communists participated in organizing the large demonstration of the unemployed in the Thirties that forced the established of committees for the distribution of cheap and also free products for the poor and unemployed.

Also, the first concentration camp in Poland -- *Carhuz Bereze* did not overlook Ciechanów: Laibl Souckover and Nathan Fizner were arrested and sent there to that torture camp.
175

Just before World War II, our *chaverim*, together with the *Bund* and *Left Poele Tzion*, organized the Peretz Library where the archives once were: A. Margolis, B. Apel and Yosl Grosbard; from the *Bund*: Wolf Kostsheva and Tchurek. From the *Left Poele Tzion*: Litwin and others.

*

The above-written is just a small part of the activities of our *chaverim* and of all branches of our Ciechanów youth that perished at the hands of the Nazi fascists, together with their near and dear ones. May lines be a modest monument for all those whom I have mentioned and whom I have not mentioned.

Blessed be their memory.

L. Naskelsker

Political and Cultural Activities

After the Russian Czarist forces left Ciechanów, we became a little more free and a renewed Jewish social life started to pulsate. A flood of increasing movements of all streams began to multiply: social, cultural and political. Such was the case in all Jewish *yishuvim* (settlements) in Poland and so it was in Ciechanów, that had, at that time, twenty thousand inhabitants. At the end of the war in 1918 Ciechanów had the following institutions and organizations: the Jewish *Kehillah*, a Merchants' society, a Bank Institution. There was a Jewish mayor, Jewish members in the city council, and Jewish policemen as well.
175 contd.

From those days there remains in my memory the beautiful Workers' Club, provided with everything that such an institution needed. Primarily a well-functioning library, overlooked by Shifra. She was a good librarian. She knew every reader and knew what to give each one to read and for study...
176

I remember the first book she gave me to read. It was *Robinson Crusoe*. "This will be good for you. Read it. You'll enjoy it, and later I'll prepare other good books for you." These were Shifra's words to me at that time, spoken with a smile.

I was still a young boy at that time and read voraciously, and soon started to learn about socialism with the help of those dear friends, idealists, of which my *shtetl* had many.

176

A meeting of Bundist groups from Ciechanów and Mlava. First row <u>top</u>: R: unknown, V. Kostsheva, Nashkelsker, T. Remboim, Kostsheva, Kleinbard; seated: Kzesla, Flata, Gzebyenaz

177

The second brother, Yidl, an energetic and determined one, "the politician" we called him, and his Party the *Bund* did indeed, because of this, put him forth as a candidate for city councilor in the elections.

The female member, M. Pafa, was a very dear young woman. From her wealthy home she came directly to the club, contributed her share of the work of evening classes that the club organized for working members, without charge. Her purpose in coming to the club wasn't merely to serve as a teacher. She was also convinced that only with social justice can there be a good world and a free world, and this is what drew her to the club that conducted its activities consistent with her ideas.

The *chaver* Voveh Burshtein was brought up in a wealthy and strictly religious home. The family hoped that their son would grow up to be a *Rov*. There came a time, though, when the *Talmid Khokhem* (religious learner) became a *Talmid Socialism*. Vaveh came to the club to give his lessons for the "lecture group" where a group of young people that the club organized were preparing themselves to be lecturers and leaders of the widely-spread social work. This widely-spread activity was carried on by the *Bund*.

I scan my brain for memories of days and years. I want to be able to recall and tell about bygone days. I want to bring out the beauty and variety of my youth club with its sports section, choral group, and so on... Where are they all: those dear idealists of my youth? Here before my eyes is a picture of a group of those young idealists and dreamers. I look at them and I feel like an orphan with a desire to say *Kadish* at the site of their graves, but where does one find the graves of these holy souls?

Once more I scan my brain. A particular page of the *Poele Tzion* movement of Ciechanów also with its own club, *Di Arbeiter Haim* (The Workers' Home). Unfortunately, I barely recall the names of those who conducted the Workers Home: Baruch Maline, and the other one -- Yosef Zilberblat of the young *Poele Tzion*, Yosef Zilberblat, a gentle blond boy, knowledgeable in Marxism Borokhovison and able to convey it, was a political opponent of mine; still, it was a pleasure to enter into a discussion with him.

There were also curious things and mischievous goings-on in the life of those days, but without doubt all these acts were closely related to certain aims that strengthened and cemented the whole active Jewish social movement uphill.

178

Group of Left Poele Tzion]

Suddenly I recall the following episode:

I jump over the fence and from there is just a hop and a skip to the friend Shifra's house. My jump over the fence has nothing to do with mischief, but rather with practicality, to save time. That's how my youthfulness expressed itself: Why go all the way around when with one jump I'm at my destination? The only barrier that separated me from the narrow alley where Shifra lived was the fence, so why should I go all the way around? --- There was no time for such a luxury.

The Chaverim of Yugnt-Bund-Tzukunft (The Friends of the Young Bund Future)

178

Regional Conference of "Tzukunft"

180   blank

181

One nice summer evening, after work, I was informed that a young man was inquiring about me. The man was staying at the only inn, by Reb Noach Mishor, where one could enjoy a tasty glass of tea with a piece of pastry such as is the custom after a journey. I went to Reb Noach Mishor's inn where I found none other than the *Yugnt Bund Tzukunft* leader of that time, and one of the editors of the Warsaw *Folks Zeitung* (Folk Newspaper), Sholem Hertz. He had come to Ciechanów to fulfill his citizen obligation as an army reservist, to service in the army for four weeks, as was the rule at that time in Poland.

A group of Tzukunft. Standing R: Gitl Singer, V. Kostsheva, I. Gallek, Frumche Loznick, Senskover, Srebnagara, Kostsheva. Seated: Yidl Bronshtein, Gevelber

We were acquainted only through correspondence that we carried on because of the newspaper *Yugnt Shtime* (Voice of Youth). I was the secretary at that time of the press committee in Ciechanów that was responsible for distributing the paper of *Yugnt Bund Tzukunft*. I quickly went to my friend Shifra, because there was the "headquarters". There people came to bring and get news. I let Shifra know that the *chaver* Sholem Hertz is in town from Warsaw.

As was her custom, she showed her joy by clapping her hands and immediately said, with a smile: "Such a guest, if even not specifically to us, we must prepare something, a bit of a *lameh* (which is what the *Bundists* of those days called a party *seudah*/meal). Right away we took Shifra's mother into the circle, a dear *Yiddish* mama, a dear mother. Everyone called her Aunt Nekhe. Everyone who entered the house such as: Sh. Grosbard, Sh. Kostsheva, Avigdor, Wolf Kostsheva and others felt like one big family.

Humble little I sneaked into this dear family, a bit of a distant one, so what? And isn't a neighbor like one of the family? -- So Shifra's mother Nekhe was everyone's aunt, and if we asked her a "banquet" was born. There was no need for special salons, as is the style today, but simply in a proletarian way as was customary then, but with warmth, with more intimacy than nowadays.

As though the news had spread through the air, *chaverim*/friends appeared from all corners and it was a real celebration. We all rejoiced together. The guest felt right at home, as with family.

I still remember the words of Sholem Hertz: "*Chaverim*, I feel so good amongst you, but aside from rejoicing with you, we have something to discuss." And soon the joyfulness got serious. Sholem reported on the Tz. K. of *Yungt-Bund-Tzukunft*. Soon we will have to submerge ourselves with all our energy in important political work.

182

After rejoicing and hearing reports, we took a walk in the *shtetl* marketplace. It started to get late. We each went our way. I remained standing for a while with the guest and he said: "The whole *shtetl* has fallen asleep, and the town clock marches on, as usual, ticking away." With a hoarse voice it struck out twelve. "A strange clock you have here." He reminded me that very early tomorrow morning I have to be at the army barracks. And one has to sleep a little also. "And I want very much to write a few words to my *kindelekh*/children."

With all my naiveté I asked: "How many do you have, may they be well." Oh, we have many. They are not only mine but yours also."

I remain standing with an open mouth, like a true small-town boy, until I gathered from the rest of his talk that he means the Orphan/Children's Home in Warsaw.

"If so," I told him, "come home with me, so you'll be able to write to the *kinderlekh*, and you'll sleep at my place also..."

What a pity that I do not have the talent to write stories and novels. I would surely not have a shortage of material nor heroes for the best and finest historical novel that would be the best contribution to world literature.

My beloved *Yiddish shtetl* Ciechanów, that was so brutally wiped out.

Vigdor Kesler (Kostsheva)

The Split in the Jewish Workers Movement

183

In the years 1918-19, when Poland was freed form the German occupation and Became an independent democratic state, opportunities arose for legalized life of cultural societies, professional organizations, political parties. That's how it was in Ciechanów also.

From the cultural club Hazamir that had existed from previous years, and also during the German occupation, different groups emerged, with different political ideologies. From them there was constructed the Zionist organization, Poele Tzion, Tzirei Tzion, and the Bund.

Each of the above-mentioned Parties had its culture-club. The Bund -- the Grauser Club. There the activities of the Yungt-Bund-Tzukunft also took place. I had an influence on the working youth. The large library and the readings that took place often brought a renewed spirit for the youth who came from bais hamedresh and from workshops.

Reading circles were founded where lecturers, together with their listeners, learned and discussed all important current events in the social and political life. Isaac Greenberg, Mlinek, Vaveh Burshtein, Aigngold, Shaiye Grosbard, Yudl and Laibish Bronshtein, were the leaders in this cultural work.

The drama group, together with the help of the Warsaw registrar, presented theater performances. Those belonging to the group were: Greenberg, Yosl Maier Perlmutter, Noske Apel, Shifra Loznik, Faige Perlmutter, Shaiye Grosbard and others. The performances took place in the large hall of the Grauser Club, or at other locations that were always packed. The group of artists became very popular in the cities around Ciechanów and they traveled around, giving performances in Proshnitz, Mlava, Makov and other cities. Those who helped a lot with the drama circle were: Moishe Klainyud, Faige Perlmutter, Malcha Pafa. They did not belong to the Bund, but did the work solely for pure cultural-literary motives.

In 1920, during the Polish-Soviet war, the situation declined decidedly. The Polish government became reactionary and started to persecute political parties that had a connection to socialism.

184

A period of repression started, including arrests, and soon all previously-won freedoms were taken away But the work in the movement did not stop. Just the opposite, with more devotion the Ciechanów youth , together with the older *chaverim* of the *Bund*, answered all appeals, circulars and decisions of the Warsaw headquarters. Our meetings, consultations and regional conferences took place normally but understandably in secret.

The Ciechanów Jewish cemetery, the small forest, private homes, these were the places where we met and made decisions about our activities. More that once our parents would wait with fast-beating hearts for the safe return of their "children" who went out at night to paste proclamations for the "May First" parade and for other political action that could lead to long prison terms.

We also had to solve difficult problems in our own ranks. It was the period when a split happened in the *Bund*. It was in the Twenties when the problem arose in the *Bund* regarding joining the "Third International" (Comintern) that put forth "twenty-one points." The Party that accepted the "twenty-one points" had to dissolve and become part of the existing landes-party.

In the *Bund* and in the Ciechanów *Bund* as well, three factions were established: those who wanted to continue with the demand for "National-Cultural Autonomy" and accept the sixteen points (of the twenty-one-one), more leftist followers of nineteen and a half points, and the so-called *Combundists* who agreed with all the twenty-one points, who also demanded to get rid of all right-wing leaders.

After weeks and months of heated discussions the *Bund* split up. A *Combund* was established. The twenty-one points group was a great disruptive force right from the start in the movement. For the Ciechanów *chaverim* it was hard to decide to which Party to belong. It did not take long, however, and with the help of literature and local and Warsaw Party lectures from two streams, everything crystallized and in a short time two opposing *Bund* Parties fought.

The previously united professional movement split according to trades. The *Bund* in Ciechanów had the influence in the tailors' union, the "Needle", later in the Garment Union. The *Combund*, together with the communists, had an influence on the cobblers, boot-makers and everything that had to do with leather, and actually called itself the leather-central that had sections in the province.

186

The tailors'-professional union "Needle" existed in Ciechanów for a length of time, and was under the influence of the *Bund*. The workers were very well organized and worked according to the union's agreement.

At the head of the union were: Noske Apel, president and Vigdor Kostsheva, secretary. The "Leather," cobbler boot-makers were not organized. They worked 12-14 hours a day and for very low pay. The *Combund* gained influence with the leather-workers. It took an interest in the conditions of the workers and with the help of active people and from the Warsaw leather headquarters there started to be organized in Ciechanów a cobbler and boot-makers' union. The *Bund*, not wanting to lose its influence with the Ciechanów leather-workers, also began to organize the cobblers and boot-makers into a professional union. The battle continued. Each Party tried with all means to prove to the workers the justice of its ideas.

185

פנקס חבר של איגוד החייטים
מיטגלידס־ביכל פון נאדל־פארריין

Member's booklet of the Needle Union

The enthusiasm and interest to improve the situation of the workers was very great on the part of the membership of both Parties. Finally, the general meeting took place. A representative of the Warsaw leather-central and a leather union was legalized in Ciechanów. The workers there were enriched by one more professional union.

After the legalization of the "Leather" the Ciechanów cobbler-bosses and workers' representatives sat down for the first time at one table, and not only did they work out better conditions for the workers with an eight-hour work day, but actually gave recognition to the cobblers and later treated them as equals.

The *Combund* later united with the communists and the further struggle in the professional workers movement in Ciechanów was between the *Bund* and communists.

Yosl Mundzak, Paris

The "Club" and Its Welfare Work for Ciechanów's Jews

187

Ciechanów was a Yiddish *shtetl*, not particularly lovely nor picturesque, a *shtetl* like all surrounding Jewish *yishuvim* in our area, with a Jewish Kehillah, religious functionaries, social benefit institutions, etc. The small river, Lidinya, with the beautiful lawns around the old historical castle in which the Polish Queen Bana, in the fifteenth century, used to spend her time, constituted the view around the *shtetl*.

A few kilometers away there were beautiful Polish pine forests and beyond there were towns and villages whose peasants provided income for the merchants and tradesmen of the urban population.

In my eyes Ciechanów was a very lovely *shtetl* that I love to this day. And though I now live in Paris, where there are thousands of wonderful monuments, palaces and gardens, I still get lonesome for that old castle with its walls, for the old Ciechanów park, for the forests of Krubinek, Ashtzislov or Gallat.

I long for that little *shtetl*, Ciechanów, because that's where I was born, there I felt the loving care of my dear parents. There I spent my youth in *shul, cheder*, and there I had the best friends of my youth. In that *shtetl* I dreamt about love and of a better, more just world.

And now, when my Yiddish *shtetl* of birth, with the once so lively *Kehillah* has been destroyed by the murderous German murderers, I want to bring into the *Yizkor Book* all that was lovely and elevating in Jewish life there. Let it be allowed for me to erect a monument for a group of young people who gave their time and energy for the benefit of all.

***

The survivors of Ciechanów Jews certainly must remember the word "Club."

What was this "Club"?

It is easy to understand that young people in their twenties do not have a desire to sleep a lot. The day is long and it stretched into the evening. There's lots of energy -- so there is a desire to create something, do something, that should be of general benefit. Possibly our parents spent their young years differently. I imagine that they spent their evenings sitting in the *bais medreshim*, learned from the sacred texts and hoped for *Mashiach ben David* to come riding on a white horse. I understand our parents very well, but our generation was more realistic, and we, the young people, occupied ourselves with other things.

After a day's work we would, in the summer evenings, enjoy ourselves sitting in the garden (near the cinema) and told stories (not about devils/spirits), discussed politics or a football game, sometimes we sang a new "Tango" but that was not all. The Polish government at that time also supplied us with work for such evenings.

188 contd.

At that time it was officially allowed to boycott Jewish stalls in the marketplace. The fascists, without any hindrance by the government, were allowed to plaster the walls of the *shtetl* with notices for the population not to patronize the Jews, because they are the enemies of Poland, the *endekes* (editor's note: *Naradave Democratzia*, a Polish anti-Semitic Party whose program it was to chase the Jews out of Poland). There was, therefore, no shortage of money to pay young hooligans, who were outfitted with green and white bands and station them beside the Jewish shops or stalls in order not to let any Poles buy. So we young people mobilized ourselves and in the evenings spread out throughout the *shtetl* to remove the freshly-pasted announcements, as well as to chase away those who were pasting them. More than once we have to return home when the sun was already rising.

Once, returning home late at night, we heard a woman sobbing. We followed the cries and entered a house where we learned that her son was very sick and the parents don't have the possibility of healing him. We immediately decided to do whatever we could to help this woman and her son in their hour of need. The sick son was a young football player, beloved by all young people.

That same night we went to the doctor and asked him to go to the sick boy as many times as will be necessary, and not to take any money from the parents because we will pay him for everything. We did not go to sleep. Though there were boys amongst us from all political streams, we nevertheless had a common language when someone needed help. We unanimously agreed to organize a ball for this purpose. Each *chaverim* was assigned a job: to prepare a hall, an orchestra, and to organize a buffet.

189 contd.

Work began: Invitations were printed and sent out to and distributed in all surrounding *shtetlech*. Our girlfriends sewed themselves white aprons in order to serve the guests. The hall was nicely decorated. The buffet stood ready with fat roasted ducks and geese, with baked goods and bottles of *schnapps* and wine. It was the first time that there were such preparations in Ciechanów. Everyone prepared themselves for a good time that Saturday evening and with the income to save the sick boy.

Dark destiny, however, wanted otherwise. The young boy died Saturday morning.

The grief on everyone's part was very great. Immediately, different opinions were expressed. The closest friends of the one who had died felt that the ball should not take place because they are in sorrow and the dead one must be brought to burial. A second opinion dominated, however, because great expense had been put out and people from surrounding *shtetlech* were coming so it should not be canceled. After a heated discussion it was decided: some of us should involve ourselves in the funeral as soon as *Shabbat* will end. The others should go on with the work that had started. The opponents of this drastic decision we gave a clear reply: True that we had organized the ball for the sick boy, but there are in Ciechanów many poor needy so that the income from the evening would go to help those in need.

In order to make protests impossible, asked the president of the *Linat Hatzedek Society*, A.V. Katz, to be in charge of the treasury and that's how it was.

A tidy sum of money was realized that was turned over to the *Linat-Hatzedek Society* so that they would be able to better assist the needy sick. They, on their part, to show their appreciation, took in one of our "Club" members to their committee.

190

That ball was a beginning of our activities to help people. We saw that there is much good work to do for the general good. We organized many such balls: for poor children of the public school to buy milk for them, and to send weak children to rest in a sanitarium.

I recall as well once at a meeting of the *Kehillah* when the question of financial difficulty was discussed, the *Rov* Bronrot expressed that if no other means will be found, an appeal will be made to the "Club" for help. That's the kind of reputation the "Club" had in Ciechanów.

The terrible war scattered all of us *chaverim* and we went in different directions. I left my dear home, my birthplace Ciechanów -- on September 3, 1939, six o'clock in the morning. Is it possible to forget such a date?

Memories and Descriptions of the Jewish Way of Life in Ciechanów

Nakhman Grosbard, Haifa

My Childhood Years and Youth Years in the Shtetl

A. Cheder Years

191

I remember Ciechanów from approximately the year 1927, when we moved there from the small shtetl Serotzk. I was still a young child then, and in my childish way was amazed at the "big city" where there are posts with electric lights in the streets and in the houses.

I was a student in the *Talmud Torah*. When I arrived there the principal, *Reb* Avraham Aaron, tested me, pinched my cheek for the "baggage" (learning) that I had brought along -- a sizable amount of *Baba Kama* off by heart. My first teacher was *Reb* Mendl, an older Jew. We, the *cheder* boys, called him "Fania" and other nicknames. He had lots of *tzores* from us. He did not overlook this, though, and hit us plenty.

We learned *Baba Mtzia -- Shanim Akhzin Bhalllit,* but our heads were occupied with something else. Through the window we could see the construction of a new house. Each day the skeleton of the roof grows larger and the workers who are laboring there look like dwarfs.

The window of our *cheder* looks out onto the Jewish cemetery where the *Ohel* (monument of a great person) of the renowned Ciechanów *tzadik* Z"L stands. There people come to deposit notes of prayer for God's grace. It is said that before going into the *Ohel*, one should knock at the door. If not, one might find the *tzadik* in his *tallis* and *tfillin,* and die of fear. (It is told that this actually happened to a student who was a non-believer...)

It is fearful to look out through the window onto the crests of the old half-overgrown and moss-covered gravestones. Still ones eyes are constantly drawn there.

Anyhow, my childish fantasy at that time was full of devils and spirits that scare one in dreams. From the *cheder* I also remember *Rebbe* Mordecai Tzinamon -- a middle-aged man with a thick black beard. He told a lot of nice stories.

192

In future years I studied in school and in *cheder* only in the afternoon. This was hard for me so

I stopped going to *cheder*. Mother did not give up, though. She hired a *rebbe* to come to the house for two hours daily. He would randomly open the *Gemara* and tell me to "recite", meanwhile catching a snooze himself, and when he awoke he suddenly started to shout at me, "*Nu*, carry on! Carry on!"

Still, I did learn some *Ivrit* (Hebrew) from him (which I later forgot). *Yiddish* came by itself. In the house we had the works of Sholem Aleichem, Peretz and other *Yiddish* writers -- the libraries of the older brothers and sisters. My father also liked reading *Yiddish* books. He was a house-painter. Winter time, when there was no work, he occupied himself with bindery (as the saying goes -- *Zibn Malokhes and Vintzig brokhes)* "seven trades and few blessings." Most of the books were *Yiddish* and as much as I read I could not satisfy my hunger for more.

There was another source of Jewish books: A pair of old folks lived in our courtyard, the old Berke with his old Berkelekhe. They lived from support money from their children in America. In their loft there was a great treasury of all kinds of story books, wonder stories of *Shpaler Zaidn*, of the Prague Maharal with the *Gollom, Firsht Reuveni*, Rabbi Akiva, Malka Shabba, stories by the Grimm Brothers and others. These I literally swallowed. The old Berke also liked to have stories read to him because he did not see so well and he did not even want to miss Kutcher's *Tzigeinerin* of the Letzte Neyes *(Latest News)*.

My mother noted with sorrow how more and more often I skip the *davening* and tuck in my *tzitzis* (this she blamed on the school I attended and on the *goyishe* books, so she sent me to evening courses of the *Poele Agudat Yisroel*. There one learned *Tanach* (Proverbs, Ecclesiastes) writing *Yiddish,* and religious morality. With these evening courses my *cheder* career ended.

It is worth noting: Up to the present I still remember lines *Biz Grinem palm-land, fun veisn land fun shnai* (From the land of green palms, from the land of white snow). In a corner of my heart I still have a feeling for the narrow river in the *shtetl* with the surrounding lawns, with the ancient castle, with the cement bridge of the "Third of May," at the long row of acacia and chestnut trees on the Aleike that leads to the railway station ...

194   blank

193

The marketplace in Ciechanów many years ago

The newly-built marketplace

195

Koshchelene Street

הגשר „למאַי"*די בריק פון 3־טן מאַי

The Bridge of the "Third of May"

196   <u>blank</u>

197

B. Roads (Highways), Streets and Alleys

There come to mind memories tied up and woven with Jewish life in a time just before its disappearance: the last act of a generations-long drama, at the edge of the tragic epilogue...

Ciechanów is remembered with its long-stretching roads (highways) leading to the wide unknown world. The fastest road (Plonsker), whose beginning is opposite a forest of crosses. "Here all roads end" -- the philosophically-tragic faded sign says on the semi-circular wall of the Christian wall. But the road, as though in spite, stretching on full of life, to the brick factory, to the small Krubin forest, to other *shtetlech* like the Pultusker road, that runs parallel to it, the road leads to the old Jewish cemetery, cuts its way to the road to the *Glinkes*, the periphery of Polish poverty and extends further, dusty, and during the rains -- a muddy road to the Jewish cemetery. There one rarely sees a living soul, other than accompanying a dead one to the final resting place. That is one of the safest meeting places for our illegal meetings.

The Proshnitzer road with its giant military barracks that attract and frighten at the same time, with their immensity and structure, with its cold build that towers up from the high walls that are so similar to each other... One can enter the barracks only when some event is taking place there -- a horse-race or a football match. At such times the band of the Eleventh Legion Regiment entertains the audience with its music, led by a Jewish bandleader...

When there is a football match *white chevreh* sneak in, not necessarily through the "parade gate" but by crawling around and around through the barbed wire gates, often catching and thus ripping off a piece of ones trousers...

At the finish of the match, as soon as the whistle blows, we Jewish boys run as fast as we can, out of breath, all the way home in order not to have stones thrown at us or be hit by the *shkotzim* (non-Jewish boys). "Home" generally means, to the streets and alleys around the marketplace where the greatest portion of Jews of the *shtetl* live.

198

At the edge of the market square, there is a proud-looking and decorated magistrature-building with a large town clock that gets wound by the old Jewish clock-maker, Melman. Every day he takes care of this. The right wing of the magistrature-building houses the city's police station. Under the building -- the long dismal prison yard, that stretches to the *electrovinia*. Opposite the neighboring house, relatives and friends come to wink to the prisoners and communicate to one another by hand signing.

Nearby is the fire hall. There theater performances take place from time to time in *Yiddish* by traveling actors and also by our own drama group with Zabelski, from Łodz, as director ever since he settled in Ciechanów. My sister Chayche also belongs to this group. For this reason I am allowed free entry to performances. There I first became fascinated with Sh. An-ski's mystic play, *Tzvishn Tog un Nakht* (Between Night and Day) and *Dybbuk* and I *shept nakhes* from the happy couplets in *Rumanishe Khaseneh* (Rumanian Wedding).

The marketplace was a Jewish cultural center. For a while there was a group of *Hashomeir-Hatzair* there, as well as a Hebrew *Tarbut* Library, the *Bais Yaacov School*, and a Free Loan Society.

* * *

Twice a week, Tuesday and Friday, was market day. On those days Jewish merchants, those who came to fairs, brought out whatever bit of goods they had, each on his stall, on the place set aside for them, and arranged the goods ready for business. The goods consisted of: boots and hats, ready-made clothing, colorful yard fabrics for women's clothes and kerchiefs, haberdashery, clay pots and blue dishes... They would exchange friendly slaps of hands, spit on their palms and the deal would be accomplished for wheat, potatoes, wood and peat while in the narrow alleys, closer to the river, there were plenty of eggs and butter, fowl and dairy and vegetable products... and around the market the narrow Jewish streets: the pharmacy (Shlonski's) and Werner's *goyishe* pharmacy (where we sometimes came to "redeem" tipping the hat respectfully, the *shtibl* on Slivke's courtyard, where father has been *davening* for some years.

From Slivke's courtyard through Slava the baker's courtyard, one exits at Nadzechna. In this street the motors of the city's electric power sounds incessantly. The mills that belong to Lubinetsky and Mundzak clatter.

199

In the evenings there is the clamor and singing of the Jewish youth organizations which had their premises there: *Hashomeir Hatzair, Hechalutz, Freiheit* and *Betar*, that later split into *Grausmanisten* and "Revisionists. The split was with a furor, scandal and fighting.

In the same narrow street was the premises of the *Bund* also. From there the pathetic voice of Wolf Kostsheva, leader of the *Bund*, was often heard. Later (at the end of its flowering period), the *Bund* moved to the *Rebbe's* courtyard opposite our house in Proshnitzer Street. In the same courtyard, in the loft of Itchele Shuster, there is the hidden rescued remainder of the great Sh. An-ski library that belonged to the

"Leftists". Until the An-ski library was closed by the police it carried on a variety of cultural and sport activities amongst the working-youth.

The Flinsker Street resounds with *Yiddishkeit*. There fowl/chickens were ritually slaughtered in the *shames* courtyard. A little way off was the *shtibl* of the Gerer *Hasidim*, the *Talmud Torah*, the *Mikveh*; then there is the wide-open space near the Jewish cemetery that sometimes serves as a cattle-market and sometimes as a football field; circuses with their acts; opposite there shine the multi-colored windowpanes of the grand new *shul*. Then there is the narrow quiet *bais hamedresh*. Further on is the *Yiddishe Street* (Yoselovicha) with old crooked houses leaning against one another, with damp walls. Nor are all the surroundings any better. There the street of butcher shops is also located, where meat and fish are sold.

From "Zabeh Street (Targova) where there live mostly cobblers and tailors, there stretches the new wide road to the railway, and then the "crown" of the city: the Varshever Street. Here people stroll every evening and *Shabbat* and *Yomtov* afternoons. Closer to the market, Varshever Street is still old-fashioned, Yiddish, similar to the nearby streets. The further one goes the more Christian it becomes: the houses taller, more modern. From here the road winds, leading to the churches and *goyishe* schools.

Varshever Street ends with a cinema, the only one. Sometimes Jewish performances or readings take place there. In the garden near the cinema one rests between strolls (so long as no *shkotzim* come to make trouble. In the last years before the war this was a common occurrence. Continuing from here one comes to the not-so-homelike Christian streets, where a very few Jewish families live also.

200

C. The Castle, the River and the Meadows

The most beautiful and interesting structure of the Middle Ages in Ciechanów is the castle. More correctly: the remains of the castle built by the Polish King Zigmund Stary for his wife as a summer residence. One explanation of this is the fact that the name stems from Uchekna Nova, the queen's name. Whether or not this is true is a problem for historians, as is the question of whether or not the bricks were made of clay mixed purely with egg-whites. This is supposed to explain the thick and unusually strong walls... However, the turrets have long ago lost their form of former days and birds build their nests there.

There is also an added wooden tower to the castle, that of the firemen. All kinds of entertainment took place in the castle. But

Jewish children generally were not allowed in there. There were a few exceptions that remain in my memory.

I recall a large gathering of the *Bund*. Wolf Kostsheva leads the whole army, dressed in blue shirts with red kerchiefs "forward to the castle!" And inside he holds a speech -- and leftist youth who are not allowed in any conditions -- get together and break down the iron gate ...

* * *

The area around the castle was a paradise on the Sabbaths for the Jewish youth who enjoyed the shade of the high castle walls that protected from the burning sun during the hot summer days.

All week card players and drunks found shelter there: but in the hot *Shabbat* days, Jewish fathers and mothers came to enjoy the fresh air, read a newspaper, and take a nap on the fresh grass. *Hashomeir Hatzair* youth did exercises/gymnastics with Hebrew commands, and *Betar* members played at Military games; and in the evening, when it got empty around the castle, the secret "left" youth groups gathered.

201

Not far from the castle there flowed the Lidinya River. Its source and its final destination is a matter for geographers. Sprint time it sometimes overflows its banks but summertime it is quite calm. Jokers used to say that the water reaches to ones ear if one stands on ones head... Women come here to wash clothes and water carriers to fill their buckets. Young people swim, leaving their clothes on the ground near the bank. Better swimmers go two or three kilometers down the way where the water is very deep. Though it was said that every year some drown in the river, it did not stop them from showing off. But the ordinary youth satisfied themselves with the part of the river that was almost completely in Jewish "territory" – from the electric power station to the right, up to the wooden bridge, the Lava.

The meadows on both sides of the river also played their part in Jewish life. Jewish sport groups used to come here to train and white *chevreh* played "football" for many an hour, with a kid's ball, often barefoot. School children did gymnastics there and youth came there to sunbathe, though there was no sand there they would lie on the grass and soak up the sun. Others relax in the shadow of the trees. There they play cards, less often dominoes, chess, carry on discussions or relax as they watch the cows munching on the grass and how young colts roll on the ground. More romantic pairs walk away further and disappear into the endless meadows and waving wheat fields.

D. The United Library Named after Sholem Aleichem

The memories of my youth prior to the *khurban*, I want to end with a description of the library that was situated in the home of *chaver* Robota.

The United Workers' Library, named after Sholem Aleichem, existed until 1938. It was established as a result of an agreement between three groups: communists, Left Poele Tzion, and Bund.

The communists brought with them the rescued remainder of books from the one-time Sh. An-ski library. The Left Poele Tzion and the Bund the books from their previous libraries.

The library that was legalized by the powers was a successful undertaking and attracted large parts of the working youth, bringing them the progressive work and the Jewish culture. Youthful workers cam to exchange books, read a newspaper, play checkers and chat with friends or have an exchange of opinions.

A tag day for the Sholem Aleichem Library

Friday evenings, political overviews were presented. Sometimes the discussion between *Leftists* and *Bund* got quite heated. The main speakers were: Yosl Grosbard and Wolf Kostsheva. In the end the *Bundist*s left the library for various reasons.

But the library was not liquidated at that time. It continued to exist and broadened its activities and influence.

The two remaining groups managed, generally, to avoid ideological disputes so as to avoid a further split that would have endangered the existence of the library. New books were purchased. Readings took place, evenings of recitation, dance evenings, Ping-Pong was played, and in general the youth had a warm place there where they could forget their troubles and become immersed in the belief that a better day was possible...

203

The United Workers' Library was like a thorn in the eye of the Polish reactionary government. One day the library was shut down, the books confiscated, with the excuse that it was a masked communist "center."

The closed doors of the United Workers' Library, the increased Jew-hatred, were like a prediction of the horrendous time that was coming. The scent of gunpowder over Jewish lives could already be felt. The tragic shadow of death and destruction got closer and closer to the *shtetl*...

Jewish soldiers in the Polish army before the start of World War II

204

Jewish Ciechanów, As I Saw It

Z. Apel

In Memory of My Unforgettable Parents, Sisters and Brothers, My Chaver Urke — Tortured by the Germans

The Teikhe (River) Street

Nadzetna -- the river street, that's how the quiet street was called in Yiddish. One end stretched to the green-covered fence of the "Broy-house" and the other met up with the Proshnitzer Street. Where Proshnitz ended and the wide road began, the road to the *shul* buildings, to the barracks and to Proshnitz, 24 kilometers away.

A long cross-street was River Street. On one side, the exit yards joined the river Lidinya and that is where it got its name. And on the opposite side: two cross-streets uphill to the marketplace and a passageway to the pharmacy street. The main passageway led through Mishlinski's long, long, yard that shortened the way. The problem there, though, was with the dogs, fearful large dogs, that sniffed out a Jewish child from a mile away.

The River Street had a magical attractive quality for us children. It was not densely built up. On one side there were fences and on the opposite side, all along the river, it was more populated, especially the part between Lubinsky's mill and Yoel's "peasant" courtyard.

Here there stood a wall, set back somewhat in the background of the street, a wall with various bricks without doors and without windows, because it served as a (storage) granary for wheat. In that enclosure, in the left wing of the ground floor, the *Hashomeir Hatzair* had its meeting-place for many years. It was called the *Izbe* by us. For us the *Izba* was the "wishing-ring" -- the quintessence of all our dreams.

The River Street dispelled all the fears that lurked in other streets. New songs rang out in River Street, fresh melodies, Hebrew words, that distinguished themselves from the ordinary and which were reinforced by the teacher, Moishe Hersh. Proud, courageous, worthy, the confident walk when the *kvutzah* marched under its flat, singing: *"Su Ness Tzionah"* ...

Years passed, and during the time we lived through great events, shattering destruction, and above all, the terrible *khurban*, the German extermination that wiped away our former homes; years when rooted truths lost their status.

205

Leaders of *Hashomeir Hatzair*: R: M. Levitzki, Sh. Trombka, I. Trombka (Yisraeli), Tobe Mundzak, Tzila Zeloner, Soreh Mlovskeh.

In the dark recesses there sparkle a few bright lights that will remain from those years, from those meetings and of those wonderful dreams. And from time to time memories of the group that left strong memories - the youth meeting-place behind, in the background on River Street.

* * *

Ciechanów, as a provincial *shtetl*, with all its good points and bad points, possessed specific characteristics.

206

It is hard to believe that Jews constituted only a third of the population. That's what the statistics showed, purposely including in the circumference of the city the parts that were inhabited exclusively by non-Jews. The center, however, the factual city-part, had a thoroughly Jewish population.

Only on Tuesdays and Fridays was the marketplace and the surrounding streets full of peasants and their wagons. They filled the Jewish stores, the Jewish shops, and created the Jewish economic position. Six days a week the Jews worked hard to earn a living, but Friday, when the sun started to set, sinking further and further into the horizon, the Zahabed Street, on the edge of the fields, a calm peacefulness descended on the street. Peasants quickly set off with their horses and wagons, as though fearing to disturb the approaching *Shabbat* rest.

And as though in response to a signal, doors were bolted, everything closed, and the *shtetl* took on another appearance -- the marketplace and all the surrounding streets.

Four stores only, on three sides of the marketplace, stood out from amongst all the others because they belonged to non-Jews. They did not change the general picture, though. They also took on a *Shabbat* appearance somehow. The city hall also took on a *Shabbat* look, as though shamed, shut off in a corner. Only the tower clock struck every quarter hour, disturbing the general peace.

There was a large *shul*, a *bais hamedresh*, many *shtiblekh* and just plain *minyanim*. There were *daveners*, but also non-*daveners*. Everyone greeted the Sabbath as they wished, each according to his conscience. The religious Jews -- with *Lkhu Nirranenah* and *shakhrit* prayers and the younger people in their groups, where their premises were. There they cast away their weekly concerns and devoted themselves to things of the spirit. Young couples, all along the Vorshever Street, dressed in their *Shabbes* clothes, strolled along in good spirits for *Shabbat*. Even accompanying the secular enlightenment lecturer for *Shabbat* from the railway station to Misher's hotel also added something to the general picture of *Shabbat*.

* * *

The river Lidinya that surrounded Ciechanów does not play a significant role in the chain of Polish rivers. Especially in recent years, after civilization interfered and redirected the Lidinya flow between two symmetrically related borders, the river shrunk even more, as though shamed and insulted for her former frolicking. Still, the meadows and lawns along the river's edge remained green and soft.

207

Spring time or summer time, the green-grass divan was destined for special purposes. Around the walls of the castle the public, old and young, enjoyed their *Shabbat*. Families used to come in masses to rest their weary bones in nature's lap. Barefoot children would splash in the swampy ditches, chasing quick-moving fish, playing with young frogs, or picked up fat green leeches, of which there were so many. It was a unique *Shabbat* experience in nature's lap.

It appeared that no one at that time was at all concerned with the ancient history of the destroyed bare walls of the castle, that remembered the days of Zigmund the First, Poland's king The majority of the *Shabbat* visitors had never stepped into the castle. The entrance was generally closed. Only from time to time was the gate opened, particularly when the firemen, the factual overseers of the castle, would arrange some holiday or entertainment. But at such times fellow Jews would avoid the castle. It smelled of drunkenness, with ruffians and hooligans.

* * *

After the wonderful *Shabbat* came the gray week. Six days of the week the Ciechanów Jews struggled with the economic difficulties. There wee some prosperous Jews, but the majority earned their bit of bread with much hardship. They earned their livelihood by the traditional Jewish trades. Most of the Jewish stores dealt with small items, a small stock, and the earnings were meager. There was no sign of Jewish industry. Aside from the four flour mills from which the roar of the motors could be heard, there was no other sizable Jewish industry.

In Jewish homes there were laborers who put in a workday of twelve to fourteen hours. Branches of families occupied themselves solely with tailoring or shoemaking, generation after generation taking over the trade, and left for their children's inheritance only a long chain of these kinds of trades. They worked to fill orders and cheap work. On market days they would put their goods out for sale at the fair.

There were some privileged tradesmen, specialists who bragged about their trade. Before the season, before a *yomtov*, we had to arrange an appointment with these men in order to be sure that the work would be completed on time.

There was a bricklayer, Avraham Elye Tautengreber. In the fall it was not easy to get him to do work. If one succeeded and Avraham Elye repaired the oven for winter, a load fell off ones mind.

There were also times in Ciechanów, and not so long ago, when a trade was a stain on the family's reputation. Time and enlightenment corrected this stance. Still, there remained traces that found their expression in insulting remarks at the expense of the tradesmen. The Ciechanów butchers of the old generation were considered amongst the very respectable men in the *shtetl*. Many of them even occupied the "Eastern Wall" and amongst the younger generation there were also no noticeable "profession-marks."

The Jewish population represented a varied mosaic: Different parties, organizations and various societies. This was a mirror of the Ciechanów community.

208

The lights of the Party premises shone over the dark, slippery, narrow streets of the Jewish poor. The communal singing of the youth echoed far and penetrated the silent walls of Jewish homes, revived, called, gave meaning and expression until... until the Germans lifted the bloody ax on our fathers and mothers, sisters and brothers, destroyed with fire and murder the Jewish population of Ciechanów.

———

209

The Shtetl in Light of My Memories
Yosl Mlotzker

Childhood Years

I am a young boy, a child of poor parents in Ciechanów. In my eyes, the city appears "immensely" large. From my Zsabe Street (that was also called the *Zsabarniak*, I do not know why), up to the barracks, seemed to me in those days so far, as though the distance was the same as to Warsaw, of which I had heard much told; and to the *tzmentazs* -- that was really like to the end of the world for me.

In the Polish district I went only when I was dragged along with the older *chaverim*. The Polish youth called me "Bailis". I did not know where they got such a name. I also did not understand why they were throwing stones at us. There was no shortage of them. And if it didn't help, and we continued on our way, the *goyim* would loosen a large dog on us, which we feared greatly, and we had to run away as fast as we could. Once, it happened that the dog, with its sharp teeth, tore my only pair of trousers. Because of this I also had trouble at home. After that I decided never again to go to the *goyishe* street.

On the contrary, though, I felt very comfortable in the nearby marketplace where, on a fair-day, one could pat a horse, or a lovely white and black little calf. All week, without any fear of punishment, I could also run after and pull the beards of the goats that belonged to the little *Rebbe* Trule, who was occupied at home, working with his pointer on the *siddurim* while he taught his students the *aleph bais*.

I loved *Shabbat* very much, the day when we are free from *kheder*, when I could stroll down to the not-so-distant Lidinya River -- there where it was such a pleasure to remove the shoes and wade in the water up to the knees. But God forbid going beyond that to Weinstock's mill. There the water was deep. One could drown there. Only grown men could swim there. When the cold winter came and the river froze, one could slide over the whole length of the river without risk. At worst, one would wear out ones pant seat because, not having any skates or sleds, we would slide down the hill, sitting on the hard snow.

210

The Fine Respected Jews

There were in the *shtetl* fine Jews whom we respected and honored, amongst them the learned *Reb* Yosele and his long gray beard. Every Friday evening he would go, in his black *capote*, from street to street, from house to house, reminding: "Jews, light candles. It's time to forget the daily business." He reminded the women to take the candlesticks out of the cabinets because the important guest, the Sabbath, is arriving.

Soon the shutters of the stores would be closed. Jews with pale faces and black *capotes* ran, some to the *mikveh*, and some already with the *siddur* to the *bais medresh* or to the *shul*, taking the children along. Nobody wanted to miss the festive *Lcha Nirannenah* and the singing of *Lcha Dodi*.

I remember our *chazzan*, who was busy all week, as I assumed at that time, with not such nice work -- he slaughtered such beautiful multi-colored poultry which could crow so beautifully -- and such beautiful ducks which did not harm anyone. But when a *yomtov* came, the *chazzan* took on a different face in my eyes. He sang with his fine voice so that it captured one's heart.

I remember, as though it had just taken place, the *Kol Nidre* singing after the deadly silence in the *bais hamedresh*. At that moment I always felt that the heavens were about to open and God Himself would appear to us in the *bais hamedresh*.

The boys particularly enjoyed the eve of *Shabbat* or *Yomtov* when they would run to the *mikveh*, open their *kapoteleh* and show their *tzitzis* at the entrance, because otherwise we were not allowed to immerse ourselves, which is to say, to dunk ourselves in the somewhat dark, warm water of the *mikveh*, plugging our nose and ears thereby, with our fingers.

211

When I was older, I once more met a Ciechanów Jew for whom I had great respect -- Moishe Lerer he was called. He gave us our first lesson on the unfamiliar letters of the aleph bais.

I did not feel any special love for most of the teachers who put so much work into making us proper Jews. They, the teachers, taught us all the commandments and statutes (dinim umishpatim) of Chumash and Gemara and the minutia of Jewish Law. All this minutia irked me because of what relationship did it have to me when my life was so poor that there was not even an egg to eat during the week An egg was too expensive for my father's purse, but that was not as important as having a piece of bread in the house.

From a Life of Religious Observance to Social Ideas and Secular Enlightenment Cultural Activity

Some time ran on. Much water flowed through the Lidinya. We grew up, had to leave the *Cheder*, school, started to work, apprenticed to learn a trade so that we would be able to earn our daily bread. And here there were fresh difficulties and problems: rich and poor, from where does the difference come in the life of various families -- the poor, who went about free all day and bought the best fish and fowl for *Shabbat* and during the week: These new thoughts had to come to a boy, and with this -- dissatisfaction and hope for a better day.

211 contd.

About all these things our older friends told us. They already belonged to a professional society. And the more we listened to their talk about the poor, hardworking, and the bosses, the more we wanted to know. The thirst for their kind of knowledge led us to listen to all kinds of discussions and read books that filled our young minds with thoughts of justice, freedom, about a different life without rich and poor.

Our thirst for knowledge was also satisfied by enlightened young men who did not spare time and effort in order to teach the younger ones who had to, because of material reasons, interrupt their studies at school. Some organized libraries. Others -- sport clubs -- so that the working boy would be able to straighten out his back from sitting at the machine.

212

It was not only the sport competitions that interested us. It gave us great pleasure to see how our *Maccabi* members parade in Varshever Street after a football match. How much pride and joy that sight gave me!

Another thing that springs to my mind is the rich library named after Sh. An-ski. There, through the works of An-ski, Peretz, Sholem Aleichem, Asch and Mendele Mokher Sforim, we learned about the life of the Jewish masses, about the poverty in the Jewish *shtetlach*, and about wealthy merchants, tradesmen and craftsmen; wagoners, who work a long week and yet did not have enough to satisfy their hunger.

In the library, through the books of Ozsheshkova, Raimont, Sinclair, Barbis, Zola and other European writers, I learned about the wide world, its many countries, nations. From Gorky's *Mother* and Zsheramsky's *Before Spring* we became acquainted with those who fight for justice and freedom. They gave us much hope for better living conditions for all citizens and also for us Jews. And the evening gatherings also helped us very much to understand many difficult problems. On such evenings, youths of various organizations, with various political affiliations, discussed, in a friendly manner, events and theories.

A Summer Shabbat Afternoon in the Shtetl

In these *Shabbat* afternoons of my youth, all of Ciechanów, after the heavy *cholent*, would stroll through the streets. Mothers, with their young daughters clad in white embroidered pinafores, with their shiny heads of hear that were washed with kerosene *erev Shabbat*, boys with white shirts and short pants, often with a ball in their hands -- all headed to the castle. There everyone enjoyed themselves. The children ran around on the soft green grass, rolling down the hills while the mothers watched over them from the distance and had *naches*. The young boys and girls went to their various organizations to meetings. Others strolled for long hours from the marketplace to the garden, in groups, until they got tired.

213

Boys and girls, with newspapers and books that they could not read at home, went to the *Gurke* where, amongst the old trees and bushes, they had no fear of an "evil eye".

My friends and I preferred to go to the small forest not far from the sugar factory. There we could rest and dream beside the quiet murmur of the Lidinya River.

The life of our mothers was quite different, full as it was with daily problems and worries. Sometimes a *tzimes* would get burnt. Another time a *cholent* would mistakenly get exchanged at the baker's. True, these were not amongst the most serious problems, but when poultry had a fault on its guts and the *Rov* concluded that it is *treyf*, it was a lot worse. In addition, there were great problems of earning a living. How does one make ends meet?

There were also happy moments in a mother's life. The wrinkles disappeared from the brows for a short time when a letter would arrive from a beloved son in a far-off land, and one would run, full of joy, to all nearby neighbors to share the news. The mothers had to share their joy. The mothers would start to dream about their beloved son's arrival on a visit. "He'll give alms to the poor when he will go to visit the graves of his ancestors, and God willing, maybe he'll make a match with the neighbor's daughter, who has long been waiting for him."

The memories of my childhood and youth quickly come to an end. How I would have liked that there be a happy end, but unfortunately it is a great tragedy. Our parents are no longer with us. Our near and dear ones perished. Almost nothing remains of the past centuries of Jewish life in Ciechanów except for one monument in the new Jewish cemetery erected in 1947 in memory of the thousands of Jews, put to death by the Nazis.

We have been left with a constant sorrow in our hearts, and through this *Yizkor Book,* compiled by the survivors of the Ciechanów Jewish *Kehillah,* we want to preserve in memory from generation to generation our past and be connected with our tortured-to-death ones, far and wide, dear and beloved martyrs of Ciechanów.

214

What I Remember of Jewish Life in Ciechanów
Avraham Perlmutter, New York

When I was three years old, my mother dressed me up in a pair of short pants, with an opening in the rear, a cap with a stiff brim, and a large *Arba - Knafos* (four-fringed-cornered religious garment worn next to the skin) with long *tzitzis* beneath a long robe, so that I should look *yomtovdik* My father took me by the hand and said to me: "Come, *khosn bokher* to *Cheder,* to *Reb* Wolf, the *melamed* in the Yiddish Street."

Reb Wolf, a Jew in his sixties, with the appearance of an old man, raised his spectacles on his forehead and said to father:

"*Baruch haba* (welcome). What good news to you have?"

"I brought you my *khosn bokher* so that you should make a *mentsch* out of him" -- my father said. After the exchange of a few words between the *Rebbe* and my father, my father said to me that he would come later to take me home.

That's how my learning in *cheder* began.

When I could already read Hebrew I was taken to a more learned teacher, *Reb* Zalman Fentsil, in the Butcher Shop Street. Why was he called Fentsil? Because his wife Chana had to help to earn a living, so she baked flat rolls for the market. So from "Pletzl" came Fentsil...

Reb Zalman was a very strict teacher. One was in fear of his mere glance. That was called -- learning respect... When I explained to father, father gave me a few slaps and assured me that "the *Rebbe* knows what he's doing." That's how education looked at that time.

Interests of the Kehillah

When I got older, my father took me to the *Kehillah* meetings that ended with a bit of a "meal" at the expense of the *Kehillah*. At that time Ciechanów had the following societies: Burial Society, Society for Visiting the Sick, Psalm Readers Society, Society for Assisting for Brides, and a Savings and Loan Society, where every needy one could borrow a few *gilder*.

Those who busied themselves with these societies were: my father, Yosl Itche Libers, Mendl Burshtein, Hersh Yoel Kiffer, Laizer Price, Yekl Klanover, Binem Malina, Binyamin Krasne, Binyamin Malina, Mendl Mlamed, Henekh Fuchs, Herschel Mai, Khune Kashnmakher, Herschel Kleinetz, Isaachar Ciechanówer,

Itche Becker, Zalmen Moishe Krubiner, Laibele Byalietofsky, Berl Mundzak, Mordechai Mundzak, Dovid Klezmer (Gurny), Noske Feldsher, Shmulek Rosen, Aba Mundshtik, Noah Misher, Nate Rosenblum, Nachman Perlmutter, Vava Burshtein, and many others. Every week a committee used to make the rounds to raise money for these purposes.

215

At the time of Moishe Rabeinu's *yahrzeit,* the Burial Society prepared two special meals -- one for the poor folk who delighted in a good piece of fish, a bit of whiskey, a drumstick of a goose... then there took place the real meal of the Society...

After such a meal the treasury was a bit depleted, so thoughts were turned to regarding how to raise fresh sums, It was decided that since it is already close to *Purim*, a few horses should be rented and the members of the Society should dress with masks and costumes on *Purim* day and ride out in their costumes, to collect funds. The parts were assigned as follows: My father and Hersh Yoel Kiffer went to the Varshever Street, all the way to the railroad. That's where the wealthier Jews lived: The Rubinsteins, Dovid Wise from the lumber yard, and others. Dovid Mundzak and Hershel Mai took the stretch from the Pharmacy Street to the barracks, and so on. And enough funds were raised for the coming year.

Jews Are Forced to Become Firemen

I remember:
215 contd.

On certain evenings, particularly summer time, the barns on the edge of the city would start burning; so too did old houses. Since the fire brigade consisted mainly of Christians and inflamed barns belonged to Christians, anti-Semitic leaflets suddenly began to appear that threatened: if Jews will not enlist in the fire brigade, Jewish homes will be set on fire, including the *shul.*

A pressure spread over the Jews: how could Jews with beards don the shirts with hats and leather belt and with an ax on their hips, run to put out a fire? This is not a Jewish matter...but after a few consultations with *Reb* Shlomo, the *Rov*, and *Reb* Yosele Dayan, it was decided that because of danger to human life Jews are permitted to become firemen.

No sooner said than done. Representatives went to the fire chief and outfits of uniforms and axes were acquired. Drills started with the water buckets, axes, the whole caboodle, like all the *goyim.*

Every Sunday afternoon, everyone was called to the exercises. My father, with his lovely beard, polished his brass hat with the number five in front, and the brass buckle of his belt that kept the blue shirt tucked in, and with the ax at his side went to the castle beside the river for exercises. Other Jews did likewise and this was followed by a parade through the city afterwards, equipped with all the tools. We youngsters would run behind.

* * *

Most of the Ciechanów Jews earned their livelihood from trade with the peasants of the surrounding villages. Tuesday and Friday were market days when peasants from the surrounding villages would come to buy and sell. Most of the peasants knew all the Jewish storekeepers and dealt with Jews in a very friendly manner. There was one *goy,* however, who really caused trouble. He was the inspector.

216 contd.

One needed a permit to sell in the market (on a table or a stall). But what Jew will take out a permit to sell only two days during the week? So people tried to avoid the inspector as much as possible. He lived on Varshever Street near the old garden, as soon as he went out of the house Jews immediately spread word in the market. "He's coming." So Jews immediately started to hide their wares and by the time the inspector arrived at the market there was already nothing there.

The Daily Life of the Ciechanów Jews
Moishe Fuchs

217

Ciechanów had very few wealthy Jews. They were wholesalers of dry goods, food products, and owners of a few mills, and of a small number of lumber yards. That was the wealthier element.

The majority of Ciechanów Jews were tradesmen, small dealers and marketers who set up a stand or a table at the market on market days. There were also Jews who, on market days, walked amongst the peasants, stuck their hand into a sack of grain, bargained, slapped hands with the peasants, and in the end, when closing the "transaction" they realized they don't have money for payment. Then the peasant and the Jew would ride to Weinstock's mill, the largest one in the Warsaw area, and they would unload the grain. The peasant would get his money and the Jew his provision.

The worst fate was that of the marketers who drove around from one fair to another. All week they traveled in rain and in snow, in frost and in fiery heat. They had to travel constantly so as not to be late for the fair. This is how they operated: Sunday they would get a loan from the Free Loan Society and Monday they would ride to Galomin; Tuesday -- Proshnitz; Wednesday -- Makv; Thursday -- Kharzil. That's what the *shtetlach* were called in the region that Ciechanów Jews traveled to in order to earn a livelihood for their wives and children.

That is how months and years passed. The energy for their lives they drew from Jewish faith; "God will not forsake."

In the evening, after a hard day of toil, the majority of the Jews in the *shtetl* went to the *bais hamedresh* for late afternoon and evening prayers (*Mincha and Ma'ariv)*, and to hear a *drasha* from a good *maggid*. Meanwhile, out of exhaustion one would have a nap. After the *maggid's drasha* they would move to *Reb* Yehuda Mashke's to hear a nice *hasidic* story about the wonders of the *tzadik, Reb* Avramele Z"L. *Reb* Yehuda Mashke doesn't keep them waiting long and he tells:

There was once a fire in the *shtetl*. Nearly all the houses got burnt. Jews remained without a roof over their heads. *Reb* Avramele stood in the street after the fire, full of sorrow, and he said: *Rebbono shel olam,* I give a blessing for the city that should there ever be a fire, God forbid, not more than one house should be burnt. At the same time I make it a rule that on *Yom Kippur* for *Kol Nidre* no women should come to *shul* because when there's a panic amongst a lot of people, many candles are burning and it could cause a fire to break out. !

218

"Do you want to know if this is true? Just remind yourselves about the fire in Velvl Remboim's mill on River Street. There was a fire! And near the mill stood a small wooden house and not a single board there got burnt - that's what Jews told."

* * *

On the fifth day of the Hebrew month of *Adar* it is the *yahrzeit* of the *tzadik,* so for the *yeshiva* boys there is a *siyum* (celebration upon the completion of study of Talmudic tractate). *Reb* Avraham Aaron Kalman is the main attendant. The *Rosh Yeshiva* says *Ahadran. Reb* Shlomo Zalman and the *Rebbe* Ziskind sing hearty *niggunim* and a delicious *seudah* meal is enjoyed. Glasses are there for a *l'chaim* and a prayer is said for his merit to protect us, Amen.

The following morning, preparations are made to receive guests from all the surrounding shtetlach as well as from Warsaw. The Strickover *Rebbe* comes. That's no small thing, because he is the grandson of *Reb* Avramele! The *yeshiva* boys each take a *tzedakah* box -- someone takes the one for repairing books. Another -- for the Free Loan Society -- another for *Linat Hatzedek*, etc. They go to the *Ohel* (monument) of the *tzadik*, knock three times with the large key. The first ones enter: the Strickover *Rebbe* and the *hasidim*. After them the Burial Society members with the learned leader, *Reb* Yosele.

All day long, men and women stream to the *Ohel*. They deposit *kvitten* (prayer notes). People pour out their bitter hearts on the grave of the *tzadik*. After a good cry they go home more at ease. They feel certain that the *tzadik* will see that justice is done and heal all the wounded hearts.

Shabbosim and Yomtovim in the Shtetl

Shabbat and *yomtov*, the Ciechanówer Jews took on a different appearance. Unrecognizable. When *Reb* Yosele sets out into the Jewish streets with his call; "*Yidn*, it's getting late, *Shabbes, Shabbes* is approaching, light candles, light candles" -- there is quite a stir. Customers are hurried out of the shops and everyone rushes: in the *bais hamedresh*, in the *shuls* or *shtiblech*. From the *shtiblech* there can be heard happy songs. *Lcha Dodi* and after the *davening* people go home, humming a happy tune.

219

Shabbat morning, when it is still dark, one can already hear from the *bais hamedresh* the beautiful psalm chant said by the Psalm readers. There are some *Shabbosim* that bring an added joy. That is when the Navidvorer *Chazzan, Reb* Laizer, comes with his choir of thirty singers to the *shtetl*. Jews prepare. First the *davening* is finished in the *shtiblech* in order to be able to hear the cantor and the choir.

* * *

Simchat Torah in the *shtetl*. The Burial Society makes a grand *seudah* (meal). A *Sefer Torah* is brought to the *shul*. The *Sefer Torah* is brought from *Reb* Yisroel Yitzhak Rimorshe's house. Women put candles on their windowsills. Men and children dance around the *Torah* that the *Rov* holds. Everyone tries to kiss the *Torah* mantle. The excited singing and dancing keep growing stronger until the *shul* is entered. In *shul* the cantor makes *hakofes*. Jews, sweating and worn out, are delighted with the bit of *yomtov* spirit that they have just experienced.

* * *

Lag B'omer. The youth of *Hashomeir Hatzair* marches in the streets with the flags, singing, until they come to the *shul* courtyard. The sound of the trumpets, the sound of the clashing cymbals, announces that the youth are coming. Yaacov Kahane and Yaacov Misher talk to the youth about the homeland of the Jewish people, about the Land of Israel. The same takes place for Herzl's *yahrzeit*, the twentieth day of the Hebrew month of *Tamuz*.

* * *

There is also another branch of Jewish youth in Ciechanów: On the Yiddish Street, in the home of Isaiah Robota, the father of Rosa Robota, who fought so courageously and was so brutally murdered in Auschwitz, there was the Peretz library. There, there gathered *Poele Tzion* who incorporated their dream of social justice with the ideal of return to Zion; *bundists*, who tied their Jewish destiny to the social-democratic future of Poland; young Jewish communists, revolutionaries who dreamed of general redemption for all future mankind and for that were imprisoned and there forfeited their young lives for an ideal.

219 contd.

That's how Jewish Ciechanów lived until the German murderers came and tragically blotted out the Jewish *yishuv*, together with all its Jewish Parties and streams.

The Idealists of the Jewish Organizations in Ciechanów
Yaacov Rubinstein

220

Jewish life in Ciechanów was very difficult. According to statistics, Jewish families lived in very cramped quarters, three to four people in a small room four by four, without any elementary conveniences whatsoever. Water was carried from the river. With one washroom for everyone it is easy to understand that there were distressful sanitary conditions.

Jews were concentrated in the center of the *shtetl*, the streets around the marketplace on streets such as: Varshever Street. Other streets were called: Yiddishe Street, Pultuska, Pharmacy Street, and a few more streets where only Jews lived!

When a Jew went beyond the Jewish area and got lost in the *goyishe* part, he felt very unsafe, and was often met with stones and with the familiar anti-Semitic call: *"Zhida Do Palestina."*

The local priests had a great influence for causing this anti-Semitism because on the basis of religion they aroused the Christians to Jew-hatred. The difficult economic situation of the Polish peasants also played a role They were stirred up by the poor farmers, who came from the villages to the *shtetl*. They tried, together with the help of anti-Semitic organizations, to get rid of the Jewish merchants/traders and the tradesmen from their place of work.

Jew-hatred constantly spread. Poles started to boycott the Jewish stores, the Jewish tradesmen, and the hard life of the Ciechanów Jews became even harder.

In such surroundings the Jewish political parties arose and each one had its solution for improving the life of the Jews... every party had its idealists who were devoted heart and soul to societal functions that they took upon themselves.

The idealists gave their free time and with their own means built organizations, institutions, religious groups, and shaped the Jewish community and spiritual life in Ciechanów

221

A significant part of Ciechanów Jews leaned towards Zionism. They understood that the solution to the Jewish problem was only through building our own national home in the Land of Israel. The idealists who were the leaders of the movement were: *Rov* Bronrot, Yaacov Misher, Avraham Vinditzky, Shlomo Rubinshtein, Garfinkl and others. They gave a part of their life for the Zion idea. They did not let any difficulty stand in their way. Their homes were open to all who wanted to support the work for the settlement of the Land of Israel. Oft times the Zionist idealists had to endure painful differences with the Ciechanówer *frumeh* Jews, who believed that only through the coming of the *Mashiach* will the Jews return to Israel. But these *frumeh* Jews, organized in the *Agudah,* had their idealists.

221 contd.

The leaders of the *Agudah* were Yoel Weingarten, Malina, Student, Yisroel Yaacov and others. They were jealous and bitter opponents of the Zionists. The leaders of the *Agudah* and their followers thought of the Zionists as criminals and fought what they thought was a righteous war. These *frum* Jews were faithfully devoted to their *Agudah* organization and its institutions.

The second Party that fought against the Zionists was the *Bund,* who believed that the Jewish problem would be resolved in Poland when there will be socialism. The leaders of the *Bund* in Ciechanów, Yidl Bronshtein, Kostsheva and others, were outstanding in their idealism and with devotion they fought for the rights of the Jewish population.

I knew the *Bundist* leader, Yidl Bronshtein, very well. The work on behalf of the community always ranked first with him. It took precedence over his home, his wife and child. The concern for the Jewish population of Ciechanów was the main thing in his life.

The *Poale* Tzion occupied a special place in Ciechanów. They were in the center between *Bund* and Zionism. The *Poele Tzion* idealists also believed in socialism, but above all they felt that Jews must have their own home in the Land of Israel, that will normalize the abnormal Jewish life. Through physical work it is necessary to prepare for the future productive Jewish life in the new home. *The first* chalutzim (pioneers) who organized the *hachshara* (training farm) for the Ciechanów youth were the *Poele Tzion* people, Templehof and Berger. They went out into the field of Berl Agradnik, and under his supervision learned to work on the land.

222

The young *Hashomeir Hatzair* organization was surrounded by love from nearly all levels of Ciechanów's Jews. The founders of this Zionist youth organization were: Herschel Finkelstein, the brothers Trombka, and Yisroel Misher. *Hashomeir Hatzair* distinguished itself by its wide range of activities: physical exercise through sport, readings and literary dictates, systematic self-education, and Zionist activities on all fronts: *hachshara*, raising funds for Zionist purposes, and preparations for going on *aliyah* to the Land of Israel.

* * *

Jewish Ciechanów was poor, but rich in idealism of its youth. Every Jewish Party in the *shtetl* had its devoted people who worked with a fanatical belief to realize their ideals.

The Ciechanówer Polish State School
Nachman Grosbard

Ciechanów in the 1930's ------ Nadzetna Street, where one end reaches the Proshnitzer Way that leads to the large military barracks and at the other end -- the Lidinya River, the wooden bridge that leads to the ancient castle...

Nadzetna is a quiet side street. Why is it so engraved in my mind? Maybe because of the *shtetl's* electric power at the other end of the street, where the river is. There we used to, with childish delight, climb on the high windows and be fascinated by the long transmission lines that run so speedily and the long row of tops of this sort of strange machines that move so rhythmically up and down, just as though a long row of hens would be standing and pecking with their beaks ... so

how does the electricity come out and how does it travel such a long distance over the wires: The children's heads used to puzzle over this.
223

There were also two Jewish mills on that street. One mill once burned down. There was a huge fire in the middle of the night that left a deep impression on my childish memory.

I remember this street so well because that's where the seven-grade state school was, a school for Jewish children where the language of instruction was Polish. All day long it was a buzzing like in a beehive, Jewish girls in black pinafores with white collars, boys with closely-shaven heads chased around and played hide-and-seek until the bell rang for going into the classrooms and the noise vanished for an hour or so, only to break out again in an even stronger noise and din.

In that school, the children learned the first steps in the spiritual life, started to learn about the world, listened in amazement to lessons about far-off lands and people that the teachers spoke about. The children nor their teachers knew what a *khurban* is approaching them in the near future, that nearly all of them would perish through the hands of the treacherous German beasts and that only a tragically small number will have the bitter fate to write painful memories.

A State Jewish School in the year 1917. In the center -- the director, Vishinsky
224

In the above-mentioned Polish state school for Jewish children, I was educated in the years 1928-1935, and because it was a school for

Jewish children, I want to devote the following memoirs, a modest contribution, a feature of the life of the Ciechanów Jews, just before the war, that the Germans burned.

* * *

The school stood in a large three-story building. The rooms were very bright, but the crowding was even greater and the classes were taught in two shifts.

In the program of the school, the main emphasis was, naturally, on the teaching of the Polish language, geography and history of Poland, and to educate a "loyal" citizen, one devoted and attentive to the reactionary regime. Yiddish was, in that school, not simply not recognized as a second language, but the teachers, themselves Jewish, absolutely forbade the children to speak Yiddish amongst themselves, even on the playground, supposedly so that they would better learn the Polish language, but more to the point -- because of the assimilatory approach and because of the view that Yiddish was a type of "jargon" and no less because of fear of the school administration. But the Jewish children did not want to abandon their mother tongue (*mameh loshen*) so, together with Polish, one could also hear the expressive Yiddish, first of all amongst the boys and in general amongst the children from ordinary homes where Yiddish was the only everyday language.

Yiddishkeit and the System of the Studies

The *yiddishkeit* of the school was expressed only in the teaching of religion, which was actually Jewish history as passed down faithfully through the *Tanakh.* For us boys who had studied before in *cheder,* see these stories from the *Chumash* and *Pasuk* that we already quite well know off by heart, so that lesson on religion was a cinch for us...

Not a word was said in school about the history of the Jews in modern times, about the Enlightenment Movement (*Haskala*), modern Yiddish literature; not one word was said about the works of Mendele Mokherasforin, not one word was said about the works of Shalom Aleichem, Peretz, Bialik, not even in Polish.
225

In the first class, many children, and I amongst them, did not understand a word of Polish, but the teacher who knew how to speak a good Yiddish was afraid to, God forbid, help us with a Yiddish word, in order for us to understand Yiddish was *treif.*

History was, understandably, first about Poland. General history -- very little. A bit of ancient Egypt, Greece and Rome. The history lesson was "saturated" with Polish nationalism and hatred of Russia, the so-called "*Moskalyes,* the destroyers of Poland."

The lessons in mathematics, geography and nature study were quite good, but there was a great shortage of maps and equipment, etc.

Singing lessons were naturally conducted solely in Polish. The majority of songs were patriotic. Yiddish songs, even in Polish translation, were not sung. So it was that Jewish children were torn away from Yiddish word, thought and feeling.

The singing lessons were on a high level, thanks to the effort and experience of the teacher, Pafa-Herman. She taught us to sing heartfelt motifs that she accompanied on her mandolin. We used to sing in two or three parts. Children who had better voices took part in the general school choir under the direction of the same teacher. The choir sang at various celebrations. There was no piano in the school. For a while there were after-class lessons in mandolin and violin, but one had to have money to pay for these lessons, as well as money to buy an instrument, and the financial possibility often did not correspond to the talent of the students.

There was also a library near the school, and the children had a special notebook in which the students had to write the moral lesson that they learned from reading the books. There was no community/social work carried on in the school. It was also forbidden for the students to be members in any existing political youth organizations. There was no organized friends help group organized in the school, as was practiced in other schools. Nobody was concerned about the conditions in which a child was studying or doing homework at home, or whether the parents have money to buy notebooks, texts and writing equipment, or whether the child comes to school well fed.

For a period of time a glass of milk was given to each child, with a cookie so that the poor children would not feel insulted, and the parents who had the means paid. There were also some poor parents who were ashamed to accept help and made strenuous efforts to pay, just as everyone else. This help for poor children did not continue for very long.

226

There were almost no recreational facilities for the children at the school. Once a trip was made to Danzig and to Zakopaneh, but only for those children who had money to pay.

Radios were still an unaffordable item for the homes and therefore it was a great joy for the children when they were invited to the teachers' lounge to listen to a radio concert. There were no undertakings where teachers and students could enjoy themselves together in an intimate and friendly way. Generally, according to the program, the relationship of the children to the teachers had to be complete obedience and, of course, compulsory respect.

There was no parents' committee to have a say in the program of the school. Parents used to be summoned once every three months for an evening of "information" in order for them to get a report about the behavior and achievement of the children. Only Polish was spoken with the parents and they were far from understanding what was being said to them.

Types of the Jewish Teachers

When I recall that Polish education for Jewish children -- I recall the types of teachers: the good-spirited, warm Jewish intellectuals, the female teachers generally more sympathetic, perhaps because of their femininity.

The female teacher of our first class was called Flata (later Hermanova). She remained in my memory as a good-natured, lovely, beautiful woman. In a childish way I was in love with her. When we went into the second class, the children were very sorry that she was leaving us. Later we got her back as singing teacher.

The teacher Mandzshainova seemed at first to be more strict. She remained our teacher until the fourth class. We grew attached to her and loved her like a mother.

227

A class in the state school with the director Yovl.

A class in the state school with the teacher Golomb

228   blank

229

Our teacher in the seventh class -- Rochele Zelaner, a wonderful woman in all respects who knew Polish and literature very well, was a very good educator. The teacher Burstein specialized in mathematics. The children who were weak in addition had grounds to consider her strict, but those students who knew what they were supposed to know, and especially those few amongst them who felt the inner beauty and even warmth in the outer cold formulas, and had the spiritual pleasure of solving difficult complicated problems, if those students are still alive -- they are certainly grateful to this teacher for her strictness.

The teacher Mondshein, whom we called *Shaini Lmelekh* (next in rank to the king) was strict, but at the same time a *kibbitzer*. He laughed at the children who spoke "jargon" (*Yiddish*). "Your language only helps you get hit by the *shkotzim* (non-Jews) -- he explained to us. The ironic destiny was that this teacher, Mondshein, should get beaten up the hooligans, in spite of his perfect Polish.

And last of all, the beloved "king" himself -- Leon Yovl, the long-time school director -- a good, soft-hearted man under a mast of strictness, better as an administrator than as a teacher. Perhaps because of the fact that for many years he carried on his shoulders the burden of the school, the constant fear of the Polish reactionary organ of the Ministry of Education, the constant fear of the inspector and the therefore fear of the children speaking "jargon" -- that they should not go to any youth organization -- all this together worried him tremendously. During the visit of the inspector, the Jewish school director humbly brought in the chair.

A fact about the seventh class: the inspector examines the cleanliness of the students. He finds one not so clean. He says, emphasizing each word: "You Jews have to take particular care to keep yourselves clean." Yovl gets red in the face, everyone's blood boils.

Jew Hatred in the School

The Jewish students suffered a lot from anti-Semitism in the school because of the anti-Semitic attitude to them on the part of the higher school authorities. I remember an event from the first class: an important guest came to the *shtetl*, the president, Moshchitsky himself. The school children came to the railway station. It was raining. We waited for hours. The Jewish children kept being moved from place to place. They couldn't get rid of the *zhidovkes* (Jews), so they wanted to at least have them off into a corner.

230

During a Polish national holiday, the Jewish children went in an organized way to the *shul*. The choir sang the Polish hymn -- *Yeghtche Polska*. The *chazzan* made a long *Mi Shbairakh* (a Hebrew prayer) for the President Moshitsky and the "friend" of the Jews -- Marshal Pilsudski. The children dispersed and went to the marketplace for the march-past. Yovel and the two prettiest girls from the seventh class (his weakness) were at the end of the file, with the large school banner that is a reminder that there is also a "Jewish" school in the *shtetl*. The special banner is huge. It is let down from the teachers lounge into the yard through the window and the "hero", the strong boy from seventh class, carries it...

* * *

What happened to all those Yovls, the Mondsheins and the Zeloners? Who of them survived? And where are the children who often acted spitefully doing mischievous acts: did go to the cinema and went to the organizations? Didn't obey though they were a little afraid, but always from the depths of their heart cherished and loved their Yiddish teachers.

The seventh class of that school naturally remained very firm in my mind. Oft times the picture of those living children appears before my eyes, my school chums, seated on the school bench, and I can almost remember the order of who sat near whom. Very few of them survived.

In Israel I met Yisroel Shlezinger, with whom I used to do my homework, and Moishe Kolko, and who else survived? On one of the first benches sat a girl, a member of *Hashomeir Hatzair*, who didn't distinguish herself at that time. Her dear memory is everlasting in the history of the uprising against the German murderers -- Rosa Robota -- this modest girl of the seventh class in the Polish Povshekhner School.

By the time we were in seventh class in the Polish Povshekhner School, looking forward to finally being free from the yoke of school, and becoming independent. None of us imagined with how much nostalgia we would look back upon those school days.

231

After finishing the school, a graduate class was started under the patronage of the school director, Yovl. Through this group he wanted to establish a contact with the school and have the youth participate in sport and cultural events. The actual aim was to draw the youth away from political activity.

To this graduate class I did not belong.

* * *

September 1939. Vacations were over but the school year had not yet started, The school benches were piled up outside. In the classrooms, instead of children, there were German soldiers. A cold, dangerous winter was approaching. It foretold no good.

On a cold December day I said goodbye to my home. Mother sobbed bitterly and father heartrendingly held back his tears. After one last glance at the school that bordered on our courtyard, I set off with other harassed and suffering Jews on a long way eastward -- a distance of thirteen thousand kilometers. On the way there I took along a pack of old clothes, and in my heart a growing longing

How I Remember the Shtetl Ciechanów

232

Yes, there once was in Poland wonderful *shtetlach* where the Jews were in the majority.

There was a shoemaker who sang as he worked, a tailor with his threads would sing away. Melodies dating back for generations still ring in my ears. But the Jews, the shoemakers and tailors, are no longer with us.

How does one put down on paper the memories of our *shtetl*, Ciechanów? How does none talk about a *shtetl* that no longer exists, a *shtetl* in which our dear ones were brutally murdered?

All of us lived there, breathed its air, the same sky that was over the heads of old and young is still there as though nothing had happened. The sun shines there, as before, and the fields are green as ever, and for us is left the memory of Rosa Robota's last word: "Revenge."

This is how I remember you, Ciechanów. A town of thirty thousand inhabitants, of whom approximately eight thousand were Jews.

The Jewish streets were situated around the marketplace. And from there, streets branched out.

On Market Street, were the magistrature, stores, workshops, the center of economic life. On Tuesdays and Fridays, market days, until sundown, there came tens and hundreds of peasants and farmers from the town and villages to sell their products. From sunrise, all the tables and stalls were in place, each one with the owner's goods on display -- clothing, butter, eggs, religious objects and necessities that were strange to us.

On a regular day the marketplace turned into a center of Jewish life. Everyone came there to carry on their business, discussing the stock market, politics, communal affairs, civic matters. The world came alive at these encounters. People came out of their homes and joined the crowd. People came and went but the discussions continued.

In the marketplace street, near one of the houses, down in the cellar there was the premises of *Hashomeir Hatzair*.

Amongst the many interesting gatherings that we had, *Hashomeir Hatzair* held a special place in our hearts. This organization started with scouting and dreams around campfires and ended with the building of the Jewish nation in its homeland.

Why were hundreds attracted to this organization? What did the boys and girls find appealing in this cellar, together with their leaders?

There was a deep feeling of Jewishness in our *shtetl*. There were communal associations that went beyond politics. People knew with their whole soul how to value the Jewish basis of their life. We didn't have any millionaires amongst us. I remember every inch of Ciechanów. though there was much poverty, even the more wealthy Jews lived modestly. No sins of the fathers shamed the youth. They behaved according to prophetic justice.

233

A Lag B'Omer Parade of Hashomeir Hatzair

234   blank

235

The youth organization did not while away its time. There was a purpose to their life as they looked ahead. No longer were we like the Jews in Mendele Mkhov Sforim's tales "like a worm in the horseradish" (a Jewish proverb).

In the evenings we used to gather and sing Hebrew songs, with words full of longing for the land full of sunshine! And the marketplace -- in our minds is all Jewish, all ours.

Varshavsky Street -- the pride of the city, named after Poland's capital, the main street on which to stroll on *Shabbat*. That's where the daily newspaper first arrived, and there everyone waited to learn the news from around the world. On that street one could see the coachmen bringing distinguished people to the railway station Here one could watch the holiday parades of the non-Jews and (let us make the proper distinction) the parading of Jewish youth setting out on their hikes outside of the *shtetl*. On this street there was the large Jewish cinema.

Were there any large show-windows? This I don't remember. But I do remember those who came to draw water at the *shtetl's* water source. Here many people gathered, water carriers with buckets which they carried on a yoke on their feeble shoulders. In the summer, plenty of water flowed, but in the winter -- it was all ice! How difficult it was to get some water, and how many tears were shed instead until we reached home safely, with pails holding a bit of water for the family's needs for the day.

But the Yiddishe street -- Yoselvich -- that street is engraved on my heart. That was the spiritual center, the heart of the *shtetl, yiddishkeit* throughout. The *shul* and the *bais hamedresh* from where the call of the *shofar* could be heard during the High Holidays. From there the *Shamesh* (beadle) would go out to call people to *Slichot* and to knock on Jewish windows to arise for worship.

And Truleh Kozo Berdl who doesn't remember? He was the *Rebbe* who taught children the *aleph-bais*. And the *Kometz-aleph* who remembers? Hebrew letters and the prayers for *Shabbat* and *Yomtovim*. Only by him did we learn these. And how many slaps did we get from his ruler on our knuckles! How many times did we repeat the same lines from the *siddur*, old and yellowed from generations who had held this! All this after we had run errands for his wife and fulfilled all his requests!

Till this day his voice rings in my ears. *"Shikses, shchotzim."* But to his credit must be said that thanks to him we learned the lessons of the aleph-bais and from him we learned the meaning of the song, *Oifn Pripichik Brent a Feierl,* and if those letters enable me today to write my memories here, may the memory of my Rebbe and teacher, Truleh ,be blessed.

From this street there rang out the prayer: *B'shana Ha-baah B'Yerushalim,* and also *Naseh Vnishma Chazak, Chazak Vamatz*
236
It happened on the *yahrzeit* of Herzl, the twentieth day in the Hebrew month of *Tamuz,* that everyone gathered to pay respect to the memory of Herzl. An emissary would come from the Land of Israel to bring us the message that "If you wish it, it is not a legend" -- the words of Herzl.

As a pledge we promised to do everything in our power to bring Herzl's words to fruition. Line after line, we paraded singing a Hebrew song. At this time there was no division, no separation between father and son, between the most pious of the *shul* and the secular enlightened ones, of the youth who belonged to *Hashomeir Hatzair*. Everyone was united here -- the ordinary folk and the head of the congregation, the *Rov* and the *Chazzan*. All were united under the blue and white flag.

In those days we knew the connection between the blue box of the Land, Land of our ancestors and the forests of Mishmar Ha-Emek for which we collected penny after penny to redeem the Land.

And we had many other streets, streets through which Jewish children made their way to school. What a long way hundreds of children walked each day. I'll never understand why the schools were so far from the center of the *shtetl* The Jews to whom the Torah was given lived in the center of the *shtetl*, but to get to the place of study was far!

All the streets appear before my eyes. Their memories are very dear to me because that's where our parents, brothers and sisters and all our dear ones died. Jews of the week round and *Shabbat* Jews, simple folk and *tzadikim*, great spiritual souls.

May their memory be bound up with the living ones here.

May we be deserving of the memory of our ancestors and may our children learn and know about the *shtetl* where we grew up.

———

The Shomer Hatzair Movement

Dvora Newman

I joined one of the groups of *Hashomeir Hatzair* when I was a young girl. The leader of our group at the beginning was Dinah Eisenberg and afterwards my sister Ludzia. If I want to recall the good days I go back in my memory to those days, the period that influenced my life up to the present day.

The meeting place was a granary with wooden pillars in the center, with damp, wet walls. It was a warehouse that we turned into a palace. It was the place where my friends and I spent the happiest years of our lives. No pouring rain, no cold or snow, no amount of homework from school could prevent us from gathering there every evening. There all our worries left us. The best evenings there were Friday and *Shabbat*. On those evenings we would enjoy ourselves, dancing, singing, reading, listening to lectures on various subjects, and playing games. On holidays we used to arrange parties. The program at the parties was singing, reading from the newspaper that we published by ourselves. As in a dream I recall a poem that I wrote for *Chanukah*. "Come, brothers, to play with the *sovivon* (top). The song had several verses.

237

We had lovely parties for important people. In my ears there ring the wonderful words of the *Ir Hashchitah* of Bialik, recited by my sister Ludzia.

Great were the preparations for these parties. I remember my friend, Dinah Rosenberg Z"L, who prepared, with her mother's help, orange peels covered with sugar. We used to go on hikes. On *Lag B'omer*, at dawn, we used to go out to the small forest singing, culminating with bugles and drums, which added much excitement. Much to my regret, my sisters and I were forbidden by my father Z"L, to go out with our group because of worry and fear that the *shchotzim* would beat us and throw stones at us because at that hour they were free from school and work. This restraint stole a lot from us, the pleasure that we would have had of going on such a hike. We used to go out by ourselves at ten o'clock in order to join the group in the forest.

For the performances we devoted much time and energy. It was easy to worry about the planning. We had the good fortune o having amongst us dramatists such as Tusia and her sister, whose voices made a great contribution to the success of the evenings.

I recall when I was a young girl, a schoolgirl, awaiting anxiously and running in the direction of the river to the Club -- the warehouse-palace. Reality is much worse, however. Just last year our friend, Zvi Finklestein, went to his eternal rest -- one of the first organizers of the *Shomeir Hatzair* in Ciechanów. From amongst the members of our group a very few are here in Israel. I often get together with them and know them well. They are honest women, sensible ones, thoughtful, good citizens and good people. They remained faithful to the education they received in the warehouse-palace.

Riva Gonska Leshed, Kfar Masarik

―――

Zionist Activity in Ciechanów

Gleaned from the Correspondence in the Jewish and Hebrew Press in Poland

The Tzirei Tzion Movement

Regarding the *Tzirei Tzion* movement in Ciechanów during 1917-1918, the Hebrew paper, *Hatzfira*, wrote:

At the founding meeting of *Tzirei Tzion Farband*, that was at that time legalized by the (at that time) occupying force of Germany, in Ciechanów, a committee of the following people was elected: N. Garfinkle, M. Vinditsky, Kviat, Rekhtman, Templehof, I. Gotfried, Rivka Kahane.

238

President of the meeting was Natan Garfinkle. Regarding the aims of the *Tzirei Tzion Farband* there spoke: Kviat, Templehof, Z. Burshtein and Kellin from Mlava. With the singing of *Hatikvah* the meeting ended.

* * *

The twentieth day of the Hebrew month *Adar*, 1917, the *Tzirei Tzion* organization of Ciechanów organized a memorial service for the *shloshim* (thirty days after the death) of Dr. Tchlenov. The memorial, attended by hundreds of people, and by the students of the Hebrew schools, was conducted by the cantor and choir at 12 o'clock noon.

The president of the *Tzirei Tzion*, Natan Garfinkle, gave the eulogy. About the life and achievements of Yechiel Tchlenov and the great loss that his death was for the Jewish people, there spoke: the member of the *Kehillah* board, Yaacov Misher, the Hebrew teacher of the Zionist school Flatzer and H. Vinditsky. Finally, the president, Garfinkle, called upon those gathered to build up the fund that was established in the name of Yekhiel Tchlenov.

* * *

On the twenty-second day of the Hebrew month of *Adar*, the well-known *chaver* Mileykovsky spoke to hundreds of people in the *shul*. His speech about Judaism, Zionism and the settlement of the Land of Israel, made a great impression upon everyone.

* * *

The *Tzirei Tzion* organization developed a broad range of activities. A library was opened. Readings in Hebrew on matters of national interest often took place.

Chaver Flatzer spoke about the various aims of the Jewish youth and *chaver* Flata, about the development in the religious sphere in various periods.

* * *

In the year 1918, the *Tzirei Tzion* movement took firm root in Ciechanów's Jewish life. The organization had its own *shul*. On the eve of *Yom Kippur* a considerable sum was collected for the settlement of *Eretz Yisroel*.

239

In general, the organization was very active in collecting money for the J.N.F. The students also gathered money for this purpose. The *Tzirei Tzion* organization planted five trees in Israel in the name of the grandfather of Yiddish literature, Mendele Mkhov Sforim. During the *shekl* campaign three hundred more were sold. Last year only two hundred were sold.

* * *

In 1918, a group of Jewish scouts visited Ciechanów from Mlava, one hundred in all. The young Zionists received the guests at the railway station with flowers and greetings. From the train to the premises of the *Tzirei Tzion* the crowd marched in a parade, decorated with flags, and sang Zionist songs. The guests wee put up at the premises of the *Tzirei Tzion*.

That same day there took place a literary musical evening that brought in 1,300 marks. The following day the scouts marched in a parade to the *shul* and there they all *davened*. Afterwards they all sang national songs.

During meals that were arranged for the guests, leaders of Ciechanów gave speeches. In the evening the guests returned home. They were accompanied by a crowd of fifteen hundred people. The visit of the young scouts made an outstanding impression on the Ciechanów Jews.

* * *

A reorganization of the Jewish Women's organization "Miryam" took place. *Chaver* Flatzer gave a lecture at this women's organization under the title, "The Undertaking of the Jewish Woman at This Time."

During the elections to the *Kehillah*, the Zionists had a large majority. From the block Zionists, orthodox and trades people, the representatives who were elected were: Vise, Misher (Zionists), Skurnik (*Mizrahi*), Rakovsky (*Agudat Yisroel*).

240

All complaints against the *Kehillah* elections were negated. The government (German occupiers at the time of World War II) confirmed the outcome. The first job of the new officers was to open the *chevra Linat Hatzedek* that served the sick and the Folks Kitchen that serves around three hundred meals free for the poor Jewish population.*

*Footnote: During the German occupation at the time of WWI all food was rationed and could only be obtained with cards. The Jewish population received a ration of sugar that was sold to the population. The earnings from its sale went, it seems, for the Free Kitchen for the Poor

Editor's note: At the third Zionist Conference, the participants were the Ciechanów delegates Natan Garfinkle and Yaacov Misher.

The Events in Eretz Yisroel in the Year 1921 and Their Echo in Ciechanów

The tragic news that came from Jaffa (the attacks on the Arabs on Jews) received the necessary response also amongst the Ciechanów Jews.

Shabbat (Perek Kdushim) 1921, a large meeting took place in the *shul*. The *Rov Reb* Chaim Mordecai Bronrot made a great speech woven throughout with quotes from rabbinic writings and *Tanakh*. With a broken heart he expressed his great sorrow at the killings of the Jews who lost their lives in the streets of Jaffa. The *Rov* told everyone not to fear, and to do everything for the settlement of the

Land of Israel in order to make it possible for a new *aliyah* of *chalutzim.*

Rov Bronrot, in his speech, sharply criticized the ultra-orthodox who campaign against gathering funds for the *Yishuv* -- against Zionism. The *Rov* called this a great desecration of God's name that can do harm to the whole *Yishuv.*

The words of *Rov* Bronrot, that came from the depths of his heart, made an outstanding impression on the crowd. Suitable resolutions were accepted.

241

A committee was formed for the Keren Hayesod in which all levels of Ciechanów's Jewish population was represented. The *Shloimai Amunai Yisroel* were also invited to the founding meeting, but their representatives did not come. Their leaders gave the excuse that they did not get notice from the leaders.

The committee for *Keren Hayesod* was established without representatives of *Shlomai Amunai Yisroel.*

Representatives of Ciechanów in the Committee "For the Kibbutz Grukhov"

In the committee "For the Kibbutz Grukhov" formed in 1934 to aid the *chalutzim kibbutz* in Grukhov and the Zionist leaders of Ciechanów who were represented were: Rosen, Barabash, Korn, Lerman and Apel.

The committee decided to build a house for the kibbutz. The newspaper *Heint* (Today) that wrote about this committee, gave Ciechanów as an example from which others should learn and in the same way take an interest in the *kvutz* of the *chalutzim.*

J. N. F. Bazaar (Keren Kayemet)

At the beginning of 1936, the J.N.F. committee in Ciechanów organized a bazaar that awakened great interest amongst the Jewish population. Hundreds of people, including city couples of the intelligentsia, attended the bazaar.

The participants in the opening of the bazaar were: I. Bialopolsky, as a representative of the J.N.F. headquarters in Warsaw, and the *chaverim* Dovid Vise, I. Korn, and Dr. N. Tov. The bazaar culminated with a banquet honoring the worthy Zionist women: Leah Vise, Soreh Misher, Rokhl Honickman and Rivka Newmark.

An Evening in Memory of Mendele Mokher Sforim's 100th Birthday

In 1936, and evening took place in memory of Mendele Mokher Sforim's birthday. Those who spoke about the classics of Yiddish and

Hebrew literature were: the president of the Ciechanów Zionist organization -- Shimon Shtern, and Kh. Stolnitz.

On September 5, 1936 elections took place for the Ciechanów *Kehillah* that resulted in the following:

Mizrachi -- 2 mandates; Hand-workers -- 2 mandates; Zionists -- 1, Revisionists -- 1; *Poele Agudat Yisroel* -- 1; and *Bund* -- 1.

* * *

At the annual General Meeting of the Jewish Society for the Protection of Children, *chaver* Leon Yovel, director of the Jewish State School, gave a report of the important work for children that the above-mentioned society was doing.

According to the report, there were three hundred children who were fed; one hundred and twenty got footwear and clothing; sixteen were sent to the summer camp *Tzentag*. More than half of the expenses were covered by the Society. The school children also receive free medical care.

Chaver Leon Yovel presented facts in his report that there are cases of children fainting in class because of hunger.

The gathering unanimously gave a vote of thanks to the outgoing committee, and in the newly elected committee women were also elected: Ruth Tov, Roselya Buland, Layidya Yovel, Salomeya Fried, Chava Hokhman, and the *chaverim* Leon Yovel, Shimon Shtern, Isadore, Mundshtein and Eliezer Hendel.

At the first meeting of the committee, Leon Yovel was elected as president of the Society for the Protection of Children, and vice-president -- Ruth Tov.

The Workmen's Club of *Bund* and *Poele Tzion*
(facts gathered by M. Tzinovich from various essays of *Hatzfira*)
Meyer Gotliber

243

During World War I a Workmen's Club was organized in Ciechanów of *Bundists* and *Poele Tzion*. But there was no peace there and they split up. Only then was the *Bundist* organization organized and there I was active until I left Ciechanów. The Grauser Library was established, named after the deceased *Bundist* leader, Branislov Grauser.

The *Bund* organized professional unions. Tailors and shoemakers went on strike and gained better working conditions. The *Bund* organized self-learning where political economics was studied. These activities took place under German occupation during World War I.

I remember a very interesting experience from that time. It was on a Thursday at a very important meeting of the leadership of the *Bund*, where it was decided to go to Warsaw and bring back proclamations. Though it was very risky at that time to travel with such things because the passengers wee inspected at the station. Still, it was decided to send me to Warsaw and meet a certain *chaver*, Karl, there on Novelipia Street, to bring a pack of proclamations.

I had to leave the very same evening. The following day, Friday, I met Karl. He introduced me to a lovely young lady whose father was a *Rov*. After eleven o'clock in the evening she took me to her parents' house. Everyone was sleep. From beneath the oven the girl pulled out the pack of proclamations and handed them to me.

That same Friday evening I was already in Ciechanów and the proclamations were distributed and distributed amongst the people, who pasted them on the walls of the houses. Immediately, on Saturday at dawn, a group of us were arrested. The German *gendarmes* questioned us, kept us in prison for one day, and then released us.

I still remember the words of the German commandant, who said to us during the investigation: "For these dogs it's a shame to waste *kugel* (in German of course).

Types and Personalities

244

Reb Laizer Borokhovich, Shtetl Chazzan and Shoichet

The heartfelt prayers of *Reb* Laizer were always so sweet and wonderful that the people at prayer were very moved by them, so much so, in fact, that he could have been called *Rebbe*. In the same way the *Hasidic Rebbe* affected the ones at prayer with his Torah and *hasidic* tales and caused his listeners to repent and return to Jewish ways, so did his singing give expression to the words, causing them to penetrate the hearts of his listeners and mend their way.

I once heard him *daven* during Passover. He sang the verses of *Barikh Dodi* and his prayer moved me so deeply that tears poured from my eyes. Always, being in Israel already, I dreamt of at least once more hearing *Reb* Laizer's prayers. And to this day I recall how beautiful he looked as he stood praying, with his combed beard, when he conducted the choir, truly like the temple *Kohen* (priest) in the time of the *Bais Hamikdash*.

The hiring of *Reb* Laizer as *Chazzan-Shoichet* was thanks to the last Ciechanów *Rov*, *Rav Hagaon Reb* Chaim Mordecai Bronrot Z'L, the former head of the *Bet Din* (Jewish religious court) in Tel-Aviv.

Amongst all his good works for Ciechanów Jewry, it is also worth mentioning *Rov* Bronrot's understanding of a good *Chazzan*. He knew that by engaging a good *chazzan* the school will have a better attendance, and that actually was the case. When *Reb* Laizer *davened*, the *shul* was packed.

Reb Laizer perished during the German annihilation.

Reb Yoel Dovid Weingarten

The light of *Reb* Yoel-Dovid shone for just a short time. He died at a young age and with his death Jewish Ciechanów lost one of its most active and finest societal workers.

245

He was active in the *Agudah* and his main aim in life was to spread the Torah amongst the people of Israel. He often put aside his own matters and devoted his time and money for communal needs. Even the most bitter opponents of the *Agudah* showed great respect to *Reb* Yoel-Dovid Weingarten, because everyone considered him an earnest person who does not want to derive any political capital from his work in the community.

The Beloved Agudat Leader -- Reb Yoel-Dovid Weingarten

The *Agudah* member, *Reb* Yoel-Dovid Weingarten, born in 1894 in the village of Glusk, near the Polish *shtetl* of Zakrochim, descended from a family of *rabbonim*, *hasidim* and important merchants. His father, *Reb* Yehoshua, gave his father a full Jewish religious education that left its mark on all the life and communal activities of *Reb* Yoel-Dovid Weingarten.

246

At the age of twenty-three, *Reb* Yoel-Dovid, who lived in the *shtetl* Yerantshin with his parents, married someone from Ciechanów and set up life there. He occupied himself with communal matters. He was one of the founders of *Agudat Shlaimah Amunai Yisroel* in Ciechanów and became the secretary of the organization of religious Jews.

Reb Yoel-Dovid devoted all his youthful fervor to this organization that he supported in every way with all the means at his disposal. As a well-to-do merchant, he helped the organization financially and influenced others to contribute funds. With his help, large sums of money were collected for victims of the Ukrainian-Petlurish pogroms of

1919. With Weingarten's help, there was carried out in the Ciechanów *Agudah* a successful campaign for *Keren Hakhinukh* (Fund for Hebrew Education)) that made it possible to establish the religious schools. His initiative, energy and temperament also expressed itself when the *Agudah* in Ciechanów collected money for *Keren Avraham* to perpetuate the memory of the Ciechanów *Rebbe Z"L.*

In 1921, when together with the help of American Jews, the Kitchen Committee was established to feed the needy Jews, we once more see *Reb* Yoel-Dovid as a representative of the *Agudah*. In this respect, *Reb* Yoel-Dovid showed himself to be Jewish-hearted to all who were in need. There was hardly an aspect of communal activity in which *Reb* Yoel-Dovid did not participate. He was amongst the founders of *Tzirei Amunai Yisroel* (later called *Tzirei Avodah*). Of the *Poale Amunai Yisroel,* of the Bais Yaacov School and other institutions. *Reb* Dovid-Yoel Weingarten supported all these materially, and for the youth of the *Agudah* he gave lectures and readings.

In the important political campaigns such as elections to the Polish *Siyum* (Government) and for the Ciechanów *Kehillah*, Weingarten took an active part. He was the Ciechanów delegate for the land-wide gatherings of the *Agudah* in Poland. In 1924, Weingarten was elected as an officer in the *Kehillah* and participated in the work of its commissions, such as : education, Talmud Torah, economy, *schita* and so on. During the *Kehillah* elections in 1931, when the *Agudah* was victorious, Weingarten was elected as vice-president of the *Kehillah* executive.

Picture of the newspaper (extra edition) that the *Tzirei Agudat Yisroel* published upon the death of *Reb* Yoel-Dovid Weingarten, 14 September 1935

With this activity of so many branches, *Reb* Yoel-Dovid Weingarten still had time for his family. He gave his children a modern Jewish-religious education.

Suddenly, an illness destroyed the normal way of life of this energetic man, and at the age of thirty-nine he died, leaving a wife and four children.

* * *

Reb Dovid Vise

One of the loveliest personalities in Ciechanów was *Reb* Dovid Vise Z"L. A wealthy Jew, a learned man of former times, well accomplished in Hebrew literature, spoke Polish well. He was well equipped to represent Jewish interests of Ciechanów.

Reb Dovid was president of the *Kehillah* many times. A devoted Zionist who worked hard and spent a lot of money for all Zionist funds.

A. D. Vinditsky

248

Reb Yantsheder der Melkhevkr

Reb Yantshe

One of the excellent and well-known people in Ciechanów was *Reb* Yantshe Robota Z"L, born in Ciechanów, whose father and grandfather were also born there. Even at his remarkable old age of ninety he was still active. He greeted everyone in friendship, treated young people as equals. The whole community respected him greatly. He was particularly punctual for *davening* in the *bais hamedresh* morning and evening. Summer time and winter time, he was the first one in the *bais hamedresh*. Very early in the morning he could be heard reciting *Tehillim* (Psalms) or studying *Mishna*. He would perform *mitzvot* large and small, do acts of living-kindness personally, particularly by visiting the sick. His work and his heart were one. He ran away from honors and anything like that. He worked hard and accepted everything with love in spite of his old age. He was happy to perform any *mitzvah*. Every year, for the High Holidays, he would travel to the *Rebbe*, Alexander, of whom he was a *hasid*.

Upon his death at the age of ninety, he was given much honor.

His nephew

———

Reb Binyamin Malina

249If we wish to express the essence of the exemplary person, *Reb* Binyamin Malina Z"L, the main description would be the words: *Ahavat Yisroel (*Love of Israel*)*.

Yes, love to every Jew in particular and to all of Israel as a whole, and a special love for every Ciechanówer resident ruled his whole being. *Ahavat Yisroel* was the main motif in all his dealings, and only love could bring out such courage, devotion and paternalism in his relationship to every Jew, and particularly to the Jews of his *Kehillah*, Ciechanów. Everyone who came in contact with *Reb* Binyamin Malina was enchanted by his walk, his respect for God, and his conduct as a spiritual Jewish aristocrat.

250

His communal activity encompassed all spheres in the life of the Ciechanów *kehillah*. There wasn't one function in which *Reb* Binyamin Malina would not be the first to throw himself into action, no matter how hard the task was. He was an example of someone who works for the good of all.

During World War I, when typhus and cholera was prevalent in Ciechanów, and the Jewish dead were, according to an order from the government, buried in mass graves together with Christians, a group of volunteers was organized, under the initiative of *Reb* Binyamin Malina, who dug up the Jewish bodies in the middle of the night from the mass graves, and gave them a Jewish burial.

The most worthy man, Gabbai of the Chevra Kadisha and Kehillah officer, Reb Binyamin Malina

Naturally this was deathly dangerous but *Reb* Binyamin was ready for everything, just as long as he could carry out his holy mission. The Germans did arrest him. They cut off his beard. He was freed and immediately restarted his work. *Reb* Binyamin also carried on help and rescue work for the sick He visited them in the hospital and thereby put his life in danger.

While the Germans were murdering Jews and the plan of the Germans to destroy the Jewish cemetery became known, which was to convert it into a field of grain, it was *Reb* Binyamin Malina who was at the head of a small group to dig up the body of the *Tzadik* in the middle of the night and to take the remains of his holy body and bring it to burial in the new Jewish cemetery.

Reb Binyamin's whole life was devoted to a long chain of devotion to Jews and *Yiddishkeit.*

* * *

All his adult years, *Reb* Binyamin was in charge of the *Chevra Kadisha,* and for a certain period he was an executive of the *Kehillah.* Under his auspices much work was done in the Ciechanów *kehillah* for the good of the Jews in general. Works such as paving the road that led to the Jewish cemetery, making a new fence around the cemetery, rebuilding the *mikveh,* and installing the most modern equipment in order to enable the modern Jewish women to practice Jewish family purification laws.

251

The house of Reb Binyamin Malina was actually a house for the wise. One could always meet there business people from all walks of life who came to seek advice from *Reb* Binyamin regarding various undertakings for the general benefit.

More than once it would happen that when a function was planned for the *Kehillah,* and everyone was uncertain and worried about where the money would come from, *Reb* Binyamin Malina, with his warm, encouraging words, would say: "Jews, don't despair' let's make a start and God will help," and with his encouragement everyone would get started and work towards the goal with enthusiasm to realize the project.

* * *

Reb Binyamin was born in Ciechanów. His father, *Reb* Baruch Mordecai, was the grandson of the famous *Reb* Abba, the father of *Reb* Binyamin's mother, one of the relatives of the Ciechanów *Tzadik Z"L,* and one of the first *Hasidim* of Khidushei Ri"on and Sfat Emet.

Reb Binyamin absorbed all the good traits of his famous grandfather, who raised him because his father died when he was a young child. He was a *Hasid* and *davened* the Gerer *shtibl.* In his work in the community, *Reb* Binyamin was very friendly to people. He greeted everyone with a smile. He had a word of encouragement for everyone. Whoever had a troubled heart full of worries felt better after speaking with *Reb* Binyamin. He was popular not only with *frum* Jews of his kind but also with secular enlightened ones, who had great respect for this *Hasidic* Jew.

Aside from the fact that he was not very wealthy, *Reb* Binyamin always had an open hand to help those in need. There were times when he neglected his own livelihood in order to do communal work. He forgave debts that poor people owed him and encouraged them, saying that when God will help them and they will get back on their feet, then they will pay their debts.

With particular love *Reb* Binyamin fulfilled the *mitzvah* of *hakhnasat orkhim*. When a night's lodging was needed for a guest, *Reb* Binyamin Malina's address was always know. Though his wife was nearly always sick, his house was always open for everyone. He would tell his children to give up their beds for the visiting strangers, and father's word was the law. The weak wife and the children never had any complaints to *Reb* Binyamin. Just the opposite -- they always helped him to fulfill his requests.

Reb Binyamin Malina Z"L, whose life was so closely tied up with the Jews of Ciechanów, together with all the Ciechanów Jews, lost their lives for *Kiddush Hashem* during the annihilation of Polish Jewry. His wife Frumet perished and his two sons -- Boruch-Shmuel and Shmuel-Dovid, and their daughter Rokhl Rosenshtein. Left living from the Malina family are: Chana-Raizl Fish, Chaim Leib Malina in America, Moishe Malina and Tziporah Aaronovich in Israel.

Wolf Aaronovich

––––––

Reb Yaacov (Yenkl) Misher

World problems, Zionism, revival of our nation on its own soil -- were *Reb* Yaacov Misher's beloved concerns, both in his private discussions and in his public appearances.

Reb Yaacov Misher was a central figure in Ciechanów. He was a member in all institutions, where he participated not only with his own work, but also with much money, and in this way was an example for everyone.

252

It is worthwhile to mention the case with the fire brigade.

There was, in Ciechanów as in other cities, a Christian fire brigade. Jews did not go there. When there was a fire in a Jewish house the effort to put it out was much less than when it was a Christian house. *Reb* Yaacov could not stand this and started to conduct propaganda for Jews to be part of the fire brigade as well, and he joined the first one. So the situation improved a lot. It was interesting to watch *Reb* Yaacov during a fire. Dressed in the blue jacket, and the brass helmet on his head, he ran around with a shiny trumpet and alarmed everyone.

Reb Yaacov was often elected as an officer in the Jewish *Kehillah* and was outstanding with his oratorical talent.

Specifically great was his devoted work for Zionism. At the first sprouting of Zionism in Ciechanów he was amongst the first who threw himself into the work. Naturally, he suffered a lot from the opponents, and he was even distanced from the Gerer *shtibl*. But *Reb* Yaacov was not discouraged by all these opponents, and worked tirelessly for the holy ideas.

253

Reb Yaacov Misher's most holy dream was to send his son away to *Eretz Yisroel* and afterwards come there himself to settle. Unfortunately, his dream did not materialize. He perished, together with millions of Jews, in one of the *lagers* or in a gas chamber.

Reb Yisroel Yaacov Student

Much has been written in this book about *Reb* Yisroel Yaacov Student. He had many *Hasidim*. It was hard for him (for *Reb* Yenkl as he was called) to pronounce the letter "r" - therefore he called his daughter "Lukhl." This name for some reason appealed to all of us and so we all called her that to this day. She wasn't insulted. Apparently the name was very dear to her. *Reb* Yisroel Yenkl didn't have much time to devote to his three daughters. He spent most of his time on Hebrew sacred texts -- little time for his livelihood that came to him with much difficulty. Deep in thought, short-sighted, he crossed the street without taking note of anyone. He didn't interfere in household matters. He depended on his daughter and agreed with them in all matters. He knew all their friends and called them all by their names. He spoke to us at home, honored us, and took an interest in our lives.

It once happened that my one-year-old daughter woke up at night because of the noise that my friends and I caused in the house late at night. The child couldn't calm down in spite of all my efforts. She didn't eat, cried non-stop. In desperation I decided to seek help from *Reb* Yisroel Yenkl regarding an *Eyin Hara* (evil eye). He listened to me patiently, calmed me, and said: "Let Dvora put the child to bed without food, let there be complete quiet in the house, and Dvora also must rest."

"And what about the prayer regarding the *Eiyin Hara*?" I asked.

"If Dvora will be quiet, everything will improve."

I listened to him - and a miracle happened. The child woke up healthy, quiet and refreshed. I was delighted. The *Eyin Hara* was ineffective, thanks to the prayer of *Reb* Yisroel Yenkl. I want to thank him. Once again he listens to me attentively, patiently, telling me not to allow loud noise in the house during the hours when the child is asleep. I thank him and go towards the door. And at that moment he says to me: "I had the impression that she is an understanding child, Dvora! I erred apparently -- she's a foolish child."

About many victims of the *Shoah* it is written in the book, *The Merit of Avraham* (Zkhuta d'Avraham). My husband did not understand the spirit in which I bought this book. In it there is an article about the father of "Lukhel", *Reb* Yisroel Yaacov Z"L, our next-door neighbor in Ciechanów.

Reb Yisroel-Yaacov Student was born in Mlava. His father was *Reb* Faivish (*Reb* Faivish Mlamed) but he lived all his life in Ciechanów.

He was a man such as is generally called "a good Yid" -- a great Torah scholar who never missed studying the *Daf Yomi* with others. He was full of *Hasidic* fervor and was always ready to rush to do a mitzvah for another Jew.

He died a tragic death.

Someone reported him and other two Jews to the Germans that he and *Reb* Avraham Friedman and *Reb* Berish Kleinetz, had removed the bones of the Ciechanów *Tzadik* Z"L and buried them elsewhere.

For this "sin" the Hitlerites hanged these three Jews in the marketplace.

Reb Natan Skurnik

Was from amongst the finest Jews in Ciechanów. A beautiful Torah scholar and learned from generations of ancestors -- a prominent merchant. Was a member of *Mizrachi*. Did much for the *Yishuv* in the Land of Israel. Gave money for the *Yishuv* even before the political Zionism.

With part of his family he was put through torture by the Germans.

A.D. Vinditsky

Adla Pafa

Adla appears before my eyes whenever I think or write about my youth, about my beloved Ciechanów. Adla always comes to mind when I think about our group of *Hashomeir Hatzair*, and many others remember this tall girl with dark eyes, friendly to everyone. Her house was always open to those who wanted to learn and make something of their lives. Adla did not base her merit on her family, but rather on her own merit, her wonderful personality, her wisdom. She knew how to get to the root of problems.
254 contd.

What was her human outlook? Adla wanted above all to be a good human being, a free soul, idealist and intellectual. She felt good amongst our group. "Here I feel I'm amongst deep thinkers and people who have a goal in life" she would say.

255

She had more education than most of her age. She knew how to be silent and her silence spoke in a friendly language from heart to heart. And when she did speak her words rang deep. She knew how to listen and was a dear friend to many.

She was an active group member with all her heart and soul, observing fully "all the negative and positive commandments."

Only in one respect did she set herself apart. Adla chose a different way. She decided to go to France to study medicine. Nobody imagined that this choice would cause Adla to perish amongst millions.

How well I remember some of her words and I shall quote them here:

> "A certain force pushes me to study, separate from what I know and my aim in life -- as though I was caught up in something over which I have no power. A person is made up of many contrasting pulls, each one pulling in a different direction. There is a curiosity within me that wants to learn and know and on the other hand to put all this aside and return to my group and to the people of my dear Ciechanów.
>
> "I'm sure that I'll come out of all this turmoil. I have seen death in my family and I know that life is nothing compared to eternity, that man is the most tragic creature. The thought of 'the end' doesn't leave him for a moment. I'll learn and discover the secret of life so that I'll be able to extend it. I'll be a physician.
>
> "When I sit in the library I feel the eyes of the young who are learning to fulfill themselves with spiritual effort, as though wanting to dig deep to discover the secret of life. I'm so happy at such moments."

This and similar thoughts Adla wrote when she was 17-18. From whence do such deep thoughts come to a girl of this age?

Her way was special, because Adla was very individualistic. In a special way and in a search for what was right -- this was her way and she constantly sought it and found it, not in the known paths. So it was in her walks and so in her life as the leader of a group she found what was special in the approach to education.

She chose as a name for the group she led *B'Tzedek Hakfari*. The choice of this name was to explain the relationship between man and his God.

The boy -- the *Tzadik* who *davened* in *shul* on *Yom Kippur*, not knowing how to read, felt privileged to be able to express himself by whistling and ran off to the nearby forest to do so.

Would he have done something like this in public?

Yes, she said. In this way it's possible to feel God's closeness and in this different way this whistling prayer of the boy was acceptable because that was his way of feeling close to God and he felt sure that he would be understood and pardoned.

We spent many hours in friendship together. We spoke about the future and dreamt dreams that took us far away.

How sorrowful it is, Adla, that your young life was cut off and you were not able to realize your dreams! You were together with all the other dear members in our life. We shall remember you always.

Riva Gonska-Leshed

256

Reb Avraham Friedman

Reb Avraham Friedman conducted his communal work quietly and modestly. We never heard him speak loudly and there wasn't a single religious institution in which *Reb* Avraham did not participate. He was very attached to his friend, *Reb* Binyamin Malina. Together they bore the responsibility of looking after the needs of the Kehillah. Here are the facts:

In the year 1920, when Haller's army spread out in Ciechanów, their first job was to torture Jews. When a bearded Jew showed up in the street, the hooligan soldiers tore out his beard, together with pieces of flesh. There was fear of going out of the house. *Reb* Avraham Friedman and *Reb* Binyamin Malina then fearlessly fulfilled their duty and went to complain to the authorities. They carried out funerals and gave the dead a proper burial. The hooligan soldiers, in return, attacked both of these men and tore out their beards.

During that difficult winter there was a shortage of heating fuel and the study of Torah could not take place in the *Bais Hamedresh*, *Reb* Avraham Friedman brought coal from his home and heated the oven in the *Bais Hamedresh*. The learners could once more sit with their *Gemaras* and the words of Torah were heard once more.

Every *mitzvah* was clear and holy for *Reb* Avraham. He made sure that there should be a hygienic *mikveh* so that the laws of family purity would be observed. He occupied himself with the Burial Society and arranged their celebrations. *Reb* Avraham's communal work was very widespread as well. He was active in the *Agudah* and was its representative in the *Kehillah*, in the *Folks Bank* and other institutions.

In the spirit of religious observance and on behalf of the *Kehillah*, he also raised his children. His daughters were active amongst the *B'not Agudat Yisroel*. One daughter, Yokhevet, was a teacher in the *Bais Yaacov School*. The son, Mordecai Eliezer, was the leader of the *Tzirei Agudat Yisroel*. His wife was active in the committee for *Taharat Mishpakha*.

257

Reb Avraham Friedman displayed great self-sacrifice during the destruction of the Jews in World War II. The Germans issued an order that the Jews must walk in the middle of the street. When a Jew forgot and walked on the sidewalk, the Germans shot him and for a long time didn't didn't allow the body to be buried at a Jewish cemetery. *Reb* Avraham Friedman risked his life and carried the murdered ones on his shoulders to give them a Jewish burial. The Germans went after him and shot and wounded him in the leg. *Reb* Avraham carried on his work with his leg bandaged.

Finally came the last chapter in *Reb* Avraham's life of holiness. Together with Yisroel-Yaacov Student and Berish Kleinetz, *Reb* Avraham Friedman carried the bones of *Reb* Avramele Ciechanówer that the Germans shamefully buried, to the new Jewish cemetery. *Reb* Avraham Friedman also buried the damaged Torah scrolls. The Germans caught him doing this "sin" and this holy man was murdered by hanging, together with the two holy men, *Reb* Berish Kleinetz and *Reb* Yisroel-Yaacov Student.

The Friedman brothers

Urku-Aaron Kostsheva

He was the leader of a group of *Hashomeir Hatzair* from 1928-31.

He perished in Auschwitz in 1942.

He was of medium height. Had a serious face, full of assurance and characteristics of a leader. Very capable -- that's what Urku was like.

In spite of the fact that he was the group's leader, and he was an example, very sympathetic, he was an enterprising man and demanded much of himself and of others. He was an observant Jew and a man of actiion. His personality left its mark on all his work and with his death there was a terrible void. He gave a feeling of security to all who were around him from the young to the old.

We called him Urku. It was a nickname lovingly spoken. His voice rang with a special warmth when he instructed the group. Still, he was pleasant and could joke as well.

How to describe him further?

258

A bright smile, two rows of fine teeth. His smile elicited confidence so that one wanted to follow him.

Urku's life was not easy. His home was not a rich one but an honorable one. There were differences of opinion in the Kostsheva family. In their store one could hear different opinions and discussions about world and Jewish problems, each with a group of followers, both of the right and the left, from Zionists to assimilated ones, the whole rainbow of outlooks. Urku was the youngest of his brothers but he was given much respect. As a youngster he already knew how to stick by his own opinion.

Urku was the leader of a *Hashomeir Hatzair* group for a number of years. He added to his leadership with his personal charm and the group gave a flavor to his young life, full of action. He was the faithful instructor of the leaders Moishe Lutsky, may he live long, head of the group Daz. I don't know how many classes Urku completed at school, how much school education he acquired, what kind of report cards he got from his teachers. His education was based on the deep sources of *Hashomeir.* He was a student and a teacher who succeeded in instilling in the young people faith in the future full of light and justice in the kibbutz. Urku built himself learning and outlook of the world and became a serious and dear individual.

Urku did not live to realize his ideas. His dreams, like those of many others, were not for him to reach.

Rivka Leshed-Gunski

Reb Avraham Aaron Kelman

Reb Avraham Aaron Kelman was born in 1883. His father's name was Yitzhak. The writer of these lines knew *Reb* Avraham from the young years on. From his young age, people already sensed that from this youngster much could be expected. *Reb* Avraham-Aaron distinguished himself already as a young boy in his serious learning. He studied at the Lomzer Yeshiva and was a good learner there. He always wanted, however, to do work with his hands and ended up earning his living as a locksmith.

Reb Avraham-Aaron was an honest man, an honest Jew, and devoted to the *Kehillah.* He devoted his whole life, his time and income for others. He could well serve as an example for learning Torah and receiving guests. He concentrated all his thoughts in implanting in the young and even in the older generation -- the love of learning Torah and *hakhnasat orchim.* The Talmud Torah of Ciechanów rested completely on his shoulders and he sacrificed everything for its existence, hired the best teachers, and though the budget increased, it did not scare him.

259

Money was never lacking. *Reb* Avraham-Aaron made sure of that. The custom of *Hakhnasat Orchim* was very important for him. When a guest came to Ciechanów and there didn't happen to be anywhere for him to sleep, everyone knew that the guest had to be brought to *Reb* Avraham-Aaron. At his place a place will never be lacking, not only for the guest, but for as many as will come. Avraham-Aaron slept it mattered not where, and gave his place and the cushion from beneath his head to the visitors. The same applied with food for the guests. From his house nobody departed hungry, and though he himself was poor and oft times hardly had what to eat himself, he always had a ready table for the guests.

It is very painful to recall the tragic death of *Reb* Avraham-Aaron. He was the first one to perish at the hands of the Germans in our *shtetl.* As he went out of his shop a "mischievous" bullet of a German soldier killed him on the spot for no reason.

D. Vinditsky

―――

A Few Lines about My Teacher Reb Avraham-Aaron Kelman

As I set out to write, at the request of the Committee of Ciechanów Jews, about the community worker, or more correctly, the one who worked on the *Kehillah's* behalf so faithfully, one who with his work on behalf of others is hard to duplicate, I must dwell on three aspects of his world. Torah and good deeds and acts of loving-kindness. I couldn't free myself from the pain in my heart even though fifteen years have passed since those terrible days when the ones most dear and close, parents, siblings, teachers, who left such precious memories with me, memories of my youth and growing up as were the days of Jewish youngsters growing up in Poland. Those days ended so inhumanly that we couldn't utter it or think about it. And those fifteen years for us in Israel. Those years of our national revival were years of our full destiny in which we saw the establishment of Israel. Like compensation by divine decree for what had happened to them there. A terrible feeling! A dreadful price. Our wise men said that we must forget the dead in our hearts otherwise it is not possible to go on living. Therefore every opportunity to memorialize the names of those who perished so tragically.

260

May they not be forgotten. And I shall try to devote a few lines to my teacher, my guide, *Reb* Avraham-Kelman of blessed memory. I remember the house, the roof of the Talmud Torah building amongst the neighboring buildings of Jewish Ciechanów, the *mikveh*, and to the right of the old Jewish cemetery where *Reb* Avremele Ciechanówer is buried. I remember also the stories about souls of departed that emerge in the *mikveh* during the night and go afterwards to pray in the great *shul* whose windows reflect the sunlight.

I remember the Talmud Torah and its director, *Reb* Avraham-Aaron. Early in the morning, he was there to open the Talmud Torah. He would be carrying his large bag that held his *tallis* and *tfillin*. His look was strict but loving. He would go from room to room in the Talmud Torah to see how the students were doing. He had a special love for the class of *Reb* Shlomo Zalman. He liked to chat with him because there was a special relationship between them. Afterwards he would put his tallis and tfillin in his office. He would check to see what repairs the building needed. Sometimes right after prayers in the *Bais Hamedresh* he would go to the Yeshiva *Bais Avraham* to hear a *shiur* given by *Reb* Avraham-Yonatan Kuzlovsky to his students.

Reb Avraham-Yonatan excelled in his explanations and would elucidate various points of view. And *Reb* Avraham Aaron got lots of *naches:* I remember times when we used to immerse ourselves together in study. And when he recognized that a student was particularly adept at learning he would do everything possible to send him away for further learning. He used to go to the parents and convince them to let their son go away to study further. And there was a saying amongst us that for *Reb* Avraham a bit of *cholent* on *Shabbat* is enough for him until the third *Shabbat* meal because of the special additional spirit he derived from *Shabbat*, and when one of the boys left to learn and trade he would be happy when he saw him in the *Bais Hamedresh* for this was Torah with *derekh eretz*.

261

And he had special love for the Land of Israel. He sent his son to *Eretz Yisroel* with the fourth *aliyah*, and every letter that he received from *Eretz Yisroel* was very special for him. And I remember all his aid and rush to do good deeds. Oft times when I was in his house I would see that his bed is made up on the floor to make room for a guest. This was the kind of person *Reb* Aaron Kelman of blessed memory was. And survivors of the *Shoah*, from Ciechanów, tell that he was amongst the first to perish at the hands of the Nazis *ymakh shmam* and that he died with his *tallis* and *tfillin* bag under his arms.

Tzvi Burshtein

———

Reb Berish Kleinetz

As a young man he was already active in the community. As a young man he was already active in the Burial Society and later in all philanthropic institutions. He was also someone who would sacrifice himself for others and sought out opportunities to do a favor for another Jew.

He was one of the holy martyrs whom the Germans hung in the marketplace.

Reb Moishe Yaacov Rakovsky

Reb Moishe-Yaacov Rakovsky was one of the great Torah scholars. He was a descendant of the Plotzker *Rov*, famous for his "iron head." He was an active member of the *Agudah* and in philanthropic institutions. Several times he was on the *Kehillah* leadership and a representative of the *Agudah* in various state institutions.

Reb Shloime Rubinstein

He was a great philanthropist and his house was always open for guests. He was active in all the Ciechanów institutions on whose behalf he worked and to which he contributed much money.
262

As one of the first Zionists in Ciechanów, Reb Shloime Rubinstein was the founder of *Mizrachi* in Ciechanów, together with Eliezer Auerbach and the writer of these lines.

He was also one of the finest members of the community and every *Yomtov* he *davened* elsewhere.

Let us recall here his wife Esther who also took part in all community philanthropies and contributed a lot of money.

He was tortured by the Germans together with his wife and only daughter.

A. D. Vinditsky

Jewish Women Personalities

The Woman Rokhl Malka Tik

Regarding Rokhl-Malka Tik, who was well-known for her wealth and goodness, many stories were told in Ciechanów. One that illustrates her personality is the following.

Rokhl-Malka Tik lived at the beginning of the 20th century in Ciechanów. She was a daughter of Mordecai Lindenberg and his first wife, whom he divorced. He carried on much business with Berlin and Moscow and had a fishing concession in the rivers of Russia and Germany.

263

His daughter from his first wife he loved very much because of her good qualities and gave her the best education of that time. When she reached the age for marriage he married her to a nice young man, Michael Tik. The father set his son-in-law up in his business and made him a manager in the fishing in the Rostov River.

Time marched on. Rokhl and Michael had three sons and a daughter. The couple lived happily. Rokhl didn't want to leave the shtetl of her birth, Ciechanów, though her husband required this because his business was somewhere in Russia. So Michael spent the whole year there and would return home for the High Holidays and bring his wife expensive gifts. In spite of her wealth Rokhl was always solitary and her time was spent raising the children and doing good for others.

Her life was devoted to helping the needy. She maintained a special cook who cooked for the family and also prepared good food for the poor sick. When someone needed a free loan or an alm it was found at Rokhl-Malka's. For every *yomtov* when her husband returned from afar he found his wife in a new outfit because her former clothes that were still in very good shape, she had distributed to poor brides.

264

She was an introvert, very absorbed in her thoughts and very attached to her daughter, who grew very good-natured.

Suddenly this greatly-loved girl became seriously ill. The mother brought the best doctors to examine her. All the Jews in the shtetl prayed for the girl's health but she grew even sicker. It reached a critical stage. Doctors said that only God could help, so Rokhl-Malka deeply believed that God would help and her inner pain she never showed anyone. The daughter was already near death and the mother kept praying in her room.

When the daughter drew her last breath the household help put off telling the mother the horrible news, but the door of Rokhl-Malcha's room opened. There she was pale and stooping, with a terrible look in her eyes, and she asked those present: "Well, can I now make the blessing?" When she noticed that the daughter is no longer amongst the living she excitedly said the blessing: "*Adonai noten v'Adonai lokeiakh*" (God gives and God takes) and so on, not shedding a tear...

The funeral took place. The mother followed after her dear dead daughter, stony-faced, silent and didn't let out a sigh.

After the *shiva* the stricken mother, after accepting the words of the comforters, told them that she feels consoled because her daughter is calling her to heaven. Rokhl-Malka started to get ill. The father, who already was staying at home after the daughter's death, didn't leave her bedside. Shortly afterwards Rokhl-Malka died, mourned by all Jews of Ciechanów.

265

The Bobe (Grandmother) Faige Lifshitz

The Bobe Faige Lifche

"Bobe Faige Lifche" -- is what her grandchildren, children, relatives and friends called her. She was the very embodiment of modesty, endless faith and spiritual elevation. She was typical of the *Hasidic* inspiration and always *Shabesdik* and *Yomtovdik*. In any group where Bobe Faige Lifche showed up, she drew respect. She spoke very little, but the soft look of her eyes had more influence on those around her than the most expressive words.

Bobe Faige Lifche belonged to the segment of the Jewish masses who grew up in holiness, purified by poverty and became strong through good deeds. She was the daughter of a great scholar and cabbalist -- *Reb* Levy Yisroel Kant.

266   blank

267

He was well-known in the learned rabbinic circles. When Faige once came to the old Łodz *Rov Reb* Eliyahu Chaim Meizl, regarding a certain matter, the *Rov* respectfully stood up when he heard whose daughter had come.

Reb Levy Yisroel's daughter had a difficult life. She was left a young widow with seven children: two sons and five daughters. The widowed mother suffered great poverty, nevertheless she gave her children the best Jewish education. There were times when there wasn't even a crust of bread in her house but the proud Faige Lifche always conducted herself honorably and respectfully. Later, when her children grew up they left for large cities to work. The daughters became textile workers in Łodz. The children provided for their mother with respect and generosity. The oldest son established a shoe business in Ciechanów and lived together with his mother.

When Faige Lifche's situation improved, she started to concern herself with poor neighbors who were starving. The assistance that she gave them was offered in such a way that they would not be embarrassed. She would eat together with them to make it seem more natural.

During World War I when Russian soldiers were billeted in Ciechanów, and amongst them Jewish soldiers, Faige arranged proper accommodation for them so that they would have good *Shabbosim* and *Yomtovim*. Also for the Russian soldiers who used to come from the front for rest to Ciechanów, Faige showed motherly love. She gave them an opportunity to get washed and provided them with fresh underwear. The soldiers, in turn, called her *mamushka dorogaya*.

To the invalids she showed endless humanity and love, whether they were incapable of work, sick or even out of their minds. She took them into her house, ate together with them, and did everything possible to improve the lives of these unfortunate sufferers.

268

With her goodness, her understanding of young people that the Zionist movement brought to her house, she endeared herself to all Jews in Ciechanów. Faige Lifshitz became a good name. All her children were called by her name, Faige Lifshitz's son, Faige Lifshitz's' daughter and so on with her grandchildren. The family grew large and each one took a prominent place in Ciechanów's Jewish community.

Faige Lifshitz died before World War II. Nearly all the Jews of Ciechanów attended her funeral.

Moishe Fuchs

My Grandmother Khana Raizl

No matter how much I write about my grandmother Khana-Raizl as she was called in our *shtetl* where there was no need to add her family name -- it will be only a drop in the sea of her aid work and of her *tzedakah* for all needs. She gave generously and anonymously. In General she was a very modest woman -- one of the 36 just people on whom the world depends and cannot live without. She became widowed before World War I after the death of her husband, Dovid Makaver Z"L, a God-fearing Jew and a *Hasid* of Rabbi Alexander. He died very young. My grandmother Khana-Raizl remained with many children. Only her eldest daughter Rokhl Z"L was married (she also perished in the great fire in Poland). Her whole life was not a bed of roses. She had to worry about a livelihood, the loss of some of her children. Still, she did not lose her spirit but continued on in the way of her family. Her house was open to everyone without exception. That's how she trained her children also: to give alms, to welcome guests for *Shabbat*. I saw this later in her son's home, my father Moishe Chaim Z"L.

I remember very well her purse that she took with her when she went out -- that was with my mother Esther Z"L from the Gutshtot household (a home well-known amongst the Alexander Hasidim in Łodz). These two went out to "visit" family of means in order to collect contributions to be anonymously distributed, and they were always greeted warmly. Everyone knew that when Khana-Raizl comes one must give -- and more than normal -- and there was no lack of needy in Ciechanów. With all this, nobody knew who the recipients were. This is how she conducted herself with the distribution of *challahs* for *Erev Shabbes* or *Yomtov*.

This was done with the help of neighbors so that nobody would know who the sender was.

And my grandmother had friends amongst all classes of people, from Zionist to *Agudat Yisroel*. One would come to seek advice in family matters and another in matters of business. Yet a third would come just to unload their troubles and everyone felt better afterwards.

Even before Herzl my grandmother was a Zionist. With all her heart she believed that it was necessary to go on *aliyah* and help build up the land. Her ideas led, on more than one occasion, to disputes and discussions with members of *Agudat Yisroel* and Gur Hasidim (who were, as is known, opposed to *aliyah*). One dispute remains clear in my mind: Grandmother asked someone why it is that every week he goes out to the market: "Why do you go out to the market? Wait at home until the Christian buyers will come to you." He burst out laughing and replied: "Do you really believe they would come to my house?" To this my grandmother replied "And if we'll sit here -- who will build our land for us -- if we won't go there and work -- nobody will help us." She didn't ever live until the day that the Jewish State was declared.

To her credit it must be said that one of her sons did go on aliyah with his family in the 20's, and was amongst the founders of *B'nai Barak*. Another son went on *aliyah* during later Arab attacks, another son made *aliyah* during the 30's and was even a manager of a business.

So some of her sons and a daughter went on *aliyah.* She derived much pleasure from every letter she got from *Eretz*. Before I left I promised to write her and tell her about every place in *Eretz*, and did so, but to my distress I couldn't continue when the Arab attacks went on.

269

All her life she also dreamed of going on *aliyah* and might have done so, but for two reasons this did not materialize. She didn't want to leave the remainder of her children in the *diaspora* and didn't want to be dependent on her children. She therefore remained behind together with some of her children who weren't able to go on *aliyah.*

She was a very pious woman, but not fanatical. She showed much patience when dealing with people. She never preached religion to others; attempted to understand everyone whether it was a discussion about the fast of *Tisha B'Av* during the time when building the *Bayit Shlishi* (Third Temple) or during a discussion with Avraham-Aaron Kelman Z"L, one of her close friends, regarding matters that according to their ideas were in a worldly realm.

She was like a second mother to me. When my father forbade me to go to a youth summer camp -- and I went in opposition to him -- I know that when I returned she would greet me with open arms.

That's what my grandmother, Khana Raizl, of blessed memory, was like.

———

My Father's Suffering for the Education of His Children
Dovid Makaver

My father suffered very much because of his desire to give his children a proper Jewish education. In the Jewish *gymnasium* in Ciechanów classes only went to grade six,. Our father Z'L, decided that we should attend the Polish *gymnasium*. Unfortunately, we had to attend the *gymnasium* on *Shabbat* also.

Our father Z"L, was a *Hasid* of the *shtibl* named after Motele Z"L. He *davened* there for many years. And I remember the responsibility of preparing his *tallis* every *Shabbat*. This deed went from sister to sister and then to our brothers.

270

Part of the Mundzak family

Destiny decreed that the *Hasidim* decided that it was a sin to study on *Shabbes*. They warned my father, and finally decided to chase him out of the *shtibl* and they did indeed stick to this decision.

My father was no longer allowed into the *shtibl* that he loved so much. He suffered quietly but didn't concede. To us children our father became a saint, a fighter for a broader education. We felt for him deeply but we also wanted to study.

My father started to go to the city *shul,* but he missed the intimate atmosphere of the *shtibl*. Finally, my father decided to build a *shtibl* in our yard. There were more than a few who understood him and came to pray together with him. We children were very happy because the suffering of our father after he was disallowed in the *shtibl* of Reb Motele Z"L was hard to witness. Jews who understood that their children needed a broader education prayed in the new *shtibl* and others joined them.

Dora Mundzak-Newman

271

Reb Yisroel Moishe Mandshik's monument that unfortunately survived only in this photo

272

Poor People

Z. Appel

The Lonely Mute

Every *Shabbat*, summer time in the very early hours, winter time in the dark predawn, father would take me along to the *Bais Hamedresh* to recite *Tehillim* (Psalms).

I recall that when I was ten years old we used to go winter time at predawn when it was quiet all around and the only sound was the crunch of the snow beneath our feet -- father and son to worship the Almighty, Creator of the universe.

Father's customary route was we would walk quickly, almost running, past Shultz' passageway, cutting through Pultusky Street, and go into the blind alley that connected the Pultusky Street with the *Bais Hamedresh* place.

There was darkness all around, and even darker in the blind connecting alley. And then suddenly there would be a fearful shout, a shout that was like the howling of a wild beast when it is wounded.

In the open space in front of the *Bais Hamedresh* there stood the mute, dressed in his usual attire, dirty clothes tied with a thick rope, his feet wrapped in thick sacks. He would jump from foot to foot and utter inhuman sounds. Nobody hinders him. He continues in this way until he has no energy left. Tired and exhausted, he enters the *Bais Hamedresh*, all out of breath. There he takes his usual place beside the door near the washbasin.

That is where he spends his evenings, Sabbaths and *Yomtovim*. Six days he would spend his days sitting in the tinsmith shop of Gelbard. Day in, day out, from morning until night, he would operate the bellows that stirred the fire. That's how he spent his poor life between the smithy and the corner in the *Bais Hamedresh* neglected by God and man.

I doubt if anyone knew his name, because he was always called -- the mute.

273

The Poor Village Wanderer and the Photographer

Dovid Kamnikofsky lived not far from the *shul* and *Bais Hamedresh* in a small low *shtibl* where there was hardly room to turn around. His wife was a sick woman who gave birth to two sons -- one a baker's journeyman, the second -- a tailor.

Dovid Kamnikovsky lived the life of a pauper. He was a tailor and he worked in the villages. Every Monday he would set out for the village with a sack on his shoulders, his wanderer staff in hand, and return home Friday for the Sabbath. Everyone in Ciechanów knew that Dovid is a village wanderer. When he would pass through the village streets, the Polish anti-Semites would point to him and say that he was an example of the Jews in Poland.

He wore a long *capote* with the round *kippa* hat on his head, *gartleh,* with a staff in his hand. The Jewish photographer in the *shtetl* photographed him and titled it "Dovid goes with his sack on his shoulders."

The photographer, Rosenstein, was a Jew whom one never saw in shul, not even to hear the best *Chazzan* nor at the best Jewish occasion. In general, he distanced himself from other Jews and villagers. Dovid, for him, was merely a curious type to photograph.

When Dovid's son returned home from the army and saw his father in the pose of Rosenstein's photograph, he went in to him and asked to take the photo out of the window display, instead of using it as an advertisement on Varshever Street. Rosenstein replied: "This is my work and no one can take it away. Kamnikofsky's son asked Rosenstein if he had gotten his father's permission. He took Rosenstein to court in Ciechanów.

Kamnikofsky's son took the appeal to Warsaw and pointed out that this is a disgrace for him and his father. In Warsaw also Kamnikofsky lost. There was much discussion in the *shtetl* about this photograph.
274

A Song/Poem Full of Love

The police in Ciechanów were in charge of sanitation. Quite often the householders would have to pay a fine for disobeying an order such as not pouring dirty water in the street on Sunday or on a Polish holiday.

But there were places that were out of sight of the police. One of these places behind the gate at the back of our yard. The space was square, with low shrubs all around. The people in the courtyard would dump their water and garbage there. All this caused a terrible stench during the summer, and in the summer -- a hazard to passersby. When I would go to my friend Khaya, I tried to take a shortcut. It was dangerous, and more than once I would fall, because of the ice of the frozen poured-out water. When I would pass this yard I would hear pleasant singing coming from behind the houses. The singing always had the same theme: "Love." The voice was that of a woman. I became curious. Once, I went into her house. From her sewing machine there arose a nice girl, dark eyes and hair. It turned out that she was a seamstress for boys. I started to recommend boys to her as customers and so it was that I got to know her better. She lived in a small room with her mother, who had bad eyesight. She was called the "Red Woman" because of her red eyes from her sickness. For periods of time she had no work. The crowding, the poverty, the dirty yard, the sick mother -- all this did not spoil the girl's spirit. She sang while she worked and continued to sing even when she had no work. And the theme of her song did not change: "Love, love."

Once she told me with joy that she met a boy. She fell in love! "And do you expect to get married soon?" I asked her.

"No, I just want to 'have a love affair' was her reply. I left the city. I heard that only for a short time did she continue to sing of love. The death of her husband in a traffic accident was the cause of her silence.
275

The Shtetl Ciechanów and Yiddish Literature
276   blank

277

Nearly every Yiddish *shtetl* in Poland got reflected in Yiddish literature. There are *shtetlech* with Jewish villagers from which there came forth portrayals by great Yiddish writers who wrote about their surroundings and people of the years of their childhood. Writers such as Sholem Asch, I.M. Visenberg, Avraham Raisen, are examples. Ciechanów also produced writers who in one way or another introduced their *shtetl* to Yiddish literature.

The *shtetl* also entered Yiddish literature through its famous rabbis and rabbinic personalities. This is how the great writer I. Opatashu memorializes in his novel *The Ciechanówer Nigun* the personage, the great *Tzadik Reb* Avreml Ciechanówer, whose great -grandson was the great American poet Zishe Landau. Landau in his poem, also mentions his great-grandfather, the Ciechanów *Reb* Avreml.

Zishe Landau was born in Plotsk but he traced his distinguished ancestry back to the Ciechanów *Tzadik* and famous rabbinic scholar, *Gaon Reb* Avreml of Ciechanów and his son, *Reb* Wolf, who became *Rebbe* in Strikov -- the grandfather of the poet Fishe Landau. (See Raisen, *Lexicon of Yiddish Literature*, 2nd volume).

Besides this above-mentioned connection with Yiddish literature, there were in Ciechanów, in the last years prior to the *khurban*, the talented writers and artists. One of these was Yosl Grosbard. His brother has written about him. This brother is himself a very talented and recognized artist who now lives in Israel.

Yehoshua Grosbard also names the following talented Jewish boys whose talents didn't have the opportunity to develop. They perished in World War II:

278

Chaim Krulik -- had a talent for drawing. Copied paintings and wanted to be a great artist. Herschel Friedberg -- copied pictures of *Eretz Yisroel*; the Western Wall, Rachel's Tomb, also painted landscapes. He died in Israel during World War II; Glass or Lass -- wrote reviews and poems and his end is not known; Nisl Kancianer -- was musically talented. Painted. Died in Israel.

In this section we bring the literary works that relate to Ciechanów Jewish writers and with the Jews of Ciechanów.

279

To the Ciechanówer

Zishe Landau

I'm not free - of my *zaides*
There's a long chain behind me;
I am not free - my every step
Is closely followed from close eyes!
Relaxed, but with a firm hand
I continue in this iron chain.

My blood feels you close, Ciechanówer
Because as was your life, so does mine carry duty.
If I want to or not, I accept it with love.

Still for this iron destiny
My heart will not fear
Because just as you, so feel I the holiness of the duty
Here is the net of duties and laws,
Oh, how many there are and joy!
And only a slave can think that an eagle
Doesn't hold his arms outstretched in his cage!
Oh, *Reb* Avraham Ciechanówer,
I, like you, stretch out my arms.

(From the book *Poems (Lider)* by Zishe Landau.
Published by "Inzl" publishers, New York, 1937).
280

The Ciechanówer Nigun

dedicated to Zishe Landau
I. Opotashu

It was already well into Friday when Wolf Landau awoke, started to stretch and remained in bed with his hands beneath his head.

Friday was his day of rest. To the editorial office where he worked, he did not go on Friday. The newspaper, an orthodox one, did not appear on *Shabbat*. On Friday Landau ate breakfast in bed. This heavy duty weighed upon him and made a demand on him.

And if you like, it wasn't a duty at all. Just listen to this -- and if the Bailer *Rebbe's* second son, the *Rebbe Reb* Menakhem Mendl, came from Poland to New York, what does that have to do with him, with Wolf? It's true that the Bialer *Rebbe* is a great-great-uncle. This means that he, Wolf, is a great-grandchild of the Strikover *Rebbe*, a blood relative of *Reb* Menakhem Mendl. In Poland these blood relatives never met. When Wolf, a boy of sixteen, came to New York, the fifty-year-old Menakhem Mendl had been a *Rebbe* for a long time. Now the *Rebbe* must be around seventy. And he, Wolf, just from the distance that separates them, these kin, his head starts to spin. Still, more than once Wolf feels that since the age of sixteen he is following in the footsteps of his great-grandfather, the Strikover. The Strikover sang hymns to God and to all the people of Israel and the great-grandchild sings songs to "girls like half-moons."

Wolf's great-grandfather, *Reb* Avreml Ciechanówer, believed that the impurity spreads itself during night-time on the tips of the fingers and can possibly touch the face during sleep, so the *Tzadik, Reb* Avreml, slept with hand gloves, and the grandchild, to spite his grandfather, dreamt about "girls' songs" and "impure matters" -- also sang the *Sefra Achra* with its forty-nine degrees of impurity, so what kind of a relationship could there possibly be between the grandchild and his grandfathers and uncles?

And yet?

281

As soon as Wolf discovered that *Reb* Menakhem Mendl is in New York, he became restless. He didn't speak about this to anyone. Not with his wife, not with his two children. He tried to ignore this bit of news, convinced himself that he had long ago forgotten about this, but as soon as he was left alone, he beheld an old man, an illustrious face, dressed in silk and satin, with beard and *payes,* his eyes -- bright. This is what he had been told about the appearance of the Strikover, the Bialer, that's how the great-uncle *Reb* Raphael looked and that's probably how *Reb* Menakhem Mendl looks.

And what about Wolf Landau?

No *tzitzis,* a head of blond hair falls on his forehead and into his blue, dreamy eyes, and in his eyes a revocative smile to people and to the world.

It happened more than once that when Wolf stood in front of the mirror combing his thick head of hair he asked himself: "What sort of connection does my revocative smile have with the Ciechanówer, with the Strikover, with the Bialer?"

On the surface -- no relationship. But deep in the soul Wolf was drawn to the Ciechanówer simplicity, to his deed modesty, when he could hide himself away from people. But I., Avraham, am a sinner. Ever since my youth people have been running after me.

For many years Wolf went around with a song to the Ciechanówer *Zaide.* The first line of the song was always on his lips, whether at home or at the office, whether in the street or when he was by himself, the song would come to him, begging for an improvement of myself.

> "Closest to my blood
> Is you Ciechanówer,
> Because just as you during your lifetime
> I feel I have a duty."

And when these lines urge him on, then he feels that for twenty years he was fooling himself; that his songs about "blue and red nightingales" were merely misleading candles that distanced him from his grandfathers and uncles, while in reality a cry begs to be expressed from within him.

> "I am not free from my *zaides!*
> From them a long chain extends to me."

282

And this chain pulled Wolf and drew him to the *Rebbe* who came from Poland, *Reb* Menakhem Mendl, who also wrote poetry in his youth.

After lunch Wolf Landau exited from the subway on east Broadway, turned in on Henry Street. It was only here that his heart rose up, fluttered, and could not calm down.

The *Rebbe* stayed in a two-story wooden house. He occupied the complete second floor.

Wolf carefully made his way up the wooden stairs that squeaked, not knowing what he would talk about to the *Rebbe*. In front of his eyes stood his great-great-grandmother, the wife of the Ciechanów *Rov*, the *Tzadikah*, Iteleh. Was she truly such a tiny little woman? And during the winter, when she would go to a woman who was after a birth, bringing a container of jam, Did her grown sons carry her in their hands?

A Jew, without a jacket, just in his *tallis-koten*, beard and *payes*, stopped Wolf.

"What good news does a Jew have?"

"Is *Reb* Menakhem-Mendl alone here?"

"Here."

"And who are you, his *shames*?"

"Yes."

"I want to see the *Rebbe*."

"Not *Shabbat*. He doesn't see anyone on *Shabbat*."

"It's not *Shabbat*."

"To the *Rebbe* it's already *Shabbat*."

"Tell the *Rebbe* that a relative has come to see him."

"What relative?" The *shames'* wise eyes looked at the shaved relative scornfully.

282

"Tell the *Rebbe* that *Reb* Mordekhai Motl's grandson came to see him."

"That's to say that you're *Reb* Strikover's grandson?"

Wolf nodded his head in the affirmative.

"Have you been in America very long?"

"About twenty years."

"Doing what, in business?"

283

"No, I work for a newspaper."

"A writer?" the shames asked, drawing out his words.

At this point the door opened, and the *Rebbe*, a tall man, slightly bent, in a satin *capote,* quietly entered, in his soft slippers, and remained standing at the door. His white socks contrasted with his black satin. The thick silk belt was loosely tied around his hips, and his wise, much-suffering face, was framed by a gray, pointy beard. He looked at Wolf as though he felt sorry for him, for how can a man destroy his own image of God form!

The *Rebbe* offered him "*Shalom*" and said:

"As I hear, you are a grandson of uncle Motl."

"Yes, *Rebbe.*"

"Your father told me that he has a son in America. You're called Wolf, named after the Strikover *Rov* Z"L. You had a great *zaide*, Wolf."

"We had an even greater great-grandfather," Wolf said.

"Are you learning at all?" the *Rebbe* asked him.

"It's a long time since I stopped learning, *Rebbe.*"

"Too bad, too bad, Wolf," the *Rebbe* said, his face clouding over, "but if you, a writer, have come to see me, come to see a relative, a *Rebbe*, you are still okay. I have faith that you will return to learning one day. And now, Wolf, it's already *Shabbes* by me," the *Rebbe* said, extending the tips of his fingers, then went into his room with the familiar Ciechanówer *nigun*, and shut his door after him.

Wolf remained standing in the middle of the room and looked toward the closed door. Did he feel insulted? No. Who knew better than Wolf how holy the *Shabbat* was for the Ciechanów Jews! After all, *Reb* Avreml Ciechanówer, Z"L, had asked that the *Hasidic Rebbes* not come to him for *Shabbat*, because if they were to come he would have to conduct himself like a *Hasidic Rebbe* while, all his life, he had stuck to the "Ashkenazi way."

And for *Reb* Menakhem Mendl? For him it was already *Shabbat*. And although it was *Shabbat* the *Rebbe* had come out and greeted Wolf with *Shalom*, said a few words to him and then had gone into his special room with the Ciechanów nigun on his lips, the *nigun* that Wolf remembered from his young days.

284

As he heard the first zmira nigun, he saw, in front of his eyes, the first Ciechanówer, Reb Avreml, hurrying Friday morning after davening, going quickly, with his shames, from store to store, checking the scales, making sure that his Jews are giving the right weights. And by two in the afternoon the Shames is already going by himself through the narrow streets, calling out: To shul, to shul."

And when Wolf descended the stairs, he was already on Henry Street, the Ciechanów zmira-nigun once more came to him, and he carried it through the streets of New York.

My Brother, the Poet, Yosl Grosbard

Yehoshua Grosbard

All of us at home knew that Yosl was growing to be a writer. Already in 1927, at the age of 22, he was already featured in a journal that appeared in Pultosk. He had a poem, *"My Shtetl"* published there and it drew the attention of the Yiddish literary critic.

Yosl was born in the year 1905 in a small *shtetl* called Serotsk, where the rivers "Bug" and "Narev" join. He would always tell that as a youngster he swam in the Narev and nearly got drowned. This connected him lovingly to the *shtetl*. As a child he moved with his parents to Ciechanów, where he completed the *folk shule* and later helped his father in his work as a house painter.

In 1918 Yosl came with his parents to Warsaw. There he worked in a metal factory, where he was badly exploited by the boss. At the same time he was active in the metalworkers' union and in the youth movement of the *Bund Tzukunft*. Later in *Komstzunft* and later in the young communists party. He studied in evening classes and studied art for awhile with the artist, Moishe Applebaum.

In 1928 Yosl came with his family to Ciechanów once more. He was active in the An-ski library, gave lectures on philosophy, communal and cultural themes; wrote and composed music for poetry for various publications in Poland as well as elsewhere, such as "Farois", "Literarishe Bleter" and "Undzer Veg." In his poetry one can feel his attachment to the day-to-day life.

285

The talented poet and labor leader in Ciechanów -- Yosef Grosbard

In "To my Song" published in Argentina's "Der Shpigl" he wrote:

> Come down from your high places
> Take off your dress of blue,
> I'll furnish you with simple boots
> And you'll walk beside me.

In his poem, "*Nem Tzunoif Aleh Vortzlen*" (printed in "Farois"):

> Let the joy of the dream fill you
> From the blade of grass and from each tree,
> Oh, try your best to understand
> The secret of -- wanting to grow and of being...

286

> The restless sweetness in the air
> Accept together with the nightingale's sweet song
> See how the bird delights
> As it faithfully builds its nest.

Yosl's attachment to the concrete life appears more clearly in his cycle of songs called "Doh" Here) published in "Farois" 1938.

> It's not only the vanished body of my *zaide*
> Dust, beneath the moss-covered stone,
> Not only the lingering fear
> Of my Mother's -- Father's present plagued days,
> But also my proud bright dream
> That springs up like a freshly blossoming tree --
> My dream of the week to come
> Is interwoven and tied to the earth -- here.

In a second poem in the same cycle Grosbard wrote:

> Right here! From this same mother's lap
> As the pine tree, poplar and the rose
> So it is that I also am from here.

It is interesting to note the theme of the cycle of songs: "*A Grus Dir Bergelson Fun Shtetl*" (Regards to you Bergelson from the Shtetl) published in "Shpigl" of Buenos Aires, 1945. The editor added the following:

"The poet, Y. Grosbard, sent us this poem in 1938. He already then felt the terrible *khurban* that was approaching the Yiddish *shtetl* and *shtetlech* of Poland. Grosbard wrote us at that time that this poem is the first in a cycle of poems called "A Grus Bergelson Fun Shtetl" that I'll shortly be sending you. We awaited the future poems, but meanwhile the war broke out and destroyed the Jewish life in Poland. From Y. Grosbard we not only did not receive any poems, but neither did we receive any word or sign of his life. Where is he to be found, this loving, sorrowful poet Grosbard who, in the year 1939, believed that "Wonders will yet appear"?...

*

288

Generally speaking, Grosbard had a struggling nature, was always ready to discuss various problems, especially those regarding literature, poetry, art and music. He loved to sing and play. He didn't like beating around the bush, as he wrote in his poem "*Aibikut's Dibros*" (Eternal Words), published in "*Yalkut Hamoadim* (B) in Buenos Aires 1943:

> There are all kinds of words, hard as granite,
> Simple ones, raw ones, that flow from blood.
> Words that strike like lightning and remain cold --
> Bengalish fire that it quickly extinguished.

Yosl hated this cold phony fire and for this reason he experienced deeply all of life's events. Just before the war, when eastern Jews were driven out of Germany, he wrote in his song, "Plitim" (Refugees) published in "*Folks' Tzeitung*" June 1939:

> These days --
> That are coursing through you
> Are flames
> Of a burning stream.

In a poem from the cycle "Here", he wrote:

> And against the dark waves of today,
> And against the enemy --
> I shall struggle with raging force,
> And fight with teeth,

With arms and legs --
Until - - -
There will arrive in my land
The brotherly hand...

In another of Yosl's poems we read:

My doubting heart never was
Believe -- that wonders will yet happen.

Unfortunately he never lived to see the day of this wonder. Recently I have received articles from friends, from newspapers and journals where there are reviews about Grosbard. I also received an article from friend Appel from the *"Forward"* of January 23, 1960. There the writer Sh. L. Shneiderman wrote the following about a trip to Yosl's place of birth, Serotsk:

"Serotsk also produced a talented young poet and artist, Yosl Grosbard who, shortly before the outbreak of war started to get attention from the Jewish literary and artistic circles of Warsaw. His deeply-sorrowful poems of the *shtetl* express the spirit of the lyricist and the eye of the artist."

"In 1939, just before the catastrophe, Yosl Grosbard wrote a cycle of poems in which there is expressed the deep worries that prevailed in his birthplace, Serotsk. It was a sort of premonition of the great khurban."

There are the poems called a "Grus Din Bergelson fun Shtetl" that I have mentioned above. Shneiderman, however, makes the mistake in thinking that Grosbard was describing Serotsk. During the 20's he was living in Ciechanów and he wrote the poem in Ciechanów, but the poem is characteristic of the majority of Yiddish *shtetlech* in Poland. That's the greatness of the poem, in that it generalizes and expressed that which is characteristic...

Everyone in Ciechanów knew Yosl in his day-to-day life when he was working hard as a house painter in order to earn a livelihood. Little did they believe how talented this young man was, but those who knew him closer felt, as they spoke with him, that he was a person who had deep feelings for the suffering and endurance of those around him. In this sense his poem, "The Woman with the Milk Pitcher." In this simple way he showed much artistic empathy and rich form.

His talent started to deepen and widen, both in poetic and artistic creation. Unfortunately, it was all to end. Together with his wife and young child and our parents he, like all our Jews of Ciechanów, were tortured and murdered by the Germans in Auschwitz.

289

Songs of Yosl Grosbard

A Grus Dir Bergelson fun Shtetl

With words from my gray spirit
A letter, I write you, in a poem
Oh winds! Carry my regards far off --
About my *shtetl,* tell all
Summer has flown away together with all the birds
The days -- filled up with grayness
The *yishuv* has huddled up together
Embraced, like children with their mother.

Gloomy autumn is now here
The sky above is patchy -- gray on gray,
All the roads are bare and empty
Full of mud after the rain.
Angry winds are now around
And are neighing just like horses
And strive to uproot hundred-year-old trees
From their deep roots in the soil.

The despair covers the narrow streets
And remains standing at the end of the alleys
And wanders back and forth
For where else does it have to go?...
The marketplace -- how old it looks in all this cold
It was once boisterous -- now a finished hero
At a table, a woman freezing stands, a Jew
And behind them the stones often shine red.

The railway station -- an indifferent local
Its walls sinking and dreaming in its stony sorrow.

290

Trains come and quickly leave
And smoke and fumes quietly rock the way
In the houses of the rich the radio plays concerts loudly
And present-day joyful music as well.
And green parrots still draw out from envelopes
Of 'katarinkes' -- the blue good fortune.

More losers now than ever
Fear and angst -- await at every door
Not only by *Reb* Gedalya are the shutters closed
It happens: in the morning night lurks here.
Oh You, great Judge so far away

Forgive my sorrowful talk
My suffering heart never did exist
Believe -- that miracles will yet happen!...

The Woman with the Milk Pitcher

In windy weather, in frost and snow
Like a part of the daily-gray shine
A dark shadow passes in front of my window
The gnarled shadow on the opposite wall --
The woman with the milk pitcher in her hand.

In houses, in courtyards with wooden steps
There await her, in kitchens, the pots and the saucepans
The old woman comes with her pitcher of milk, early
          each morning
And fills the utensils with milk
All alone, in her old age, she makes her rounds.

291

> For *groshns* that she gathers each day in this way
> She brings home for the nourishment herring and bread.
> She chews up her food with her toothless mouth
> That's how she spends her old years, she and her
>   pitcher.
>
> Like birds that have flown from their nests at summer's
>   end
> Across oceans, to warmer lands,
> So children have long ago parted
> And an aching heart is left...
> At least if the birds would return next year
> And greet us happily with twitter and tweet,
> But children have vanished like stone in the sea
> And mother is left alone with a broken heart.
>
> Recently, in the dim light, at my window a while,
> The old woman with her pitcher there stood
> She motions with her hands, giving me to understand:
> "Just think about this -- Is it really possible, that which
>   is written
> That one will no longer be able to sell the bit of milk
> That it's finished!
> No longer to climb stairs, go from house to house?"
> And she ends with a piercing crying again:
> "All that's left is a rope on one's neck,
> And simply to expire thus."

(Written in 1938, published in "Der Shpigl", Buenos Aires January 1945)

292

Shimon Stern

Tears

The following poem was written by the youngest brother of the great poet, Yisroel Shtern. Shimon lived many years in Ciechanów, where he was active in the Zionist organization as well as culturally. He wrote poems. Some appeared in the journal, "Shprotzungen" in the late 1920's in Warsaw.

Yisroel Shtern had another brother, Hirsh. (He was called "Hershele"), a well-known figure in Warsaw's Writers' Union. He was on friendly terms with everyone, was a fine singer of folk songs. Many of them he composed for the famous folk-singer, Kipnis. He also spent much time with his family in Ciechanów. By trade he was a boot-maker.

This poem "Tears" Shimon dedicated to his artist friend Yehoshua Grosbard.

Holy are those who cry
When days approach like messengers of doom
Of years loaded with pain
Of growing-up years,
When such a childish fear strikes
Without reason, not making sense.
"Without reason, not making sense"
When a mother stands at the bedside of her dying child
And there is no proper place for her heartfelt prayers --
So she cries and cries
And her hot motherly tears fall
Upon ice-cold stones
Upon ice-cold stones
When days start to press upon the old man
And choke,
When minutes dance around him
Words remain empty
Like shadows of a fading light --
God of mercy and grace
And he cries and he cries
Holy are those who cry.

293

Drawing of the Grosbard family in Ciechanów on Proshnitzer Street, by Yehoshua Grosbard

294   blank

295

The Son and the Grandchild of the Ciechanówer Rebbe, Reb Avremele

Avraham Pinkhas Unger

The Ciechanówer *Rebbe, Reb* Avremele Landau, had a son, *Reb* Wolf, who was greatly beloved by his father's *Hasidim*. Finally, some of the *Hasidim*, mainly those of Warsaw and Łodz, crowned *Reb* Wolf as their *Rebbe*, and they chose the city Strikov for the *Rebbe's* place. Strikov is only three miles from Łodz. At that time there were already two railways in Łodz. One went to Warsaw, the other to Dombrove, Bendin and Sosnowitz. From Dombrove a train went to Ivangrad and passed through Keltzer and Radomer provinces. This helped a lot for Keltzer and Radomer district *Hasidim* to come to the Strikover *Rebbe.*

The *Hasidim* built a nice large house in Strikov for their *Rebbe*, and a large *Bais Hamedresh* as well. It was called "The Cold *Bais Hamedresh.*" In addition they also built a smaller *Bais Hamedresh*. In the large *Bais Hamedresh* they *davened* only on *Shavuos, Rosh Hashana* and *Yom Kippur*, because on those *yomtovim* several hundred *Hasidim* came to the *rebbe*. The small *Bais Hamedresh* was long, with many windows on both sides, with a large bookcase. There they *davened* on week-days, on *Shabbat* and also on the *Yomtovim* -- when not many *Hasidim* came -- *Pesakh* and *Sukot*. On one side of the *Bais Hamedresh* there stood a large house with a gate through which one entered and there was a second door for entering the *Bais Hamedresh* and the *Rebbe's* house.

On the other side of the yard there was an orchard. In there stood a hut with tables where the *Rebbe* rested after a walk in the orchard. In the huts the *Rebbe* received wealthy *Hasidim* and *rabbonim* who came to ask the *Rebbe* for advice regarding their *Kehillot*, or to discuss Torah matters with him. At the end of the small *Bais Hamedresh* there stood the *Rebbe's* house where the *Rebbe* greeted the *Hasidim* who came to him. In this house the *Hasidim* also bade the *Rebbe* farewell when they departed for home.

To the *Rebbe, Reb* Wolf, all kinds of *Hasidim* came, rich and poor. Religious functionaries also came, *rabbonim* from smaller and larger cities, cantors, young men who boarded at their in-laws, and so on. Some of the young men came to the *Rebbe* asking for ordination to be rabbis.

The *Rebbe's shames* was called Groinem. His job was to select the *Hasidim* who would sit at the *Rebbe's* table. After *davening*, Groinem once more called out each *Hasid* by name to join the *Rebbe* at his table. He seated the *Hasidim*, each one at his place, and when the *Rebbe's* sons and sons-in-law were seated, Groinem would call the *Rebbe*, telling him that all are seated at the table. He returned and called out: "Quiet please, the *Rebbe* is entering." All, like one man, rose to their feet. The *Rebbe* said *Kiddush* over a large wine-cup. Wine kept being added to the *Rebbe's* cup so that there would be enough for everyone. Some Hasidim hid the wine of the *Rebbe's kiddush* cup to bring it home for a sick one, so that he should drink from this wine and recover.

The *Rebbe* washed his hands -- and after him the *Hasidim*. The *Rebbe* made the *Hamotzi*. Everyone got a piece of his *challah*. After this the *Rebbe* got a large platter of fish so that he should have enough so that there would even be some left over. After the *Rebbe* finished passing the fish around to all those who were at the table, Groinem placed the platter with the remaining fish in the center of the table. A grab was made for the remaining fish by those who were not sitting at the *Rebbe's* table. They had finished eating early so that they could come to the *Rebbe's* Torah talk on time.

296

When the *Rebbe* was giving his Torah talk it was so quiet that one could hear a pin drop. When the *Rebbe* finished his Torah talk he would call upon a *Hasid* who had a good voice to sing *zmirot*. After the blessings the *Hasidim* danced until it was time for the afternoon worship. After that they ate *Shalosh Seudah* and *davened* the evening prayers.

After evening prayers the *Hasidim* came to say farewell to the *Rebbe*. Each one would leave a note with his wishes (a good livelihood, to marry off a daughter, health) and thereby left a contribution.

When *Reb* Wolf died his son, *Reb* Motl, became the *Rebbe* in Strikover, but he didn't have half the number of *Hasidim* as his father. Many of the Strikover *Hasidim* started to go to the Alexander *Rebbe* who up to that time was considered a small-town *Rebbe*. Other Strikover *Hasidim* started to go to the Sakhochover brilliant one, *Reb* Avremele, and still others to the Gerer *Rebbe*.

297

The *Rebbe*, *Reb* Motl, was very learned, knew the *Tanakh* very well also. He knew many chapters of *Tanakh* off by heart. He could also read and write *loshen kodesh* very well, as well as other languages and was the author of two books. One book was called: *Ki Mordecai Doresh Tov*.

Once the *Rebbe* saw me reading a Hebrew newspaper (at the *Rebbe's* house). He asked me where I got it. I told him that a few fellows subscribed to it. There was something that I didn't understand in the paper, so I would ask the *Rebbe* and he would explain it to me.

I learned by *Rebbe Reb* Motl and also in the *Rebbe's* house itself I read many books, both Yiddish and Hebrew ones. Often the *Rebbe* would see me reading a book or a newspaper but he didn't comment.

(From the book, *My Hometown Strikove*, published by "Arbeiter Ring" New York 1957.)

Yehoshua Podruznik — The Ciechanówer Writer

Yehoshua was born in Ciechanów in 1894 into a *Hasidic* family. He learned his Yiddish studies from his father, Yitzhak, a Gerer *Hasid* who also had an interest in modern Hebrew and Yiddish literature.

At the age of 13 Yehoshua and his parents left for Antwerp. There he completed high school and then worked in the diamond industry, studying at the university at the same time.

Podruznik started his journalistic writing at the age of 16 as a correspondent for *"Friend"*, where he regularly worked until the outbreak of World War I, when the newspaper ceased. At the same time he published several articles in the Parisian *"Neyem Journal"* ((New Journal) and in the *"Yiddisher Velt"* (Jewish World) where one article concerned the National Language Question in Belgium.

Together with the engineer Y. Lifshitz, Podruznik published a monthly journal in 1913, called *"Der Yidisher Student"* (the Jewish Student) that was the first attempt at a periodical that would unite the various thousands of Jewish students of eastern Europe who studied in the west European universities.

298

During that period Podruznik, together with M. Lipson and I. Krefliak, edited the first Jewish newspaper in Belgium as well. It was called *"Der Ma arev"* (The West), a weekly that was published only four times.

At the start of World War I Prodruznik left for London, where he worked for *"Di Tzeit"* (The Time). Then he went to New York. There he worked at various times in *"Tog"* (Day), *"Tzukunft"* (Future), *"Vahrheit"* (Present). He was on the editorial board and publisher of a large work, *"A Togbukh fun Der Milkhomeh"* (A Diary of the War). He also wrote feuilletons in *"Kurds"* (Art), at one time translating the novel, *"Roiteh Lily"* (Red Lily, Farlag "Yiddish", New York).

When Jabotinsky founded the Jewish Legion, Podruznik joined. After World War I he returned to London, where he once more worked for *"Di Tzeit"*, was one of the founders of the monthly *"Renaissance"* under the editorship of Leo Kenig, and in 1920 ceased his journalistic work and founded *"Das Internatzionale Tzeitungs Bureau"* (The International Newspaper Bureau) -- an institution that made a name for itself with its bibliographic collections. This newspaper bureau served various governments in historical and community societies and so on. Podruznik collected over a million excerpts from newspapers and journals that have a connection with Jews.

In 1924 he also edited an English journal devoted to the profession of journalism.

For the last five years Podruznik is working on a large five-volume undertaking on the theme: *"Moderne Yiddishe Merkverdikeytn"* (Modern Jewish Matters).

(Source: Zalmen Rai in -- *Lexicon Fun Der Yidisher Literatur*, Philadelphia, vol. 2, p. 842).

Zalmen Raisen's *Lexicon*, as is well known, only includes biographical information up to the year 1928, when this was published. Regarding the further life of Podruznik we discovered the following: He is carrying on with his newspaper bureau to the present day, in partnership with his son.

299

300	blank

301

In the Years of the German Extermination of the Jews

The Polish Preparation for the War

Binyamin Appel

Already in the first months of 1939 we started to feel that something evil was awaiting us. We knew what Hitlerism signified for the Jewish people. We felt a dark cloud descending upon us

The Polish state was preparing for war. In Ciechanów, committees were formed to protect its residents during air raids. The population was taught how to extinguish fires when the enemy bombs the shtetl. Commanders were appointed for every courtyard. Every courtyard was ordered to have a reserve of sand and water to extinguish the fire. The windows had to be pasted with strips of paper.

Jews stock up on food. The situation is tense. People stop thinking about a livelihood. Stores are abandoned. One thing is on everyone's mind: What will happen to us Jews when war will start. The terrible suspense sweeps before our eyes; everyone runs to hear news on the radio.

Every day new politicians arose, predicting when war would start and what its nature would be. There was only one thing that we did not foresee -- that in our century there would be found, in cultured Germany, beasts in the form of human beings who would be insatiable in their thirst for Jewish blood...

On August 25 the conscription order was issued. Men up to the age of 40 must enlist in the army. One day before the outbreak of war a commission went from house to house in Ciechanów to check if proper preparations had been made to extinguish fires. The commission also informed everyone that the following day -- Friday -- there will be a general drill: our planes will fly and drop incendiary bombs throughout the city and the population must be ready to put out the fires. Everyone prepared for the "General Drill." Some Jews were given white armbands and were appointed as commanders.

That sorrowful Friday, September 1, 1939 arrived. In the morning the German planes appeared and shot down with machine ammunition. Everyone went out to see, and Poles declared that there's no reason to fear. "They are ours." Soon, though, we found out the bitter truth that war had started.

302

In the afternoon several planes were already spotted and bombs started to fall on our *shtetl*. That same Friday Mlava was also bombed and nearly half the city was burnt. People started to run in all directions.

Shabbat morning refugees started to arrive from Mlava, some in wagons and some on foot. Many remained on the road. We sent wagons to bring them to Ciechanów. We tried to greet the Mlava Jews and housed them temporarily. It didn't last long though. A few hours later we Ciechanówers also became refugees.

The wealthier ones were the first to run away in wagons. The representatives of the Polish government who were supposed to protect us also ran away. The panic in the *shtetl* was great and no one knew where to run. From hour to hour the shooting became closer. In every house everything was packed in readiness to leave, but the question remained -- where to?

The mood was very oppressive. From somewhere a rumor spread that when the Germans conquer a city they gather all those men who are capable of fighting, and they are shot. My family forced me to run away. Not having any other choice, I started off on foot in the direction of Warsaw.

On the main road leading to Warsaw I saw in front of me the whole misery of war. The roads were full of people: Jews, Christians, young and old, everyone running. The German planes fly quite low and shoot at the civilian population. People fell the way stalks of wheat fall in a field beneath the scythe. The roads wee covered with thousands of shot bodies.

The Germans in the City — The First Jewish Victims

Monday, September 4, the Germans captured Ciechanów. The following Jews perished when the *shtetl* was captured: Yenkl Renboim was shot. Shimon Garfinkl, a bookseller, was returning from *davening* when a bullet shot him; Pesakh Lipsky's son was shot right at home.

303

We soon found out about the *khurban* that the Germans brought upon Jews in other places: Mlava was half-burnt; from Proshnitz all Jews were sent out. From Poltusk also the Jews were sent out and half were shot on the way.

Two days after the capture of Ciechanów the German military called all the Jews to the *shul*. A German officer spoke to the Jews to voluntarily leave Ciechanów. He promised them assistance if they would leave, and assured that it would be better for us if we leave.

A brief consultation took place amongst the most prominent Jews of the *shtetl* and the word was not to leave. One of the assembled called out: "We were born here and here we will get lost." The German representative replied: "If you choose to remain here, know that you have no rights. You will have to carry out all commands that we issue, and you come under the Nuremberg Laws."

The crowd dispersed and the cruel life under German rule started. Everyone had great fear. The German acts of vandalism started. They spread the *Sefer Torahs* out on the sidewalks; the *shul* and *Bais Hamedresh* in which generations of Jews had sent their prayers to the Almighty the Germans converted into a factory for the repair of automobiles, and the seizure of Jews for forced labor started.

Jews are seized for forced labor in the marketplace

304

The work wouldn't have been so hard, but in addition to the work they beat us, and they sought the most difficult work with which to torture the Jews.

Every morning the Germans ran amongst the Jewish houses and grabbed Jews for forced labor. People started to hide. In every house a hideout was made in the loft. Woe to those Jews who were dragged out of their hiding places. They were beaten and tortured without pity.

At the same time we lived in great fear because we heard that all the Jews of the surrounding *shtetlech* had been sent away: Nashelsek Drabnin, Ratszeans, Zuramin, Ripin, Shierptz. The expelled Jews were sent in the direction of Warsaw. They weren't allowed to take any of their belongings. Every day we were ready to become wanderers, but the expulsion was spared for us for the time being.

Jewish refugees who had been expelled, and had run away on the road, we took into our crowded homes.

Jews who are laboring under the supervision of the Germans

305

The Germans started to take over in our *shtetl*. A mayor and many police came and they established order. First they established a *Judenrat* with Ben-Tzion Ehrlikh at its head. Every resident had to register both with the *Judenrat* and with the German police, and everyone received a card with the mark: "*Yude.*" They stopped seizing people for forced labor.

A command was given that every Jew from the age of 15 on must present himself each morning in the marketplace for work. It was woe to anyone who didn't appear. The Germans already had prepared lists of the Jews who were then in the *shtetl.* From the marketplace groups of Jews were sent off to labor.

Murder, Terror and the Destruction of Jewish Homes

At the beginning of 1940 a Gestapo member shot a Jew in a murderous way. There was a Jew in our *shtetl* by the name of Avraham-Aaron Kelman, a religious Jew, the supervisor of the Talmud Torah. In the years prior to the war he accomplished much for Jewish education. Avraham-Aaron gathered all the *melamdim* in one place, and under his supervision all children were taught, rich and poor alike. He also provided all the poor folk, strangers, with a place to eat and sleep. For the arrested ones -- kosher food and food for the spirit, such as a book or a religious text.

The first *Shabbat* of the year 1940, right in the morning, Avraham-Aaron went out of his house, dressed in his *Shabbes-capote* and his silk hat, as he was accustomed.

There were two exits in the house of Hersh Berman where Avraham-Aaron was living: one to the marketplace, the other to the Optaik (Pharmacy) Street. He wanted to look out to see what was going on outside, when one of the Gestapo called to him. The Jew was terribly frightened and withdrew into the house. The German followed him and shot him near the door. Just as he was clad, so he was buried. His death made a deep impression in Ciechanów.

That winter there were terrible frosts. Jews suffered bitterly and their ears and the fingers on their hands froze as they worked.

306

In the second month of 1940 a command was given that Jews must wear yellow patches, and must remove their hats when they meet a German. The *Judenrat* was responsible for carrying out this order. The yellow patches were round, 10 centimeters in size. One patch had to be worn in the front, on the left side of the chest, the other on the shoulder.

An order was issued that Jews must not walk on the sidewalk, only in the gutter. This was connected with morale and physical pain, because winter time when the snow melted, one had to splash about in the puddles. Besides, the Jews didn't have proper shoes.

The situation got increasingly worse. Whoever could and had the strength tried to run away. Everyone wanted to save their life. The wandering, however, was also very dangerous because there was a command that no one must leave Ciechanów without permission. Every resident was registered, yet many people risked going into Australenko where the Russian border was, and so they crossed over into Russia.

Furthermore, an order was given to beautify Ciechanów. The Germans wanted to establish Ciechanów as a "residential" city of the captured territories and refashion it according to the German style. Meanwhile they started to tear down houses and this affected mainly the Jewish residents. First on the Warsaw Street on one side: from the marketplace up to the cinema, the houses were torn down in order to widen the street. The work was carried out by Jews. Women were also taken to do this work.

The tearing down of the Jewish houses brought new suffering for the Jewish population because the better homes were seized by the Germans. When a house was going to be torn down, the owner was notified one hour in advance. During this hour the house had to be emptied; if not, the Germans confiscated everything that was there and gave it to the Poles. Many Jews had to live without a roof over their heads in the winter. The *Judenrat* started to create order and assigned residences. Five families were placed in a single dwelling. Unfortunately, the shortage of living quarters was taken advantage of by the Jewish *makhers*. Whoever had money to pay the Jewish quartermaster got a residence immediately. Whoever didn't have money lived in a stall or in a loft.

307

The tearing down of the Jewish houses.

308   blank

309

Reb Yishaiyeh Cohen beside his destroyed home

The *Judenrat* also formed a labor force that provided the Germans with men and women each day. For the distribution of labor the same principle applied. For money one could remain at home and whoever didn't "bribe" had to work without pay every day.

The distribution of food for the Jews was according to ration cards. Five *deca* bread was distributed each day per person, and ten *deca* meat for a week. The meat was not *kosher* because Jewish slaughter was strictly forbidden.

No private trade existed. Craftsmen were not allowed to work without a permit. The poverty was horrendous. People starved. They started to sell their household belongings to the Polish population for meager food. The Poles got rich from Jewish belongings.

The German forces also forced the Jews to relinquish their best clothes that were then sent off to Germany.

The Open Ghetto and the Lasting Hunger

It appears that the Germans couldn't tolerate the fact that the Jews had good relationships with the Poles so they ordered that the Poles must not mingle with the Jews from the time when the Jews were given a quarter where only the Jews were allowed to live while the

Poles had their quarter. There was no fenced ghetto in Ciechanów. Jews also got a Jewish doctor that the Germans sent, and the Polish doctors were not allowed to visit Jewish patients.

Because of the crowding and uncleanliness in which Jews were forced to live, various sicknesses broke out amongst them. Jews died of hunger, frost, catastrophic lack of nutrition. The Jewish quarter looked like a Jewish cemetery with living dead.

The terrible hunger caused certain persons with weak characters to serve the Gestapo. Some of the cobblers, tailors, "buried" their goods. There were other Jews who dealt with life necessities that were called "special" products. The Jewish snitchers would bring these items to the Gestapo and get well paid for this. Ciechanów Jews didn't occupy themselves with this ugly work, but there were certain refugees from the surrounding *shtetlech* who created problems for us in this respect.

310

Jewish property robbed by the Germans in Ciechanów

Under such circumstances we lived in great fear for the morrow, and waited patiently and hoped for a change.

On June 22, 1941, when war broke out between Germany and Russia new hope arose. "Politicians" explained that such a situation would not last long. There was talk that an end must come, "either life or death." The mood was that we would perish with them. The Germans ordered shelters to be built in every courtyard. Fresh work arose for the Jews. In every courtyard shelters were made. In the evening every window had to be blacked-out so that no light should be seen. After six in the evening nobody was allowed out in the street.

311

The city and all around the city was built with new houses. Complete quarters were constructed and occupied by Germans. Various German firms established themselves here and forced Jews to work there. These German businessmen discovered that Jews are also capable of working and this was a great wonder for them. They met good Jewish craftsmen. A German newspaper that appeared during the occupation in Ciechanów praised the "good Jewish craftsmen."

I worked for the above-mentioned Germans and they asked me, "how is it that a Jew can work?" I explained to them the misconception with which they had been living.

With the command to walk in the gutter and not on the sidewalk, more than one Jew paid with his life. The Germans deliberately ran over a Jew, angrily complaining for not clearing the way for them.

Soon a command came to drive out of Ciechanów those Jews who are weak or too old to work...

The First Deportation of Ciechanów Jews

On December 11, 1941, the Germans sent 1200 Jews out of Ciechanów to Neustadt, where there was a closed ghetto. We all were very frightened. We knew that this deportation would not be completed without victims.

The assembly point for the deportation was in the castle. The *Judenrat* brought together a group of people, so-called militia, who were appointed by the Germans to keep order in the castle so that beatings would not take place. German murderers arrived, drunks, with sticks in their hands. They stood at the door where everyone had to pass and they beat every Jew fiercely. Many of the unfortunate ones were incapable of mounting the wagon by themselves, so they had to be lifted on to the waiting wagon. This wasn't enough for the murderers so they shot one of the Jewish militia -- Alba Blum. He fell dead from the murderous shot while he was trying to keep order. Some of the people died on the way because of the beatings. The Germans informed the *Judenrat* that if one of the deported ones will be found, he, together with the people with whom he would be found, would be shot.

The "selected" ones, so to speak, those who remained in Ciechanów, attempted to help the deported ones in any way possible, but our help wasn't able to ease the needs of the unfortunate ones.

312

The Deportation of the Ciechanów Jews

Some of them returned on foot to Ciechanów. Whoever the Germans caught on the way, they shot. In Ciechanów they caught Aaron Kirshenbaum, who was hiding with his daughter in the loft of his in-law, Aaron Gelbard. They were arrested and a brother, Binyamin Kirshenbaum, was also dragged in. He was the secretary of the *Judenrat.* They were all sentenced to death.

***

In the year 1942 the hunger and death increased. People died of hunger and cold. The Germans appointed a new head responsible for overseeing the Jews. He was a murderer. Every day he beat men and women. One evening after a rain, he went up to a place where Jews were living and called out: "All Jews must come out." Later he sent one of his men to make sure that no one had hidden. He went from house to house and found five Jews hidden in a loft.

The Jews, who already looked like dead, were brought down. They were terribly beaten. They were arrested and sentenced to death by hanging. With great pomp the Germans ordered a gallows to be erected.

313

They called the *Judenrat* out, as well as all the Jews of Ciechanów, and in the presence of all they forced Jews to hang the five Jews.

When I recall this frightful incident my body shivers. Children stood witnessing the hanging of their fathers and they weren't allowed to cry. The murderers looked into the eyes of each and every one. It was prohibited to cry. The five victims hung for three hours, from six to nine in the evening. The names of the martyrs are: Simkha Sodek, Dovid Mlotzker, Teiblum, Velvl Grudover's son, and a young man from Proshnitz. I have forgotten his name.

Under threat of being shot, Jews were forced to witness the handing of their brothers

314

Germans Destroy the Jewish Quarter and the Jewish Cemetery

The destruction of the houses continued. Before long all the houses where Jews had lived were destroyed. The Jewish street, the *Bais Hamedresh*, the *shul*, one side of the marketplace, half of the Warsaw Street, the street of the Jewish butchers. No sign remained of human habitation. The Germans also started destroying the old Jewish cemetery that was holy for everyone because of the *Tzadik's* grave that was there. The Germans destroyed the fence, later the monuments; the *Tzadik's Ohel* remained and was used as a chamber for storing work tools.

A brief meeting took place and it was decided, with the approval of the religious leaders, to remove the bones of the *Tzadik* from the *Ohel*. The opportunity was taken advantage of on a Sunday when no one worked there. Very early a few *frum* Jews went in. They dug and took out some bones because there were so few, placed them in a container (which the writer of these lines had made) and buried it in the new cemetery.

The following day the *Ohel* was destroyed so that no trace remained that there had once been a holy place here. More than seventy-one years Jews from all over the world had come to the *yahrzeit* of the *Tzadik.*

The same year, *Rosh Hashana -- Yom Kippur,* The German guard of the Jewish quarter, a gruesome murderer and sadist, gathered all the Ciechanów Jews and went together with them all to the new cemetery. There he commanded them to chop down all the monuments and destroy the fence. The place was transformed so that no one could recognize what had once been there. A case occurred that some *Sefer Torahs* were rescued and there was no place to hide them, so a few Jews went to the cemetery (before it was liquidated). There they dug a pit and buried the *Sforim*. The Germans found about this and ordered the Judenrat to bring the people who buried the *Sforim*. The Jews were arrested and they paid with their lives. Their names are: my brother, Mordecai Appel, Shmuel-Yaacov Pozarek, Yosl Shtifenholtz, Kalman Bagreber.

***

315

After *Succot* we felt a chill in our bones. Rumors started to spread that the remaining Jews would be liquidated. One didn't want to believe that the end is approaching. We convinced ourselves that it couldn't be this frightful. Still, the fear gave us no rest. We felt that our days are numbered. But we were so tired out that the worst decree no long bothered us. We were ready to go to our death with joy. We envied the dead.

We build bunkers in which to hide

316

The Final Liquidation of the Ciechanów Jews

On November 1, 1942, the bitter order came that all Jews must, on the following day, Sunday, leave Ciechanów. The tumult was great, not only on the part of the Jews but also on the part of the Germans, because all the Jews were working for them and they had no one to fill these vacancies. The Germans started to intervene with the higher powers to postpone the evacuation for another few days. Apparently this appeal was effective. A second order was issued stating that we remain until November 6.

On Tuesday, November 4, 1942, eighteen hundred Jews were expelled from Ciechanów. They were divided into two groups: those capable of work and those not. The first group, those capable of working, were lined up in rows of one hundred, each hundred with an elder who was responsible for them.

The following morning, Friday, the remaining Jews assembled in the castle. Young and old gathered there. There the Germans selected older people, men and women. They were lined up against the wall and shot. Amongst them was the religious leader of Ciechanów. The rest of the people were put on wagons and dispatched to the Mlava ghetto.

My family and I were in the second group that left Ciechanów. It was already quiet in the street. Nobody was seen -- no Jews Poles. I left the city forever, the place where I had lived most of my life.

According to what I know, the first group was sent to Auschwitz and the second group to Treblinka. I managed to avoid the gas chamber and I was sent from lager to lager.

317

The last expulsion of the Ciechanów Jews. Germans drive out the Jews

The death march in the Ciechanów fortress

318   blank

319

אויטאָס מיט ייִדן פֿאָרן פֿון מאַרק צו דער באַן, וואָס וועט זיי פֿירן צום טויט

מכוניות עם יהודים נוסעים מכּכר השוק לרכבת ומשם למחנה המוות

Trucks with Jews depart from the marketplace to the train that will take them to their death

The last road to death

320 blank

321

Monday, April 30, 1945 will always remain a day of remembrance for me and for all those who were liberated that day, a day for which we had waited so long.

When I realized that I am actually free, I started to try to figure out where in the world I stand, whom have I lost. I saw my loneliness and those whom I had lost forever.

In that great *khurban* I lost my most beloved and dearest. I won't let your memory be forgotten. I will guard your memory as long as I live. When I write these lines I picture everyone. The tragic events have not faded from my memory. I still live with them even though I'm in America ten years now and I'm not bad off. But my present good life cannot wipe from my mind those tragic events which we Jews endured. May the bright memory of our homes in the old country, and that of our dear relatives and friends who perished in the name of *Kiddush Hashem,* never be forgotten by us.

———

322

My Experiences in World War II

The Underground Movement at the Beginning of the German Occupation
Noach Zabludowicz

I was born in Ciechanów in 1919. My father, Moishe Aryeh, was a merchant, and my mother kept house. Both perished in Auschwitz. We were eight brothers and one sister. My five brothers and I are in the land. The sister and two brothers were tortured to death in Auschwitz.

At the beginning of 1940 I was in Ciechanów under German rule. One day the German Military commander called all the Jews together at the *shul* in our *shtetl*. When all were gathered, he gave a speech and declared that in a short time his Military would leave Ciechanów and in its place there would arrive a German civilian leadership. At such a time the situation of the Jews would get worse and he would therefore advise us to leave Ciechanów and to cross over to the Soviet side. He declared his willingness to provide us with comfortable transportation.

In reply one of the gathered Jews said in German: "Here we were born and here we will get lost." At the command of the commandant we all went home. Shortly thereafter the German Military did leave and German civilian powers took over, consisting of S.S. and other police formations. As city mayor, a German by the name of Rot was appointed, as well as a German commander of the region.

The German occupiers restricted the area in which Jews were allowed to live. An open ghetto was established in the center of Ciechanów. Jewish property was confiscated: goods, houses, jewelry and all valuables.

Ciechanów was not included in the general-government. The Germans called this section the "New Residence Place," and the name was changed to Ciekhenau. The Germans tore down the Jewish homes and the Jews had to move to other quarters, and as a result we ended up living in terribly cramped quarters, sometimes three, four families in one room. Mail no longer reached us Jews so that we should no longer have any contact with the outside world, so that we wouldn't know what's happening elsewhere.

323

We, the youth, organized an underground organization. We met often to discuss means of protecting ourselves from the terrible decrees. Those who took part in the organization were my two brothers: Pinkhas and Khanan, Moishe Kolka, Godl Zilber, Noah

Eisenberg, Yosef Eisenberg, Motl Bergson, Yisroel Likhtenstein and Dovid Shmidt. Noah and Yosef Eisenberg are no longer alive.

Playing the Role of a Volksdeutch and Actual Contact Man for the Ghettos

The Germans issued a decree that forbade the Jews to work as chauffeurs and in general to carry out any kind of work. I didn't pay attention to this decree and approached the German leader of the transport, Kesler, introducing myself as chauffeur by trade. He examined me and confirmed that I am suitable for him, and gave his approval for me to get this position.

After working for him for a short time, when I saw that my work pleased him, I told him the truth, that unfortunately I can't work for him because I'm a Jew and Jews are not allowed to be chauffeurs. To this he replied: "Don't worry, you'll work as my chauffeur and I'll make all the arrangements for you. A few days later he came to me with a permit in the name of Zabludowicz, but instead of Noah there was the name Robert and underlined that I am a *volksdeutch*. The contents of the permit were as follows:

"Dem Kraftfuhrer Robert Zabludowicz, (Volksdeuttscher) is gestatet dem Lastwagen 32439 zu furen. Die Gen aehmigung ist erteitt, dass am Reichsdeutsche Kraftfuhrer ein Mangel ist."

("The chauffeur Robert Zabludowicz, a Volksdeutch, is permitted to drive the auto 32439. This permission is granted because there is a shortage of Reichsdeuttsch chauffeurs.")

At the bottom the red stamp of the regional commandant for communication was added. During that period I was on the road all week except for Shabbat. On Shabbat he allowed me to return to the ghetto, when I would meet with the chaverim to whom I would report on my activities. I also got instructions on how to conduct myself the following week.

I was in constant contact with the ghettos in Mlava, Neustadt, (Nova Miasto), Plonsk, Vlodava, Plotzk, Schenegov and others. I brought them information about everything that was happening.

324

There were instances when the Germans transferred the Jews from one ghetto to another or to do forced labor in the lagers. There they lived in terrible conditions. They were transported on wagons, on back roads, and they tried to hide. Those who were caught were shot immediately. During my trips with the German vehicle I saved many of these unfortunate Jews, some of whom I knew and others whom I did not know. Quite a few I took back to the ghettos from which they were taken for slave labor.

In 1941 the Germans expelled fifteen hundred Jews from Ciechanów, chasing them to Neustadt. Because of the crowding and hunger, many died. Many families were successful in returning illegally to Ciechanów.

Once, my Ciechanów *chaverim* asked me to save the Cohen family, whom the Gestapo was seeking. I agreed to this, and *Motzei Shabbat*, at midnight, I told the Cohen family to wait for me in a courtyard. I wanted to take advantage of the Saturday night because at that time my boss and his family were in Tilsitz. But just that Saturday he remained in the city. It was very dangerous to do something like this. Relatives tried to convince me not to attempt this, telling me that I'm endangering my life and the life of all my family. I didn't heed these warnings, however.

I got Avraham Baumgart to assist me. My auto was standing in the courtyard where Kesler lived. In order not to awaken my boss, I didn't ignite the motor. The two of us pushed the machine out onto the road. There, I started the motor and set off. Around midnight I reached the spot where the Cohen family was waiting. I took them all in the auto and set off for Neustadt.

I knew that on the way to Neustadt there were two turnpikes that are guarded by German gendarmes. I knew that there we were in great danger. However, there was no other way. As we approached the turnpike, I started to pick up speed. I put on the strong headlights and then weakened them (flashed them on and off). At the same time I signaled in the highest octave. This all had to signal that I'm traveling on an urgent mission and have no time for delays. I was successful with this behavior, and in this way we successfully reached the gate of the ghettoNeustadt.

325

The Jewish police who guarded the entrance on the inside didn't want to let in the people whom I had brought. My pleas and explanations were of no avail when I told them that I and my family were in great danger -- that every moment was very crucial. However, they refused to open the gate. I climbed over the fence and was immediately held by the Jewish police. Then I told them that I want to see the head of the *Judenrat*. One of the policemen accompanied me to the head, who was asleep in bed.

I woke him up and told him what was happening. He gave an order to open the gate immediately and to take in the family. Around three-thirty in the morning I returned home. It was like *Tisha B'Av*. Scared, they were sitting there crying. They thought that for sure the Germans had caught me.

Hangings in Ciechanów Ghetto

At the command of the Germans in Ciechanów, all the men had to line up each morning at seven o'clock in front of the city hall. From there people were sent to various forced labor. When the mayor (a German) arrived, all the Jews had to take off their hats and say in a chorus: *"Gut morgn, Herr Bergermeister."* ("Good morning, Mr. Mayor"). To this he replied: *Gut morgn, shveine."* ("Good morning, swine"). He checked the rows and whoever displeased him he hit with a rubber cudgel. The cudgel had a lead tip. After such a treatment the Jews were sent off to work. For work the pay was nine marks per day. From this scanty pay for forced labor the city treasury deducted fifty per cent for their funds.

People worked from dawn till dusk. In the ghetto people lived in terrible crowding. In one room -- several families. Beds had to be mounted one on top of the other; four levels, one on top of the other up to the ceiling. In the evenings the houses had to be blacked-out because from nine o'clock on it was forbidden to go out on the street. After nine the Germans made "inspections" in the houses.

326

There was a German in the Gestapo by the name of Rosenman who used to enter at night and wherever he found a man sleeping with a woman, he dragged him out of bed and asked him why he was sleeping with a woman. The man answered that he is doing so because there's no room to sleep separately. After such a reply, the German, revolver in hand, forced the man to go outside so that they could take their place with the woman and have intercourse. (Because of the crowding, several families lived in one room).

One night in 1942 this Rosenman, with a group of Germans, wanted to enter a courtyard where there was the house of the Jew, Lucatz Brink. The door of this house was locked. The gang, with Rosenman at the head, knocked down the door and shouted that all the men and women must go out. Everybody assembled in the courtyard. Rosenman selected five men: Teitelbaum, Sadek, Rumianek, Malotzker, Galadzer. The sadist led off these three deathly afraid Jews to the police station and accused them of sabotage -- supposedly because they didn't want to go to work. The fifth week the Germans again called all the Jews to gather at the marketplace. There the Germans erected a gallows and hung the five Jews.

Avraham-Aaron Kelman, a Jew, a *Talmid Khokhem*, the principal of the Ciechanów Talmud Torah, was walking one *Shabbat* morning, with his *tallis* under his arm, to *daven*. A German stopped him on the way and told him to stand still. Apparently the Jew didn't hear him, and walked on. The German shot him from behind, in the head, and the Jew fell down dead on the spot.

The Germans carried out other murderous acts on the Kirshenbaum family and other Jews. This was after fifteen hundred Jews, including Kirshenbaum, his wife and two children were deported from the Ciechanów ghetto and brought to Neustadt. After some time the Kirshenbaum family managed to escape from there and return to the Ciechanów ghetto. They hid in the house of their in-law, Aaron Gelbard. When the Gestapo discovered this they immediately arrested the whole family: Aaron Kirshenbaum, his daughter Rachel, the in-law and Kirshenbaum's brother, Binyamin, the treasurer of the *Judenrat*, because he didn't inform about the illegal return of the Kirshenbaum family to the ghetto.

327

The memorial plaque of the Ciechanów martyrs who were hung according to Eichmann's order

A funeral in Ciechanów ghetto

328   blank

329

To this group of victims the Germans added a Jew called Eliyahu Lindberg. He was accused of sabotage because during work he was told to bring a spade and he apparently, not understanding, brought a pitchfork.

These unfortunate Jews were detained for five weeks in Ciechanów prison. Afterwards they were transferred to Navidvover ghetto. There they were publicly hung in the presence of all the Jews.

People who witnessed the German murders told that the rope with which Gelbard was hung tore. The murders took another rope and hung him a second time. The daughter of Aaron Kirshenbaum didn't allow herself to be led to the gallows so the Germans shot her on the spot.

The Jews: Yisroel Yaacov Student, Avraham Freedman, Berish Kleinetz, were arrested by the Germans because they found a *Sefer Torah* hidden amongst the graves.

These Jews were held in prison for some time, then on *Krulova Buni* Square, a gallows was erected and in the presence of all the Jews the two martyrs were hung. Yisroel Yaacov Student died in prison from a heart attack. The Germans didn't allow for the arrangement of the martyrs. Only four Jews occupied themselves with the burial. I, and also the closest relatives of the family were the four. The hands of the martyrs were tied behind with barbed wire. The Germans ordered that they should be thrown into the grave in this way. The grave was the one in which the four *Sefrei Torah* had been found.

At the request of Kleinitz's son, the Germans allowed the father to be buried in another grave beside his grandfather. The others were simply cast into the grave. Only their shoes were removed.

*

One *Shabbat*, in May 1942, I was in the Ciechanów ghetto. Two new Gestapo men arrived. We heard that they were terribly cruel. They beat women, children, old folks, making no distinction and without any reason. When these sadists appeared on the street all the Jews scattered.

330

I remained standing and did not remove my hat in the presence of a German as was the rule here in the ghetto. One of the Germans started shouting at me in a brutal manner:

How dare I not remove my hat in his presence?" I replied, not knowing at the time what a dangerous thing I was doing. They became outraged and wanted immediately to take me and tie me up.

I started to run and suddenly bent down. The Germans, who were chasing me, tripped over me and fell. I took advantage of the moment and started to run faster. I succeeded in hiding in a courtyard. I lived with my family at that time in a courtyard with Kesler.

The next day I got an order from Kesler to bring, for a day's rest in the ghetto, the few Mlava Jews who were working in the nearby village, Bielin. When I was driving these Jews, I passed the courtyard where my mother lived. I found her in tears. She told me that the *Shturmfuhrer* Lisker had been searching for me. He carried on and created a scandal for my not being at home. Kesler, who heard the row of the German, found out from him the story of my running away, and this from his own son, one of the two who had chased me.

The *Shturmfehrer* demanded that I report to the police (German). Kesler replied to this that I am one of his responsible and best workers and he asks that this order not be carried out. My boss promised him that tomorrow he would detain me in his own house and he, the *Shturmfehrer* should come and do with me whatever he pleases. Kesler asked of him one thing -- that after I receive my punishment I should return to work for him. The brutal German agreed to this.

Regarding this exchange between the two Germans, I was informed by my mother. According to Kesler's order, I brought the Jews back to the Mlava ghetto. I also brought along a Jews from the Ciechanów ghetto, by the name of Alter, who was being sought by the Gestapo. He was from Mlava. In Mlava, as in other ghettos that I frequented at Kesler's command, I behaved like a German. My outfit was also typically German.

When I brought the Jews to Mlava, a Jewish policeman approached me. He pardoned himself and asked me in German if I am the chauffeur who had brought the Jews from Bielin. When I replied in the affirmative he invited me to the commandant of the Jewish police. He also did not know that I am a Jew.

331

The commandant asked me in German if I had brought a Jew by the name of Alter. At this time he brought Alter to me. I declared that I'm not sure if he came with me. Soon a Jewish policeman entered, the nephew of Alter, who knew me from prior to the war. He said to me in Yiddish: "Noah, you brought my father from there and you'll take him back." I understood the intention of this Jewish policeman. He had sent his father to Ciechanów in order not to have to care for him, and I'm the one who brought him back.

Meanwhile everyone discovered that I was a Jew and the attitude towards me naturally changed. The Jewish policeman who had wanted to get rid of his father threatened me that he would report me to the Gestapo. To this I replied that I also can inform the Gestapo about this. It's enough that by bringing this Jew into the ghetto I had acted dangerously, without any reward whatsoever, and I would not take this Jew back because both in the Ciechanów ghetto and on the way there, the Jew's life is in danger. Other Jewish police intervened and Alter remained in the Mlava ghetto.

The End of My Term with the Germans and the Grueling Inquest in the Gestapo

At the appointed hour I brought back the Jewish forced laborers to Bielin and drove back to Ciechanów. At home I was informed that there's a search going on for me. It's very bad. The commandant of the German police categorically demands that I report to the police.

Having no choice, I reported to the police (German), giving my true name, Noah Zabludowicz. The German demanded that I tell him what had happened between me and the Gestapo. I told him the truth. The commandant ordered that I be given a beating.

332

A policeman led me into a separate room. There I was ordered to strip naked. I was ordered to lay down on the table. Two of them beat me on my naked skin and one of them crunched the blows. From the terrible pain I began to cry. Someone opened the door and ordered the beating to stop.

When I put my clothes on my beaten body, a policeman entered the room, a *Volksdeutsch*, called Gottesman. This rogue knew me very well. He asked me what I was doing here. The policemen started to talk amongst themselves. They were interested in knowing from where he knows me. To this he replied that I'm from the "Kesler-Bande" and that there we have "A Jewish Government" and that there we do whatever we like. We even have a radio, he said. There was a sentence of death at that time for possessing a radio.

The police commandant, Lieutenant Lifker, started to question me about whether I had really listened to the radio. The *Volksdeutsche* had reported on Sara Altus, who was working in the household of Kesler, that she and I had listened to the radio. We were both arrested and kept under watch. Our hands in chains, we were led to the Gestapo. During the inquest I did not admit to listening to the radio. The commandant of the Gestapo beat me mercilessly and threatened me that I wouldn't exit from there alive. After the first inquest I was taken to prison.

Two weeks later the questioning began once more. The torture continued from seven in the morning to seven in the evening. In this manner I had to go through the streets with terrible wounds on my whole body. A Gestapo guy was guarding me with a revolver in his hand. He threatened to shoot me immediately if I tried to get away from him a distance of more than three feet. In this manner I was brought back to the Gestapo.

Once more sadistic beatings were given to me. A Gestapo officer finally took me away from this torture. He gave instructions that I should be brought to him and meanwhile not to harm me. He "invited" me to his room and very politely told me to sit down and treated me to a cigarette. In a very delicate manner the officer addressed me, calling me very politely, "*Herr* Zabludowicz." With the same courtesy he told me to tell him everything that had taken place.

333

I told him everything. The German asked me if I know what kind of punishment was coming to me for this. When I replied that I know, he said that the punishment is much worse than I can imagine, but he is ready to help me, even free me from my punishment, if I tell him one thing: I should tell him who in Kesler's house listened to the radio. After I will tell him I can go home.

In Kesler's home there really was a radio receiver. Whenever Kesler was not at home I would put on the radio at midnight and listen to news from London in Polish. Kesler also listened to the same radio station in German, but later than me -- around two in the morning. Naturally, I explained to the Gestapo officer that I have no idea of what is happening in Kesler's home. "All week," I said, "I'm on the road, and only come to Kesler in connection with my work."

The German officer tried, with all kinds of delicate means, to win me over. He wasn't so interested in torturing me, but rather to find out from me who was listening to the radio at Kesler's. He interrogated me for two hours, and I remained with the same story: "I don't know about anything."

In the midst of the interrogation there suddenly appeared four Gestapo men in the room, each one with a different excuse, and the interrogation continued. One of those who entered called out to the officer: "Release him. Just hand him over to me. One, two, three, and I'll finish him off." Then my interrogator once more turned to me:

"Good that you didn't fall into his hands. He would have finished you off right away."

The second part of the interrogation started. The polite German officer suddenly became a sadist. All four suddenly ordered me to lay down on a stool on my belly, knees down on the floor, my head pressed to the back of the stool. One of the officers grabbed my head between his legs. A second one stood on my feet and two beat me with cudgels. This probably continued for about twenty minutes.

I couldn't endure and cried out, struggling as much as I could. The stool broke and the two sadists that were holding me fell. Then they madly grabbed the legs of the broken stool and started to beat me even more murderously and I was left there in a state of unconsciousness. The murderers poured a pitcher of water on me and I revived.

334

Three of them left for lunch. One, by the name of Kraizl, remained and continued with the interrogation. He started to do "gymnastics" with me. There was a tall built-in-oven in the room. He commanded me to climb up and down on the oven. With my tortured body it was very hard for me. After a few times I fell down exhausted. I pleaded with him to shoot me, but he replied that it's a shame to waste a bullet. ""You'll crap one way or another anyhow," he said with laughter. The bandit kicked me with his steel-tipped boots and knocked out all my teeth.

Soon the other three torturers returned and with fresh energy started to torture me. When all this didn't help they put handcuffs on my hands. The handcuffs were tied with electrical wire. An electric shock immediately ran through me. My hands started to shake. The Germans beat me murderously while at the same time shouting mockingly, telling me to remove my electric handcuffs that where still clamping my hands. The suffering was enormous.

This is how they treated me for an hour and a half. Around seven o'clock in the evening the torturers started to say amongst themselves that they have to bring "Sara," (Sara, the second one accused of listening to the radio). She was then in prison. The torturers told me to get dressed and put myself in order, but I couldn't move my hands. All my fingers, all my sinews were broken. My body was covered with wounds. They took me to a tap and told me to wash. At that moment they brought in Sara.

The door of the interrogation room was open and I heard everything that was taking place there. The Germans told the tortured woman that I have already confessed and have also said that she had listened to the radio. Sara didn't let herself be misled and argued that she had worked at Kesler's as a cleaning woman, and had never heard the radio. The sadists also applied their sadistic treatment to the unfortunate woman. With this torture they ended the day, and we were led to the prison.

335

With Poles in the Lager - Sansk

In the prison where I was confined there were fifty-five people, Poles. All of them related to me properly and treated me like a brother. I was all beaten up and in a terrible state. Wounds and sores covered my body. There wasn't an unharmed spot anywhere. For fourteen days my prison-mates applied compresses on my wounded body. For this they used the water that was sparingly given for drinking.

Amongst the arrested ones was the former commandant of the Polish police. He was called Roman. In 1940 he was sentenced to death. He had succeeded in running way from the Warsaw citadel. In 1942 the Germans caught him again. He sat in prison with his hands handcuffed. We spoon-fed him. Once, at his request, I removed a nail from his pocket. He taught me how to undo the lock of the handcuffs with the nail. I did as he instructed me, and the handcuffs opened. By the same means I closed the handcuffs. One morning I opened his chains. In the afternoon, during the walk, he succeeded in running away.

After working for him for a short time, and after a few brief conversations with him, I understood that he was an opponent of the Nazis. He even introduced himself as a social-democrat, but he was afraid to open his mouth when the German mayor of Ciechanów issued an order at the end of 1940 to destroy 28 wagons and destroy the horses of the Jewish owners. Kesler requested that this all be given to him. He did get them.

Kesler lined up the wagons in his yard. He erected stables for the horses. He had a locksmith shop and a smithy. There he repaired his trucks and the wagons. The horses and wagons were used for city work for which Kesler got properly paid. The profit that Kesler earned, after deducting the expense for maintaining the horses and wagons, Kesler gave me to distribute amongst the Jewish wagoners, the former owners of the same.

337

Naturally this was all done secretly. When the German forces discovered that he had hired me, a Jewish chauffeur, he was arrested. A court case took place and he was freed. He proved that he had made good use of the Jewish chauffeur. While the Jews were being driven to Auschwitz by the Germans, Kesler stood in the yard and cried. I don't know what happened to him later.

In the Death Camp, Auschwitz

I arrived at Auschwitz 7/11/42. At first I worked in the train station crew that worked at loading and unloading goods from the wagons and trains that arrived at the lager. In 1943 I, together with my brother Khanan, was transferred to Block 24 where we were house-supervisors. In this block there were the 'privileged' of the lager, mainly Poles: cooks, butchers, bakers, musicians who played in the orchestra, and others. They received food parcels from home and didn't need the lager food. My brother and I took the food rations for Block 24 from the kitchen and brought it to Block 16, where my third brother, Pinkhas, was. There we divided much food amongst the hungry Jews.

***

One day in May, 1944, the Jews of Bendin, Sosnowiecm. I was a witness to the following murderous act of the Germans: I saw a German standing with his gun ready to shoot is leading a woman with a girl of five or six. At that moment a commandant came out of the woman's lager. The German soldier stood at attention and reported that he has a woman and a Jewish child from Bendin who had hidden with a Pole.

The commandant asked the woman if she was a *Juden*. To this she answered in Polish that she doesn't understand German. After repeating the question a few times, and receiving the same answer, the *haupt-shturmfuhrer* got angry and grabbed a revolver. At this the child ran up to the feet of the German and cried, begged for mercy. The sadist lifted up the child from the ground, kissed her on the forehead and then shot her. When the mother began to cry, he shot her also.

338

At that time the Germans brought two transport trucks with children to Auschwitz. Male and female teachers accompanied them. They were all well-dressed. Upon their arrival they sang German songs. They were immediately led to the gas-chambers and crematorium.

A half-hour later I went in the same direction and I heard from one of the *Sonderkommando* (those who worked at the crematoriums) that the Jewish children were from Bialystok, and from there they had been taken, together with their teachers, to Theresienstadt (Czechoslovakia). There they got education, clothing, good food, and in 1944 the children were brought to Auschwitz to perish. The children were led to a shallow channel in which a fire was burning. The Germans threw them in and they were burnt alive.

The Uprising in Auschwitz

The mutual help of the Ciechanówers in Auschwitz made an extraordinary impression on those arrested in the lager. The underground movement in Auschwitz started to take an interest in us. I found out from Moishe Kolka about this and all of us Ciechanówers joined.

At that time I worked as an electrician. Every day I went out to Birkenau to do electrical work. Thanks to the possibility of moving around in the lager, I took upon myself to be the contact between the various lager sections. I was also in contact with the Poles who came from the city of Auschwitz to the lager to work. Through them I made contact with the A.K. (Polish underground party).

There was also an ammunition factory in Auschwitz called "Union." There only Jews worked: women separate and men separate. Work was done in three shifts. There was no contact with them. They all lived in Birkenau lager.

From the leadership of the underground movement I got an instruction to make contact in any way possible with trustworthy people who work in the ammunition factory, "Union," who can help us to acquire arms and ammunition for the underground.

339

After a short time I managed to make contact with one of our own - - Rosa Robota. She worked in the clothing section in Birkenau lager. She organized a group of women who worked in the "Gunpowder Pavilion." Twenty girls, endangering their lives, hid between their breasts small packets of explosive material. Rosa received the "transport" and gave it to those who worked hidden in the wagons in which the bodies of those who died in the barracks during the night were carried. Close to the crematorium the secret arms supply was organized. We also assured that those who endangered their lives in gathering arms and explosives should get better food. We worked in this way for a year and a half.

We also bought arms from the Poles and paid with gold and silver. That's how we prepared for the rebellion in the terrible extermination lager that the Germans had built, where Jewish lives were burned en masse.

340

Ciechanów Jews in Auschwitz

L. Silver, Montreal

The last days in the ghetto prior to the final liquidation destroyed the city and we built the new city. We believed that they would not send us out because all the males from the ages between fourteen and sixteen, and females between fourteen and fifteen, worked, and were registered on jobs. But apparently the murderers didn't have enough blood and the turn of the Ciechanów Jews came.

It was *Shabbat* morning in the last days of October, 1942. I lived on Tilsit Street at that time (once called Shlonska) when my neighbor, Shalom Stolnitz, came to me, with a deep sigh and tear-filled eyes, and said to me: "All the Jews who find themselves in the Ciechanów area must leave by November 1."

We immediately understood what this meant. It is a death sentence. I went outside and saw how everyone was going about, wringing their hands and crying. Desperate cries were heard: "Jews, let's not leave. Better we should die here." With the help of the *Judenrat*, however, the Germans succeeded in filling the transports. One transport of one thousand, five hundred people capable of hard work were taken to Aubershlezia in November 1942. Those in that transport were: my mother, sister, my bride's brother, parents and myself. There was talk that this was supposed to be a "good" transport that is headed for work in the factories.

We traveled for two days. The crowding in the wagons was so great that there was no room to stand or sit. We received no water. Since everyone still had something from home, it was a little easier to survive.

I saw how they were led to the gas-chambers

Friday morning, November 9, 1942 we left Ciechanów. On Saturday, late in the evening, we reached Auschwitz. We all shuddered when we saw that we are totally surrounded by Gestapo and by dogs. We heard their mad shouts: *"Raus fun di vogn ir hunde!"* (Out of the wagons, you dogs).

341

I saw how a Gestapo man threw out through the window my friend Wolf Kostsheva's two children.

There is great shoving. Beatings are being administered from all sides. A wild scream is heard: "Leave the bags on the ramp. Men, women, children separate!"

An *Obershturmfuhrer* stood and pointed with his hand: left and right. Ten minutes later four hundred men and a small number of women went to a lager. Nine hundred people, including two hundred women, the Germans loaded onto trucks and took them to be burned. Amongst them was my mother and my bride's parents.

The murderers lined us up, five to a row, surrounded on all sides by S.S., and in this way we were led to the lager.

At one o'clock in the morning we reached the lager. We were led into a large room. Immediately block leaders came, and to assist them block elders and *kapos*. Blows came from all sides. They shouted: "Hand over everything you own! In five minutes everyone must be naked. Money and all other valuables must be deposited in the containers that had been pre-arranged. Shoes and underwear you must throw into one heap."

This had to be done immediately, quickly, because the *kapos* were going around amongst us with thick sticks and murderously hit those who didn't want to undress.

My hair was immediately cut off. There was no bath nor water for washing oneself. A pair of shorts was tossed to me, with a small jacket and a shirt. As soon as I put it on it tore. I also got something for my head but it was too small. I got wooden clogs that didn't fit and wouldn't get on. For requesting a larger size I got struck with a stick. From all this I understood where I was.

They counted off a group of fifty and handed us over to a block-elder, a tall, strong fellow, with a wild look in his eyes and a stick in his hand. The sleeves of his shirt were tucked up, his collar undone. His whole body and his hands were covered with tattoos, like an old criminal. His name was Albert Neiman.

He led us into a barrack with an open roof that let the rain in. The windows were also open. He divided us so that there were ten of us in a section. Some got a bit of straw. Most of us slept on stones. We didn't get any blankets.

342

Each one was occupied with his own *tzores*, with what awaited him. One could hear sighs and painful cries: "My wife, my children, my mother." I myself lay on the asphalt for hours and cried: "Woe is me, my mother is being gassed and burned, and possibly I will also end up that way."

Then we heard the mad shouts of the block-elder and his helpers: "Get up. Outside for roll-call."

It was dark, four o'clock in the morning. We were chased from all sides. I couldn't grasp what was happening. In order to avoid getting hit I also went out.

We were lined up ten in a row. The mud reached to our knees. It was raining. I had lost one shoe. My jacket had no buttons and it was open. The rain poured non-stop, and I was shivering. I regretted that I didn't go with my mother and all my acquaintances. Why should I suffer and be tortured to death.

We stood for more than an hour and they tortured us with commands; "Stand up, get down."

Finally, seven o'clock in the morning a block-leader showed up. We were brought back to the same room where we had been the previous day and there we were called out according to the letters of the alphabet. Since my name began with an "S", I stood until nine o'clock in the evening without food or water. Around ten o'clock I got two potatoes and a bit of cold water. Before I started to eat I heard a shout: "Out of the block, line up in fives!"

One hundred and twenty men were taken into Block 16. There I found many Belgian Jews, very honest people, mostly older people, between twenty-five and forty years old. All together in this series: 71.000. The block-elder was a Jew by the name of Mandek from Warsaw, a "Narvikher," his representative, Yosele, from Radom. His "specialty" was to give "25" with a thick stick on the behind. Whoever got hit by him didn't go to work the following day because he was carried off to the "sick-bay." That's how hundreds of people were led to their death by him. He was shot in 1943 for trying to bribe a block-leader.

The first night in the new block, as soon as I fell asleep, screams were heard immediately: "Get up!" It's three o'clock in the morning and I quickly dressed. We were called out for roll-call that lasted until seven.

343

In the Komando-Crematorium Number 1

After the roll-call we were surrounded by *kapos* and foremen with sticks in their hands. We were grouped into komandos. I ended up in the komando: crematorium number 1. The *kapo* was a German, dressed in a Russian winter coat with a stick in his hand. He was called Hercules. He had four Polish foremen, four actual bandits.

We came to the "work-place." There crematorium No. 1 was built. The *kapo* called out all the new arrivals. I wanted to approach but a Polish Jew grabbed me and held me back. I didn't know why, but I soon understood that this Jew saved me from certain death. The *kapo* gathered 25 Jews (French and Belgian) and told them to sing loudly. Then he and his foremen chose 16 Jews and declared: "Since they sang so well, they'll get good work. Meanwhile let them rest."

Before lunch each one got a pail of clay and they were told to go up high where the chimney of the crematorium was being built. This was a small narrow space surrounded by boards. I stood below where the cement was made, where I would observe everything. As the Jews were going up and hanging onto the boards, the Polish foremen, who were standing on either side with a hammer, hammered quickly and the boards broke down. All 16 Jews with the pots of clay in their hands fell and were killed on the spot. The *kapo* and his foremen laughed uproariously and let it be known these are Jews who had never worked and therefore they fell down.

The murderers immediately commanded Jews to drag away the dead ones. At work one also got killed. The other Jews were cruelly beaten.

When we returned, the Jew who had saved me told me that every day they do the same. They command that Jews sing, noting at the same time who has gold teeth...Then they are sent up high. They fall down and the Polish *kapo* aid pulls out their teeth together with flesh, using pliers. This is turned over to the S.S. For this the *kapo* gets *schnapps.*

344

I got into the komando of Barrack B. There it was somewhat better. I met a French Jew from the 53.000 series, whose name was Moritz. He helped me a lot. Later I worked in Birkenau.

The suffering from hunger was terrible. We would stand at roll-call two or three hours. In the evening we got our midday meal at the workplace, where the mud reached to our knees because the ground was like clay. When I put down a foot, I could hardly lift it out again, with great difficulty. We had to eat standing, 10 people in a row, in order that a control should be possible to assure that no one gets fed twice. There was no water at all, and the bowls were dirty, full of mud.

When we went into the block we had to quickly get up on our sleeping bunks. At night, when we would fall asleep from exhaustion, a piece of bread and 10 grams of margarine would be tossed to each of us. But the block-elders cut this in such a way that the largest portion was always left for them. Each of us was lonely and it was deathly risky to go to someone in another block. If "a stranger" was found there he would be killed immediately.

*

It was already November 15, 1942. Many of us are already gone. Many of our transport turned up in Block 7. Amongst them were: Avraham Shrenkster, Yekhiel Skurnik, Motl Kuchinsky and others. They said that if their wives and children are no longer alive, they should also not live. From Block 7 one is immediately sent, after two days, to the crematorium. An auto comes and the people are taken away. In five to seven minutes you're dead. Later the bodies are burned. Death, they said, is the best savior. Anyhow, there were no chances of staying alive.

I already wanted to accompany them but I wanted to see my sister and my bride at least once more. I found out that they work for a komando "S.S. - Unterkunft." There they have very mean Polish *kapos* and foremen. Beatings go on all day. If a Jew comes to them from anywhere, they finish him off immediately. In spite of all this, I went to that komando.

I met my bride and sister in Auschwitz.

345

On November 18 komandos were going out as usual. We came to the gate. The music played according to the beat of the komando: *Mitzer* up, hands down. We enter, like the proudest soldiers." Our hearts were beating because who knows: he will be sent back dead and he will no longer hear the sad music. Finally we reach the stand. My heart beats with joy yet with sorrow. Finally I will see them -- my sister and my bride. I didn't eat the piece of bread. I gave it to the foreman so that he would take me with the group that works together with the women.

To the women whom I knew from Ciechanów, I had already given a sign to tell my sister and my bride, who stuck together, that I'm present and am working as a paver.

Finally I saw two young women dressed in men's uniforms of Russian prisoners and in their grim top and trousers. Their hair was shaven, heads covered with a kerchief. On their feet -- one wooden shoe and one rag-sandal. Their faces were pale and thin. Their eyes looked at me sadly. When I saw them from the distance my heart started to beat faster. Tears started to flow from my eyes.

I didn't want them to see my fallen spirits, so I scratched my hand with something so that the physical pain should disguise my inner suffering. They couldn't approach me because this was asking for death. However, they did notice me wiping the blood off my hand with my cap. They removed the kerchiefs from their heads, tore them in half. With one part they again covered their heads and in the other half wrapped a piece of bread of 20 grams and a piece of turnip of 10 grams. They passed this to me saying: "Take this, Laibl. We have enough. Hang on. Better days are coming." My sister wanted to say something else, but the S.S. appeared and she immediately went away.

I followed them with my eyes and I wept. I didn't cry so much because of my own condition, but because of their suffering. Who knows, I thought, whether their suffering is not in vain. It was then that I decided that as long as they live, I also must live.

I avoided seeing them for two reasons: first of all, I was told that they always carry half a loaf of bread that they don't eat themselves but want to give to me. I didn't want to take this. Secondly - Khana, my bride, asked me why her brothers don't come to see her and I didn't want to tell her that they are no longer alive. The younger brother, Maier, was murdered in the komando of crematorium No. 1, and the older one, Motl, volunteered for Block 7 -- the death block.

346

Sad and difficult days passed. Every day there remained fewer of us. It is difficult to describe the hunger. I grew thinner and thinner from day to day. Another terrible enemy appeared -- lice. Since there was no water we couldn't wash. The lice multiplied, and we couldn't sleep. We struggled with them throughout the night and couldn't find a solution.

The Death Transport

During the first days of December, 1942, I worked on the construction of crematorium No. 3. That day there was a frightful *kapo*: a German, with a red insignia, called Max. When he was drunk he would lash out at anyone who came his way. One day he killed two people with a spade. They were both people whom I knew from Ciechanów. One was Steinberg, the second, Kzivansky. I was very despondent and tired because we Ciechanówers carried them back from work. This was the last honor that we could give them.

No sooner had I fallen asleep when I heard shouts in the block. We're being chased to the roll-call, driven with sticks. I went out naked. A terrible snow storm was blowing from all sides. The frost was burning. I didn't know what happened. Finally Yosele, the *kapo's* helper, came and said: "We want thirty of you men to load the dead onto the trucks, and if you don't provide this number the whole block (all of you) will stand out here until the trucks will come. This will take another three hours. If volunteers come forth we'll allow the block of people to go back in."

Nobody wanted, after a hard day's work, to load, at midnight, the dead, and to get up pre-dawn to go to work after that. But what could we do? In the lager one doesn't ask such questions. Thirty men volunteered and I was amongst them. We loaded 800 dead. So it was every day.

Later a block-leader chose twelve men. I was also amongst them, and we were led to the women's lager -- Block 25, where we were instructed to remove the dead. This gruesome picture that I saw there remains before my eyes to this day. I seemed to turn to stone and didn't know what to do. Approximately 70 women, mostly Dutch, lay in a state of dying. Mice were eating them, sucking their living blood. An S.S. man with a thick stick stood there and shouted. *"Raus mitn drek!"* (Out with this garbage). "Put a move on -- if not" – he struck with his stick on our heads -- "you'll go together with them."

347

German extermination of Jews

German extermination of Jews

348   blank
349

German extermination of Jews

I hold a leg. It's impossible to move them because in their expiration they are grasping hands. I have no strength so I stand up. Then I got struck with a stick on my head. I get covered with blood. Binyamin Zigmund noticed this. (He was from Ciechanów, who was killed while working in the lager). He said to me in Polish: "Give me your hand and I'll help you. If not, he'll kill you." Finally I succumbed.

My acquaintances wiped the blood off me with snow. I pulled something out of a sleeve and wrapped the wound. It was too dangerous to go to a doctor. For uttering the word "sick" one would immediately be burnt. For not going to work one would also be taken immediately to Block 7. Those were the difficult days that I lived through in December, 1942. It's no wonder that from our transport more than half had by then perished.

A Woman's Transport for the Gas Chambers, Amongst Them My Sister and My Bride

350

It was mid-December, 1942. The new arrivals told me that it was *Shabbat-Chanukah*. I worked in the *kise* komando (gravel pits). This komando was working on the route through which the transports were brought for gassing and burning. There were no finished crematoriums yet. They were being built. Those who were brought were taken into a white barrack that had a sign above it *"Badeh Tzimer,"* (Bathroom), *"Eingang"* (Entrance) and *"Oisgang"* (Exit). Nobody exited from there. There all were gassed and removed to be burnt in the pits.

It was around twelve o'clock noon. A snow smarted in the face. The foreman didn't pay much attention to the work. We spoke amongst ourselves about what we used to eat on *Shabbat-Chanukah.* The greater the hunger, the more one talks about food. My neighbor pointed out to me: "Look, a large transport is being taken to be burnt."

Since I was working beside the railway, I had the opportunity to observe. I was stunned to see a transport solely of women, all dressed in Russian thin clothing. I noticed a lot of familiar girls from my *shtetl* amongst them. All with eyes red from crying. I heard desperate cries: "Why must we die so young?"

I shiver from the cold. Tears stream from my eyes. What's happening here? Suddenly I hear a shout: "Be well, Laibl," and someone tosses gloves to me. That was the last time I saw my sister and my bride. They weren't crying, but huddling to each other, their eyes looking at me. Their faces were as white as snow. It must be that from so much crying they had no tears left. I heard desperate cries: "Revenge for our innocent lives that they are extinguishing."

351

I had no control over myself that day. I felt very weak. Right after roll-call I thought about going over to the electric fence. There stood a German guard. He will notice me, and thinking that I intend to run away, he will shoot me. Fate wanted me to live, however. I stood in front of the barbed wire and the German didn't shoot. He merely shouted "Up" and again "Up." I lost consciousness and fell down. I lay there all night.

In the morning I was found and dragged to roll-call. As the house-*kapos* were my acquaintances, they didn't beat me.

To Eat to the Fill Just Once and Then Die

Sunday, December 20, a few acquaintances met: the brothers Kostsheva, Sholem Stolnitz and others from Ciechanów. We decided that since our lives were aimless and without any chance, we shouldn't go on suffering. We should sign up for Block 7. This is the easiest death. Of course I agreed with this proposition, but since I was told that on the Christmas eve each one gets a loaf of bread (if it wasn't long to then), I decided to wait. At least once in my life to eat to the full and after that, die. I lived to that day...

The first day of Christmas, at 7 in the morning, the familiar shouts were heard: "Roll-call. Whoever won't line up will be beaten to death."

We all lined up. Who could know what the bandits might do with us on their holiday. We were led outside of the lager. There we were commanded: "Everyone take in your clothes some sand and carry it into the women's lager."

From both sides the block-leaders and elders arose, *kapos, kapos'* assistants, foremen, Poles, Russians, Germans, also S.S. with dogs. Together they built an aisle, a passageway of sorts. Through this space we had to pass with the sand that we were carrying.

352

It's easy to imagine what a hell this was. How could we save ourselves from the brutal blows? Nothing helped. Blows struck from all sides. The dogs bit. I thought that from this hell I wouldn't come out alive.

During all this the two brothers Galgiel (their correct names I don't remember) came close to me and said: "Laibl, get an additional man and as soon as one will get struck with a blow and fall down, the four of us will grab him and immediately take him into the lager. In that way we'll avoid the blows."

It only took a few minutes and one got a blow with a club on his head. He got covered with blood and fell down. Since he had stopped the "march" we grabbed him right away and carried him into the lager. We informed that he was dead. That Christmas night celebration of the Germans cost 148 dead and 200 beaten, but no whole loaf of bread was seen.

On the second night of Christmas this was repeated. It cost us more victims. I managed to hide. A Slavic Jew helped me -- Engl, a very good person.

On the 28th of December Mandek, the block-elder, went away. As his replacement a German block-elder with a red insignia arrived. His name was Tzimer, a terrible murderer. His friend was Alfred Kihn, also a German from Block 17, a cold-blooded murderer. He murdered the brothers Wolf and Aaron Kostsheva and Mordecai Shirensker. The first two were his barbers. After they shaved him, if something displeased him, he immediately killed the barber. He beat to death more than 100 Ciechanówers. Itche Bergson he also murdered. Let his brothers and sisters who are still living know that their brother's murderer was Alfred Kihn. He was tall and strong.

The first Sunday when Tzimer became block-captain he called for a roll-call and told everyone to run like horses. Four hundred Jews (most of them from Germany) who didn't run properly he immediately sent to Block 7 to their death. He had a particular weakness for murdering brothers. He killed the two Peretz brothers, two Slod brothers. As soon as he killed one brother, this German would seek the second one and strike him dead. It was a miracle that Block 16 (my block) was taken away for a komando that was called "Canada." Who they were, whether people from Canada or others, I didn't know at the time. Only later did I get to know them better.

On January 4, 1943, I, together with all the inmates of Block 16, was transferred to Block 15. The block-elder was a Pole called Vladek -- tall, blond, a priest. His assistant, Yuzshek, was also a Pole. The block-elder was a terrible bandit. To this day I can't understand how a person who is a priest can change so drastically.

353

Before roll-call and after it, we stood "knees bent." To get our food we had to approach on our knees, ten in a row. When he chased us into the block it was the same all over again: in a row and on bent knees. He was most pleased when he could inform about a larger number of dead. He instructed that they be laid out in a row and with great pleasure he walked by them and then came into the block like a hero. In March, 1943, in a transport of Poles that went to Germany, he was murdered.

Tortured Jews Try to Help Their Suffering Friends

On January 10 I got sick. I was feverish and didn't know what was happening to me. I was working in the new lager that was being built. Every day I gave my ration of bread to the foreman so that he would let me sit on my knees which I was making the bricks. At night I felt so bad that I decided not to go to work the following day. Come what may, let them take me to Block 7.

Itche Lindberg from Ciechanów took an interest in me. He was a neighbor of mine back home. He came to the lager with two sons, boys of 16 and 18. One of them lost his life at work and the second was taken to the "Shtrof-komando." There he was hung. All the Jews who were in the Shtrof-komando were hung in a row.

Itche said to me: "Laib, I have lost everything. You are the only acquaintance who remains. Hang in there. It will pass. I'll help you." He really did help me. He brought me some hot coffee and in the morning a bit of soup.

Since I was sleeping in my clothes and had "dirtied myself" Itche brought me a pair of pants right away. He had removed them from one of the dead.

Twelve days passed that way. My fever disappeared but I was very weak. In addition, my left foot had suffered frostbite. I got wounds. I couldn't tie my shoes and go to work.

At that time we were transferred to Block 14. A transport arrived with people from Bialystok and Grodno. Transports started to arrive from Czechoslovakia also. It became more crowded. On a bunk where six people formerly slept, sixteen to twenty now had to sleep. For roll-call 1200 people lined up. We were awakened before dawn. Until seven the house-*kapos* were busy arranging the rows.

354

After roll-call they arranged the komandos. Itche and I went to the work of gathering the dead. We hid amongst the dead. We lay that way until ten o'clock. Later we went elsewhere where we stayed until roll-call.

We existed this way for four weeks until once, February 1, a large action took place. All those who had hidden from work were sought. We were caught. We were eight men in hiding. We were pulled out. Blows struck us from all sides. That's how we were chased to Block 7.

I knew that I was lost and didn't know where to run. My heart told me, "Laibl, save yourself." The question was how. We were surrounded on all sides. As we were running we passed Block 14. There Moritz was standing, someone I knew, a house-*kapo*. He was standing on guard as I shouted: "Moritz, save me." He replied that he can only let me through. He told me in which direction to run. Itche and I went through. But I couldn't run because of my wounded foot. Itche went in. Russians with clubs encircled me. They struck me on the shoulders and head. They chased me in the direction of Block 7.

As I was running, desperate, with blood trickling down on me (wishing to lie down in the mud and die) I heard a shout in Polish: "Leave him alone. He's my worker." This was the shout of the *kapo* of the wood storehouse. He knew me also. He took me in, gave me water for washing myself and told me to work. Later he told me that I could go out to roll-call. There I met Itche, Mordecai Singer, Pshigoda and Peretz. Here's how they saved themselves: they grabbed sticks and pretended to be foremen. In this way they succeeded to avoid death.

In the middle of February, 1943, we found ourselves in Block 13. The house-*kapo* was Adek, a French Jew, born in Poland. He was brutal.

355

There were seventeen men sleeping in one bunk. Whoever was sitting couldn't get up. Whoever was laying down couldn't stretch out. The hunger was great. The lice ate us up alive. We were always hungry. Noon time we were given some raw green vegetable. We all got dysentery from this. There was nothing we would do about this and we were helpless.

Every day the block-captain commanded: "Whoever can't go to work, stand aside." Around ten in the morning everyone was assembled, undressed, and without footwear all were taken to Block 7. From there people were led en masse daily to the gas-chambers and then to the crematorium. We couldn't go to work, but as long-time inmates, we already knew when the record-writer comes to write things down. That's when we went away.

Some time passed in this way. Itche Lindberg's and the brothers Galial's dysentery got worse. At the end of February the Germans took them to Block 7. They comforted the unfortunate ones by telling them that as soon as they would get better they would be returned. That's how I lost my only and best friend.

I appealed to the record-writer, Engel, whom I knew, to send me to Block 7, but he didn't want to, and assured me that better times would come.

On March 1, 1943, an order was issued: "Lunch is to be eaten at the komandos, that's to say, at work." This was bad. What were we to do? I asked Moritz what to do. He said that he has no advice for me. "You have already lived through so much," he said to me. "Summer's approaching. Things will improve. Maybe a miracle will happen."

I consulted with the last two from Ciechanów: Singer and Pshigoda. We decided to go to work in the crematoria-komando, number 4.

The Stubborn Struggle for Life and Existence

After six weeks of avoiding work I once more went out, as though for the first time, to work. The musical orchestra had grown meanwhile. It was playing to the beat. The lager head was standing at the gate. The one in charge of reporting, the well-known bandit, Shilinger, treats me better than before. After all, I'm an old hand. I have an early number and I'm treated better. I get easier work. I just have to be careful that the *kapo* and the head-*kapo* don't find me standing idle.

356

It's a little warm now but the pain in my foot does not ease. The wounds are tied up with various rags. I've been suffering this way since January 15. Everything is sticking to the wound. As soon as it got a little warmer my foot acted up and I felt the smarting. I was as thin as a stick - a candidate for Block 7.

At the next reduction when the komando was reduced, I was thrown out. Then I had to go to a "fishing place Kenigsgroben." It was

4 kilometers away. The foremen, who were all Russians, took away our bit of bread for every little thing. Whether we worked or not, they told everyone to bend down and gave everyone 10 strokes on the behind. Once more things were bad.

We were taken to Block 15. There the roofers-komando was, amongst whom a few Ciechanówers worked. I appealed to them for help because I can't endure any more.

I went out to work with the roofers for the first time. This was in the women's lager. It was said that there it is possible to "organize something," that's to say, one can manage to get a piece of bread, a bit of soup. Women didn't interest me at that time. We worked in Block 3. It was an empty block. It was already lunch time. The work is light. My *landsleit* do everything possible so that I won't have to do heavy work. But I had nothing to "organize."

After lunch the *kapo* calls us over and gives us a wagon. He told us to transport bricks from Block 25 to Block 27 to make a floor. There were three of us. On the way, while we were bringing the bricks, the block-elder from Barrack 21 says to bring her bricks then she will give us bread and marmalade. We accepted her suggestion and worked speedily. One wagon load went to her and one to Block 17. At Block 25 a Polish woman came out and asks me in Polish if I want to sell her the wagon. She needs it to bring meals and coffee to the sick. I didn't know what to reply, and told her that I would give her a reply later.

My working companions went to Block 21 to get the bread and marmalade for me as well. When they returned I asked for my portion. One of them told me that they didn't want to give the bread. The second one was the representative and he said: "Take a look at him. He wants bread and marmalade. It's his first time in the komando and already he wants to eat like us. Can't you eat bricks?" he shouted. "I'm going right away to tell the *kapo* that you don't want to work," and they all went away.

357

Later the woman came once more and asked if I'm selling the wagon. I answered "Yes." I suddenly became brave and didn't ask anyone. In the evening my working companions told me that I should take the wagon to Block 17. I took it to Block 25 instead. The woman brought me an apron full of bread. I hid the bread wherever I could.

The next day we were divided into two groups. One group went to do roofing in the gypsy lager, the second -- in the women's lager. I was afraid to go into the women's lager because of the wagon, so I asked to go to the gypsy-lager.

It was already warmer and once more one wanted to live. The work was light. The noon meal was somewhat better and more and the komando, a good one. But what does one do when I was told that with sick hands and legs one could go to Block 12. There, there are doctors who can help. Where to take water, though, to wash my feet? How do I get rid of the lice? I'm ashamed to go to the doctor in such a condition. Still, I want to live.

One Sunday evening I took the *shmates* off my foot, together with the bandage that had already been stuck to my wound for three months. I started to shiver throughout my body when I saw that my foot was covered with wounds on which there are parasites...There was no water so I washed the wound with my own urine, cleaned off the parasites and put on another pair of slippers that I got from Yehuda Kalflus. He worked in the Canada-komando.

Early the next morning I went to Block 12. There Dr. Caplan saw me. He bandaged my wounds and told me to come every second day. If not, I will develop gangrene. I went bandaged up for a long time and the wounds on my foot started to heal. Meanwhile, I started to suffer from something else.

A transport of Greek Jews arrived and they brought with them a contagious disease which I caught.

***

358

On April 10, 1943, the situation in Birkenau improved. The morning roll-call no longer took place. It was no longer permitted to inflict blows. New toilets and bathrooms were installed. There was more water. I don't know why the situation took a turn for the better.

On the first days of *Pesach* we didn't work. We were taken to the bath. For the first time I got underwear. In short, I once again thought I would survive. Why the situation improved I don't know to this day.

I was very weak, thin, and all kinds of ailments struck me. No wonder I got sores. I couldn't walk. An operation was done on my foot. I got three days rest. But the sores increased and I couldn't walk.

On May 10 I was taken to Block 8. There I lay until May 23. To my good fortune, an order was issued at that time not to gas any prisoners with early numbers who are in the lager. My friends gave me food through the window.

I left the "hospital" but two days later I got sick again. A terrible swelling developed on my operated foot. The 12th of June, 1943, I had to go to Block 8 once more for another operation. I suffered terrible physical pain At that time the Poles, Czechs and other Aryans had the right to receive parcels from home. In Block 8 (hospital) I got a bed near the Aryans. There I became friendly with engineer Tolochko, a man of 72, a fine man. He got many packages from home and he helped me a lot. Noon meals I got from the Ciechanówers who worked close to Block 8.

I started to regain my strength. I felt that I was getting stronger. My wounds started to heal gradually. I could already walk. The old lager was moved to a new block. Where we had been, women were put in. The "sick-house" was transferred to a new lager – Block 6. Two Jewish doctors headed this block-hospital, Caplan and Antesko -- a Rumanian Jew who came from France.

359

The doctors told me that they cannot keep me any longer in the hospital. The house-elder, someone I knew, and Tolochko, promised to find me easy work. It so happened that at that time a barber and a tailor were needed in a newly-formed block. I went there. It was quite good for me. I did tailoring for the block-elders.

Dr. Mengele Sends the "Sick" Jews to Be Gassed

The Herosim of a Jewish Girl

On August 8, after midnight, I was sitting in front of the block when I noticed that all those who had left the lager in the morning were returning. I asked what had happened. I was told that Mengele had chosen all the Jews and had sent them back. Everyone knew nothing good could come from this.

An hour later the same Mengele came with the lager-elder and gave an order: "All the sick must get out of the block." From Block 15, 115 Jews were removed. The same in other blocks. From the lager healthy and sick were brought (mostly healthy). They were stripped naked, led to Block 14 to the empty barracks.

In this way more than 1400 people were gathered. They were kept in the washroom until ten in the evening. The following day, when autos with S.S. leaders arrived, they were all taken to be gassed and burnt.

That same August, nine transports arrived from Obershlesia, Zaglembia, Bendin and Sosnowiec. A small number went to the lager; the remainder, around seventy per cent, were taken directly to the gas chambers.

At the beginning of September one of the largest selections took place in the lager. I saw how all were stripped naked and Mengele, together with the lager leader, Shwartzhober, stood there and all the skeletal survivors pissed in a row in front of them. The lager leader indicated with his hand: "Left," "Right." Right was designated for the gas-chambers. Those to the left had their numbers recorded and were led to the blocks for work.

Sunday morning, I saw the terrible scene of the Jews being led to the gas-chambers. An S.S. officer went in the front with a pistol in his hand. Following him were four S.S. with upheld guns ready to shoot. Every five feet at the sides, S.S. with dogs, and the unfortunate went in the middle. In rows, and with terrible cries, the screams: "What did we do to deserve to die?" I had the opportunity to count 1700 Jews, that is 17 groups, all from the lager. They went on their last way to the gas-chambers.

360

In September, 1943, many transports arrived that went directly to the gas-chambers. Since Block 15 was close to the gas-chambers, not more than thirty steps away, I could observe everything.

When the German mass murderers had everyone assembled in the yard of the crematorium (approximately 1500 people). They were told to strip and that is how they were led into the bunker of the crematorium. First to go were the women and children. Horrendous screams were heard and calls of *Shma Yisroel*. Some shouted: "Murderers, kill me. What do you want from my child? What sort of crime did it commit?" Others called out: "Save my children." These cries were superhuman. When they were already inside a "subordinate" came over, dressed in a gas-mask. He opened the two small windows and through them inserted the poisonous contents. Then he closed the windows and left.

Afterwards the doors were opened and the dead were thrown out. The mothers were holding their children tightly. In crematorium number three there were sixteen ovens. In every oven five people were thrown. Fat ones burned for fifteen minutes, skinny ones -- half an hour. The *Sonderkommando* already knew how to regulate so that the burning would not take more than twenty minutes. They put in two people: one fat and one skinny. In this way eighty people were burnt in the crematorium every twenty minutes.

One night we were all shocked. We went down from our bunks and saw a transport that had arrived from Cracow. The unfortunate ones probably knew that they were going to their death. I heard two young girls singing the song: "Was I born from a stone, was it not to a mother that I was born?" Others sang *Hatikva* as well as the *Internationale*. The S.S. murderers laughed. The blood froze in my veins. I didn't sleep all night. I lay awake thinking: Why are so many of us dying? Why are we being tormented?

I asked to be sent back to the lager. My request was granted and I was sent to Block 29. There I met Shaya Kalflus from my transport. I was given food and a place to sleep. It was better for me than before.
361

In the evening, for roll-call, Victor from the work-assigners came and sent me to Block 28 in the "Watch" komando. The block-elders were Jews. One was called Shafron. Conditions in this block were better than in the old lager. In the morning we got coffee. The main person in this komando was Mendl Goldberg at that time. He received me well because I had an early number. He took me into the tailors where sacks were sewn. The work was not hard. I was able to endure. I got two liters of food. The hunger was no longer so severe. I started to get used to this life.

In October, 1943, it got "cozier" in the lager. A transport solely of Americans arrived. These were Jews who hadn't managed to return home in 1939 when war broke out. The International Red Cross interested itself in them. They got help as internees. They were gathered and were supposed to be taken to Switzerland. That's what they said. The Gestapo had told them so. But they were taken to Auschwitz.

Once an unusual case happened. In the transport there was an American artist, a beautiful woman. When a group of Americans were told in the evening that they are going to bathe, she asked: "Where are those who want to bathe before us?"

Near her stood the bandit, the report leader, Shilinger, pistol in hand. The woman was very beautiful and she didn't want to strip naked in front of them. She covered her breasts with her dress, and asked the murderers why they don't go away, since she's ashamed to strip in the presence of males.

The German bandits, though, had very little regard for the innocent blood of the victims. They wanted to mock the figure of the beautiful, refined woman. One of them went over to her and tried to pull her skirt off. She, quick as lightning, grabbed a stool and struck the German on his hands. The revolver fell from his hand. At that moment she grabbed it and shot at the Germans. Shilinger dropped dead immediately and the second one got badly wounded.

After the death of the bandit Shilinger, things eased up somewhat in the lager. The second report-keeper was somewhat milder.

I was still working in the "weaving shop." In the month of November, 1943 men started to be grabbed -- women as well.
362

The report-keeper, together with the lager-elder, chose whoever they pleased and sent them to Auschwitz. There the men were castrated. Many familiar men started to appear, castrated. They said that after such an operation there's no point in further suffering to survive. The fear of this operation and its aftermath was tremendous.

In December the castrations eased off somewhat. Christmas was again approaching. The "Aryans" received many packages from home, but we continued to go hungry. The first day of the holiday we didn't go to work. It was much better than the former Christmases and at the same time very sad. In the lager those whom we knew from 1942 were no longer living.

That's how 1943 ended, a bit easier than the past year. I was also able to breathe a little easier.

A New Year and New Transports to Be Gassed

The first of January, 1944, the *kapos* made a roll-call only for Jews. We, the old inmates, already knew what this signified. They already needed new victims. They can't culminate their holidays without drinking some more Jewish blood.

Everyone was gathered and shoved into the "washroom" where they were forced to strip naked. Then, as before Mengele stood with his subordinate -- *Obershturmfuehrer,* who was also a doctor, Tila. They pointed "right," and "left." This didn't take more than fifteen minutes. From the small number that we were then, they chose 560 to die. The following day the *kapos* and block-elders chased the victims who ran naked, and put them on trucks, taking them to the gas-chambers.

In this gruesome, horrible way, the new year started for us in Auschwitz, after we had already suffered so much. We felt that a hard year was in store for us. I had a premonition that the bandits wouldn't give us any rest, for they want nothing less than to finish off all of us. Rumors were heard that the Russians are attacking the Germans heavily, causing the Germans to pull back. Since they can't win the battle against the strong enemy, they'll take the Jews, the weak and despondent.

363

On January 18, 1944, there was talk that the following day none of the Jews would go out to work. We understood that this means another selection.

On January 19, three o'clock after midnight, I couldn't sleep. I was thinking about two years in Birkenau lager where we had suffered so much; so much beatings and *tzores.* I feel somewhat healthier but who knows what kind of plans the German murderers have prepared in order to finish off the last remaining Jews in Auschwitz. Never before had this thought plagued me as much as that night. Who knows if this is not my last night of life?

Finally we had to get up. I washed myself, ate well, wanting to appear presentable on "Judgment Day" that would be in a few hours. It's possible that I suffered in vain so much for so many years. But maybe...

At 6:00 a.m. everyone appeared for work, all except the Jews. Once more they are waiting for their turn for life or death. At seven o'clock the block-elder announced that all Jews must line up, completely naked, and wait until the commission will decide whom to send to work. In the lager there were very few Jews at that time in the same healthy condition as I was. The whole Block 28 stood, in this way, from seven in the morning until one in the afternoon, six hours they stood naked and waited. We were 148 Jews.

At one o'clock we heard: "They're coming." My heart was beating. I want to live. I'm capable of working. After surviving for two years in Birkenau, I want to live to see better days. And then -- the wink, the short word: "Right," "Left" will soon decide whether I'll live or not.

"Achtung," the block-elder shouts. The bandits get closer. The lager leader, Shwartz, comes over. *Obershturmfuehrer* Tila, the lager boss, two block-heads. All these constituted the commission. Each person goes up to them, stands at attention, and turns around: that was all, this was decisive. In those few seconds one's fate was decided.

Dr. Tila indicates with his finger, holding one hand between the buttons of his coat with only the index finger showing: life or death. In the course of ten minutes he had sent 120 to their death and 28 to live. I was amongst those assigned to die.

I had survived here for two years, gone through tens of selections, had regained my health, and now when I'm feeling better I must die? No, I'm not resigning. I tried to appeal to my *landsleit*. They had money, and with money it was possible at the last moment to bribe the bandits, but the *landsleit* tell me that it's all the same. Tomorrow we'll all go. I try to convince them that we must fight and not lose hope.

364

All day I ran from one to the other. I appealed to Herbert, the record-keeper from the weavery where I worked. He said that he would do everything possible to save me as a good tradesman.

After the roll-call, the sentenced ones were taken to Block 27.

In the evening of January 19 I was led into the block of the sentenced ones. That night I'll never forget. There were 375 Jews. At first everyone was arguing. Each one wanted to fight, destroy, burn, but not die easily. Everyone knew that tomorrow trucks would come and, naked, we would be taken to the gas-chambers.

The terror was unimaginable. A Jew from Bendin was standing and shouting: "Jews, in what way are we better than our wives, children and parents? They all died as innocents, so why should we live? What's our life worth anyhow? There's no point in fighting for a foolish existence when all our dear ones are gone."

Gradually everyone calmed down. People wanted to sleep one more night as human beings because tomorrow there won't be a sign of us. The crematorium burns everything. I couldn't sleep, though. All night I was plagued by the thought of gas-death.

It was seven in the morning. People drink. I'm amazed at everyone as I watch them drink so close to death. I don't want the coffee because the pleasure of drinking just adds to my desire to live. I want to get it all over with and let there be an end to this cursed life.

At eight in the morning the lager-elder, Daniash, entered and called out a few names of tailors, cobblers, locksmiths. They are called back to work. Once more my heart starts to beat quickly. Perhaps I'll be amongst the lucky ones. Maybe I'll have pull and I'll stay alive for the time being. The lager-elder comes once more and calls other numbers. I see that I'm not called.

I start to resign from life. My waiting seems long and foolish. Totally exhausted, I fall on the bunk, sum up my life in the silence and prepare to die. Resigned, I think: It's useless to fight. Naked, watched by so many S.S. who are armed with the most modern weapons, what can I do? I try to imagine myself being gassed. I'm choking. I'm being burnt.

365

From Death Row Back to Life

Suddenly I hear a call: "Laibl!"

Mendl Goldberg from the weavery is here. I get up. It's true. They're calling me back to work.

At twelve noon, January 20, I was rescued from death. I returned to work at the weavery. I live, but for how long I don't know. In the evening everyone from Blocks 20 and 27, 850 Jews, were stripped naked, guarded by S.S. arrested Reichs-Germans: political, criminal, block-elders and *kapos*. With clubs in their hands, the unfortunate ones were driven to death. The helpers of the murderers often beat the naked ones more fiercely than the S.S. themselves. The helpers carried out their "work" with satisfaction and attentiveness like beasts. These were Reich's Germans, political and criminal elements, who carried out the work of murdering the Jews. On their conscience rests the lives of tens of thousands of murdered Jews in the lagers alone.

After the selection of January 19 it felt like a cemetery in Birkenau. The remaining Jews were downhearted. Each one thought that these were their last days. There was no escaping death. I worked in the weavery. Life got a wee bit better. I had enough to eat, to wear, and gradually the mood picked up.

All this was thanks to a girl from Ciechanów, my relative, Rosa Robota. She made an effort to meet me in the weavery, gave me advice and food. We also spoke about the most recent selections and about our situation. The family members of Rosa Robota, those who find themselves in America, should be proud of the heroic deeds of this woman. It is a great privilege, for me also, to belong to this family who nurtured such a woman as Rosa Robota.

She was a beautiful young woman, nicely built, 23 years old. She fought for her life until the very end against the bandits and she perished as a heroine.

366

In 1944 she was working in the clothing section near crematorium 1. In the *Sonderkommando* of Crematorium 1 there were people who had started to "organize" arms in preparation for an uprising. Rosa Robota came to an understanding with the girls of the "union" komando who manufactured ammunition for the *Wehrmacht*. She got ammunition from those girls and handed it over to the organizers of the uprising.

Of course, every move could mean death, but this ammunition led to the uprising and to the destruction of the crematorium, which made a great impression in all the Auschwitz lagers.

After the liquidation of the crematorium in Birkenau, the S.S. arrested a girl and she betrayed it all. Rosa and two other Jewish girls were arrested. For months the S.S. tortured her, beat her body with clubs so that she was beyond recognition. All the brutal torture that the S.S. could think of, she endured. She didn't betray anyone. In the last days of December, 1944, she was hung. Proud, to the extent that her strength would allow, she went to her death like a heroine. Honor to her memory!

***

Meanwhile my life went on quietly. I worked in the weavery. There was food to eat. According to the conditions to which I had already acclimatized myself, it was good. Most important -- I had secured another shirt for myself so that I could change from time to time. Though I washed it with cold water and dried it beneath the bunk on which I slept. Transports for gassing came less frequently. By this time there were already fewer Jews in Europe.

The Ciechanów Transport from Theresienstadt and the Hungarian Jews

I found out that the festival of *Purim* was approaching. From experience I knew that at the time of Jewish festivals the bandits need some Jewish blood. *Erev Purim* there were already rumors that the whole Ciechanów (Jewish) transport that is in the "Czech" lager will be burnt. Who was this Czech transport?

In August, 1943, there was brought from Theresienstadt (Czechoslovakia) a transport of four thousand Jews. There were whole families. They were all taken to a lager. There they were divided into blocks, according to the families, and their blocks were called "Czech families lager" – lager B; our lager was marked lager D, a work lager.

367

Those from Theresienstadt were very intelligent, well educated people. The women were lovely, the children clean, well-dressed. They were allowed to keep their hair. The men also didn't have their hair shaved off. They set up schools where lectures took place. When there was an "action" this lager B was not involved. One could think that the Hitler bandits want to let the Jews of this lager live.

In March, 1944, an order came from Berlin that the whole transport must be gassed. Once more there was a panic. Every one of us understood that if the Czech transport is to be gassed and burnt, we also don't have any hope. We certainly want to emerge alive from this hell, I thought over and over again.

A day after *Purim*, that is on *Shushan Purim*, at night, S.S. once more were put on guard, armed with machine guns. Assisting them were block-heads (Poles), *kapos*, Germans. All of them surrounded the Czech-Jewish families: children, elderly, young, beautiful girls. With clubs they were chased onto the trucks that were as always readied for this purpose. That's how they were taken to the gas-chambers and, from there, their bodies were taken to be burnt.

One of the *Sonderkommando* told me about this. He worked at the gassing. The people went calmly to the bunker to be gassed. They kissed and said farewell to one another. They called out to the S.S. – "Today we are going to our death, but we are sure that you will come after us." Singing *Hatikvah* and the Czech hymn, the Czech transport perished. This was in the month of March, 1944, *Purim*.

The month of April, 1944, it was just before our great festival of *Pesach* was to take place. What will they demand from us now? Very few Jews remained in Birkenau. Only in a few kommandos, where the majority were Poles, Russians and Russian prisoners-of-war. Very few Jews worked in the weavery. Many were sick in the infirmary. One saw few Jewish faces, nevertheless the Germans will find their victims, I thought.

368

On the first day of *Pesach* all the Jewish women and children who were in the infirmary were loaded onto the trucks and taken to the gas-chambers. This wasn't enough for the murderers, though. They also needed the healthy ones who were weak from the work. These also were driven to death.

In the month of May the komando (of Birkenau lager) was building the railway line into the lager. The skeletal men worked day and night. A line was being built that was intended to connect Birkenau with the gas chamber and crematorium. Day and night whole train wagons of wood kept arriving. The crematoriums were put in shape. The ovens and the chimneys were enlarged.

Something was being prepared. Huge pits were being built. Those that the murderers covered up after the crematoriums were built were enlarged. Who are they now preparing to bring from Poland, Greece, France, Belgium, Holland, from Europe? I kept thinking. Were there still people left to destroy? Whose turn would it be next? But one didn't have to wait long for the answer.

At the end of May the first transports of Hungarian Jews arrived. I could observe their arrival very well from close proximity. The first transports came from Zibenburgen, Munkach. It had been a very long time since I had last seen these types of Jews. The older ones were *frum*, with beards and *payes* and *arba-knafot*, in long coats with their *tallisim* in their hands. They went together, apparently in family groups: men and women, holding children by the hand. They were separated on the spot: left and right, women separately and men separately. Every transport had 2000 people. In ten minutes the S.S. doctor decided the fate of tens of thousands of Jews.

From every transport approximately seventy per cent were sent to the gas chambers to be burnt and the rest to the lager to suffer. Day and night transports came and left. An empty train left and a full one arrived.

The crematoriums in Birkenau worked non-stop, twenty-four hours a day. At night the sky was lit up from the fires of the crematoriums. It was so bright in the lager that everything could be seen. Everyone could smell the smoke and fumes of burning human flesh. I saw the people enter and saw their end go up in smoke.

369

Two months passed in this way: July and August, until the Germans had brought 450 thousand Hungarian Jews -- women, children, babes -- together with their mothers.

I also saw, in the lager, the Hungarian women who remained alive. These were mainly women between the ages of eighteen and thirty. In rows of five they were led to hard labor, slender, clean and well-dressed, in spite of all they had been through. They carried satchels or rucksacks with them. That's how they went when they were led to the baths as well, immediately after they arrived. There they were forced to strip naked. Their hair was cut off, their clothes taken away and dressed in sleeping apparel, striped pants and wooden shoes. After this procedure they were led back, in rows of five, from the bath to the lager.

Whoever saw these women, these lovely Jewish girls, just a few hours before, could not recognize them after this: shamed eyes, sad faces. They held one another by the hand because it was hard for them to walk in the wooden shoes.

They were in lager No. 3, 12-15 women on one bunk. They slept on the bare boards, beneath broken roofs. The rain poured in, wind and cold -- a terrible hell for the women.

At four in the morning they were driven outside, almost completely naked. They stood hours long this way for roll-call. There was no water there. The toilets were open and the women had to relieve themselves in front of the eyes of the strange men who regularly worked there. Every second day selections took place amongst the women. They were forced to stand naked a whole day. We, who worked in the weavery, saw all this.

Since there was no roof on the bunks for all the women, many lay naked on the ground. The unfortunate women were led en masse to be burnt. Their burning went faster than usual because fresh transports were constantly arriving. Since the bandits were busy with exterminating the new arrivals, they left us alone in the weavery.

370

Transports of Łodz Jews with Mordecai-Chaim Rumkofsky, the Jewish Elder

In September, 1944 when the Russian offensive reached Prague, near Warsaw, the Germans started to liquidate the last ghetto where Jews still worked. Tens of thousands of Jews, whole families, were then brought to Birkenau. Pale, weak, hungry, they were directly brought here, together with the workshops. They brought along the sewing machines and other working tools because they were told that they are being taken to Germany to work.

Sixty to seventy per cent of the Łodz Jews were immediately gassed. The remainder were scattered for work. Together with them arrived the Jew-elder of the Łodz ghetto, Mordecai-Chaim Rumkofsky. He and his family had to stand and see how "his" Łodz Jews are burnt.

Then the Germans tortured the Jew-elder and his family and finally led them into the gas chamber and destroyed them all.

After the Łodz transports few Jews arrived in Auschwitz; the Germans reduced the *Sonderkommandos*. When the transports arrived 800 people worked in a *Sonderkommando*. Now the majority remained without work. Each time that a transport was gassed, the S.S. reduced the *Sonderkommando* by liquidating half of their crew. Many were liquidated on the spot. Others were transferred to Auschwitz to clean clothes of the gassed and burnt people, or to sort the clothes after them.

When the transports stopped coming and the *Sonderkommando* knew what awaited them, their people started to organize themselves and prepare for an uprising. It was all the same, though. They knew that they would be shot.

The three hundred men who were chosen for the "transport," the majority from the *Sonderkommando* from crematorium No. 3, understood that they were being taken to their death so they disarmed the S.S. on the way and the battle started.

Those who rose up set the crematorium on fire by throwing in a few grenades. The crematorium started to burn. The arrested ones began to run away. The workers at crematorium No. 1 came to their aid. The men of this workforce threw the head *kapo*, a German, into the crematorium while he was still alive. They disarmed the guards, with pliers ripped open the barbed wire, and escaped.

Soon larger numbers of S.S. arrived with tanks and machine guns. A battle started. Thirteen S.S. were killed. Amongst the badly wounded of the *Sonderkommando* there was one from Ciechanów: Yankl Verona, who greatly distinguished himself in the uprising.

After the failed uprising the management of the lager, with the bandit Yosef Kramer at the head, started to liquidate Birkenau lager as well as the weavery, that is to say, my turn came.

On October 26, 1944, I was sent, with the last transport that left the lager Birkenau, to Oranienberg. We were 2000 prisoners, all Jews.

After traveling for two days we arrived at night in Oranienberg. We were taken into a large hall of a factory that had been bombed a short time before. There, airplanes were manufactured. It was a large storehouse of asphalt and iron. The windows were open and it was terribly cold, impossible to warm up. At night an alarm went off every two hours. We had to get up five times during the few hours and run out to hide in the forest that was near the lager. There was very little food to eat, but we did not work. We were in Oranienberg for two whole weeks. There our better clothes were removed from us, those that we had received at Auschwitz. We were given concentration camp clothes. There we found all kinds of prisoners: Reichs-Germans, criminals and political ones. Many of us got sick because our clothes had been taken away from us. Finally we were taken to Zackenhausen. We were there for only a few days.

This transport was divided in two: one part to Buchenwald, the second part, where I was -- to Dachau. We were one thousand one hundred men. We traveled by water for three days. Each one got half a loaf of bread and some cheese. That was all the food we got in those days.

It was cold and we were on the hard floor. We weren't allowed to get up because there was a watchman guarding us who checked our every move. Finally, after dragging ourselves for three days, sick and broken, we reached Kaufering near Landsberg. It didn't take long before we were liberated there.

———

372

Ciechanów Jews in the Uprising in Auschwitz the Last Days of the Ghetto

Moshe Kolko

At the end of 1942, the German press from time to time reported on heavy fighting on the eastern front and also about the regrouping of their army. The news also reached the Jews in Ciechanów.

In the evenings, a few of us, close neighbors, gathered at the home of Moishe-Reuven Vina, who had a good knowledge of German, and he told us the news from the German newspapers. We looked at the map and made calculations, figuring how long it would take for the Germans to reach us.

With the hope that it would not take long, we made peace with all our *tzores* and with all the decrees that the Germans came out with every day. We went voluntarily to work in order to save our lives. At first the Germans didn't pay us and we survived by selling some household item from time to time. Later Jews got paid, but only half the pay that Polish workers got. The Germans paid them 34 *fenigs* an hour while Jews got 17 *fenigs*. We were satisfied with this, though. "As long as it doesn't get worse," everyone thought. We were all sure of the German defeat.

The Germans bought produce from the peasants, such as potatoes, cabbage and other items, and from this they gave the Jews small rations. They also gave peat and coal to heat the houses. Jews became so optimistic that they started to store produce for the winter.

When Noah Zabludowicz was freed, this was also encouraging. However, the hope did not last long.

November 2, 1942, was the last day of the Jewish *Kehillah* in Ciechanów. An order was issued that all Jews must leave the *shtetl* and can only take handbags and food for a few days.

373

Immediately the mood in Ciechanów became nervous. With anxiety one asked the other: "Where will we go?" No one knew what to reply to this painful question.

According to the order of the Germans the Jewish population was divided into two transports -- one that travels straight while the second went to the Mlava ghetto. Everyone wanted to go with the first transport because it consisted mainly of young people. This was considered a good sign, because young people were certainly being sent to work.

Jews ran to Ben-Tzion Ehrlich, the Jew-elder of Ciechanów, asking to be listed for the first transport. Whoever he chose to, he inscribed in the first transport.

We started to pack our bags. Tradesmen took their work tools Perhaps they would be put to work, in which case they would have their tools handy. Clothes were packed and everyone put on as many layers of clothes as possible. Each child was given a bag to carry. A day before being sent out, I wrote the last letter to my parents, who had been sent out a year earlier to the Neustadt (Nova Miasto) ghetto Tearfully I had parted from them. Intuitively I felt that I would no longer see them.

Assembly point at the castle. Germans lead Ciechanów Jews to their death
374

November 5th, a Wednesday, we appeared at a lager barrack that was on the *Zborniak* (assembly point) at the new railway station. We remained there all night. The following morning the Germans told us to hand over all our money and jewelry and keep only 20 marks per person. Anyone found keeping more money will be shot instantly. That was the German order. This terrible order was immediately carried out. They found that Shalom Lubinetski had more money and they shot him immediately.

In Closed, Sealed Wagons

This wasn't the end of the atrocities of the Germans. As we marched out of the lager a Gestapo tore out of Urka Kostsheva's hands her child and murdered it on the spot.

In sealed wagons, with tiny barred windows, we were taken to an unknown destination. The wagons were so packed with people that it was hardly possible to stand. We traveled three days this way. Many times the wagon was detained on side roads. All three days we weren't given food or drink. Children cried. People fainted as they looked at the passing fields and trees. Everyone asked the other: "Where are we? Where are we going?"

In the wagons people said the blessing for the new Hebrew month *Kislev*. It was *Shabbat*. They recalled that the month of *Kislev* was a month of miracles and in this month the miracle of *Chanukah* happened. "Maybe a miracle will also happen with us," we encouraged ourselves.

On a side railway line somewhere bordering on a field, the train came to a stop. Everyone stood at the barred, tiny window to see where we were. Shortly after, we heard marching soldiers singing in the distance. The singing got closer and closer. Suddenly it got light. All around the train electric lights went on. The approaching soldiers close in from all directions and surround the train with machine guns. Some Germans open the wagons and greet us with wild shouts: "Out of the train and leave your bags!"

Wild shouts deafen us. Our blood freezes in our veins. Armed S.S. meet us with mockery and beatings.

375

After we lined up five in a row, men separate, women separate, the selection began. Those who endured this selection will never forget; that will torture us day and night in our nightmares. A German stands in his high boots. Thousands of exhausted Jews, mothers with their children, pass in front of him. Older people moan. The stone-faced German motions with one finger: "right and left -- life and death." Families separate. Children run to their parents and cry. A woman says goodbye to her husband. A father embraces his son. Everyone cries so that it breaks one's heart.

Dr. Baron, at one time the only doctor in Ciechanów, could not bear the German cruelty. Together with his wife and child he swallowed the poison that he had prepared.

From the whole transport 600 men and 300 women approximately remained. The remaining Jews, elderly and children, were put to death in the gas chambers that were closed into two village houses in Auschwitz in a forest in the Polish village Biezeyinki that was especially rebuilt for this purpose. The Germans killed the children at the edge of the forest.

After the selection we came to Birkenau lager near Auschwitz. Women were taken to the women's lager and we – to a men's lager. All our belongings were taken away as well as our clothes. Then we were lined up to have our hair shaved. Wherever there was a spot on a body that had hair on it, the hair was plucked out because the razors were dull.

When we were let out we were given old torn clothes that were marked with a red stripe in the length and breadth. Of course, the clothes didn't fit the one who got them. I got a pair of long pants with a short top, one leather shoe, the other wooden, and it was small...

That same evening we were taken to Block 29. Here it was hell on earth. The block-elder, together with his helpers, beat mercilessly whoever was within their reach. The mocking and shouts reached to high heaven.

Finally we lay down, five men to a reconstructed horse wagon. Not far from me were Ben-Tzion Ehrlich, with his son Avreml, who were choking their cries and clung to one another.

376

After a short time certain people were taken out and kettles with a kind of liquid were brought, tea supposedly. Nakhum Blum was one of the distributors. It's interesting that after traveling three days on the train, without water, nobody could drink because it was brewed from strange leaves. It was simply poison.

The following morning we were chased out of the block very early. A light rain was falling. After we had been standing a few hours and soaked to the bone, after the roll-call, the block-elder, a well-known German criminal -- started to explain to us why we were brought to the lager. He pointed out that we didn't come to live in the lager but to "crap" all the sooner. After his talk we returned to the block. Then we were taken to a place where we went through the registration ceremony.

Special prisoners from the lager tattooed a number on each one's left arm. From that moment on we ceased to exist as people with a name. We became a number. The first Ciechanów transport, in which I was included, was signified with the number 73 thousand and on, and the second transport that came from Mlava was signified with the number 75 thousand and on.

Late at night we were taken to a second block, the ninth block, where there were only Jews. Only the block-elder and the *shreiber* were Poles.

We got the first bit of food, that consisted of rotten potatoes. The distribution of food was accompanied by blows. The next day those who had signed up as tradesmen: carpenters, electricians and others, were sent to Auschwitz, in the main lager.

I won't describe the death lager Auschwitz here. There, millions of Jewish victims were swallowed up. There is a sizable literature about Auschwitz. Here I only want to describe the suffering, pain and heroic uprising of the Ciechanów Jews in this atrocious death lager. First the intellectuals were sent there from the surrounding countries: Poles, French, Dutch, Czechs. They were killed massively by the Germans, and after a short time only singular ones remained.

377

Afterwards all kinds of Poles were brought, amongst whom there was no lack of criminals, anti-Semites who were always ready to torture Jews. When they saw that they were being rewarded for their murderous acts, they helped even more and became devoted partners of the Germans for the mutual aim of destroying the Jews.

In the middle of 1942, Auschwitz became an assembly point for the victims, particularly for the Jews whom the Germans were preparing to murder immediately. Jews who were brought to Auschwitz at that time were quickly converted to ash. People from all lands also came, though their lands were not yet occupied by the Germans, but they remained stuck in lands from where they could not return home.

In the Hell of Auschwitz

The transport of the Ciechanów Jews belonged to these first mass liquidations that were carried out in Auschwitz in 1942.

After being in the lager several days, many Ciechanówers gave up the struggle against the cruel reality. The cold, hunger, beatings and hard labor broke the physical state and morale of the people. From day to day the number of the Ciechanówers grew fewer and fewer. If anyone remained alive it is just by chance.

Once, while returning from work, we weren't allowed into our block after roll-call. A *kapo* appeared and started to pull out people. Everyone tried to hide but later, when it was noticed that the *kapo* had a sign on his arm that be belongs to the clothing-cell, tens of people started to push towards him, I also. He took a look at me, asked where I worked before coming to the lager. "At construction work," I replied. He added me to the chosen ones.

The group consisted of 40 people. We went to work in the clothing storeroom. Laibl Galel was also with me and both Hak brothers. We were taken to another block where there were mainly Poles. Conditions there were much better, the blocks heated and the food better. Working at the clothing we could also dress in warmer clothing and better shoes.

378

A few days later selections took place. The weaker ones were taken out and gassed. *Shabbat Chanukah*, 6 weeks after arriving in the lager, nearly all Ciechanów women were taken to gas chambers. Just a few miraculously were saved.

I started to look for an opportunity to be transferred to another lager. The contagious diseases, typhus, diphtheria started to spread. Under these circumstances I met my good friend from Warsaw. We talked and agreed to go on a transport that was being selected to be sent off. We didn't know where it was headed for, but we didn't care, anywhere -- just to get away from this death-lager. We had to undergo a medical examination for which we had to strip naked and leave our clothes outside. We were already standing at the door, freezing from the cold. Suddenly the *shreiber* called that everyone can return to the block. No more were needed and we could dress and return to our block.

Late at night, when I was already in my bunk, the light suddenly went on and the *shreiber* of the block called out that those up to the age of 19 should step forward. I quickly stepped down and got in line. It was my luck to be sent on the transport.

The next day we didn't go to work. In the afternoon we were taken out of our block. Outside, there were around 2000 young people, all Jews. A civilian German with a *kapo* carried out the selection. They told everyone to march past and those who pleased them they told to step aside. From the 2000, they chose 240, I amongst them.

We got our bread ration, and under the guard of S.S. we were taken to Auschwitz. There was another Ciechanówer with me, Shmuelek Oysteriak, Eliyahu Oysteriak's son. We were taken to Block 7A in a bricklaying school, and here our *tzores* started anew.

The block-elder, a well-known German criminal, started, with the help of the overseer, to cause us *tzores* of the worst kind. We started to get frequent punishment, such as doing knee bends for hours on end with our hands on high. Food was taken away from us We were beaten and shouted at. It was like a crazy-house.

379

From the abnormal and poor food many of us got sick. We started to suffer from diarrhea that nobody could avoid. Every morning when the overseer saw at roll-call that someone doesn't feel good or that their night-layer is not "clean," they would be sent to the "sick-house" and from there nobody returned. That's what happened to Shmuelik Oysteriak. He was sent to the "sick-house" and never returned.

The diarrhea didn't spare me either. I held back with my last bit of strength. I didn't drink the water and used it instead to wash my underwear with it. More than once I put on wet underwear and went this way to work. In this way I managed to get through the first winter in the "bricklaying" school. Later the opportunity arose for me to work in the hospital.

After a few weeks I was transferred to work at disinfecting where the clothes of the prisoners were disinfected before they were washed. Here I worked nearly to the end, that is, up to the time the Russians arrived in January, 1945. There wasn't enough food, but I didn't suffer there from the cold or the filth.

The Lifestyle of the Prisoners in Auschwitz

Generally, the Polish Jews had more endurance than those of other lands. The Jews of Poland, until they came to Auschwitz, had already gone through a "school" of Polish anti-Semitism, German cruelty and ghetto torture, hunger and sickness. The knowledge of Polish and German also helped the Polish Jews a lot. Because of all this they were more able to overcome the hellish existence of Auschwitz than the Jews of other countries.

Amongst the Polish Jews as well as the Slovakian Jews there were those who lost their humanity. In the women's lager in Birkenau the Jewish women of Slovakia were indirect helpers to the cruelty in the lager. These were mainly young women who completed their education in the lager surrounded by electrified barbed wire, so what is the wonder that their hearts were poisoned by the German methods?

380

The most horrifying work in the lager was burning the dead corpses. The unfortunate ones who did this work called themselves *Sonderkommandos*. At first, Russians did this work. That was at the time when tens of thousands of Russian prisoners died of hunger.

When the Jewish transports began to arrive, the Germans put the Jews to work burning the dead. Doing this frightful work were some Ciechanów Jews. When someone would meet them by chance, they bemoaned their bitter destiny.

From time to time the Germans would change those who were working at the crematorium by murdering the former workers and selecting new ones. The old ones were supposedly "transferred to another place and on the way they were murdered, or they were choked in the barracks where they slept.

Once, the Germans didn't succeed in carrying out their plan. The workers in the *Sonderkommando* (as they were called), made an uprising and fought heroically. Some Ciechanów Jews distinguished themselves in this battle. They were Yukl Verona and Shimon Altus.

*

Noah Zabludowicz, who used to come to Birkenau often because of his work as an electrician, brought us the bad news. At the beginning of 1944 the Germans brought thousands of Jews from Poland and Hungary. They went directly to be exterminated. In a matter of days they had turned into heaps of ash. Only a small percentage came into the lager.

We, those arrested in the lager, lived through days of inner turmoil and deep pain in those days. We thought that the murders would no longer affect us, but we made a mistake. The new murders affected us terribly. Every day we looked towards the ovens with the hope that the chimneys would not be emitting the thick smoke that poisoned the air.

For people who weren't in Auschwitz, the problem will certainly arise: How could a few thousand German criminals cause such a fear for a camp of 150 thousand people? Why didn't they rise up against this hell?

381

An answer to this painful question can be found in the precise killing-machine that the Germans erected in Auschwitz.

Projectors lit up every step at night, machine guns, electrified barbed wire and police dogs caused a dreadful fear in every lager prisoner. And in addition to these so-called technical means, the lager apparatus that was installed according to the most modern methods of the German murder "science."

The organization for murdering people crushed the prisoners and sucked out their physical and spiritual marrow. The fear of the two-legged German beast seeped into the senses of the tortured ones. The Auschwitz prisoners had two dreadful enemies: the German beasts did not distinguish between guilty and innocent, and the national hatred of the Jews that was prevalent amongst the prisoners themselves.

No German leadership could have ruled over the tortured ones in the lager if not for the antagonism of the prisoners themselves. The more the antagonism grew, the easier it became for the Germans to rule over the people.

When, in 1943, an end was put to gassing the sick and weak of other nationalities, the mass extermination of Jews started. For Christians there was still a spark of hope of being freed, but for Jews it was clear that only death could free them. When a Pole or a Czech ran away from the lager and they came to a city and mingled with its residents, they could depend on their help, but when a Jew ran away he had no one to turn to.

The social composition of the prisoners in Auschwitz varied. Amongst the prisoners of other nationalities there were a number of Polish activities of various underground movements who fought against the German fascists. These prisoners knew why they were sent to Auschwitz and therefore they started to get organized, adjusted to the conditions in the lager so that could carry on their fight against the Germans. We Jews, however, were a mass of people who had been torn away from their homes because of the only sin that we were Jews. That tied us together spiritually -- physically and morally broken, degraded so low.

When the first winter in the lager passed, and it began to get warmer, it felt somewhat lighter. The days got longer and warmer and every ray of sun brought with it a bit of hope. After roll-call people used to get together in the lager, discuss the situation, news was passed around from one to the other.

382

The Encounter with Ciechanów Jews

The first one I met in the lager was Motl Bergson from Ciechanów. I rejoiced to see him. We exchanged talk of our experiences as well as talk about the Jews of Ciechanów in recent days. Bergson came to Auschwitz from the German lager Zaksenhausen and thanks to his acquaintance with some prisoners, he managed to get into one of the best working places -- that of loading bread.

From him I also discovered that Noah Zabludowicz is also in the lager with his two brothers -- Pinkhas and Khanan. In their block I met others from Ciechanów: Godl Zilber, Yaacov Rosenthal, Yisroel Lichtenstein and his brother Yeshayahu. After that we met often.

At Noah's it became the meeting place of all Ciechanówers. Yitzhak Laib Kleinetz, Yehoshua Gelbart, Mordecai Belovich; Gedalya Vina also came. Others were: Eliyahu Kohn with his son Moishe, Nakhman Ustriak, Dovid Shmid, Barukh Zeloner, Adjulek Kersh, Moishe Gelbart and some others whose names I don't remember.

We started to help one another with bread, clothing, or with "pull" in certain cases to get better work. In time, Noah Zabludowicz and his brother Khanan managed to get jobs as house attendants in one of the best blocks in the lager. The prisoners of that block didn't take the food of the lager. They were mainly Poles who got food parcels from home. They would give the lager food away not only to the Ciechanówers, but also to other prisoners.

After a certain time the block was liquidated and Noah was returned to his former work as an electrician and his two brothers, Pinkhas and Khanan, went to work in a mechanical laundry not far from the place when I was working.

At the same time, through Mordecai Bielovich, we met a young fellow who had lived recently in Mlava but from Ripin originally. His name was Laibik Braun, a dental technician by trade. He worked as a medic in the hospital. Laibik often gave us medication and salves so that we could avoid going to the hospital.

383

He became one of our best friends in the lager.

We Prepare for the Armed Uprising against the Germans

We were sure that the German defeat would come and that then they would want to murder everyone in the lager in order that there shouldn't remain anyone to tell the world what crimes they had committed against mankind. We therefore started to talk about an uprising of the lager prisoners. For this, though, we needed connections and support from outside.

We knew that there was an underground movement in the lager, well organized with political prisoners at the head from various countries. We didn't have an approach to them, however, nor did we know how to take the first step.

Once, going from the roll-call, I met the *shtube dinst* who was in the same block as me. His name was Shimon, a Polish Jew who lived in France before the war. After speaking to him at length about the condition of the Jews in the lager, I told him that the youth who are with us want to do something in order to gain some power to be able to prevent the Germans from killing the remaining Jews.

Shimon looked at me sternly and asked me if we would be ready to organize small groups and gather information for the underground movement. I immediately agreed that not only that, but we're ready for other undertakings as well. At that point he told me of the existence of an underground organization to which belong prisoners of various nations: Germans, French, Poles, etc. He told me to meet with one by the name of Bruno.

I was very surprised because the person he indicated to me was someone I knew very well. He had been working with me for a few months. I spoke with him often and it never entered my mind that he was one of the main people in the underground movement in Auschwitz.

384

Bruno was a German Jew, not very tall, with fiery dark eyes. He always made an impression on me of a quiet person, but in the course of time I learned that he can speak when he has to. I also noticed that he had many German friends, political prisoners, who come to him to hear his opinion. Since 1933 he had been in various lagers and was known as an anti-fascist fighter. Shimon had purposely sent me to Bruno because, as it proved to be, he had been appointed by the underground to leave the lager. After a time, he and two others ran away.

At first my connection with him consisted merely of passing on information, military and political. Bruno checked up on me for some time to see with whom I was meeting and who my friends were.

In his book, *Vidershtand in Auschwitz*, that appeared in Germany after the war, Bruno writes with much praise about the Polish Jews who joined the underground movement in Auschwitz.

On pages 12-13 of his book Bruno points out what the underground in Auschwitz put forth:

"Not to be led to the gas chambers." "When you'll be loaded onto the trucks to be brought to the gas chambers, all should jump from the trucks at the train station Obershlesia-Cracow, and carry on a fight with the S.S. bandits."*

In the ranks of the Jews this last proclamation resounded well and it became a means for gathering the active Jewish forces.

The narrow circle to whom I conveyed Bruno's proclamation were: Noah Zabludowicz, Mordecai Bilovich (Aaron Gelbart's son-in-law), Laibl Laufer, a Slovakian Jew, Yisroel Gutman from Warsaw and Laibek Braun from Ripin. More recently he had lived in Mlava.

We, on our part, extended the framework of our activities, increased the number of our people, and asked Bruno to assign important tasks to us. I informed him about our supplies factory D.A.W. Bruno warned us not to conduct any action on our own.

*Bruno Baum, *Vidershtand in Auschwitz*, a report of the international anti-fascist lager action, Winnie Publishers, Berlin, Potsdam.

385

The Organization of the Uprising in Auschwitz

In order to maintain contact with the people, we needed support. We appealed to Motl Bergson, who worked in the bread supply. He enabled us to carry this through. At his place all Ciechanówers found an open door. He helped everyone in every way he possibly could. There was also a German Jew with him, Yaacov (both had come from the German lagers). He knew nearly all the Ciechanówers. When anyone asked him where he was from he said: "Ciechanów."

Being somewhat supplied with food, we were able to carry on further with our work. We started to think about sending one of our *chaverim* out of the lager. Once, after a talk with Noah Zabludowicz, he told me that he is ready to run away together with Avraham Boimgart.

Noah was the most suitable candidate because of his "Aryan" looks and also because of his experience in the former lagers.

I came to an understanding with Bruno in this regard and he agreed that Noah should leave the lager. I requested from Bruno names of people on the outside who act as contacts with those who run away. He sent me to one in Block 1, a German Jew called Max. From him I got the necessary addresses that I had to memorize. At the last minute the plan was not carried out because the dangers grew greater and the chances of getting out of the lager became slimmer.

Noah continued his contact with the women's lager. There also we met a Ciechanówer girl, Rosa Robota, Shaya Robota's daughter, who joined the underground movement.

At the same time some Ciechanówers were sent to Birkenau. Amongst them were: Godl Zilber and Baruch Zeloner. Unfortunately, Zeloner didn't survive long He got sick with typhus and died.

In 1944, large transports were sent to the lagers in Germany. Noah was supposed to be amongst them but his brother Pinkhas, who knew the work representative, succeeded in rescuing Noah from the transport.

At the time that preparations are being made for the general uprising, it was decided that the Jewish group should supply the explosives from the munitions factory "Union", in order to make bombs.

386

The job was entrusted to two *chaverim* from our group: Yehudah Laufer and Yisroel Gutman. But the matter encountered great difficulties and great dangers. All efforts were in vain. It remained to make contact with the small women's group that worked in the gunpowder-factory where the grenades were prepared.

The Jewish women who worked there were always strictly controlled and it was forbidden for them to meet with prisoners of other barracks, especially with men, so that it was very difficult to come into contact with them. After a consultation it was decided to send Noah to Birkenau to make connections with the women's groups of the gunpowder-factory.

Noah knew that Rosa Robota is in contact with the women who transport the explosive material that is handed over through them to Rosa. She, in turn, gives it to Godl Zilber, and from him the material goes to the *Sonderkommando*. The material gets put into a container of acid, that is used for welding iron.

Rosa promised to help. It didn't take long and contact was established. During a pause in the work the women put a bundle of dynamite at a pre-arranged spot. All the work was done during the night shift, when the control wasn't so strict.

In the morning when the workers came from work, I awaited them, and from a Hungarian Jewish acquaintance I took half a loaf of bread. In that bread there was a packet of dynamite. I kept it at my work place and later gave it to a German Jew who worked at the railway station.

The dynamite that was handed over to the *Sonderkommando* by Rosa Robota was handed over to a Russian technician, Borodin, and he produced bombs in preserve cans. The bombs were hidden in various places.

The Uprising and Its Tragic End

Noah, when returning from work to the lager one day, informed us that the *Sonderkommando* was preparing for an uprising. At that time the Germans stopped exterminating the Hungarian Jews. The Jews from the *Sonderkommando* already knew that the Germans will kill them all. The experienced ones already knew from previous transports that the Germans had supposedly transferred to other places to work, and in the middle of the way they killed the Jews. For this reason the *Sonderkommando* decided not to wait any longer.

The day that news got out that a transport would be sent out, consisting only of men who work in the *Sonderkommando*, the uprising broke out. In the period of a few minutes around 600 people who worked in *Sonderkommando* were involved in the uprising. Crematorium 2 was exploded and burnt. The *kapo*, a German, who was known for his atrocities, the rebels threw into the burning oven while still alive. In hand-to-hand fighting 4 S.S. were killed and some others wounded. Around the crematoriums it looked like a war zone. The enclosure was torn up and the people ran off.

All the S.S. who were in the area were recruited. All the kommandos that worked outside of the lager interrupted their work and came to the lager. Immediately a roll-call took place. S.S. men ran around like poisoned mice. They hadn't expected anything like this: that they would have to defend themselves against the Jews.

Unfortunately, the prisoners from other larger-parts didn't come to help the rebels of the *Sonderkommando*. The end was that the Germans gained control of the situation. The uprising of the *Sonderkommando* remained a symbol of revenge and an inspiration for all the prisoners. The Christian prisoners started to conduct themselves with a certain respect towards the Jews.

The Germans murdered all those who had participated in the uprising. Amongst those murdered were the Ciechanówers: Yukl Verona and Shimon Altus and others. Only a few, who hid and only appeared again after a few days, remained alive.

The inquest connected with brutal torture that the Germans conducted proved that the explosives that the rebels used came from the ammunition factory. This information the investigators got from informers who worked in the factory. The suspicion in giving the prisoners explosives fell on a few women who worked in the gunpowder-factory.

388

They were arrested and taken to Block 11 in Auschwitz. After several days of grueling questioning and terrible torture, they broke down. Amongst the arrested women was Rosa Robota.

Pinkhas Zabludowicz, who often found himself at the entrance of the lager, once noticed Rosa Robota being led in the lager to Block 11. Fearfully we thought that she would not be able to bear the merciless torture and that she would divulge the names who were in contact with her or with other girls. Every morning I saw her go out of the lager in the political section.

Once, after a roll-call, it got dark in the lager. Such blackouts were now frequent in the lager because of bombings. During the blackout I was standing with Yukl Rosenthal at my place of work. We noticed two women supporting a woman. An S.S. man was going along with them, taking them to Block 11. We recognized Rosa. When they had gone a few feet away we started to shout: "Rosa! Rosa!" so that she should be aware that we know where she is. We thought that maybe the Germans had purposely made a blackout so that no one should see the condition in which Rosa was returning from the political section.

We were also worried about the *chaverim*, Laibl Laufer and Yisroel Gutman, who worked in "Union." Their arrest could bring great misfortune to the underground movement in the lager and this through Jews.

A Visit with the Tortured Rosa Robota and Her Heroic Death

As I have already mentioned, my workplace was not far from Block 11 where the bunker was. Yaacov Kozelchik, a Jew from the Bialystok area, was the *kapo* for Block 11. He used to come in to us often to wash, and each time he would tell about the four Jewish women, amongst them Rosa also, who get tortured in his block. He helps them with whatever he can, but unfortunately he knows their fate.

I met with Noah at that time. I told him about the condition of the tortured women. He decided to talk to Yaacov to find out if he could possibly arrange for one of us to go in to Rosa's bunker and hear from her personally what the situation looks like. Yaacov agreed that Noah should go in to her, taking along a good bottle of whiskey and a *vurshtin* in order to bribe the S.S. man who is always in the block.

389

The visit was arranged for the evening. Noah took everything along. Yaacov took him into the block and introduced him to the S.S. as a friend who came to visit him. They started to drink until the German fell asleep. Taking advantage of the opportunity, Yaacov grabbed the keys and led Noah through the dark corridor to Rosa's cell and the following is what Noah wrote in his memoirs about that visit:

"I was privileged to see Rosa a few days before her death, for the last time. At night, when all the prisoners were already asleep, and when it was forbidden to go about in the lager, I went down to Bunker 11 and saw the room and the dark corridors. I heard the groans of charged people. I shuddered. I went by way of the stairs where Yaacov led me until we came to the cell where Rosa was. Yaacov opened the door, let me in and locked it again and then disappeared.

"When I got used to the light, I noticed, lying on the cold cement, a form, wrapped in torn clothes. She turned her head towards me. I hardly recognized her. On her face one could recognize the pain and torture that she had endured at the inquest. After a few minutes of quiet she began to speak. She told of the sadistic methods that the Germans use at these inquests. Nobody can endure it. She also said that she takes all responsibility on herself and she will to the last. She didn't betray anyone.

"I tried to comfort her, but she didn't want to hear. 'I know what I did and I know what awaits me,' she said. She asked that the *chaverim* continue their work. 'It's easier to die when one knows that one's work continues.'

"I heard a squeaking of the door. Yaacov told me to go out. I said farewell to her. That was the last time I saw her."

*

Shuddering, I stood outside and waited for Noah. I was afraid that he might have a failure. Finally the door opened and he came out. From his face I could recognize that the visit to Rosa's cell made a strong impression on him. He couldn't free himself from that impression for a long time.

390

Once, when the women were being taken to the washroom, I succeeded in speaking with her. She told me that for the last few days they weren't taking her for interrogation and she no longer needs food. She doesn't know what will happen further.

When a few days had passed, information was given to the "Union" factory that all the women must leave work early and return to the lager. The women immediately understood that something would happen. True enough, the Germans hung four women that day. Two, they hung in the ammunition factory "Union" and two in the women's lager. The women immediately understood that something would happen. True enough, the Germans hung four women that day. Two, they hung in the ammunition factory "Union" and two in the women's lager. Amongst these two was Rosa Robota.

From what the women who were present at that bestial act afterwards told, Rosa went to the gallows and sacrificed her young life.

*

In his already-mentioned book, *Vidershtand in Auschwitz*, in the chapter *Fir Topfere Medals*, Bruno Baum describes the heroic death of the four girls.

At the interrogation about the hand-grenades that were prepared by the *Sonderkommando*, the S.S. proved that the explosives were taken from the "Union" store of gunpowder. Because of the information of the bandit, Shultz, eight women were arrested. They were freed after terrible torture at the interrogation. It was only after the proof given by *kapo-* assistant Koch that four girls were arrested who worked in the day-shift in the gungunpowder store.

In spite of the sadistic torture at the interrogation, the arrested girls were silent and didn't divulge any names.

"The execution of the girls was ordered. They were to be hung in the women's lager No. 1. The night before the execution we succeeded, through a connection, in speaking with one of them. We were in a bunker at night (a cellar in which those who were sentenced to death were kept) and spoke to a girl of around twenty. We wanted to comfort and strengthen her but she tried to give us courage to continue our fight. She told us that she is proud that she participated in the uprising. She will die in peace. We knew that these heroic girls will be silent to the grave.

391

The following day she was hung during roll-call in the women's lager. She died quietly, calling out: "We'll take revenge."

"Who were these girls? They were young Jewish girls between the ages of 18-22. They were from Poland. In 1939 they went into the ghetto. In 1942 or 1943 they came to Auschwitz. Immediately upon arrival their parents and sisters were taken away from them and sent to the gas chambers. They were the only survivors of their family and immediately joined the Jewish group of 300 prisoners who were in contact with the uprising organization. On January 6, 1945, an end was made, by execution, to the lives of these heroic girls.

Nobody who was in Auschwitz will ever forget these heroic Jewish girls."

*

The above quote from Bruno Baum's book does not give the names of these four heroic Jewish girls who, in Auschwitz, participated in the truly heroic struggle against the German murderers.

We Ciechanówers who were in Auschwitz knew one of these heroines very well -- our Rosa Robota from Ciechanów. It remains for the researchers to find out the names of the three young Jewish heroines who sacrificed their life in the fight against the German bestiality in Auschwitz.

New Hangings, and the Tumult of the Germans Because the Front Was Getting Closer

At that time the front was already at Cracow and all along the shore of the Veisl. Frequent air raids occurred in the vicinity of Auschwitz, where the German heavy industry was located. No bombs fell on the lager.

Once, when the prisoners were outside the lager, an air raid took place and the houses in which the S.S. lived were hit. A bomb also fell somewhere where there were lager workers. Sixty people were killed. Quite often, during such raids, the Germans came into the lager because there they were more secure than outside. This situation encouraged us. We were sure that their defeat would come very soon.

392

In order to make a connection with the Russian front that was 60 kilometers away from the lager, it was decided to send out a small group of people. For this purpose two Austrians and two Poles were selected. They were at the head of the underground movement. They prepared a long time for this and made contact with a friend of theirs, an S.S. man, in the lager. He was to take them out. He betrayed them, however, and the whole group were captured and sent to Block 11. After lengthy interrogation and torture, they were hung in the lager.

It was already the end of 1944. Their death left a deep sorrow in the lager. It greatly affected the work of the underground fighters.

The Germans, while awaiting the approaching Russian attack, that was likely to strike any day, started to liquidate everything that was connected with their criminal acts. Large transports of clothes, shoes and gold were sent to Germany. Fearing an eventual uprising, the Germans from Auschwitz and from the surrounding lagers transferred all the Poles to Austria and Germany. Hundreds of lager people were put to work to destroy the crematoriums. In the furnace of the laundry the Auschwitz files were burned, a total of a million files.

There was a great tumult amongst the S.S. in Bunker 11. S.S. who didn't want to carry out the orders were arrested. At night, Russian rockets lit up the sky for hours.

We went out to work daily in order to show that we aren't interested in what was going on around us. Every day brought greater hope, and this went on until January 16, 1945.

Late at night all block *shreibers* were called out and were told to prepare to evacuate everyone.

The next day, we Ciechanówers gathered at Motl Bialovich's room and discussed the new situation. Because of the quick advance of the Russians, there might be a possibility that we will be freed in the middle of the way, though we knew that marching in the cold and frost would cost many lives. We supplied ourselves with warm clothes and food, and on the 18th of January we were led out of Auschwitz.

393

Because of the breakup of the blocks we got separated. Some went to Germany and I, Motl Bialovich, Yehoshua Albert and his brother Moishe, and Yehoshua Lichtenstein, were led away in the direction of Austria.

The German Bestiality before Their Final Defeat

After walking for four days we came to a train station where we went into open wagons. We reached Czechoslovakia. The population there brought us food and hot coffee. The Germans, our guards, chased away the good Czechs and even fired shots over their heads.

After traveling for several days we reached Austria and were taken to the Mauthausen lager. Here fresh *tzores* started for us. Our clothes were taken away from us. We were kept in a block for two weeks, not sent out to work. We had to line up for roll-call almost naked.

Afterwards, we were sent in a transport of a few hundred people to Abenze in Upper Austria. There fresh troubles started: stone-digging in the mountains, which was very hard work. Hunger, cold, beatings and mocking were daily events. We were isolated from the world around us.

After being in the lager for two months, I decided to go to the sick precinct. It wasn't so easy to get in there, however, Hundreds of people were waiting for a place and for a bed to become vacant. Finally, I got a place as the fourth one in a bed. In the same bed there was also the Ciechanów teacher of the *Yavneh School*, Petrikus.

Once, at the end of April 1945, he got off the bed and fell down. I picked him up and put him back in bed. Laying there together with him, I asked him to move a bit but he didn't answer me. I touched his cold body. He was no longer alive. A few days later Moishe Gelbard could not survive the hunger.

A Tarnover Jew told us about the situation in the lager. He had come to visit his sick father who was in our block. He told us that nobody is going out to work. Those who do go, return at noon. The S.S. are very irritable and lost.

394

It was also told that the lager leader appealed to the prisoners that in order to prevent the loss of lives, everyone should go to the bunkers that were dug out in the hills. The lager *shreiber*, a Czech, replied that no one would go. After a brief consultation, he agreed that we should remain in the lager. The intent of the German murderers was to blow up all the bunkers together with the people in them.

In the middle of the night we were suddenly awakened. A man came in who addressed us in Polish: "Where is the block-elder?" Out of fear none replied. He went into the room where the block-elder lived and he found two large pots of food there. He immediately divided it up amongst us and said that tomorrow a different block-head would come and that in another few days the Americans would come and we should remain as calm as possible.

The next morning one of the sick noticed a white flag on the crematorium. With my last bit of energy I went down from the bed to see the flag. Two days later the first Americans entered. It's easy to imagine the jubilation. They immediately started to send the sick to various hospitals. With food they made a big mistake: the food that they sent to the lager was not good for the sick, and hundreds of people died from it.

The Americans noted the situation and thereafter only sent such food as the sick could digest. After being in the hospital for half a year

I felt completely well. I started to realize my youthful dream of coming to the Land of Israel.

So it was that, through Italy and Cyprus, I reached *Eretz Yisroel*.

395

Ciechanówer refugees in Vilna at the start of the war

The German extermination caused a great wandering in the occupied areas, as is well known. As long as there were no closed ghettos, Jews ran from place to place in order to escape the brutality of the Germans. Many of the refugees also came to Vilna. Amongst them was a group of Ciechanów Jews.

Unfortunately we don't have any information about the life of the Ciechanów Jews in Vilna during the war. The group photograph that remains shows that they kept together. Ciechanów readers of this *Yizkor Book* will probably recognize their friends or close relatives in the photograph.

396

Uprising against the Germans

In various forms, expression was given to the uprising of the tormented Jews against the Germans and against their extermination of the Jews: the acts of sabotaging the German orders, giving mutual help to one another in the lagers, organizing food, medical help. In all these ways the Jewish uprising against the Germans expressed itself. The armed Jewish uprising stands out. It was possible only under certain conditions. When Jews could get ammunition.

The fight against the Germans, the Jews carried on in all the above-mentioned ways. They also took part in the armed uprising, not in Ciechanów, but in the death-lager -- in Auschwitz and in occupied France. In both of these struggles heroic persons stand out, who sacrificed their lives with their martyr deaths. One of them was the heroic girl, Rosa Robota.

The (signed) A.V.I.

397

Rosa Robota -- the heroic martyr

398   blank

399
Top square:

> With love and pride we cherish in our hearts the memory
> of our dearly beloved
> ROSA ROBOTA - H.I " D
> who after taking revenge on the German murderers
> perished heroically.
> We shall always cherish her pure and holy spirit
> as a sign of courage for the sake of her people.
> May her soul be bound in the bond of eternal life.
>
> Her uncles and their families in Israel and elsewhere
> Yosef Trombka and his family (Detroit, U.S.A.)
> Yechiel Yisraeli (Trombka) and family, Israel
> Shalom Trombka and family, Israel
> Mordecai Yisraeli (Trombka) and family, Israel.

Bottom square: A similar *Yizkor* for Rosa Robota by the survivors of Ciechanów.

400

Rosa Robota

Her Life, Struggle against the Germans and Her Death as a Martyr

In the history of the daring uprising struggle that the tortured Auschwitz prisoners conducted against the German mass-murderers — Rosa Robota wrote a chapter of heroism, courage and perseverance and elevation of morale and martyrdom. In the Jewish literature of martyrdom the term martyr is used very sparingly, but Rosa Robota earned this by her acts in Auschwitz and can rightfully be called a martyr.

*

Rosa Robota was born in Ciechanów to fine parents who had lived in the *shtetl* for many generations. She had one brother and one sister. Rosa completed the *Folk Shule* with distinction.

Beloved by her school friends because of her goodness, devotion and true friendship that she showed her friends, she already in the sixth grade organized a school-group that, after finishing school, joined *Hashomeir Hatzair*. The group -- Hene Greenbaum, Sonya Gurna, Chaya Mundzak, Lola Kirsh, Rukhche Kirshenzweig, Melekh

Zilberstein, Moishe Shlesinger, Noah Isenberg, Shepsl Galk and Shmuel Viezba -- formed a special *kvutza* in *Hashomeir Hatzair*.

Parents of Rosa Robota

401

Rosa Robota and her friends in Ciechanów before the war. Rosa - second from right, standing

During the German extermination the *kvutza* did much to ease the need of the tortured Jews.

Rosa had her second home in the *Hashomeir Hatzair* organization. Many of her friends went to the *kibbutzim* to prepare themselves to fulfil the dream to make *aliyah* to *Eretz Yisroel*. Rosa strove for this also, but because of difficulties at home she had to temporarily go to a *Hechalutz hachshara*. Meanwhile, the German extermination came and this destroyed all her efforts.

When the Germans destroyed Ciechanów, Rosa was a young girl. She and her sister were seized for work where the governor had lived before the war. The two young girls were tortured at work. Soon Rosa and her family lost their home. The Germans destroyed the house where they lived, together with the whole Jewish quarter.

402

The tragic ghetto life started. Rosa and her family moved in with relatives.

In the ghetto Rosa participated in various consultations of the young Jewish people regarding the preparation of an uprising, but conditions in the Ciechanów ghetto were not ripe for this. Rosa was always going around enraged because she couldn't avenge the suffering of the Jews.

In November 1942 Rosa, together with the Ciechanów Jews, was sent to Auschwitz, the extermination-hell. During the "selections" -- when some were chosen to go to the gas chambers, while others were found fit for work -- Rosa was amongst those for work. She was sent to work not far from the ammunition factory "Union" in Auschwitz. There a large number of women were working, amongst them young girls from Ciechanów. Some of them, with Rosa Robota at the head, volunteered with heart and soul for the underground movement, against the Germans, that the tortured prisoners organized.

As has already been mentioned in the memoirs that are in this *Yizkor Book*, the Ciechanów Jews in Auschwitz stuck together as much as possible in the notorious German torture-lager. They found out about the existence of the underground movement and made contact with it.

The organizers of the uprising, who knew that there are Ciechanów girls employed in the production of ammunition, hinted to the Ciechanówers to establish contact with the women they knew in order to get explosives. Here Rosa came on the scene, with her wonderful personality. She took upon herself the dangerous, life-threatening role of getting explosives for the underground in Auschwitz.

Noah Zabludowicz of the Ciechanów group established contact with Rosa, and as Moishe Kulka has written, Rosa promised her help. It didn't take long and the contact was made. During a break at work, the women placed a bundle containing dynamite at a pre-arranged spot. All this was done during the night shift, when the control was not so strict.

403

In the morning, when the workers returned from work, I waited for them and took a half loaf of bread from a Hungarian Jew whom I knew. Inside the bread I found the packet. I hid it at my place of work and later gave it to a German Jew who worked in the railway station.

The dynamite, that was handed over to the *Sonderkommando* through Rosa Robota, was then given to a Russian technician, Borodin, and he constructed bombs in cans of preserves. The bombs were hidden in various places.

Much has been written about Rosa Robota's devotion and struggle against the Germans, and her heroic death. To all this we want to add an excerpt from a publication that Raya Kagan wrote in *Yediot Yad Vashem*, Number 15/16 (entitled "Four Who Were Executed"). Raya Kagan, the prisoner in Auschwitz, and one who also took part in the uprising, wrote:

"As is well known, a small group of young Jewish girls helped, with heroic deeds, particularly in the Auschwitz conditions, to explode one of the crematoriums in Auschwitz. The group consisted of four girls: two of them, Tosca Esther, and Regina, worked in the manufacturing of ammunition at "Union" in the section called *gunpowder kommando*. A third girl, Ella Gertner, worked in the office of this section. Rosa was not connected with "Union." She was active in the underground movement in Birkenau and she was given the risky job of establishing contact between the underground movement and the girls who work in the explosives section.

Rosa got the gunpowder from Ella Gertner after she stole it from the factory "Union" and she turned it over to trusty hands of the men's lager in Birkenau.

The publication of Raya Kagan's article was written mainly to explain how the Germans discovered the participation of the girls in the underground movement in Auschwitz. Regarding the arrest and the torture that Rosa Robota endured, R. Kagan wrote:

404

"Rosa Robota was arrested. Apparently the S.S. considered her one of the initiators of the whole action, and she (Rosa) drank from the cup of agony. She was forced, by the Germans, to reveal who were the closest links to the uprising. She gave the name of a *Sonderkommando* to whom she had given the package of explosives, but that one was no longer alive." All the interrogations were made in the barrack where I worked. I saw the girls. I heard the cries of the tortured ones that filled the whole barrack. In my eyes, just as in the eyes of Yisroel Gutman,* Rosa Robota stands in all the grace of her heroic acts.

*Yisroel Gutman, author of the book, *Anashim v'aifer* (People and Ashes) in which the experiences of Auschwitz are described, as well as the armed uprising, with the heroic participation of Rosa Robota.

In the brochure *Kehillat Ciechanów Bkhurban Vmavet shel Rosa Robota* (Kehillah Ciechanów And The Death of Rosa Robota), there is the following description about the heroic deeds of Rosa Robota and the girls who supplied explosives to the underground fighters in Auschwitz:

Noah Zabludowicz made contact with the women who worked in the ammunition factory. He organized a group of girls who had to collect explosive material and transport it to a safe place in order to use it at a precise time. At the head of this group was Rosa Robota. She carried out her mission with great devotion. She herself kept the explosive material, risking her life. Her eyes burned with revenge when she was able to do something concrete against the enemy. She also supplied bread for hungry women.

She was very beloved in all women's lagers and many women put themselves at her service, regularly supplying explosives. Noah Zabludowicz was responsible for the ammunition. Every evening the material was taken out through the *Sonderkommando* to the crematorium. That's where the safest place was.*

*The brochure, *Kehillat Ciechanów Bkhurbana vmavet giborim shel Rosa Robota* (Kehillah of Ciechanów during the khurban and the heroic death of Rosa Robota), a brochure in Yiddish, published by the committee to memorialize Rosa Robota. The brochure included submissions by: Yekhiel Yisraeli (Trombka), Noah Zabludowicz, and Moishe Kolko. Material gathered by Noah and Moishe Kolko. Edited by Moishe Fuchs, Tel-Aviv, 1952.

405

After the failed uprising the Germans killed all who had participated in the struggle. Amongst them there were also some Ciechanówers. The investigation, during which torture was administered, conducted by the Germans, naturally revealed that the explosive material that had been used came from the ammunition factory. The interrogators were given this information by informers who worked in the factory. The suspicion of supplying the explosives fell on several women who worked in the gunpowder section. They were arrested and taken to Block 11 in Auschwitz, where they were terribly tortured. Amongst these was Rosa Robota.

The failure of the uprising, the thinning of the ranks, arrests and torture, cast a disturbing fear on the Auschwitz prisoners. Everyone awaited their death in the gas chambers. The Ciechanówers were particularly affected -- the small group who were connected with Rosa Robota and knew how she was being bestially tormented by the Germans. Everyone wanted very much to see her before her death as a martyr.

With the aid of a Jewish *kapo*, there was success in getting drunk an S.S. man who guarded Block 11, where the tortured women were, and Noah Zabludowicz got into the cell.

In the previously-mentioned brochure -- *Kehillat Ciechanów Bkhurban vmavet giborim shel Rosa Robota*, the following moving description of Rosa's thoughts and feelings in the torture chamber in the last hours before the execution:

Rosa Robota in the death chamber

"In a dark cell Rosa sat naked. Her body was murderously wounded from beatings and blood was running from her wounds. She was deep in thought and hardly felt her physical suffering. She made a reckoning with herself. Every day of her 23 years flashed before her eyes. She saw pictures of her whole past. One thought burned in her mind:

Was it worth it?

She recalled the *shtetl*, her parents, friends, the surroundings in which she lived, hoped and dreamt of a better future.

406

And now all is finished. The Jewish people are wiped out. And she falls into great despair. She questions herself: What did I fight for? Did the people-eaters really succeed in annihilating our people? Will Hitler's will be fulfilled, that one will be able to see a Jew only in a display, or are Jewish youth alive somewhere? And there, in the distant land of Jewish dreams of a new Jewish life, there must certainly be youth that can't come to terms with the thought that, God forbid, we cease to exist as a people.

The youth of *Eretz Yisroel* is rushing to the fight against those who want to kill us all. Rosa recalls how, in her group at *Hashomeir Hatzair*, she learned the mighty chapter in *Tanakh* where Ezekiel, the prophet, describes his beautiful vision, and as though through a dream the words spring from her: Will these bones live? And she answers herself with Ezekiel's words: "See, I instill breath into you and you will live. Yes, I will restore you, put flesh upon you, cover you with skin and put breath into you and you will come alive. See, I open your graves and will raise you, my people, from the grave and bring you to the land of Israel.

Ray of hope arises in her deep suffering and sorrow:

My people, you shall once more live. There is no power that can destroy you. You shall be in your land. My suffering was worth it, just as long as my dear people will continue to exist.*

*From the brochure: *Kehillat Ciechanów Bkhurban vmavet giborim shel Rosa Robota*. In this quoted passage, stylistic changes have been made.

*

A few days later the Germans in Auschwitz gathered together all the women who had worked in the "Union" factory to witness the hanging of the four women, amongst whom was Rosa Robota. As was later told by the women who were present at the execution, the Ciechanów Jewish martyr went stoically and proudly to her death. This was at the end of November, 1944. (According to the memoirs of Bruno Baum the execution was carried out January 6, 1945).

At that time the Polish *shtetl* Ciechanów was already without Jews. The grandchildren and great-grandchildren of those Jews who had, hundreds of years ago, built up their *Kehillah* in the Polish settlement on the edge of the Lidinia River, were tortured by the German occupiers with all kinds of terrible means and led to their death.

The small number of Ciechanów Jews who remained alive, living in Israel and in other parts of the world, will never forget the torture of those of their *shtetl*, the martyrs, heroes who fought against the Germans with every possible means to prevent their destruction.

A. V. Y.

407

The Partisan Gavriel Avshanka

Gavriel Avshanka was a very close friend of mine only in the last pre-war years. We all loved him dearly because of his open-heartedness. He was strong, healthy and full of the joy of life, always ready to help a friend in a time of need if at all possible.

On the third day of the outbreak of war we left our home, Ciechanów, and together with him and his family ended up in the distant Stalingrad steppes.

A few months later Avshanka and his family left the village in which we lived temporarily, and went to Rovno in western-Ukraine. They probably thought they would live better there, but to their great disappointment, they were fooled.

Immediately after the outbreak of the German-Soviet war, in June 1941, the whole territory of western-Ukraine was occupied by the Germans. The suffering of the Jews immediately began: ghettos, yellow patches, then the annihilation. In the city of Rovno alone eighteen thousand Jews were murdered.

Gavriel, when he beheld the bloody enemy, decided not to forfeit his life so easily. He went to the forest and joined the partisans, where Jews and Russians fought together against the Germans and their Ukrainian helpers. They carried on for many months in the forests in the vicinity of Sarny, always on the move. Many times there wasn't even a crust of bread to eat. The partisans decided to send out a few *chaverim* to search for some food and also to get some medication for the sick and wounded partisans. Volunteers, amongst them our Gavriel, came forth. He didn't like to be left out of the action. They set out.

408

Gavriel Avshanka

In the dark of night the partisans went to the nearest village, where all were asleep, in order to force the village-elder to give food for the partisans. They surrounded the house of the village-elder. Gavriel knocked on the door. Steps were heard, the sound of a lock turning, and at the same time there was a shot from a revolver. The shot was deathly for Gavriel. In spite of his strong, herculean body, he could no longer utter a word when the *chaverim* came to his aid. His eyes were shut forever.

The partisans took revenge for their murdered friend. Two grenades were thrown into the dwelling from which, after some shooting, large tongues of fire started to break out. The well-aimed bullets of the partisans didn't let anyone get out alive. After seizing the necessary food, the partisans took the dead body of their friend and returned to their base. At the open grave they all paid respect to the fallen hero.

This happened in the village Matzienlis, not far from the city Sarny, in April 1944. A few days later the territory was liberated by the Russian army.

————

Shlomo Zalman Kahane

Shlomo Zalman Kahane, with the nickname Yuzshek, I knew from before the war. He was the son of very poor parents; his father, a tailor. He worked in Ciechanów

From his early days he dreamt of a free, just world, without exploitation of one person by another, of a world where work would be a pleasure, not a hardship. In order to reach his ideal and principles, he joined the ranks of the communist youth movement that was illegal. He knew that he had chosen a long and difficult way, but the belief in a better tomorrow was very great for him and no difficulties scared him.

Shlomo Zalman Kahane

In the fight against the Polish fascist government, he gave most of his best young years cooped up in prison, constantly suffering, yet he didn't break down, always was full of the joy of life and beliefs. The secret police didn't leave Kahane alone and he was forced to leave Poland and left for Paris.

410

There also, Kahane didn't have an easy life. He had difficulty getting a work-card. Finding living quarters was also not easy and in addition to this there was the problem of how to earn a living. Shlomo Zalman worked late into the night and still made time to be active in the professional union to improve the living conditions of the workers.

When the Germans occupied France, Yuzshek, in spite of his poor health as a result of his imprisonment in Poland, threw himself, together with his French *chaverim*, into the underground fight against the enemy.

After the victory over the German mass-murderers, when everyone started to breathe freely once more, Kahane was already very sick. He had to go into a sanitarium where, full of belief in the struggle for a better tomorrow, he died in July 1946.

Ciechanówers in Paris paid their debt to this idealistic fighter against nazism and fascism and took his bones to the brother-grave of the Ciechanów *landsmanschaft.*

————

Menakhem Kalenberg

Menakhem Kalenberg, son of a religious family, was well-known in Ciechanów. He attended a *yeshiva* in his young years or in the *Bais Hamedresh* studying *Gemara.* For many years his father didn't occupy himself with earning a living. The mother provided for the family.

Menakhem, as a loyal son, helped his mother carry her heavy burden.

I knew Menakhem from my earliest childhood years. We were neighbors and also learned together at the *cheder* of *Rebbe* Zachs. Later, our paths parted. I went to the *Povshekhner* School, but for Menakhem's parents this was like turning him into a *goy,* and he remained in *cheder.* Still, every time we met, in addition to a good-morning, we would always have something to talk about. In general, Menakhem was a happy fellow and loved people.

Longer, hard years passed. In 1946 I was in Łodz. There I discovered that my *chaver* Menakhem is sick. Naturally, I went to visit him. At that time he was staying with one of our *landsleit,* Dinche Krimke. Great was his joy when he saw me. We exchanged memoirs of our war years.

Almost in tears, in his customary hoarse voice, he said: "You see, if our folks wouldn't have been so foolishly misled in 1939, and they would have escaped to Russia the way we did, we wouldn't be so lonely, and they would also have survived the war. The first days of the war I begged my parents to leave Ciechanów. I had a feeling that we must run away. They didn't want to listen to me, however. I therefore said goodbye to them, took my *tfillin* and left the place of my birth; went to far-off Russia and worked there. Afterwards I was also mobilized into the Russian army. That was already at the time when the Germans began to retreat.

In one of the battles, already on the cursed German soil, I was wounded and sent to a hospital, but to the present day I suffer with my legs.

"And now, Yosele," he continued, "after I didn't find any of my family in Poland, I dream of going to *Eretz Yisroel*. I'll find suitable work and be able to live amongst our own people."

When he spoke these words, his pale face regained color and beamed.

Destiny, though, did not want Menakhem to reach *Eretz Yisroel*. En route to the land of his dreams, and in Paris, he got seriously ill and entered the Jewish hospital. He sent searchers for his *landsleit,* but when the emissary came to *chaver* Melotzker, who immediately went to the hotel, it was already too late. The sick one had died a day before (May 2, 1948).

Yosef Mundzak

On February 23, 1949, the committee of Ciechanów *landsleit* in Paris published the following announcement in the Parisian *Freier Press* (Free Press):

412

Committee of Ciechanówer and surrounding area *landsleit* invites all members and friends to honor the two Ciechanów *landsleit* SHLOMO KAHANE, former resistance fighter, and MENAKHEM KALENBERG, former soldier in the Red Army, who are being buried in the brother-grave of the Ciechanówer *landsleit* and of those in the surrounding area, February 25, 9:00 a.m., at the main entrance of the Banye Cemetery.

This announcement serves as an invitation.

The Committee

Honor to their memory

SHLOMO KAHANE AND MENAKHEM KALENBERG OF CIECHANÓW HAVE THEIR BONES BURIED IN THE BROTHER-GRAVE

Two of our *landsleit* are being buried in the brother-grave, February 25, 9:00 a.m. These are SHLOMO KAHANE, very well-known in the 11th (lager) under the name Yuzshek. In spite of his poor health, he took an active part in the underground movement until he was confined to bed. One year after the liberation he gets torn away from us.

MENAKHEM KALENBERG left his home town Ciechanów after the arrival of the Germans and enlists in the Russian army. Fights from Stalingrad to Berlin. In Berlin he gets wounded and has a leg amputated.

In 1948 he arrives in Paris. He enters the Rothschild Hospital, where he dies in a short time, after much suffering.

The Committee

Honor to his memory

———

413

Funeral in Paris for Shlomo Kahane and Menakhem Kalenberg. Yitzhak-Leib Kleinetz delivers the eulogy

414

A Speech by Yitzhak-Leib Kleinetz at a Yizkor Evening of Ciechanówers in Paris

Beloved sisters, brothers and friends:

You know me for a long time, and so you know that this is not an orator speaking to you, but blind destiny wanted me to be the one amongst you who must, with a broken heart, always remind you of the suffering of our dearest whom the German murderers tore away from us and destroyed. Believe me, for such a speech I don't have to make any preparations, nor fabricate anything. When the day of *yahrzeit* comes, everything that has gathered in my memory pours forth. But how is it possible to tell it all? And as much as my memory allows, I see all the *tzores* that they -- our dear ones endured until their death as holy martyrs.

As long as I live I will always remind, so that we do not forget, who were the murderers of our dear ones: fathers, mothers, sisters and brothers, innocent suckling-babies, and I ask you, my dear friends, to convey all this to your children because this must not be forgotten.

Everyone has to know how the German murderers tortured, shamed, shot, hung and burned the six million of our Jews...

We Jews of Ciechanów and the surrounding area have a special chapter in our great *khurban*. I am the only survivor of those on whom there has fallen the great and heavy task of being responsible for the unfortunate Ciechanówer population and also to concern myself with it. I am very fortunate to be able to say to you all that my conscience is clear. To the extent that it was at all possible, I fulfilled my community-role in such difficult abnormal times. I have carried everything out and have done everything to lighten the burden of my fellow brethren. I want to say hereby that I worked along with the *Gemina* that was formed at the beginning of the war, which included: Yudl Bronstein, Pinkhas Wilk, Wolf Kostsheva, Binyamin Kirshenbaum, Ben-Tzion Erhlikh and myself. I must also add that the above-mentioned Erhlikh (who was also called "Zemele") was forced by the Germans to be in charge of us and he was the only one who faithfully carried out all the orders of the Germans and thus deserves to be cursed by all Jews.

*This *Yizkor* talk was given at a *Yizkor* evening in Paris that the *landsmanshaft* -- " Friends of Ciechanów and the surrounding areas" arranged. Though the facts and descriptions that are presented by the speaker also appear in other memoirs in this *Yizkor Book*, the speech remains an important documentary, valuable as a genuine final farewell of a tortured Jew who participated in (*Gemina*) *Judenrat* in Ciechanów.

415

As soon as the Germans entered Ciechanow they gathered the whole Jewish population at the *shul* and there a soldier explained to us that Ciechanów must become *Judenrein*, and advised us to leave the *shtetl*. "Go," he said, "wherever you like -- but don't remain here because following the army the S.S. will come and they won't play around with you." To this our beloved *Chazzan* Laizer Barukhovich replied: "where do you want such a community as ours to go? We were born here and if it is so destined, we'll die here."

Woefully, regrettably, we didn't take advantage of the opportunity to leave for Lomze, where the Russian army received the Jews in a friendly manner and even helped those who had run away from the Germans. Now we see, if a few Jews remained, and they definitely lived under difficult war conditions, they rescued themselves by fleeing eastward.

We remained in Ciechanów, and immediately the Gestapo began to send for us and demanded that we give them a large contribution of money. It was very difficult to gather such a sum because the wealthy Jews had left Ciechanów in order to save themselves, some to Warsaw, others elsewhere. Still, we paid, believing that this was all that the Germans were demanding. But after the first contribution there came a second, a third and many more. Soon orders came that were meant to disgrace us.

A Jew became an inferior being.

We had to work for the Germans as well as for the Poles without getting any pay, not even food.

Unfortunately the *Judenrat* also had to supply work-hands for the robbers. Unfortunately there were always the same people who went to work. Gradually they became weak, working beyond their ability, going hungry, and weren't capable of fulfilling the quotas. For this they got beaten, wounded, so that often they would come home with smashed faces so that our mothers couldn't recognize us.

We hoped, though, that the situation would improve, but once we had to supply 500 strong men and we didn't know where they were being taken. Since this number couldn't be supplied, two of the *Judenrat* were arrested: Pinkhas Wilk and myself.

416

We didn't believe we'd ever see our families again. For such sabotage one could get the death penalty, but a miracle happened, and after they beat us up, broke our bones, they sent us home with the words: "See you next time."

They started using methods that caused us to be fearful, so that we would carry out all their murderous orders all the faster. The Germans often arrested us, beat us and sent us home, "until next time." Of course, it was no privilege to be a member of the *Judenrat,* but they kept us in their grasp, not freeing us. "When we won't need you, we ourselves will relieve you from your post," the German sadists used to stipulate.

Later, an order came from higher up, that Ciechanów is to become a large city center of south Prussia, with a typical German appearance. In the spring of 1941, with the help of unpaid Jewish work-hands, the Jewish quarter started to be torn down. Just imagine the sad situation of the Jewish population that had to leave their old homes, some quite comfortable, others very scanty, but nevertheless their own old homes. There was great crowding as several families moved into one house, and when there was a lack of houses people ran, like livestock, into barns.

Jewish holy sites, such as the *Bais Hamedresh* and the *shul* were brutally damaged. There was no more Godliness there – just room for the German horses and autos. Even the Jewish cemetery was destroyed. Our religious folks thought that a miracle would happen because the once-famous great *tzadik* Avremele was buried there, but the time of miracles was over. A few Jews from the Holy Burial Society dug up the holy bones and took them to the new cemetery.

The whole period of the German rule we weren't allowed to make any purchases in the Polish stores. We, the *Judenrat*, managed with much difficulty to get some cast-off food for the Jewish population. We opened a store for which I was responsible. A Jewish bakery also existed where there was permission to sell to each Jew 250 grams of bread daily. The one responsible was a very good young man, Motele Baumgart. Meat was something we hardly ever saw because the Polish butchers ruled over this and very rarely threw us a bone.

417

Imagine, dear friends, what kind of meals we ate in those days. But if we could more or less exist, it was because of our cooperation, in spite of the German enemies.

But the situation kept getting increasingly worse. The tortured Jews kept on getting weaker and we were constantly required to produce more work-hands. A series of epidemics broke out that spread death daily.

By bribing the German mayor we managed to set up a "hospital" in an empty garage, under the direction of a doctor who had come from elsewhere, by the name of Baron, a one-legged man, who helped with total devotion to ease the misery of the sick.

The work got harder and harder. The very young children were taken away from their mothers at work, and when they had no more strength to work, they were beaten on their naked bodies -- both boys and girls as well as women. That's how the sadistic Germans tortured our mothers, sisters and children. We didn't know where to look for help, still we didn't totally lose hope.

And once people started to say that through our city, Serotzker, Jews were being led through on their way to Germany. We weren't allowed to go outside to witness how our brothers are being led away. But the following day when we went outside we saw many of the poor Serotzker Jews murdered in the street. All that was left was to give them a Jewish burial.

We received exact information that from Pultosk also, Jews were driven out. In Makov, Mlava, Plonsk and Neustadt, ghettos were being built where the whole Jewish population would be placed. But in Ciechanów the Germans couldn't erect a ghetto because all the Jewish homes had been destroyed and the Jewish population lived in lofts, cellars, stables, where Poles also lived.

In the second harsh winter of our tragic lives a fresh decree was announced -- to send all those incapable of work to Neustadt. Can you imagine the sorrowful situation? From every family parts are torn asunder. It's very painful and there is no end to the cries of despair. The period of preparing those incapable of work endures, and it's clear to us that sooner or later the same fate awaits us, and in order to destroy us both physically and mentally the enemy commands that we provide five innocent Jews to gather the whole population of Ciechanów where the former *Bais Hamedresh* and *shul* place was, and the representative of the *Judenrat* with myself amongst them, must hang these five unfortunate brothers on the prepared gallows. Furthermore, none of our *Kehillah* must let out a moan or a cry, because for such a transgression one gets shot on the spot.

418

Our eyes beheld all this but our hearts, without sobbing, cried. Can you imagine our tragic situation: It was only the next day that the hung ones were given a Jewish burial. Naturally, I didn't tell you everything. It's impossible for us to tell all, but there already were shot Jews in the *shtetl* before.

Then the gathering of "those incapable of working" began at the large castle, and they got many lashes as they were loaded onto the wagons. Aba Blum, at that time, distinguished himself in assisting. The Germans shot him on the spot for helping the old and the weak.

Every day brought fresh and more horrible *tzores* than the previous one. The German murderers went from house to house and took whatever they liked while at the same time doing the cruelest and dirtiest acts about which it is hard to speak. Our beautiful Ciechanów girls had to strip naked in the presence of their parents, and in that way had to dance for the soldiers, and if a strange man was found in the house he had to rape the women. The two-legged brutes in uniforms of German soldiers, view the "spectacle" and clap bravo.

Every dawn we lived through such despicable acts. Then came days when our mothers and fathers were called to the marketplace and get beaten on their bare skin and we had to witness these scenes also. Believe me that every one of us wishes for death, but unfortunately it didn't come.

Finally came the total destruction of Jewish Ciechanów: the *shtetl* had to become *Judenrein* and with great speed and fierce German haughtiness, Erik Kokh, the *Gauleiter* (area commander) of Bialystock and Ciechanów, carried out the destruction of the Jews.

Transport after transport left Ciechanów daily to the death camps, and at that moment we lived to see soldiers, pure Aryans, from the *herren volk*, with frozen feet, hands, noses and ears; and the hope of the so-long awaited freedom was once more awakened for us. We blessed the hands of the Russian avengers who struck powerfully at our mutual enemy.

419

The *Gauleiter* Kokh loaded the Jews on the horse-wagons, some in the direction of Mlava. In the wagons many were choked to death by lime. Other elderly Jews were brought to the so-called "hospital" in the garage and there they were shot en masse. The remainder, amongst whom I also found myself, was sent to Katowitz to work. We also were fooled, however, The train brought us to the tragically-known Auschwitz.

Dear landsleit:

I know that I have caused you much grief by my telling you about your tortured nearest and dearest who were so cruelly destroyed by the Germans. Pardon me, because if not I, not a person but number 733734, a survivor, can tell you all this it is so that "you will remember what Amalek did to you." Remember forever who the murderers were of the six million innocent Jews, our dear mothers, fathers, brothers and sisters. Remember who wanted to do away with all our people.

420

Two Processes against German Mass Murderers Who Carried Out the Torture and Extermination of Ciechanów Jews

Yitzhak-Leib Kleinetz

At two trials of German mass-murderers the sadism, murder and evil that the Germans committed against the Jewish population of Ciechanów was exposed: at the Eichmann trial in Jerusalem and in the court case in Warsaw regarding Erik Kokh, the former *Gauleiter* Ober-president for eastern Prussia and former chief of civil service of the areas including Bialystok and Ciechanów. In both trials Ciechanówer Jews were witnesses, survivors of the German extermination.

At the Eichmann process in Jerusalem, Noah Zabludowicz was the witness. His testimony, recorded at the court proceedings, under the number 1-43/BF 41 file 06 -- takes up 12 typewritten pages. Zabludowicz's oral testimony at the Jerusalem court case was greatly condensed, but in the condensed form as well the witness presented the whole sadistic cruelty, murder and killing that the Germans committed against the Ciechanów Jews.

A particularly strong impression was made by Zabludowicz's telling of how the German hangmen carried out the act of once hanging four Jewish men publicly in the marketplace, and a second time seven Jews. The prosecutor, Hausner, asked the witness for exact information about the German hangings of the innocent Jews, their names and the exact dates when the beastly murders were carried out.

After Zabludowicz's testimony, Hausner took out from the files two telegrams that were sent from Berlin to Ciechanów and read them for the court.

The first telegram, dated April 17 1942:

"To Gestapo office in Ciechanów: According to the order of *Reichsfuhrer* of the S.S., the *sonderbahandlung* of the Jews Zalman Lipski; Moishe Bayman, Dovid Tzimmerman and Abraham Itscovich must be carried out.

Signed: Obersturmbahnfuhrer Eichmann"

421

The second telegram dispatched from Berlin, May 23, 1942:

"The *Reichsfuhrer* of the S.S. orders the hanging of the following Jews in the ghetto of Ciechanów: Shmerl Goldberg, Yona Eliaf, Raphael Braun, Mendl Rubinshtein, Moishe Levin, Dovid Brikovsky and Dovid Zemliadin. They must be hung in the presence of their race-brothers.

"I request a report about the execution of the hanging."

Signed: In auftrag -- Eichmann, S.S. *Obersturmfuhrer**

*The names of those who were hung, given in the two telegrams, are definitely different than those hung in Ciechanów as given in the previously-given memoirs.

*

The declarations of witness Noah Zabludowicz were widely commented on by the press in Israel and abroad.

*

At the court case against Erikh Kokh, that took place in Warsaw, the murderous acts that Kokh committed against the Jews of Ciechanów were confirmed.

Immediately at the start of the German occupation of Poland Erikh Kokh, one of the leaders of Hitler's "National-Socialist Workers' Party" and Himmler's confidant, with the rank of *Gauleiter*, was appointed by the German powers as *Oberpresident* of the so-called eastern-Prussia. In the area of east-Prussia there were included the Polish regions of Bialystok and Ciechanów. Erik Kokh became the chief of Bialystok and Ciechanów region. Ciechanów became an east-Prussian city with the name Tzikhenow.

422

The *Gauleiter* and Nazi, Erikh Kokh, started to Germanize Ciechanów with all the means of the German extermination. All the acts of murder, robbery and killing of the Jewish population of Ciechanów were organized and led by Erikh Kokh. He ruled over the life and death of Ciechanów Jews.

At the court case in Warsaw one of the miraculously surviving Jews of Ciechanów -- Fianka, proved, with his testimony, the mass-murderer's activity that Erik Kokh carried out in Ciechanów. He himself, the *Gauleiter* and Nazi, tortured and shot men, women and children, Jews and non-Jews.

The Warsaw Polish court sentenced to death the German mass-murderer.

(signed) A. V. Y.

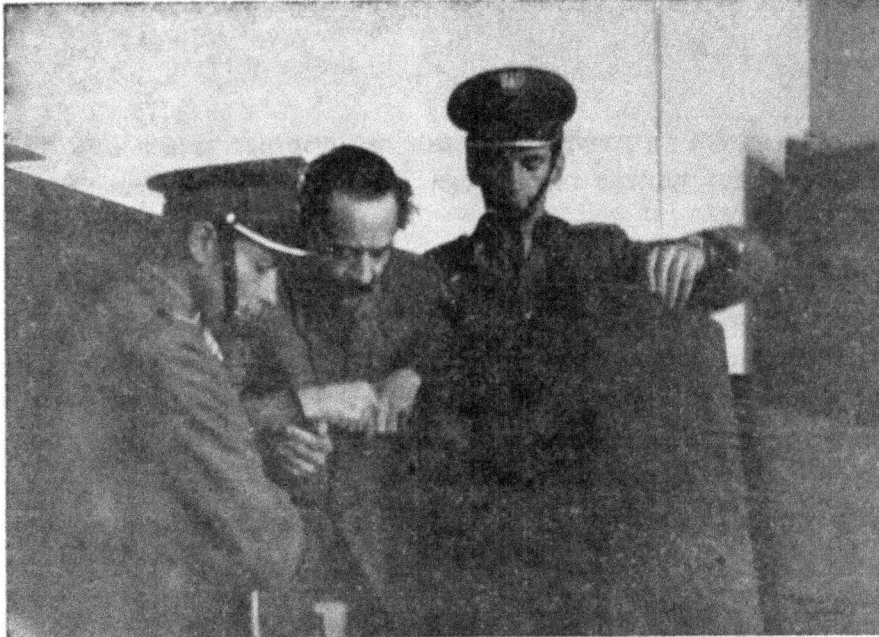

The mass-murderer, Erik Kokh, during his trial in Warsaw

423

Families and Individuals of Ciechanów Tortured by the Germans

Who can console us when the catastrophe is so great? Our beloved family, our pride, our light was so tragically torn away.

And we live? Is it possible to call this living? When our dear mother, who endured so much *tzores* in her life until she established her family-nest, raised a family, in whom many took pride, Mother dear, whom did you harm in your life that brought upon you such a punishment?

You defended everyone justly. You accepted all *tzores* with love, helped everyone who was in need, carried your heavy burden and never complained, served God and faithfully strove to live to have some *naches* from your children.

You went proudly to your martyrdom, and comforted others on their last way. Oy, how we miss you. Woe is us that we have lost such a dear treasure.

*

Our beloved sister, ROKHEL YEHUDIT, most beautiful, your goodness is hard to describe: Everyone honored you and your modest behavior. You had just started to build your family nest. Whoever had any aggravation found an open heart and you helped everyone.

424

You lit up the street when you arppeared with your two lovely sons, Ephraiml and Dovidl; so much beauty, warmth and goodness, so much hope we put in you. How vile your murder the murderer of your children must have been.

*

Our brother, Avraham Yosef -- you always had a harsh life, worked hard in order to provide honorably for your family. In your quiet manner you strove for a better and nicer life. You hardly managed to enjoy life at all when the murderers murdered you, your wife and child in such a brutal way. Who can understand the world that allowed so much evil to be perpetuated.

Levy Binyamin -- Levileh you were called. A pale, delicate young boy with dreamy eyes and a good-natured smile on your lips. We remember your dreams: Justice, fairness, a world without exploitation, a Jewish state, brotherly love, these were your goals. We remember your lectures for religious working-youth in Łodz.

Top, r to l: parents Ephraim and Frumet Khaya Fuchs.

Second row: Yosef Fuchs and his wife; Rokhl (Fuchs) and Shlomo Sokolover.

Last row: Levy Binyamin, Ephraim and Dovid - the children of Rokhl and Shlomo

425

You inspired everyone. Just like a prophet you arose to give hope to everyone. Our mother, who loved you so dearly, *shept naches* from the child she had in her late years, and we, brothers and sisters, were convinced that here was someone who would grow up to give hope and courage to all those who suffer. And who more than us knew that you had not yet enjoyed life at all?

Your tragic death has no equal in martyrdom. In the last moment, when we still had a little hope that people who were capable of working would be saved, and our mother pleaded to be saved, you decided that "wherever she will go you will go and a *Shma Yisroel* was heard from the dear mother and son when they went to their holy death.

That's the kind of family that we lost. Is it possible to express our sorrow in words?

May these lines serve as a memorial candle for our dear ones whom we miss so much.

The remaining survivors:

Leah Piaskovsky (Fuchs) - Argentina

Shmuel Fuchs and family - Israel

Malka Bromson (Fuchs) and family - Israel

Mindl Fuchs - Israel

426

The Glinovyets Families

With great respect for the victims, with deep sorrow and flaming anger against the tormentors and murderers, I want to mention the small Jewish *yishuv*, GLINOVYETS, a *shtetl* where there lived around 15 families that the Hitler-murderers destroyed.

I myself was born in GLINOVYETS. From my young years on I lived in Schlegova until I left for Paris. With great respect I want to mention the names of families and individuals.

The Family of Shimon Moskowitz

My dear uncle, Shimon Moskowitz with the yellowish beard, was a Jew whom many Ciechanówers knew. He was always concerned with the welfare of all and let himself be known in Ciechanów, Proshnitz and Plonsk when he collected money for the wedding of an orphan girl.

There were six Markowitz brothers in Glinoyvets, all merchants -- Eliyahu Sokolovsky - a tailor, Moishe Cohen - from Ciechanów,

Markowitz, the Goloms – merchants; Menashe's three sons - horse dealers, Yaacov Becker, who was born in a village near Ciechanów where various villagers lived, the *Shelmniakes* they were called. What precious Jews. It was never too hard for them to help someone in need on the way, or to have something ready for a guest to eat.

From the small *yishuv* in Glinovyets there remain living one of the Markowitzes who is in Poland. From Moishe Cohen's family there are alive today, if I'm not mistaken, two sons in America. From Shimon Moscowitz two sons remain alive -- one in Paris, the youngest in America.

Let the names of those who perished be mentioned in this *Yizkor Book*: Warm Jews - Shimon Moskowitz, together with his wife and son; Yaacov Sholem Sokolovsky and his family; Eliyahu Sokolovsky and his family; Rokhl Fogelman and her children; Moishe Cohen, with his wife and children; Yaacov Becker and family; the children of Bezalel and his family; Menashe's sons and their families.

From the martyrs whose names I don't remember I beg pardon for not mentioning them. They all remain in my heart. To my very last breath I'll remember my birthplace with its dear Jews who lived in Glinoyvets.

———

427

A Memorial Candle for My Close Ones

Shlomo ben Avraham Zvi Hershkowitz

Please allow me, in this long row of memorial candles for our unforgettable martyrs, to bring in a few candles for my own and close ones.

My Father

To the Torah he would be called up as *Reb* Chaim Zvi ben Eliezer Aryeh. At home mother called him simply Chaim Hersh. In his young years he was a heated follower of the Gerer *Rebbe*; later - a hot *Mizrachi* member. He was active in the Zionist organization and received from the *Keren Hayesod* a certificate with gold letters. In Serotsk my father was in charge of the Holy Burial Society for some time, also for the *Linat Hatzedek*. In his fifties he was the *shofar* blower in Ciechanów for Rosh Hashana. I remember him as always having gray hair and a gray beard.

He was a very hard worker. In his young years he had several trades: a bookbinder, a glazier, a baker, a small businessman, operated a tea-house, made soap. Many years before I was born my father was a house-painter. It used to be said about my father: "He has golden hands and makes birds on the walls." Father also painted signs and ornaments on ceilings.

My father kept himself in good health, had a mouth of healthy teeth, read without glasses and clattered on a ladder during his work, but at night he would be dead tired. Often, at the Friday evening table, he would fall asleep in the midst of singing *zmires*. He loved *zmires*. He was, after all, a *baal tfillah* in the High Holidays. Various visitors came to him, amongst them a certain *Chazzan* who always brought a new *nigun* to the *shtibl* for *Shalosh Seudas*. My father would sing the new *nigun* with those present.

The *khurban* came. Father worked as a painter for the Germans also. When I was in the Soviet Union as a refugee, I received letters from home with the signature at the end of the letter, *Vash etyetz*, your father. How much longing and love those two simple words expressed!

And until the day of my death the thought will plague me that my father, with his bold enduring nature would certainly have been able to cross the border and live out his years of labor in the Soviet Union, and maybe would even have lived to come to the land of his dreams -- to *Eretz Yisroel*.

428

My Mother

My mother, Henia-Mirl -- maiden name Blumberg, always used to tell about her prestigious ancestors. Her father was a great Torah scholar, *Reb* Nachman Eliezer. Her brother was Berish -- *Rov* of Skompe, and her nephew Ben-Tzion -- *Rov* of Ziramin. Mother, the same age as father, was hardly gray at all, but she felt much weaker than father.

In her young years she was a woman of valor who worked to help my father in all his efforts to earn a livelihood. Poverty -- a frequent visitor at our place, came and went and returned again, and mother "breaks her head" to make ends meet, to make sure that our home always looks decent, not to have to, God forbid, ask elsewhere for help; on the contrary -- we should quietly help the needy with *tzedakah*, and for Shabbat there always had to be fish and meat prepared, even in winter, the worst time, when there was no work.

In preparation for the High Holidays, though, there was always plenty of work and the best of everything was prepared at home. Then mother "*shept* some *naches*" when there would arrive and gather together sons, daughters, grandchildren...

For mother, *frumkeit* and virtue are one. Mother always sought to justify everyone, and understandably for her own children also, when they caused her regret. She knew that they had good hearts. They aren't out for themselves but want to improve the world. "But what harm would it do to observe some *Yiddishkeit*?" mother argued.

Mother read the *Tzenah Urenah* and "magic" books in *Ivreh-teich* (Hebrew translated into Yiddish). She also enjoyed when someone would read Sholem Aleichem to her. She didn't sing as well as father, but she remembered a mass of Yiddish folk-songs and many stories, jokes and proverbs.

For mother, with her soft, delicate nature, who always trembled about the fate of her children even in the "good" years, who always feared to go past a policeman, the arrival of the Germans in Ciechanów made an oppressive impression. Her instinctive fear of the forthcoming danger affected us all, even father, with his strong character.

It will always remain firmly in my mind, her sad darkened face, with her tear-filled eyes, when she accompanied us -- me and my sister Khaheye, and sister Soreche and her husband Avreml Margil and their daughter -- to the horse-drawn wagon that took us away on a long course of wandering.

My Brother Yosl

My brother Yosl, happy, friendly, worked from a young age at a variety of jobs. I remember him as an excellent room-painter. He was very good at everything. Whatever his eyes saw, he could paint. He drew nice pictures, was musically talented, played mandolin and sang sentimental songs as he worked. He was a good chess player -- was also interested in mathematical problems and formulas.

He was an auto-didact, full of knowledge in various fields but especially in the field of literature, philosophy and Marxism. He gave outstanding readings on these subjects, particularly about the young Jewish poets that were so close to him because he was a poet, had poetry published in various publications, and was preparing for publication a book of poetry.

Father, who was quite upset at this heretic was, deep in his heart, proud of him. When Yosl was in captivity with the Germans father buried the notebook with Yosl's creations deep in the ground -- God have mercy perhaps? Maybe there will yet be a normal life.

Yosl returned from German captivity. He was forced to paint for the Germans. (Maybe he wrote poems in secret).

At the age of thirty something, together with his wife, child and all Ciechanów martyrs, he was murdered by the Germans.

My Sisters

The eldest one was Liba, was smart, loved life, a dear person, in spite of the harsh trials of life. She didn't live in Ciechanów, but every summer she used to come for a few months with her two young daughters Aidl and Rokhle to mother and father for vacation nearby. Aidl, beautiful somewhat phlegmatic, grew stern and modest. The young stubborn Rokhle was raised by *bubba* and *zaide*, studying at the Ciechanów school and grew up to be a dancer.

During the war they ended up in Bialystok and shared the fate of the majority of Bialystok Jews.

My middle sister -- Khaiche, was delicate and very capable. She acted in a drama group, drew and painted on kerchiefs, had a passive nature. Saved herself from the Germans by going to the Soviet Union and there she perished from the hard life.

430The youngest sister was Pearl. She had a fiery nature. She remained at home with mother and father and perished at the hands of the Germans.

My Friends from My Youth

Mendl and Feivl were my friends from my youth. Mendel Kronenberg was the son of a neighbor close to my age. We grew up together. His parents used to go to markets. There, life was very hard since they were always traveling. Mendel's father, a Ger *Hasid*, always complained that I had also made a heretic of his eldest, Yosl, and even the young Shayeleh with the dark burning eyes... The last time I saw them was in Bialystok and since then their traces have disappeared.

Feivl Sumko came to Ciechanów from Proshnitz with his *zaide*, a carpenter, in a Jewish hat and curly *payes*, rosy cheeks and clever eyes. Our first acquaintance took place when we were trying to solve mathematical problems and riddles. Afterwards Feivl, Mendl and I became a threesome. Feivl's *zaide* also objected to his coming to me for fear that I would corrupt him. But Feivl's close house-friends had already "corrupted" him -- the books of Marx and Engels, Plekhenov, Zitlovsky and Belshe.

We read together, discussed heatedly and "solved" world problems in the kitchen beside the oven...Our friendship deepened through spiritual closeness, through spending time together in the illegal circles, in the progressive An-ski and Sholem Aleichem library and at home at the chess board.

This is what Feivl wrote me during the war when I was in the Soviet Union: "Our situation is developing as follows: I come into your house often. It's your mother and I who feel your absence the most."

Oh how painfully we suffer, we the survivors -- from the tragic absence of you -- numberless fathers and mothers, sisters and Feivls, who perished in the flames of Hitler's German hell.

431

Nakhman Grosbard

Grosbard family

432

The Family Where There Was the Cradle of Zionism in Ciechanów

One's hand trembles when one recalls that the large Trombka family was murdered in the most terrible way. We still remember our father from the time when we were very young children. He was one of the most faithful Alexander *hasidim*...He named his children after his *Hasidic* rabbis. My mother, Rokhl, came from Rotchons. She was an industrious woman who, unfortunately, became a widow at a young age. With much sacrifice she provided for her children. She raised them in such a way that they were an example for others.

Brakha -- the mother of the Trombka family in their bakery

Avraham Trombka, His Wife Raizl and Children

Many Ciechanówers surely remember the respected Jew with the long Herzl beard, a *Hasidic* man who carried on the tradition of our father. Though he was an Alexander *Hasid* he was one of the pioneers of the *Mizrachi* in Ciechanów. He gave a lot of *tzedakah* and did a lot of communal work. He built a fine household. His son, Moishe, was one of the founders of the *Mizrachi* in Ciechanów. In a bestial manner his family perished at the hands of the Germans.

433

Faige Robota

Faige Robota -- wife of Yishayahu Robota -- the mother of the heroine Rosa, was a pioneer of Zionist thought. Already in Czarist times she risked giving her home for a Zionist library, for Hebrew courses, etc. She raised her children as staunch Jews, fought for the establishment of Israel. Her education resulted in such a great heroine as Rosa, the pride of the Jewish people in general and in particular for Ciechanów. Raizele, our pride and joy, we see you as a young, attractive girl, a lovely flower that lit up the surroundings. How bitter it is for us that your young years were cut down so early. But we are so proud of your martyrdom. We shall never, never forget you.

Yekhezkl Trombka

Which Zionist, or any of Ciechanów doesn't remember Yekhezkl Trombka? He was amongst the founders of the Zionist movement, *Keren Kayemet, Keren Hayesod*. All Zionist activities were conducted by him. He was put to death by the Germans.

Raizl and Avraham Trombka and their children

434

Pinkhas Trombka

All the children in our household were busy: Avraham in *Mizrachi*, Faige in *Bnot Tzion*, Yekhezkl in general Zionist activities, Yekhiel-Sholem and Bayla in *Hashomeir Hatzair*; however, one had to eat also. Pinkhas took this responsibility upon himself. He worked hard all his life to provide for the family in an honorable way. His memory will always be cherished by us.

Yehoshua was sick for many years. We were all broken-hearted about his illness; he lived until the war, was tortured and shot by the Germans.

Trombka family

It is impossible to describe our pain at the loss of our dear family. Our eyes are already dry of tears and there are no words to express sorrow. May it be a consolation for our *kadoshim* that the survivors are following the footsteps of the Trombka family in Ciechanów.

435

Trombka Brother and Sister in Israel and Elsewhere

Rokhl-Leah Kostsheva

Rokhl-Leah Kostsheva -- a very religious woman who watched over family purity in Ciechanów, was responsible for supervision in the *mikve*. All week she got to know all levels of Ciechanów Jewish life. Rokhl-Leah knew all those in need, the sick, the widows and orphans.

Bringing help to the sick and the needy was Rokhl-Leah's holiest work. She went to visit the sick, cooked noon-time meals for the hungry, and brought it to their homes. The downhearted found hope in her.

Though she herself was very *frum*, she had understanding for her modern children. Parties were formed in her house.

During the German extermination Rokhl-Leah tried to continue to help people. She appealed to her children in Detroit, U.S.A. to form an aid organization for the suffering Jews in Ciechanów. Funds did come

from America. This was secretly distributed by a committee including
Rokhl-Leah and Wolf Kostsheva.

Yisroel Moishe Pudlovitz

Maier Becker (Zalaner) and his family

436

A memorial page for
AVRAHAM GOLDSHMIT
CHAIM YOSEF BERMAN (Teshak)
LIBER BERMAN (Liber Shnider)
DOVID BORNSTEIN (Listofar)
DOVID FUCHS, son of Henekh Fuchs
signed by the Ciechanówer *Farein* in Detroit
president: MOISHE LESER
secretary: VIGDOR KESSLER
An eternal curse on the slayers and murderers

437

Memorial Page for the
Parents and their three children
who were together put to death in the death camps

top l to r
LEAH 1893-1942 MOISHE-ADYA 1888-1942
bottom
MENAKHEM 1934-1942 ISAKHAR 1930-42 KHANA
   1927-42
signed by the brothers ZABLUDOWICZ and their families in Israel

438

Memorial Page for
> Father YAACOV KALFUS
> Mother KILAH
> Our Sister SARAH
signed by YOSEF and YESHAYAHU KALFUS, in Israel

Memorial Page

Our Parents, REB YEHOSHUA BERMSON and his wife
        SHASHA;
Our Sisters, MIRIAM RIVKA, her husband and their
        daughter, TRANA
signed by DAVID BERMSON and Family, in Israel
        LEAH SHLESINGER (BERMSON) and her Family, in Israel

439

Memorial Page for
  Our Father, SHALOM ZELIG SHLESINGER
  Mother, ESTHER
  Brother, MOISHE
  Aunt, ORPA ROSA
  (Picture: top row are of ESTHER and ORPA;
  bottom row are of SHALOM ZELIG and MOISHE
signed by ROSA SHMID SHLESINGER in Israel

439

Memorial Page for Our Parents YOSL TATENGREBER
   died Yom Kippur 1935
   Mother, FAIGE; Brother, GERSHON, his wife and
     children
   Sister, ZLOTE
   and
   ESTHER LEAH (LANYA) TATENGREBER
   Our Lanya (Leah) did not want to leave her children in
     the Medem Sanitarium in German-murderous
     hands. Together with the children she perished
     the 22nd of August, 1942.
Signed by BRONCHE TATENGREBER (HOFFER)
    MENDL HOFFER (Detroit)

Memorial Page Our Parents ,
   YITZHAK MAIER AND LEAH FUCHS
   Brother, AARON and his wife RUKHCHE
   Their Children,
   AVIGDOR, BINYAMIN, ESTHER , SHLOMO, SORCHE
     and PAULA
   Sister, HENIA and her husband DOVID GOGL
   Their children:
   ROTZE, BAILCHE, CHAIM, YAACOV, YITZHAK MEYER
     and PINKHAS
   Sisters
   MINDL and her husband HERSHL SENTZKOVER
   Their children
   YITZHAK MAIER, ROKHELE
   Sister
   GITL and her child MOISHELE
   Sister Nekhe
signed by SIMCHA and YAACOV FUCHS, in Montreal

440

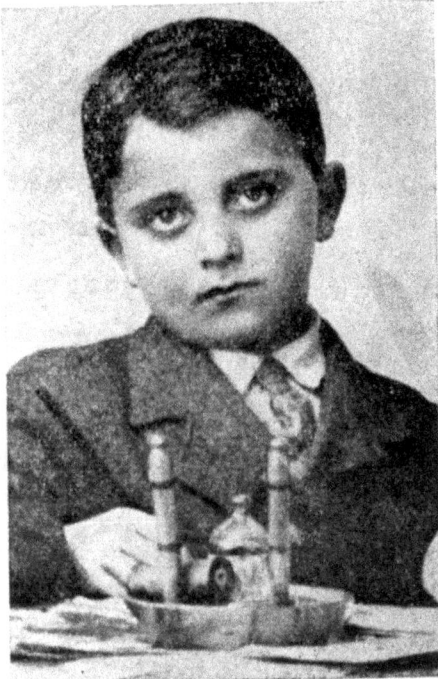

Memorial Page for
l to r: AVRAHAM PISAGE who perished in May, 1944;
TUVYA PISAGE, who perished in January 1944
signed by TOLA PISAGE AND FAMILY in Israel

Memorial Page for

Mother, NEKHEMYA APEL; mother SHAYNE BAYLE

Sister, PESYA and her husband MOTL EISENBERG and four grandchildren

Brother, ITCHE APEL and his wife TSIPEH

Brother, MORDECAI APEL and his wife ROSA and their five children

Sister, BRONCHE APEL, her husband ITCHE and two children

Those tortured to death in Auschwitz

My wife, KHANA APEL, perished November 15, 1942;

My son, YEKHEZKL - born30.5.1930, perished 15.11.1942;

My son, BERL - born 15.7.1934, perished 15.11.1942;

My daughter, Shayne Bayla - born 22.9.1939, perished 15.11.1942

signed BINYAMIN, NOSKE AND YOSEF APEL IN AMERICA

441

Memorial Page for the DAN FAMILY

top l to r - SOREH MINDL and HENEKH,
our Parents;
Brother, AVRAHAM and YEKHEZKL;
Sisters GITL and TZIRL
signed: the surviving brothers YITZHAK, FEIVL, SHOLEM and
MOISHE DAN

Memorial Page

l to r PEARL and MELEKH GASTAMSKY
who will always be remembered with love
by their daughter, AIDL GASTAMSKY-STEIN in Detroit

442

Memorial Page

Parents: MENDL and ESTHER KIRSHENBAUM
Brothers: SHMUEL BERL and EZRIEL SHAYELE
signed HARRY and LEAH KIRSHENBAUM

Memorial Page

Father: ELIYAHU LOZNIK, who died in Otwask, Poland, May, 1928

Mother: NEKHE, died in Ciechanów, 1928

Like a tree that spreads its roots, that's how their children are spread in various lands: America, Mexico, Canada and Lima, Peru, but we who were born in Ciechanów carry the chain of our parents' love for everything that is Jewish.

signed by SHIFRA LOSNIK (KESLER) in Detroit, LAIBL LOZNIK (LESER) in Detroit, MOISHE LOZNIK (LESER) in Detroit.

FAIGL LOZNIK (SILVERBERG) in Montreal, Canada

VIGROD LOZNIK, in Lima, Peru; FRIMCHES children in Mexico: YONA, DOVID, MOISHE, EPHRAIM, CRYSTAL

443

LIBER BERMAN
one of the founders of the Ciechanów *Farein* who died in
1944 in Detroit, U.S.A.
signed by TZERKA BERMAN, HYMIE BERMAN, Detroit, TED
BERMAN, Cleveland; daughter MOLLIE BERMAN,
California

Memorial

          for our beloved family who perished in the German lagers
          lovingly remembered are:
          Father - YITZHAK GROSKIND; Mother, CHAVA;
          Sister, ESTHER; Brother, YAACOV

signed: CHAIM GROSKIND, Detroit

          In memory of my dear parents
          ZISHE and MOISHE REUVEIN VINA
          who perished in Auschwitz, may their mention in this
Yizkor Book serve as a gravestone for me and my children

signed: their only son, GEDALIA VINA, Detroit

          In eternal memory of our parents
          Father, FISHL BEN ELIYAHU MUKOVSKY, died 1929
          Mother, TZIPE BAS CHAIM VELVL, and our sister SARA
who perished in the *Shoah.*

Signed: BATYA SHERATSKI, Israel

          May this *Yizkor Book* be a permanent memorial for my
dear Mother
          NEKHE (AVRAHAM-NATAN TEITELBAUM'S daughter,
          who died in Ciechanów in 1941; and my sister SOREH-
LEAH,
          who perished in Auschwitz.

Signed: LAIBL MONDRI, Detroit

444

Memorial Page for

ROKHL-LEAH and Father, SHLOMO KOSTSHEVA)

With sorrow and honor we will always remember our dearly beloved ones, whose awful fate was the same as that of millions of our people who were murdered by the hands of the German killers:

Mother, ROKHL-LEAH; Brother, MOISHE-CHAIM, his wife and children; cousins, WOLF KOSTSHEVA AND FAMILY; YOSEF-LAIB KOSTSHEVA AND FAMILY; EPHRAIM-HERSH KOSTSHEVA AND FAMILY; URKE KOSTSHEVA AND FAMILY; SOREH-FAIGE KOSTSHEVA AND FAMILY.

We remember our father, Shlomo Kostsheva, who died 1920

sister, SOREHCHE who died 1927

sister, GITL who died 1931

signed: ISAAC KOSTSHEVA (KESLER)

SHAYA KOSTSHEVA (KESLER)

VIGDOR KOSTSHEVA (KESLER)

SHMUEL YAACOV KOSTSHEVA (KESLER),

Detroit.

―――

With great sorrow I will always remember my parents:

Father, AVRAHAM SHABLOVSKY, died 1920;
Mother, SOREH RIVKA; brother, DOVID HERSH, his wife
and three children, brother ZELIG; his wife and
three children whose life was extinguished by the
German murderers.
Signed: the only survivor - YOSL SHABLOVSKY, Detroit

With much love we remember our parents
Father, DOV LISTOPAD, died *Heshvan* 24, 1929
Mother, LIBE, died *Shvat* 21, 1950
signed: AVREML, MOISHE, YUKL and YOSEF-HERSH
LISTOPAD, Detroit
FAIGL LISTOPAD (BERMAN), Los Angeles
ROSE LISTOPAD, Los Angeles

445

Memorial Page

With great respect we remember tortured martyrs who
were tortured to death in Auschwitz
VELVL GALADZSHER, born 1889
BRYNA GALADZSHER ULEVNIK; HINDE GALADZSHER,
born 1908; CHAYA GALADSHER, born 1910;
ZELIG GALADZSHER; SHMUEL ZALMAN, hung in
Ciechanów.
signed: YISROEL GALADZSHER AND FAMILY, Israel

In memory of our dear family
Father, DOVID MELOTZKER, brutally put to death in
Ciechanów by the Germans; Mother, ROKHL-
LEAH; sisters, HINDA and HANA
signed: son and brother AVRAHAM and YAACOV
MELOTZKEER, Israel

Honor to the memory of our dearly beloved parents
DVORA and MOISHE KAHANE; sister, HINDE-PERL; and
AVRAHAM, brutally murdered in the German
lagers.
Signed: DOVID LEON SHEPSL and MORDECAI
KAHANE, California

In memory of my dear family
Father, SHLOMO KULKA; mother CHAYA NEKH; sisters,
ROKHL and MINDL; cousin, TZERKA
SENTZKOVER.
Signed: MOSHE KULKA, Israel

In memory of my husband, our father
SHABTAI BEN BORISH (SAM SHINE) who died October
1958 in Detroit.
Signed: ESTHER and LARRY SHINE

446

Memorial Page for

MOISHE SHWARTZBERG

A memorial for the holy martyrs
Father, MOISHE SHWARTZBERG.
Mother, ESTHER-LEAH; brother, ZELIG.
Put to death at Auschwitz.
With sorrow and broken hearts we will always remember
them.
Signed: GITL SHWARTZBERG (BOON), Detroit;
DVORAH SCHWARTZBERG, New York

We mourn the following: our parents,
LEIB and TOVA SHLESINGER; our brothers and sisters
and their families -
BELLA and her husband PERETZ AIDLITZ and their
children
SHMUEL MOISHE, HINDA-LEAH and FISHL; CHAIM and
SARA-FAIGE and their son YOSL-DOVID; ROSA,
her husband and children; SHLOMO ZALMAN and
his wife ROKHL; YISROEL SHLESINGER.
Signed: NAKHMAN-YEHUDA and MISHA SHLESINGER,
Israel

In memory of our dear ones:
Father, DOVID-YOSEF GONSKA; mother, ESTHER-
ROKHL (SAFIRSTEIN), our brother, AARON
GONSKA; sister-in-law, MANYA GONSKA
(YUSLOVSKI), their children, TZASHE and
MOISHE.
Signed: AVRAHAM-YEHUDA GOLD (GONSKA), U.S.A.
HANA FINK (GONSKA), Ber-Sheva, Israel
RIVA LESHED (GONSKA), Kibbutz Kfar Massarik

447

Memorial Page for

YENKL & TEMEH BURSHTEIN

With deep sorrow we remember our dear ones:

Father, YENKL BURSHTEIN, died 1926, (pictured to the left of mother, TEMEH); brother, PESAKH, died 1946 in Detroit; brother MOISHE, died 1958; and our mother, TEMEH, who perished in the lagers of the German murderers.

Signed: UREKE BURSHTEIN (KESLER), Detroit; KHAYA BURSHTEIN, Israel

Father, FAIVISH SHRAGA SHFAT, died 1927; mother, GITL; sister, HANA-SOREH, a widow; ALEXANDER ZISHE WEINGART, died 1931.

We remember all those of our family from Ciechanów who never got to Israel but were murdered by the German killers and whose grave site is unknown. The children: YEHOSHUA, ESTHER-MALKA, LIBA and MANYA; sister RIVKA and husband LIBL WEINGROD and their children, SHMUEL and FEIVL; brother, SHIMON and his wife NEKHA and their children; my brother, YISROEL and my sister RELEH; my wife's family - her parents, YOSEF and FRIEDA SARBINGUREH; the brother, SIMKHA BINAM and his wife, HENCHEH, who perished in the *Shoah*; my sister TZVIYAH, who died in Israel; my brother MOISHE; my sisters, MIRIAM, SHINCHEH; my brother YANKELEH.

Signed ALTER and ELKEH SHFAT, Israel

448

With great sorrow we heard about the premature death
of SHMUEL EISENBERG (in picture) who died in
Los Angeles November 20, 1959 at the age of 44.
Signed: your aunt and uncle MASHEH and BINYAMIN APEL, Detroit

---

In memory of our dear parents
ELIYAHU and RIVKA OISTRIAK; sisters, SOREH, KHAYA,
TZIRL, TOIBEH; brothers, SHMUEL, MOISHE and
PINKHUS AND FAMILY who perished at the hands
of the German murderers in 1941.
Signed: YESHAYA, NAKHMAN and wife ROKHL, Canada

In eternal memory of our dear parents: AVRAHAM-
NATAN SKURNIK; ESTHER LEAH (maiden name
LAKH); my brothers, YITZHAK-AARON, YISROEL-
BER and DOVID; sister, SHAYNEH-TRAYNEH.
We mourn forever over your tragically-shortened lives.
Signed: sons, LAIBL and YEKHIEL SKURNIK

449

Memorial Page for:

GOLDA & YISROEL ALTUS

We honor the memory of our dear parents
Mother, GOLDA ALTUS, died October 943;
Father, YISROEL ALTUS, died June, 1943.
They were founders of our Ciechanów *Farein* in Detroit.
Signed: IDL-AVREML and NAKHMAN ALTUS, Detroit.

SOREH-FRIL CITRON (KVIAT) (left) ,

LEVY-YISROEL KVIAT (center)

HANA-ITAH BINKORN (KVIAT) (right)

We commemorate our brothers and sisters, born in Ciechanów. Pictured are LEVY-YISROEL KVIAT (IN CENTER), died in his youth in Łodz; at left SOREH-FRIL CITRON (KVIAT) died in U.S.A.; HANA-ITAH BINKORN (KVIAT) perished in the *Shoah* with their children YAACOV and TZIPORAH.

Signed: DVORAH HENDL KVIAT; BRYNA BUTSKA KVIAT, MOISHE-PARAKH KVIAT AND THEIR FAMILIES, Israel

450

A memorial for the holy martyrs

Pictured are all those mentioned: the dear mother and grandmother, HANA-RAIZL MEKUVER; SARA SHECHTER-MAKUVER, her husband and children; ROKHL BLUMSTEIN-MEKUVER, her son DOVID and daughter TZIRL; MOISHE-CHAIM MEKUVER and his wife ESTHER (GUTSHMID) and their son NATAN-YEHUDA.

Signed: the children and grandchildren, brothers and sisters and their families, Israel

In memory of our dear parents:

YOKHEVET and CHAIM ZISHBIK who died in New York.
Signed: the children AVRAHAM-MOTL ZISHBIK, Detroit;
RAYEH ZISHBIK (LESER), Detroit; SOREH-LEAH
ZISHBIK (FISHLER), Los Angeles; FAIGL ZISHBIK
(ZIVYETZ), New York

Instead of a gravestone for our dear ones

Parents: WOLF-KHANUKH ZILBESHTROM; our mother,
SARA, who died in Israel; our sister TEMA and her
husband KHANUKH MUNTSHTOK and their
children; our brother YIDL and his wife MANYA
(BIALISTOK) who perished in the *Shoah*. We will
never forget them.
Signed: their sisters and their children ROKHA, GOLDA
and CHAYA AND FAMILIES in Israel

451

In memory of the LUXENBERG FAMILY who are no longer alive.

Signed: the LUXENBERG FAMILY in Israel (No identification is given for the men and women in the picture).

In memory of my dear family who perished in the *Shoah*:

Father, DOV BEN MENAKHEM-MENDL PUDOLOVITZ; mother, SHIFRA, daughter of SHLOMO (KOSTSHEVA); sister BRYNA, brother ELKHANAN-MENDL who died before the war; brother DOVID; grandmother DINAH; uncle PINKHAS AND FAMILY, aunt LIBA AND FAMILY

signed: YISROEL-MOISHE PUDLOVITZ AND FAMILY, Israel

We mourn for the loss of our family members whose grave sites we do not know
Dear parents: ITCHE and TZIPEH; the sisters and the brother, MASHA, MOISHE and SHAYNA who perished in Auschwitz
and LEAH who was shot in the forests of Keidan on her way to Israel.
signed: the only remaining survivor of the family, ZELON APEL, Kfar Menakhem

452

We mourn the tragic death of our dear ones AVRAHAM ANTEKS AND HIS FAMILY: our sister-in-law; YEHOSHUA GREENBAUM FAMILY.

Signed: PESAKH ANTEKS AND FAMILY in Israel

To the eternal memory of our dearest who perished at the hands of the German murderers: my sister KHAVEH GEZUNTHEIT and her husband AVRAHAM SHRENSTKER AND CHILD; my sister, ROKHL GEZUNTHEIT.

Signed: THE GEZUNTHEIT BROTHERS, Mexico

With sorrow we recall our dear ones

Mother, the *rabbanit,* FAIGE-MATIL BRONROT and her daughter, SHAYNA-DVORA BRONROT

signed: the survivors of the BRONROT FAMILY in Israel

To the eternal memory of the families NOTEH ATINGER and his wife MANYA (ZILBERSHTROM); LEAH GARFINKEL (ZILBERSHTROM) AND THEIR CHILDREN

No sign has been left of these dear ones

signed: sisters ZILBERSHTROM AND THEIR FAMILIES in Israel

To the eternal memory of our dearest ones who perished at the hands of the German murderers: My dear mother, SOREH MANDZSHOK; brother, AVRAHAM MANDZSHOK

signed: KHAYA KOZSCHNITSKY (MANDZSHOK) and ROKHL GEZUNTHEIT

453

Honor to their memory. Father, AVRAHAM ZILBER
(AVREMISH-BARON), died *Heshvan* 25, 1945 in
Siberia
Mother, ESTHER, perished in Auschwitz
We shall always remember their love and devotion

signed: LAIBL ZILBER, Canada; DOVID ZILBER, Detroit, GOLDA
ZILBER, Canada, BAYLA ZILBER (SHER), Canada

For an eternal memory to the souls of my brother and
sisters who died a martyr's death: SHLOMO, SARA
and DVORA (SOKOLOVER) AND THEIR FAMILIES,
who were murdered during the *Shoah*
signed: their sister ESTHER LANDAU (SOKOLOVER),
Israel

With a broken heart I recall my family who perished:
Father, the great communal worker, REB YEKHIEL
      MAIER SOKOLOFF; my mother, TOVA
      SOKOLOFF; my sisters, KHAYA AND MALKA.
I'll never forget you.
Signed: MOISHE SOKOLOFF AND FAMILY in Israel

454

The unforgettable **MARGOLIS FAMILY**
Father, mother, sister and brother: HIRSH-CHAIM
    MARGOLIS, KHAYA-NOMI, HUDUS YETA and four
    grandchildren of the sons: ITCHE and LAIZER
    murdered by the German fascists.

We shall never forget you.

Signed: the only survivor of this large family
    AVRAHAM MARGOLIS AND FAMILY, Israel

In memory of my dear parents YOSEF and RADZSHE
    TZEITOG (ROSEN); sister, SOREH; brothers
    HERSHL and DOVID
Our sorrow for your martyrs' death will never be stilled.
    We shall remember you with greatest respect.
Signed: the brothers PINKHAS and YAACOV TZEITOG

To the eternal memory of our parents
HILLEL KAPOTA AND ALL THE FAMILY who perished in
    the *Shoah.*
We shall never forget you.
Signed: ESTHER   MIR   KAPOTA,   Israel;   RIVKA
    ROSENBLUM KAPOTA, New York

To the eternal memory
of the souls of mother and father HERTZL and KHAYA-
    SARA ROSENTHAL; sister RIVKA and brother-in-
    law SHIMSHON NEMARK and their children who
    were brutally murdered during the *Shoah*
signed: their sons, YAACOV ROSENTHAL AND FAMILY;
    their daughter DINAH LETZTER AND FAMILY in
    Israel

455

We mourn the terrible tragedy that happened to us at the hands of the Germans. Our dear family (in an assortment of pictures at the side).

Parents: REB BINYAMIM MALINA and his wife FRIMA KHAYA; brothers and sisters and their families: HANA-RAIZL FISH (MALINA); BORUKH-MORDECAI MALINA and his wife; their daughter, AYDL; ROKHL-YEHUDIT ROZENSHTEIN MALINA and her husband YAACOV and the children; SHMUEL-DOVID MALINA and his wife

signed: MOISHE MALINA, Israel; TZIPORA ARONOVICH (MALINA) and her family, Israel; CHAIM LEIB MALINA AND FAMILY, New York; and the whole family in the Diaspora.

We mourn for our close ones who were tragically torn away from us: picture of mother, PESYA MILOVSKY and sister FAIGE MILOVSKY-KAHANE; (not shown are: BASHA MILOVSKY and her children: AVRAHAM, LEAH AND NEKHE, FRAU NEKHA MILOVSKY-FUCHS

signed: MOISHE MILOVSKY, Israel

456

We memorialize the names of our dearest ones who
perished so tragically at the hands of the
Germans: in picture:

Parents: ZELIG and SARA PARMA; brothers ELIEZER
and FEIVL; sister, MIRIAM; cousin PEARL
PERLMUTTER

We shall never forget you.

Signed: YAACOV and TOVA PARMA, Israel

In memory of our dear parents
AVRAHAM ELYA and DINAH SREBNAGURA; sister,
    ESTHER SREBNAGURA, who perished at the
    hands of the beastly German murderers.
We shall never forget them.
Signed: KHAVA KRIGER, LAIBL SILVER, TZIVYE
    VARONSKI, MOISHE SILVER

In memory of my beloved family
Father, YOEL-DOVID WEINGARTEN; mother, MIRIAM;
    sisters, PESACH, KHAYA, NOMI; brother,
    YITZHAK SHMUEL
signed: daughter and sister ESTHER MALOTSKER-
    WEINGARTEN, Israel

457 to 472   Necrology

Ciechanów Necrology

This Necrology lists Ciechanów Jews (*Aleihem HaShalom*) who were known to have been murdered by the Germans during the Shoah, 1939-1945.

The following list was transliterated from Yiddish, and represents the collective knowledge of the surviving, organized Ciechanów Jews in Israel, France, and the U.S. in 1962.

It must not be considered definitive.

This English version was prepared by Allan Eliyahu Mallenbaum, Chairman of the Rosa Robota Foundation, Inc.

Some conventional spellings and contemporary pronunciations have been employed although the common Yiddish pronunciation and printed alphabetization from the original Necrology were followed in most cases.

<u>Note To Researchers:</u> *Original Polish name spellings and original Yiddish pronunciations* **were different** *from the names we know today!*

<u>*ALEPH*</u>
[Used to transliterate some **A, O,** and **E** names into Yiddish]

Abrentsh	Chaim
Abrentsh	Devora
Abrentsh	Malka
Abrentsh	Feivel
Abrentsh	Shlomo
Adamski	Avrohom
Adamski	Chava
Adamski	Yitzchak
Adamski	Yisrael
Adamski	Moshe
Adamski	Rivka
Adamski	P'nina
Olovnik	Yisrael
Olovnik	Shmuel

Osterreik	Eliyohu
Osterreik	Devora
Osterreik	Chaya
Osterreik	Yitzchak
Osterreik	Modechai
Osterreik	Feivel
Osterreik	Rivka
Osterreik	Shmuel
Osterreik	Sara
Osterreik	Chana
Ostri	Zelik & Family
Ostri	Moshe Yosef & Family
Ohrbach	Yocheved & Family
Avshanka	Adam
Avshanka	Miriam
Avshanka	Gavriel
Avshanka	Moshe
Avshanka	Sara
Eisman	Yaakov & Family
Eisenberg	Avrohom
Eisenberg	Breina
Eisenberg	Mordechai
Eisenberg	Chaya
Eisenberg	Leibel
Eisenberg	Mottel
Eisenberg	Roize
Eisenberg	Noah & Family
Altus	Avrohom
Altus	Aharon
Altus	Devora

Altus	Hershel
Altus	Chana
Altus	Yosef
Altus	Yitte
Altus	Yaakov
Altus	Yaakov-Leib
Altus	Yitzchak
Altus	Moshe
Altus	Frumme
Altus	Sara
Altus	Rochel
Altus	Rasheh
Altus	Shaindel
Altus	Shimun
Altus	Moshe
Altus	Bela
Altus	Binyomin
Altus	Nosson
Altus	Rochel
Altus	Sara
Altus	Kalman
Antkos	- - -
Offenheim	Gadalyahu
Offenheim	Abba
Offenheim	Dovid
Offenheim	Lea
Offenheim	Avrohom
Offenheim	Sara
Offenheim	Eliezer

BET

[Used to transliterate most **B** names into Yiddish]

Bokser	Eliezer
Bokser	Eliyohu
Bokser	Binyomin
Bokser	Sabina
Bokser	Pesse
Bokser	Rivka
Bordovitsh	Eliyohu Meir
Bordovitsh	Botze
Bordovitsh	Dovid
Bordovitsh	Chana
Bordovitsh	Yechezkel
Bordovitsh	Leibel
Bordovitsh	Feige
Bordovitsh	Eliezer
Bordovitsh	Devora
Bordovitsh	Hadassa
Bordovitsh	Yaakov
Bordovitsh	Nachum
Botshka	Dovid
Botshka	Lea
Botshka	Yisrael
Botshka	Shlomo
Biezshoner	Binyomin
Biezshoner	Hinde
Biezshoner	Yisrael
Biezshoner	Lea
Biezshoner	Mordechai
Birenboim	Yitzchak
Birenboim	Miriam

Birenboim	Yisrael
Birenboim	Lea
Blum	Abba
Blum	Reuven
Blum	Raizel
Blum	Temme
Blum	Sara
Blum	Nachman
Blum	Devora
Blum	Neche
Blum	Simcha
Blumshtein	Chaim
Blumshtein	Devora
Bergson	& Family
Berlinki	Meir
Berlinki	Devora
Berlinki	Hinde
Berlinki	Nechama
Berlinki	Rochel
Berlinki	Shlomo
Berka	Yishachar & Family
Berka	Alter and Family
Bronshtein	Aidel & Family
Bronshtein	Dovid & Family
Bronshtein	Avrohom
Bronshtein	Brocha
Bronshtein	Chaim
Bronshtein	Mordechai
Bronshtein	Rivka
Bronshtein	Sara

Bronshtein	Shimun
Brash	Mordechai & Family
Brash	Fishel & Family
Brenner	Slomo
Brenner	Gittel
Brenner	Chaya
Brenner	Chana
Brenner	Yitzchak
Brenner	Fela

GIMMEL
[Used to transliterate most **G** names into Yiddish]

Gozavski	Eliezer
Gozavski	Dovid
Gozavski	Chaim
Gozavski	Yitzchak
Gozavski	Shaindel
Gotteiner	Elimelech & Family
Gottleiber	Yosef
Gottleiber	Rochel
Gottleiber	Shmuel
Gottleiber	Moshe Dovid & Family
Gottleiber	Mattis
Gottleiber	Feivel
Gottfried	Moshe & Family
Gottfried	Shmuel & Family
Gottfried	& Family
Galadzsher	Velvel & Family
Golombik	Yitzchak
Golombik	Lea
Golombik	Brocha

Golombik	Zindel
Golombik	Leibe
Golombik	Rochel
Golombik	Miriam
Goldberg	Avrohom
Goldberg	Brocha
Goldberg	Henne
Goldberg	Mendel
Goldberg	Moshe
Goldberg	Feige
Goldberg	Feivel
Goldberg	Temme
Goldberg	Rochel
Goldberg	Avrohom
Goldberg	[Dentist] & Wife
Goldshtop	Devora
Goldshtop	Chaim
Goldshtop	Yitzchak
Goldshtop	Sara
Goldshtop	Yocheved
Goldshtein	Esther
Goldshtein	Efraim
Goldshtein	Beila
Goldshtein	Zev
Goldshtein	Chaya
Goldshtein	Yosef Hersh
Goldshtein	Menachem
Goldshtein	Mordechai
Goldshtein	Tsluvke
Goldshtein	Shaindel

Goldshtein	Shimon
Goldshtein	Chaya
Goldshtein	Yitzchak Meir
Goldshtein	Faiye
Gallina	Gedalyahu
Gallina	Devora
Gallina	Zelik
Gallina	Chana
Gallina	Moshe
Gallina	Roize
Gallek	Leibel & Family
Gallek	Yaakov & Family
Galka	Kalman & Family
Garfinkel	Mendel
Garfinkel	Avrohom
Garfinkel	Devora
Garfinkel	Yisrael
Garfinkel	Lea
Garfinkel	Nosson
Garfinkel	Feige
Garfinkel	Abba
Garfinkel	Yosef
Garfinkel	Chaya
Garfinkel	Simcha
Garfinkel	Velvel
Garfinkel	Dovid
Garfinkel	Shimon
Garfinkel	Zev
Garfinkel	Tova
Gutman	Yosef & Family

Gurni	Eliezer
Gurni	Devora
Gurni	Hadassa
Gurni	Hirsh
Gurni	Chava
Gurni	Chana
Gurni	Yiddel
Gurni	Yitzchak
Gurni	Zishe
Gurni	Lea
Gurni	Tzvi
Gurni	Hershel
Gurni	Sholom
Gurni	Rochel
Gurni	Yechiel & Family
Gzshevyenazsh	Moshe & Family
Gelberd	Aharon
Gelberd	Henne
Gelberd	Chana
Gelberd	Yosef
Gelberd	Miriam
Gelberd	Sara
Gelberd	Moshe & Family
Gershenovitch	Berel
Gershenovitch	Lea
Gershenovitch	Meir
Gershenovitch	Devora
Gershenovitch	Deena
Gershenovitch	Chana
Gershenovitch	Yeshayahu

Gershenovitch	Feige
Gershenovitch	Frumme
Gershenovitch	Rivka
Gershenovitch	Shlomo
Gershenovitch	Simcha
Gershenovitch	Yosef & Family
Gershenovitch	Yitzchak & Family
Grossbard	Yosef & Family
Greenshpan	Yechiel & Family

DALET
[Used to transliterate most **D** names into Yiddish]

Dombek	Chaim & Family
Dan	Yeshayahu
Dan	Gittel
Dan	Leibel
Dantus	& Family
Daniel	Chaim
Daniel	Efraim
Daniel	Brocha
Daniel	Golde
Daniel	Dovid
Daniel	Henne
Daniel	Miriam
Daniel	Sholom
Dzshik	Dovid
Dzshik	Rivka
Dzshik	Gittel
Dzshik	Chana
Dzshik	Yeshiyahu
Dzshik	Miriam

HEH
[Used to transliterate some **H** names into Yiddish]

Honigman	& Family

VAV
[Used to transliterate most **V** and **W** names into Yiddish]

Vosk	Orish
Viatrak	Chana
Viatrak	Mendel
Viatrak	Breina
Viatrak	Devora
Viatrak	Lea
Viatrak	Moshe
Viatrak	Sara
Vilenberg	Binom
Vilenberg	Dov (Bertshe)
Vilenberg	Henne
Vino	Moshe Reuven
Vino	Zisse
Vino	Yosef
Vino	Hillel
Vino	Yeshayahu
Vino	Yaakov
Veingarten	Yoel Dovid
Veingarten	Miriam
Veingarten	Pesse
Veingarten	Yitzchak
Veingarten	Nemmi
Veintrab	Volf and Family
Veintrab	Chanoch
Veiss	Dovid and Family

ZAYIN
[Used to transliterate most **Z** names into Yiddish]

Zabludovitch	Moshe Leib
Zabludovitch	Lea
Zabludovitch	Chana Hinde
Zabludovitch	Yishachar Ber
Zabludovitch	Menachem Mendel
Zabludovitch	Boruch
Zabludovitch	Chana
Zabludovitch	Yeshayahu
Zabludovitch	Rochel
Zagatzker	Mordechai
Zaloshnitza	Chaim
Zaloshnitza	Devora
Zaloshnitza	Mendel
Zilber	Avrohom
Zilber	Aizik
Zilber	Chaim
Zilber	Chana
Zilber	Yente
Zilber	Mendel
Zilber	Shaindel
Zilbershtram	Isser
Zilbershtram	Boruch
Zilbershtram	Devora
Zilbershtram	Arye
Zilbershtram	Yechiel Hersh
Zilbershtram	Bronya
Zilbershtram	Brocha
Zilbershtram	Neche
Zilbershtram	Feige

Zilbershtram	Shlomo
Zilbershtram	Shmuel
Zinger	Chava
Zinger	Chana
Zinger	Chaya Bayle
Zinger	Avrohom
Zinger	Nemmi
Zshelaner	Nachman
Zshelaner	Simcha
Zshelaner	Sara
Zismanovitch	Yitzchak
Ziskind	Shlomo
Zshbik	Hersh and Family
Zshbik	Dovid and Family
Zshita	Bella
Zshita	Devora
Zshita	Zev
Zshita	Rochel
Zshelaner	Rochel
Zshelaner	Feige
Zshelaner	Meir
Zshelaner	Avrohom
Zshelaner	Blumme
Zshelaner	Binyomin
Zshelaner	Dvora
Zshelaner	Gitte

TET
[Used to transliterate most **T** names into Yiddish]

Tottengreber	Avrohom Eliyohu
Tottengreber	Devora

Tottengreber	Chana
Tottengreber	Feivel
Tottengreber	Rivka
Trambka	Yehoshe
Trambka	Pinchas
Trambka	Moshe
Trambka	Miriam
Trambka	Raizel
Trambka	Tzviya
Trambka	Avrahan
Trambka	Brocha
Trambka	Devora
Trambka	Chaim
Trambka	Chana
Trambka	Yechezkel
Trambka	Yitzchak
Trambka	Avrohom
Tshechanover	Binyomin
Tshechanover	Devora
Tshechanover	Dovid
Tshechanover	Chaya
Tshechanover	Chaim
Tshechanover	Chana Hinde
Tshechanover	Yishachar Ber
Tshechanover	Yishachar
Tshechanover	Leibe
Tshechanover	Mendel
Tshechanover	Mordechai
Tshechanover	Moshe
Tshechanover	Nosson

Tshechanover	Leibe
Tshechanover	Pesse
Tshechanover	Rochel
Tshechanover	Simcha
Tshechanover	Rivke
Tshechanover	Raya

YOD
[Used to transliterate some **I, J** and **Y** names into Yiddish]

Yentshmen	Chaim
Yentshmen	Yosef
Yentshmen	Yehoshua
Yentshmen	Malka

KAF
[Used to transliterate most **C** and **K** names into Yiddish]

Cohen	Avrohom
Cohen	Chava
Cohen	Mordechai
Cohen	Sara
Kahana	Eliyohu
Kahana	Lea
Kahana	Zelig
Kahana	Shmuel
Kahana	Shlomo Zalman
Kvitaika	Chaim
Kvitaika	Leibe
Kvitaika	Blumme
Katz	Chaim
Katz	Chava
Katz	Tzvi
Katz	Moshe

LAMED
[Used to transliterate most **L** names into Yiddish]

Lach	Yehoshua
Lach	Feige
Lach	Chaim
Lach	Chaya
Lach	Yitzchak
Lach	Feivel
Lubinietski	Sholom & Family
Luksenburg	Dina
Luksenburg	Yitzchak
Liberberg	Hinde
Liberberg	Aizik
Liberberg	Miriam
Liberberg	Moshe
Liberberg	Nachman
Liberberg	Sara
Littman	Volf
Littman	Breine
Littman	Miriam
Littman	Nachum
Littman	Rivka
Lichtenshtein	Shmuel
Lichtenshtein	Fraida
Lichtenshtein	Esther
Lichtenshtein	Devora
Lichtenshtein	Yehoshua
Lichtenshtein	Yente
Lichtenshtein	Faibish
Lichtenshtein	Chana
Lichtenshtein	Elke

Lichtenshtein	Rivka
Lindenberg	Yishayahu
Lindenberg	Eliyohu
Lindenberg	Hinde
Lindenberg	Chava
Lipski	Breinne
Lipski	Shimun
Lipski	Shlomo
Lipski	Chaya
Lipski	Raizel
Levetal	& Family
Lemberg	Dovid
Lemberg	Pesach
Lemberg	Ekiba
Lemberg	Chomma
Lengalka	& Family

MEM
[Used to transliterate most **M** names into Yiddish]

Malina	Boruch Mordechai & Fam.
Magnashever	& Wife
Makovski	Temme
Makovski	Yaakov
Makovski	Leibel
Makovski	Tsiril
Margolis	Avrohom
Margolis	Moshe
Margolis	Chanuch
Margolis	Chaya
Margolis	Yehoshua
Margolis	Nemmi

Mondzshak	Moshe
Mondzshak	Leibel
Mondzshak	Chava
Mondzshak	Chana
Mondzshak	Chaya
Mondzshak	Feivel
Mondzshak	Yisrael
Mondzshak	Mordechai
Mondzshak	Hinde
Monshtok	Yisrael
Monshtok	Hershel & Family
Monshtok	Abba
Monshtok	Devora
Monshtok	Chana
Monshtok	Nachman & Family
Mishor	Hershel
Mishor	Devora
Mishor	Henne
Mishor	Hadassa
Mishor	Miriam
Mishor	Moshe
Melavski	Avrohom
Melavski	Bashe
Melavski	Gittel
Melavski	Lea
Melavski	Neche
Melavski	Feige
Melavski	Pesse
Melaver	Dovid
Melaver	Vavtze

Melaver	Chain
Melaver	Reuven
Melaver	Roize
Melotzker	Dovid
Melotzker	Rochel Lea
Melotzker	Chana Gittel
Melotzker	Moshe
Melotzker	Rivke
Melotzker	Hinde Rochel
Melotzker	Mordechai & Family
Melotzker	Berel & Family

NUN
[Used to transliterate most **N** names into Yiddish]

Nagor	Gedalia
Nagor	Penina
Nagor	Rivke
Novogrodski	Eliyohu
Novogrodski	Devora
Novogrodski	Dovid
Novogrodski	Hadassa
Novogrodski	Zev
Novogrodski	Chana
Novogrodski	Yaakov
Novogrodski	Meir
Novogrodski	Miriam
Novogrodski	Simcha
Navre	Sara Feige
Navre	Shmulik
Navre	Chanhalle
Nachtigal	Nachum

Nachtigal	Dovid
Nachtigal	Yosef
Nachtigal	Lea
Nachtigal	Nachman
Nachtigal	Rachel
Nirenberg	Hershel & Family
Naiar	Mordechai & Family
Neiman	Yechiel & Family

SAMECH
[Used to transliterate most **S** names into Yiddish]

Sabal	Yoal
Sabal	Devora
Sabal	Chana
Sabal	Lea
Sabal	Nosson
Sadzovka	Yechezkel & Family
Sadek	Eliezer
Sadek	Beile
Sadek	Henne
Sadek	Hershel
Sadek	Chaim
Sadek	Chana
Sadek	Yitzchak
Sadek	Mashe(!)
Sadek	Rivke
Sadek	Rochel
Sadek	Sholom
Stopien	Mattos
Stopien	Chaim
Stopien	Tsaddok

Stopien	Chana
Stopien	Rochel
Stopien	Sholom Bendet & Family
Student	Yisrael Yakov
Slod	Boruch & Family
Slod	Devora
Slod	Zelig
Slod	Yakov
Slod	Shlomo
Slod	Dovid
Slod	Miriam
Smalazsh	Berel
Smalazsh	Zisse
Smalazsh	Hersh Volf
Smalazsh	Feivel
Smalazsh	Yosef
Sentzkaver	Simcha
Sentzkaver	Devora
Sentzkaver	Dovid
Sentzkaver	Chaim
Sentzkaver	Chana
Sentzkaver	Rivka
Sentzkaver	Yitzchak
Sentzkaver	Tzerke (!)
Sentzkaver	Rochel
Sentzkaver	Boruch
Sentzkaver	Hersh
Sentzkaver	Mindel
Sentzkaver	Rivke
Sekola	Velvel & Family

Seratzk	Altter and Wife
Skoza	Chaim
Skoza	Gutta
Skoza	Avrohom
Skornik	Nosson
Skornik	Esther Lea
Skornik	Shaindel
Skornik	Dovid
Skornik	Meir Lippe
Skornik	Miriam
Skornik	Yechiel & Family
Srebnagora	Binyomin
Srebnagora	Devora
Srebnagora	Yitzchak
Srebnagora	Freida
Srebnagora	Simcha Binnem
Srebnagora	Moshe
Srebnagora	Mindel
Srebnagora	Simcha
Srebnagora	Shaintshe(!)
Srebnagora	Eliyohu

AYIN
[Used to transliterate some **E** names into Yiddish]

Ettinger	Notte & Family
Elboim	Binyomin
Elboim	Esther
Elboim	Chanoch
Elboim	Yitta
Elboim	Maks
Elboim	Nemmi

Eliasavitz	Boaz
Eliasavitz	Gedaliahu
Eliasavitz	Zev
Eliasavitz	Chaya
Eliasavitz	Leibe
Eliasavitz	Moshe
Erlich	Ben-Tzion & Family

PAY / FAY
[Used to transliterate most **F** and **P** names into Yiddish]

Fagazsheletz	Chaya
Fagazsheletz	Chaim
Fagazsheletz	Bella
Fagazsheletz	Devora
Fagazsheletz	Dovid
Fagazsheletz	Zelik
Fagazsheletz	Yakov
Fagazsheletz	Yitzchak
Fagazsheletz	Yishachar
Fagazsheletz	Rivka
Fagazsheletz	Rashe
Fagazsheletz	Shifra
Fagazsheletz	Sara
Fazner	Meir & Family
Fazner	Pesach & Family
Fazner	Avrohom Meir & Family
Fazner	Yitzchak & Family
Fazner	Hershel & Family
Fazner	Aitshe(!) & Family
Fazdshorek	Shmuel & Family
Fazdshorek	Rivka

Fazshdzsharek	Zalman
Fazshdzsharek	Yitzchak
Fazshdzsharek	Rochel
Fazshdzsharek	Rivka
Fater	Yitzchak
Fater	Shmuel
Fater	Devora
Fater	Chaya
Fater	Eliyohu Leib
Fater	Zalovka(?)
Fater	Abba
Fater	Feivel
Palloch	Chaim
Palloch	Yoel
Palloch	Malke
Palloch	Mendel
Palloch	Mordechai
Palloch	Moshe
Palloch	Rivke
Palloch	Sara
Fanfil	Shlomo & Family
Paktshik	Devora
Paktshik	Yitzchak
Paktshik	Peretz
Farma	Eliezer
Farma	Dina
Farma	Zelik
Farma	Zissel
Farma	Hershel
Farma	Miriam

Farma	Feivel
Farma	Sara
Fodalavitsh	Berish
Fodalavitsh	Safra
Fodalavitsh	Breina
Fodalavitsh	Aharon
Fodalavitsh	Dovid
Fodalavitsh	Dina
Fodalavitsh	Pinchas & Family
Fuchs	Eliyohu
Fuchs	Yona
Fuchs	Aharon
Fuchs	Avigdor
Fuchs	Binyomin
Fuchs	Devora
Fuchs	Rochel
Fianka	Chaya
Fianka	Yosek
Fianka	Yakov & Family
Fianka	Esther
Fianka	Tova
Fianka	Chava
Fianka	Miriam
Fianka	Pinchas
Fianka	Rochel
Fianka	Brocha
Fianka	Mordechai
Fianka	Menachem
Fianka	Simcha
Fianka	Yechiel

Filot	Moshe & Family
Fiekarek	Aharon & Family
Fisherman	Shmuel Lieber & Family
Feffer	Yitzchak
Feffer	Israel
Feffer	Devora
Feffer	Chaya
Perlmutter	Yosef
Perlmutter	Yakov
Perlmutter	Feivel
Perlmutter	Perl
Perlmutter	Leibak
Peretz	Chana
Peretz	Shlomo Dovid
Peretz	Leibe
Peretz	Rochel
Peretz	Breina
Peretz	Zelik
Peretz	Pinia
Peretz	Yeshayahu Yitzchok
Peretz	Baile
Peretz	Shlomo
Peretz	Nechemia
Peretz	Yocheved
Peretz	Rochel
Fried	Binyomin
Fried	Chaya
Fried	Yitzchok
Fried	Mendel
Fried	Rivka

Friedman	Avrohom & Family
Friedman	Yehoshua
Friedenberg	Zerach & Wife
Friedenberg	Efraim
Friedenberg	Michal (!)
Friedenberg	Avrohom & Family

TZADDI
[Used to transliterate most **TZ** and some **S** and **C** names into Yiddish]

Tzukerman	Altter
Tzukerman	Gittel
Tzukerman	Dovid
Tzukerman	Hershel
Tzukerman	Nachman
Tzukerman	Rivka
Tzinaman	Mordechai
Tzinaman	Chana
Tzinaman	Rivka
Tzinaman	Chaim
Tzinaman	Yakov & Family

KOOF
[Used to transliterate some **K** names into Yiddish]

Kahn	Yeshayahu & Family
Kozshik	Devora
Kozshik	Chaim
Kozshik	Chana
Kozshik	Yitzchak
Kozshik	Mendel
Kozshik	Miriam
Kolakavski	Mordechai & Family
Kaloska	Devora

Kaloska	Yosef Hersh
Kaloska	Yisrael
Kaloska	Miriam
Kalenberg	Menachem
Kalfus	Yakov
Kalfus	Kayla
Kalfus	Sara
Kamianer	Yosef
Kamianer	Malka
Kamianer	Rize
Kamianer	Shlomo
Kanarek	Leibel & Family
Kanarek	Binyomin
Kanarek	Chaya
Kanarek	Chana
Kanarek	Fromme
Kanarek	Rivke
Kanarek	Shmuel
Kostsheva	Urka & Family
Kostsheva	Volf & Family
Kostsheva	Moshe Chaim
Kostsheva	Miriam
Kostsheva	Moshe Nachum
Kostsheva	Lea
Kostsheva	Avigdor
Kostsheva	Avrohom
Kostsheva	Itta
Kostsheva	Devora
Kostsheva	Penina
Kostsheva	Rashe

Kostsheva	Shifra
Kostsheva	Esther
Kostsheva	Tova
Kaplan	Avigdor and Wife
Karetka	Sholom
Karetka	Yehuda
Karetka	Henne
Karetka	Devora
Kutner	Simcha Dovid
Kutner	Leiba
Kutner	Yitzchak
Kutner	Meir
Kutner	Miriam
Kutner	Esther
Kutner	Yosef
Kilka	Simcha
Kilka	Chaya Neche
Kilka	Rochel
Kilka	Mindel
Kuska	Aharon
Kuska	Moshe
Kuska	Rochel
Kuska	Rashe
Kufiatz	Devora
Kufiatz	Yitzchak
Kufiatz	Pesse
Kufiatz	Shmuel
Kirshenboim	Aharon & Family
Kirshenboim	Mendel & Family
Kirshenboim	Binyomin & Family

Kirshenboim	Moshe
Kirshenboim	Feige
Kirshenzweig	Monish
Kirshenzweig	Blumme
Kleinyod	Mendel & Family
Kleinman	Yitzchok
Kleinman	Leibe
Kleinman	Aharon
Kleinman	Hershel
Kleinman	Chaim
Kleinman	Mendel
Kleinman	Chana
Klenietz	Berish
Klenietz	Miriam
Klenietz	Meir
Klenietz	Dina
Klenietz	Rivka
Klenietz	Chana
Klenietz	Moshe
Kelman	Avrohom Aharon & Family
Kronenberg	Golde
Kronenberg	Hershel & Family
Krulik	Leibel
Krulik	Peretz
Krulik	Chava
Krulik	Henne
Krulik	Moshe
Kremer	Nachum
Kshivanovski	Boruch

Kshivanovski	Eliezer
Kshivanovski	Hershel
Kshivanovski	Lea
Kshivanovski	Rivke

RAISH
[Used to transliterate most **R** names into Yiddish]

Robota	Yeshayahu
Robota	Feige
Robota	Sara
Robota	Roize
Robota	Chaya
Robota	Yakov
Robota	Yisrael
Radzinovitsh	Avrohom
Radzinovitsh	Gutman
Radzinovitsh	Chana
Radzinovitsh	Yitzchak
Radzinovitsh	Feige
Radzinovitsh	Rivka
Radzinovitsh	Shlomo
Radzinovitsh	Sara
Radzinek	Dov
Radzinek	Hinde
Radzinek	Yakov
Radzinek	Mordechai
Radzinek	Feige
Rozmarin	Dov
Rozmarin	Devora
Rozmarin	Chanoch
Rozmarin	Miriam

Rozmarin	Rivka
Rozenshtein	Yochanan & Family
Rozenblum	Kalman & Family
Rotenberg	Shimon & Family
Ramek	Chona (!) & Family
Rubinshtein	Shlomo
Rubinshtein	Esther
Rubinshtein	Rivka
Romianek	- - -
Riba	Chaim
Riba	Berel
Riba	Yitzchak
Riba	Devora
Riba	Mendel
Riba	Rashe
Riba	Sara
Riba	Avrohom
Remboim	Devora
Remboim	Chaya
Remboim	Yosef
Remboim	Yitzchak
Remboim	Abba
Remboim	Yakov
Remboim	Mordechai
Remboim	Menachem
Remboim	Velvel & Family

SHIN

[Used to transliterate most **Sh**, and **Sz**, and some **Sch** names into Yiddish]
[Note: Where **Sch** represents **Sk**, the name will be found under *Samech*.]

Shano	Chaim
Shano	Mendel

Shano	Malka
Shano	Miriam
Shafft	Michal (!) & Family
Shaffran	Binyomin
Shaffran	Devora
Shaffran	Yosef
Shaffran	Nachum
Shaffran	Rivka
Shultz	Menachem
Shultz	Chaim
Shultz	Mordechai
Shultz	Nemmi
Shultz	Feivel
Shultz	Chava
Shultz	Zishe
Shulrif	Dovid
Shulrif	Golde
Shulrif	Hershel
Shulrif	Chana
Shulrif	Chanan
Shulrif	Rivka
Shulrif	Rochel
Shulrif	Shalom
Shuster	Shilom & Family
Schvartz	Dovid
Schvartz	Chana
Schvartz	Yente
Schvartz	Yakov
Schvartz	Miriam
Schvartz	Nachman

Schvartz	Reuven
Schvartz	Yakov Dovid
Shtutzki	Yechiel
Shtutzki	Rochel
Shaiman	Baruch
Shaiman	Dovid
Shaiman	Chanoch
Shaiman	Yehoshua
Shaiman	Malka
Shaiman	Miriam
Shlamovitsh	Dovid
Shlamovitsh	Chana
Shlamovitsh	Sara
Shlamovitsh	Devora
Shlamovitsh	Yisrael
Shlamovitsh	Yitzchak
Shlivka	Yakov
Shlivka	Chana
Shlivka	Yorre
Shlivka	Menachem
Shlezinger	Chaim
Shlezinger	Feige
Shlezinger	Yosef-Dovid
Shlezinger	Gittel
Shlezinger	Yosef
Shlezinger	Yakov
Shlezinger	Yisrael
Shlezinger	Libbe
Shlezinger	Masha
Shlezinger	Roize

Shlezinger	Slomo Zalman
Shlezinger	Simcha
Shmichovitz	Berel
Shmichovitz	Leibe
Shmichovitz	Moshe
Shmichovitz	Tziril
Shmichovitz	Temme
Shmichovitz	Yitzchak
Shmichovitz	Pinchas
Shmichovitz	Roize
Shmichovitz	Rochel
Shmichovitz	Shmuel Hersh
Shmichovitz	Sara
Schmidt	Avrohom
Schmidt	Avrohom Michal
Schmidt	Aizik
Schmidt	Eliyohu
Schmidt	Efraim
Schmidt	Beile
Schmidt	Dov
Schmidt	Dovid
Schmidt	Hadassa
Schmidt	Hinde
Schmidt	Hersh Yosef
Schmidt	Chana
Schmidt	Yosef
Schmidt	Yakov
Schmidt	Mindel
Schmidt	Malka
Schmidt	Mordechai

Schmidt	Miriam
Schmidt	Feivel
Schmidt	Rutke
Schmidt	Shaindel
Schmidt	Michael
Schmidt	Tova
Schmidt	Reuven
Schmidt	Shimon
Schmidt	Elke
Schmidt	Zlate
Shnaidavski	Dovid
Shnaidavski	Esther
Shnaidavski	Nachum
Shnaidavski	Pesse
Shnaidavski	Shabsai
Shreiber	Sender
Shreiber	Avrohom
Shreiber	Eliezer
Shreiber	Chana
Shreiber	Lea
Shreiber	Malke
Shreiber	Rochel

May Their Memory Be For A Blessing

In Ciechanów after the Destruction

473

Immediately after the destruction a few Jews started to return to Ciechanów. They came from the death camps, from hiding. Each one hoped to find some trace of their dear ones, thinking that by chance someone may have survived. So the few Ciechanów Jews met and talked about the catastrophe that they had lived through.

The destruction of Ciechanów Jewry could be seen all over. The bones of the martyrs were strewn everywhere. With the Jewish gravestones, roads were paved. The pain and sorrow of those who returned was great. They strengthened themselves and set up a committee that took upon itself the holy task of giving the bones a Jewish burial and to bring back as many as possible of the damaged gravestones.

With the help of the newly set up Polish government, the work was carried out. The bodies of the tortured ones were exhumed. They were put into coffins for their eternal rest in brother-graves in the Jewish cemetery.

After completing the holy work, those who returned erected a memorial from the shattered gravestones, a reminder of the great destruction that the sadistic Germans brought upon the Jews. A garden was planted around the memorial and it is cared for to the present day. This was the final act for the dead that the survivors performed for the Ciechanów Jewish martyrs. Afterwards, these few survivors left Ciechanów, the place where they were born or raised, their home place, that was turned into a Valley of Death by the Germans for the Jews.

The last Ciechanów Jews left for Israel, America and other countries throughout the world in order to build new lives and to carry on with Jewish national life.

Signed: M.P.

The photographs that follow were taken on the spot. They are a documentary confirmation of the German bestiality in exterminating the Jews that spread out also on the graves of the Jews who died in peaceful times, and on the gravestones.

474

Survivors who returned

475

Survivors who returned gather gravestones that were scattered in Ciechanów streets

476

Survivors gather the bones of the victims

The coffins carried to the Jewish cemetery

477

At tthe open graves at the Jewish burial in the Ciechanów cemetery

At the cemetery after the burial

478

Exhumation and burial of the tormented Sarah Altus   The bones in the coffin

479

The coffin in the cemetery

The new grave

480

The monument for the Jews of Ciechanów who perished in the _Shoah_.

After giving the remains a Jewish burial the survivors erected a monument made of the gathered gravestones that were desecrated by the heinous Germans. With the erection of this monument the history of Ciechanów Jewry on Polish Ciechanów soil ended forever].

481

Ciechanów in 1956

Riva Gonska

Of this small town I will tell a few things in memory of all my dear ones who were wiped out, to my best friend Adele Pepe and to each Jewish home in this Jewish town which will light and remember the past and from which we drew out future life. It has been my heart's yearning ever since to see the town once again, to see and not to forget. I wanted to go over the whole place, to feel every corner where I'd grown up, to see with my own eyes and to be as one in a spiritual way with the past. I wanted to search. Perhaps a person would be found, or something which would be able to tell me how it happened. How were the dear ones, relatives, our birth-giving parents, brothers and sisters and all of the Jewish community wiped out. I wished this very much and so it was.

In the midst of the summer of 1956 I visited Poland and my hometown of Ciechanów. I knew very little on my coming to Poland, only what I'd read. However, as much as I read, the information didn't match my childhood memories or past feelings and didn't fit the present general picture of Ciechanów.

New Poland was, in my mind, a new building project after the destruction, with new busy streets, streetcars and a renewal of spiritual life. However, what about us with our special lives -- what about the Jewish town, the Jewish school, language, prayers on holidays, the Jews in the synagogues, in the market, and at work? And what about the youth? All those aspects which marked our childhood experiences. Through some unrealistic, secret yearnings I wanted to see them all, so that it was worth knocking on every door, approaching every person who remained, to release all the orphan-like sorrow in the hearts of those who were from this place. I hoped to absorb the feelings of the past and to see every person in his place at the time of his suffering and torture and to know he stood the test of those times and that the bonds of national brotherhood were not broken in those insane times. I will ask people, maybe they remember how it happened. Where are the lively youth? Where is their final resting place?

An unexplained fear fills me despite my clear decision that no matter what, I am to see the city of my birth. Fear of what? I had pleasant memories of childhood and youth with every place connected to a youthful tale, so that I thought the skies of the city were the most beautiful in the world. The big house on the main street, the most beautiful of houses, the public park full of charm, the old house where I grew up which stood on the main street and especially the big yard within which are hidden the sorrow and happiness of tens of children who grew up in those yards. I retained all the beauty of this city and now was afraid to be disappointed. After all, I've seen the big world. What if the value of all that was precious to me will be minimized and a vacuum created in the place of this majestic period, above all, that of a Jewish family, dear Jews, memories of whom are still engraved in my heart? The old one in his *kitl* on *Yom Kippur* standing outside the synagogue saying "Next year in Jerusalem." G-d willing, I will meet some Jews there.

482

I was fearful lest it be difficult for me to deal with the extent of destruction and the national and personal orphan-like loss. Fear that I would not find anything I was searching for and that the break [down] would be immense, the biggest in one's life.

There are two train stations in Warsaw, one being the main one and one in the east from which one goes on to Ciechanów. I boarded the train on a rainy and gray day even though it was the month of August, mid-summer. It was Friday, the market day in the city. Lots of farmers and especially farmers' wives got on the train with their baskets as in the past, to sell their produce. At every station wave after wave board and disembark from the train. The ticket-checker was calling the names of the stations and with every name, a chain of memories. Memories of people who were and are no more. I barely had room between all the people. Conversation was about prices, produce and untimely rains. I asked here and there some routine questions without disclosing my background. Some of the girls spoke of clothing prices and I asked them if the new regime and its changes is to their liking. One of the types of gentiles whom we knew in the past, who at the look of their eyes a chill would go through my body for the hate of Israel which is in their eyes, answered, "I tell you, one thing good we have today is when I go into a store and they tell me how much a dress costs, I know that's the price and I pay it. No more are there those Jews who took us for all they were worth. Once when we paid we knew we were paying too much. We finished with them forever." A classic response from those days, which apparently is not related to the regime, heard in the time of grandfather and father. Will it really be repeated in all generations under all regimes?

The ticket-checker calls the station for Ciechanów. In the area opposite the train station stands an "auto", questionable if it is a transport car for the transporting of cattle, or one which reminds me from my childhood used in transporting the gypsies. Now instead of horses, a motor. The rain turns everything ugly, both the clothing and the wind. My eyes follow those going into the auto. I muster all my memory. Maybe I'll see some figure whom I'll recognize. The arguing farmers pile into the car. The auto takes them to the city, to the distant market. I imagined my entry into the city differently. I became one of the travelers. Two stops are made along the way -- one near the new garden and the other on the main street upon entering the market, where everyone gets off. I also disembarked and stood at the side of the way not knowing where to turn. I looked around everything so familiar and yet so strange. This is the main road on which we strolled and walked back and forth on holidays and *Shabbat*, in our best clothing, in holiday spirits. Here is the big house of K, and in a few more meters opposite, according to all the signs, should be the big yard with our house towards the back. I enter; however there is no sign of the house. The place has changed. There is a new house. This was the first "isn't" I saw. Beside the sidewalk is a familiar house and upon it a sign, "Watches repaired here."

483

I entered and recognized the man. It was our neighbor from back then. I asked him if he still remembers the Jewish man who lived in this yard before the war -- an old man with a red beard who had two sons and two daughters. I told him I am one of those daughters. He remembers, lifting his eyes from the watch. He remembers the G. family but his father remembers even better. And he tells me, "It was on one day in September or October. The Germans put out a flyer that all the Jews in the city must leave their homes, young, old and babes, women and men, divided by age and sex. The elders had to run to the fort where it would be decided what each one would have to do. All the men up to middle age were put on the car to go afar.

Many women and children were shot in view of fathers and husbands. Amongst them my sister-in-law and her children. Your mother went with the other elders to the central place. They hurried her along, but she couldn't keep up and tripped here and there. When she fell a German shot her on the spot.

You should know that they led an honest life. I heard many stories about the Jews of the town. We also didn't have it easy. We suffered much with many casualties. In this town there is only one Jew who remains. He lives opposite. Go to him, maybe he can tell you more.

I left dumbfounded and decided to get my wits about me before another encounter. I entered the plaza in front of the new city hall. The nicest building in the city today. I wandered around and passed all the streets which led to the market. Nothing had changed. Every house familiar, though a bit smaller and old-fashioned, perhaps from age or from suffering. All of a sudden I saw a sign with the names of the past Jewish owners: Z. It is possible that there was a mistake. I knocked at the door and entered. Despite the early hour there was a kerosene light. The house so recognizable was totally different outside than from within. This was not a Jewish home. Sacred pictures and beside them two thick wax candles. An old woman sitting and sewing. I asked her if she has any connection with the name on the sign outside. "No, ma'am. There were many empty homes after the war. All the Jews left or were killed. Many came from afar and got the empty apartments. My children were also killed and I am here with my grandchildren. There is no point looking for Jews here. There are none. There is only one, go on the street...." She also sent me to the one, the only one remaining. On the main street on the corner stands the house so well known to me with the bakery in front. In the yard is a red brick house. One of the dearest families and my soul-mate friend lived in this house. I wanted to walk again on the same path I'd walked so many times in the past, where my childhood and young dreams were woven -- my dreams and hers, my friend Adele. The house stood, cold, awakening memories but rejecting. The power of a house, bigger than that of a person. It absorbs and rejects and remains as is. The people living there now know nothing of the previous occupants.

I went to the home of the remaining Jew. I was welcomed by a young man who went through the whole hellish experience while still a young boy, the concentration camp, and exterminations.

484

Like many youngsters his age he witnessed the horrid annihilation, the ovens, the millions of pairs of shoes, the burnt clothing and the many skeletons of his people and his townsmen. He lives but cannot free himself from the nightmare in which he lives. Those are the eyes that have seen it all, and will certainly not see much joy, and happiness will not be found in them. He told me of many survivors, who left the town, of those who emigrated and of a few who went to HaEretz. He told me of the heroism of Rosa Robota, may her memory be blessed. Everyone knew of her and was proud of this daughter of our town. Of those I ask him about, he knew only a few. He was after all only a boy then. I went through the whole town with him in all directions, each road big and small, and all remained as was. The house in which hundreds of Jewish children studied remained as was. Only the children are missing. It seems that any minute a familiar face will appear from the gymnasium, the market or whatever. The roads are full of people and particularly carts harnessed to horses. The sidewalk is narrow, as is the road. The stores along the roads are small. There are no storefront show windows, rather glass dripping rain. The impression of everything is sad and monochrome, with no light, much mud and plaster. The old homes stand close one to another. The park is as if nothing happened. The benches stand as does the hill above the park and children are even running in the paths. Only a few new homes were built by the Germans near the gymnasium, two-story homes with a garden around according to best German tradition. Now the city's wealthy live in them with radio, telephone and baths. Once, a telephone was had by only two of the townspeople. And a radio by the same number. I couldn't say who the rich are now. In the vicinity of the cemetery there was once a shack, a place where there was a *Shomeir Hatzair* meeting place. The place stands empty, the windows closed with boards. Perhaps people hid out there in bad times. When you go around and want to see the cemetery, you simply can't. I will probably not get there. There is destruction and damage. I didn't go because I couldn't bear the horrors that a living person's eyes could see. I turned quickly and took off.

After this I understood. In this place no Jews would live. The living left because it is not possible to create new life. Here there remains only one artifact of the horrid period that lives in the memory of the past and tries to live on. He will also not start a new generation as there is no place here for a Jewish baby. There is nothing on which to raise a Jewish child. On that we agreed.

I saw the whole town with all the bravery and pain with the words of the song of the great poet: "Rise and go to the city of killing and come to the gardens and your eyes shall see.."

I saw with my own eyes, and felt, and left with the ache of a Jewish orphan for what has been done to us. I saw one of the places where the dawn will never see a Jewish town because a Jewish child will never be born there.

485

Ciechanów Jews throughout the World

Supplement to the *Yizkor* Book

486   blank

487

Landmanschafts and Aid Activities

The Ciechanówers in Israel

From 1920 until the outbreak of war a large stream of Ciechanówers left for Palestine. People from all Zionist groups went on *aliyah*: *Hashomeir Hatzair, Hechalutz,* General *Zionist,* etc. The Ciechanówers contributed a great deal to the building of the land. In all aspects of the building they participated: in industry, agriculture, in the city and in the settlements. Like all *olim,* they went through the thorny path of building *Eretz Yisroel*: that is -- hunger, sickness, epidemics, guarding and defense, danger of attack by the Arabs. The Ciechanówers drained swamps, made the barren land fruitful with their blood and sweat.

We organized ourselves as a special Ciechanówer Landsmanshaft, as a result of the bloody war in 1939. When we received the first news of the *khurban* of our *Kehillah,* when we received the first cries for help from our brethren, who managed to save themselves from the great catastrophe and from those who were scattered in the Siberian forests in Russia, some of the community decided to do whatever was possible to help the unfortunate ones.

Appeals for help reached our honored *Rov, Reb* Chaim Mordecai Bronrot Z"L, who was living in Tel-Aviv at that time, and to the Kahane family, who were amongst the first to go on *aliyah* to *Eretz Yisroel.*

At the beginning our *Rov* Z"L, thanks to his contact with various institutions in the country, sent parcels with the assistance of his son Yaacov. The Kahane family also sent parcels on their own initiative. However, when the appeals for help increased, the first aid-committee was established with the *Rov* as honorary chairman; M. Kleinyud, secretary; members-at-large: R. Kahane, Y. Bronrot, S. Fuchs, Moishe Porakh, Shulamit Porakh, D. Newman, Bryna Pulus, Z. Aronovich (Malina), Kh. L. Ostry, A.D. Vinditsky, A. Fried, F. Friedenreikh, V.H. Zilbershtrom.

The committee arranged the first impressive memorial service for our *Kehillah* and appealed to America for urgent help. We immediately received $100, and shortly thereafter another $200 as well as parcels to distribute to the survivors who came to the land and to send help to those in need who were still scattered throughout Europe.

The aid work grew. More and more *olim* came to *Eretz Yisroel*. We received little support from abroad. The economic situation in the land was critical, and to our great misfortune, our dear active member, Moishe Kleinyud, was torn away from us prematurely at a young age. Still, every *oleh* was received warmly and received primary assistance. We started to think about constructive help for our brothers in order to establish them in the land. Those who were especially active at that time were: Malka Bromson (Fuchs), Noah Zabludowicz, and others.

The Plan for Establishing a Gmilat Hesed Fund Becomes Ripe

The Ciechanów community heard that *Frau* Mazur, the daughter of Avraham Klinger of Ciechanów, wants to establish a memorial for her family who perished. A committee of Ciechanówers approached her and influenced her to establish a *Gmilat Hesed Fund* (Free Loan Society), with a considerable sum for the Ciechanówers in Israel, to be named after her parents. She then gave $300. Another Ciechanówer, who didn't want his name disclosed, contributed a larger sum, and these donations were the foundation of the *Gmilat Hesed Fund*.

The *Gmilat Hesed* soon became a large financial institution that helped constructively to establish all the Ciechanów *olim*. Money came from various sources, mainly from New York and Detroit.

Our *landsleit* in New York came up with a plan to establish a special housing project for Ciechanówers who had come to Israel. They raised several thousand dollars for this purpose, but this grand plan was connected with so many difficulties that they had to give it up. They had already sent the money to Israel to a specific institution. After much effort we succeeded in getting the money back and with it, to enlarge the *Gmilat Hesed Fund*.

*****

The last balance of the treasury is as follows
Gmilat Hesed Society of the Ciechanowers in Israel
Founded in memory of the Klinger family

Balance as of 31.12.61

Active		Passive	
In bank	2,986.31	Capital	14,768.62
Owing	12,630.00	Keren Ezra	177.00
		Keren Hasaifer	635.69
		Zakhayim	35.00
Total	15,616.31		

Income		Expenses	
dues from America	440.00	Memorial	145.00
Sons of Abraham	1,797.50	Postage	64.97
from American relief	375.60		
donations	317.00	Supplies	60.00
from the bank	30.30	Postage	20.00
		Miscellaneous	1.40
Total	2,675.40	**Total**	291.37
minus expenses	291.37		
Total	1,384.03		

		Loans distributed in 1961	
on hand as of 1.1.61	12,349.59		
net income for 1961	2,384.03	12 x 300 ..	3,600
other income	35.00	32 x 400 ..	12,800
Total	14,678.62	44 = **Total**	16,400

488

Members of first society from Ciechanow in Israel to help survivors

Including: Chaim Leib Charif-Estry, Malka Bramson, Rivka Kahane, Moshe Frach-Kveit, Noach Zabludowicz, Shmuel Fuchs, Yakov Bronrot.

489

**Members of first society from Ciechanow
in Israel to help survivors**

Including: Moshe Shlossinger, Yisrael
Galadosher, Yakov Kahane, Dvora
Paulos, Yichiel Yisraeli-Tromkbi,
Noach Zabludowicz, David Bramson

This *Yizkor* Book of the Destroyed *Kehillah*

Community activists decided to publish a large book in memory of the
destroyed Ciechanów *Kehillah*. We gathered material for over ten
years. Some of it was in New York where some Ciechanówers wanted
to publish a *Yizkor Book*. Our dear friends in Detroit, a small group of
Ciechanówers, but with a strong will and devotion for this project,
helped a lot in making possible the publication of this *Yizkor Book*.
Binyamin Apel and his family, who visited Israel, were the deciding
factor in this matter.

We received back the material we had sent to America and at a
large meeting of Ciechanówers, in honor of Binyamin Apel, the
foundation was laid for the large undertaking, namely, the Ciechanów

Yizkor Book. A book committee was formed with: Moishe Fuchs, Yehoshua Grossbard, Yaacov Bronrot, Moishe Kolko, Noah Zabludowicz, Yaacov Rubinstein, Zola Apel and Riva Gonska. Those abroad who contributed much energy for the book are: Moishe Lesser and Binyamin Apel from Detroit, and Yosef Mundzak from Paris.

Yaar Kdoshim -- Martyrs' Forest

The Ciechanów *landsleit* wanted to memorialize their destroyed *Kehillah* with something that would symbolize the destruction of our dearest ones and at the same time do something for the new Jewish life in the State of Israel. So, we turned our eyes to the Judean Hills. When you arrive at this place you get a feeling of holiness. The heroic history of our people rises in front of you as it lived in its own land. In those ancient hills one feels the connection between the past and the present -- the eternal Jewish history throughout all generations.

This wonderful part of Israel, the Israeli government decided to transform into a forest as an eternal memory of the six million martyrs.

492

Every *Kehillah* plants trees in the name of the destroyed.

In "Yaar Kdoshim (Forest of the Holy)"

Ceremony of planting trees in memory of the destroyed Ciechanów *Kehillah*

A detailed list of those who perished is found in the archives of *Keren Kayemet* (J.N.F.). A special stone with the name of each *Kehillah* and country is in every pathway of the forest.

On the 27th of *Nisan*, the day of the uprising, representatives of all the Jewish *Kehillahs* from all over the world gather, and a large memorial service takes place in memory of the six million martyrs.

We also, the Ciechanów *landsleit* decided that our *Kehillah* must also be memorialized in this martyrs' forest. Much effort went into collecting money in Israel but the greatest help we got from our dear *landsleit* in Detroit who helped and who were the first in all our fund-raising. Our Parisian *landsleit* also planted a number of trees in this forest.

*

The committee of the *Gmilat Hesed Fund* became, in time, a general Ciechanów committee. Additional people became active: Yekhiel Yisraeli (Trombka), Tzaduk Ostry, Moishe Shlesinger, and others. The committee broadened its activities, arranged memorial programs with suitable content. In the early days we still had at the memorials the presence of the patriarchal figure of our *Rov, Reb* Bronrot Z"L. After his death various personalities were invited, such as: *Rov* Tkherz and others.

At the gatherings various suggestions were made. Through the iniative of Yosef Trombka we published a brochure in memory of the heroine, Rosa Robota. A committee of the following participated in its publication: Yekhiel Yisraeli, Noah Zabludowicz and M. Kolko. Moishe Fuchs edited the brochure, which was widely distributed amongst the Ciechanówers in Israel as well as abroad. As a result Ciechanówers in many lands got in touch with the Ciechanów committee in Israel. New projects were undertaken by the *landsleit* in order to memorialize the Ciechanów Jewish martyrs.

494

A banquet in honor of the guests Binyamin Apel from Detroit and Tenenbaum from Paris;

495

With great respect we recall the founders of the Ciechanów committee in Israel who have gone to their eternal rest:

Rov Chaim Mordecai Bronrot

Like a faithful father, he was tied to the survivors of his *Kehillah*. As long as he was here with us in Israel we didn't feel our homelessness so much. In the midst of his fruitful and creative work he was taken away from us. May his memory be blessed.

Tenenbaum greets Binyamin Apel and his wife

Moishe Kleinyud

A quiet, introverted person, he was very active already in Ciechanów in cultural work. He was the secretary of the Ciechahow *Farband* in Israel, and worked tirelessly for the good of all. He departed from us in his early years.

A. D. Vinditsky

A precious Jew, a *talmid khokhem*, he was one of the founders of *Mizrachi* in Ciechanów; was a delegate at Zionist congresses; a fighter for the idea of peace in the world. He published brochures, appealing to all world leaders, regarding peace. His writings about various types of Ciechanówers are found in this book.

Golda Mazur

Golda Mazur laid the foundation of our *Gmilat Hesed Fund* by contributing a sizable sum. She was the wife of the Warsaw *Kehillah* president, *Reb* Eliyahu Mazur. But enjoying life in another place, she wanted to memorialize her parents and family who lived in Ciechanów -- the Klinger family. Through her initiative the *Gmilat Hesed Fund* for our *landsleit* was established. In addition to the sum that she gave originally, she covered nearly all the expenses of the Fund during her lifetime.

496

Shulamit Porakh

Shulamit was one of the founders of our committee. Her house was always open for the participants who were active on behalf of the Ciechanówers.

A. Fried

One of the people who was always ready to be active on behalf of others. He was one of the first to work on behalf of the Ciechanówers.

Wolf Henekh Zilbershtrom

He was one of the founders of the *Gmilat Hesed Fund* in Israel. He was a loyal and devoted member of our committee. His work on behalf of the Fund is described in this book.

*

In the framework of our review about Ciechanów in Israel we want to thank all those who are carrying on activities for the benefit of the survivors of Ciechanów and in memorializing the destroyed *Kehillah*. Presently there is an effort being made to build, in memory of Rosa Robota, a culture-house in her name in a *kibbutz* in Israel and we hope that abroad there will be interest in this too.

A Ciechanówer in Israel

497

A memorial service in Israel for the martyrs of Ciechanów

Presidium during a memorial service

498

Assembled in the hall

Assembled in the hall

499

A memorial service for Ciechanów martyrs in 1961

500

A memorial service for Ciechanów martyrs in 1961

501

The Ciechanów Landsmanschaft in Detroit

Hitler's rise to power in Germany, the increased anti-Semitism in Poland, including pogroms and acts of hooligans, the appeals for aid that came from our dear ones on the other side of the ocean gave us no rest in America. The Ciechanówers also felt that something must be done for our *landsleit* back home.

So our people got together: Chaim Yosef Berman (Teshok), Sam Cohen (Mendl Patzier's son), Liber Berman, Isaac Glass (Khilek Shuster's son), Avraham Goldshmid, Yisroel Burshtein (Yenkl Shakhemuk's son-in-law), and decided that the Ciechanówers must organize an aid institution. The next step was to appeal to the Ciechanówers in Detroit until it became possible to organize the first gathering.

A temporary committee was established for the purpose of organizing a *landsmanshaft* group. There were difficulties because of the differences in the world view of our Ciechanówers in Detroit. There were amongst us extreme leftists to extreme right, and a significant number of religious Jews.

In spite of these differences in thinking, everyone began to work immediately. Such a small group as ours arranged various events such as: banquets and picnics, at which our members, men and women, worked very hard in addition to their personal donations, in order to raise more money.

Already at the first meetings the matter of aid for Ciechanów political prisoners was raised. They were in Polish prisons. For many of our members the whole matter was not understandable, particularly for those of the older generation.

We had to make our aims of our *farein* clear. Ours were definitely different from the activities of other similar organizations. Besides the similar activities of our *landsleit* on the other side of the ocean, we also carried out cultural events.

We were very fortunate in this respect. Many of our members were *Yiddische yidn,* nationally inclined, members of national-cultural organizations, knowledgable about Jewish life.

502

We took advantage of this and organized talks, lectures, current events, discussions, occasional book reviews. Those who participated in these were: Yosef Trombka, Isaac Kesler, Dovid Fuchs, Toba Dregner and her husband, Moishe Listopad, and others, young and old.

The meetings took place in private homes around dining tables. In this way the desire was established of working together and enjoying ourselves together as *landsleit.* The so-called loneliness, that every immigrant feels deeply, vanished. The longing for a bit of the old Ciechanów was stilled: a word, an expression, an anecdote, even a nickname – anything that reminded one of childhood years -- warmed the hearts of the Ciechanówers. All were like one large family. Automatically we became closely bonded. We invited one another to *simchas* and, God forbid, to other occasions...We shared our life experiences both in joy and in sorrow. ..

At the same time our members were active in other organizations: *Yiddisher Kultur Farband* ("IKUF'), *Sholem Aleichem Folk Shule, Arbeter Ring* (Workmens' Circle), as well as in literary groups.

When war broke out our *landsmanshaft-aid* even accompanied the refugees to Shanghai. After the liberation, when news reached us about the *khurban* that the Ciechanówers, together with all the Jews of Poland had endured, we gave thousands to help the freed ones of the lagers. Our aid to Poland consisted of: parcels, food, medication, money and clothing and continued even when no other organization was still sending money there.

Our work also adjusted itself to the new conditions. When Israel became our land, the assistance was directed towards Israel. We sent money for the *Gmilat Hesed Fund*, *Yaar Kdoshim* and, more recently, for the *Yizkor Book*. We are also proud that we were one of the few groups who supported Israel in its War of Independence.

In summing up our *landsmanshaft* activities:

As soon as the need of our *landsleit* overseas became very great, the work progressed rapidly. The sending of parcels, letters and the contact that was established with those of our fellow Ciechanówers from back home, were instrumental in forging the *landsmanshaft* contact.

503

Ciechanówers in Detroit

Executive committee

Committee members

504

Meeting of *landsleit.*

Ciechanów Jewish survivors of the lagers upon their arrival in Detroit

505

Reception for Moishe Porakh during his visit in Detroit

Landsleit [compatriots] of Detroit

506

We want to mention here some of our people who devoted much time and effort for the *landsmanshaft* organization: Yisroel and Vita Bornstein; Liber and Tzerka Burman; Yuzek and Frau Glass, who did so much, including the most difficult work, to raise money, raised funds themselves and packed parcels.

After the *khurban*, when Jewish Ciechanów no longer existed, and after some of our members died, the work ceased. We might have stopped existing, just as did many similar organizations in America, had it not been for the arrival in Detroil of a group of young refugees with Binyamin Apel and Laibl Mandrl at the head.

They started to awaken anew the old and tired members, who worked very hard to draw the newcomers in and help them adjust. We must mention: Dovid Silver (Avreml Baron's son), Ostriak, Yosl Pshibalovsky, Groskind, Avreml and Nakhum Altus, their nephew Yisroel Altus, Gitl Schwartz (Moishe Zemiker's daughter), George Vina. When Isaac Kesler returned from his visit to Israel, we started to work with renewed energy for the institutions that our *landsleit* established in Israel: Free Loan, Martyrs' Forest and the *Yizkor Book*.

507

We also dreamed about forming a central Ciechanów organization. The New York organization had a wonderful group that included: Yisroel, Moishe and Zelig Krasne; the Malinas, two Klein brothers, Voveh and Yidl Burnshtein. A small group was active in Chicago. In Montreal there is also a small but good group.

But in spite of all efforts, there was no success in establishing such a central committee in America. Each group conducts its own activities: memorial services and banquets are arranged. Perhaps because of the *Yizkor Book*, the contact will once more be established amongst the Ciechanów *landsleit* who still have much to do in order to memorialize their betrayed *Kehillah*.

Let us not forget that we also in the small *shtetl* have, by our way of life, contributed something to the wider world.

The Ciechanów Farein In Detroit
Moishe Leser - President
Victor Kesler - Secretary

508

Ciechanowers in Paris and Surroundings

After World War I, when Poland became independent, the situation in all Polish cities and *shtetlech*, in spite of all expectations, grew much worse. The economic anti-Semitism robbed the Jews of their livelihood. The young people had no future to look forward to. The hooligan attacks on Jews also increased. Naturally, Ciechanów was no exception and Jews, particularly the young, left the *shtetl* and emigrated. They left for America, *Eretz Yisroel*, and especially for nearby France.

In France as well, the life of the new immigrants was not easy. They had to seek employment, go to various government offices to get work-permits. Many of them had material difficulties. More than one had to sometimes spend the night on a park bench. In these circumstances, the idea arose amongst the newcomers to form a *landsmanshaft* to offer mutual assistance to one another as much as possible.

In the beginning of 1928, therefore, the first "Fraternity of Ciechanówers And Nearby *Shtetlech*" was formed. The included *shtetlech* were Plotsk, Proshnitz, Mlava, Noshelsk and others. The main purpose was mutual assistance for local Ciechanówers as well as help for those who were suffering in Polish prisons for various political ideas.

The Ciechanów "Fraternity" carried on very useful activities for eleven years, up to the time of the outbreak of World War II in 1939. At that time the number of Ciechanówers in Paris was around seventy families.

The terrible war also brought great *tzores* for the Jewish population in France. The brutal acts of the Hitlerite murderers were not strange to us, though we were in France then. As foreigners nearly all Jewish men volunteered for the French army to fight against humanity's enemy, against Hitler and fascism.

Exactly one year later, when France capitulated, before the German attack on the Soviet Union, the first racial laws against Jews began. After the arrest of the first five thousand Jews, a great portion of the Jewish

509

population began to flee to the so-called "free zone" (south zone), where the Vichy government ruled, in order not to fall into German claws.

But it didn't take long and all of France was occupied by the Germans, and with this began the German extermination of the Jews of France. Jews were arrested *en masse*. Various lagers were established by the Germans and to these were sent men, women and children, and from there to Auschwitz.

The resistance against the Germans grew stronger. Jews, together with large numbers of French, fought against the occupiers. Aid committees were also established to help Jews with false "Aryan" papers, with a hiding place. In this resistance movement our *landsleit* also participated.

Shlomo Zalman Kahane, in spite of his poor health, took an active part in the resistance against the Germans right to the end.

We paid with two young lives of our Ciechanówers. These were the two heroes who were shot by the Hitler brutes, namely: Shimon Bronstein (a son of Laibish Bronstein) and Bernard Coopershmid. They perished aged 20 and 21.

Landsmanshaft Activities after the Liberation

The joyous days arrived when the Allied forces, together with the resistance fighters, gave the death-blow to the Germans. Our hearts started to beat harder. We waited with bated breath, thinking that at any moment our dear ones would return, parents will find their children, children – their parents, but unfortunately a terrible picture unfolded for us.

Only a handful returned. We suffered horribly by this and thought it was the end of the world. But the will to live is stronger than everything With an iron will we started to reconstruct our destroyed homes. Slowly the few remnants, survivors of the lagers, started to return. Jews who had survived in Soviet Russia came to France. They told us the tragic news of our destroyed homes. The survivors who returned from the Soviet Union to Ciechanów and the surrounding *shtetlech* did not find anyone in the Poland they had left. Their first place of destination was France -- Paris.

For us, the very few survivors who still lived here, every new returnee, Chiechanow *landsman*, was a real treasure, a brother with whom we rejoiced. We helped and did everything in order to give him the first primary aid.

A new problem arose. We organized all our forces, though we ourselves were shattered from our experiences that we had suffered through in France. So, with the help of the Parisian *Yiddish* newspaper we gathered all the Ciechanówer survivors and formed the *landsmanshaft* with the name: "Friends of Ciechanów and

Surroundings," whose first undertaking was: to give the necessary primary aid to those who had come from various lagers.

The first meeting of the newly-formed *landsmanshaft* took place September 28, 1946. All surviving Ciechanówers were present, as well as survivors from the surrounding *shtetlech*: Mlava, Proshnitz, Makov, Schegova and Plonsk. After a very serious exchange of ideas, a committee of the following was elected: President - Yosl Mlotzker; vice-president - Henekh Perlmutter; secretary - Laibl Rosenblum; treasurer - Yitzhak Leib Kleinetz; auditors: Moishe Weinstock, Frau Faige Asherman (Sadiker) and Traister. The first objective of ours was to help establish, even though temporarily perhaps, the new arrivals, to provide them with legal papers and work permits. All this was connected with great difficulties. We had to pay for hotel rooms, where the survivors lived temporarily.

The committee formed: a commission to help the sick -- whose task it was to visit a sick member -- and a loan fund that issued loans without interest.

With the establishment of the State of Israel we, like other

511

Jewish organizations and "societies," participated in the great fund-raising for the *Haganah,* and at various oportunities collected food and other items for our brothers in Israel.

Frequent banquets and farewell evenings were arranged for the Ciechanówer who volunteered in Paris to fight for the independence of Israel.

At all undertakings related to helping Israel we take an active part. We did this, for example, by buying a sum of loan certificates.

Ciechanówers in Paris say farewell to their *landsman*, F. Tanenbaum, upon his departure for Israel

512

We also purchased 260 trees to plant in the Martyrs' Forest in memory of the Ciechanów Jews who perished.

*

In response to our announcement, all our *landsleit* come to the annual memorial for our nearest and dearest who perished, our martyrs. Every year the *El Malei Rachamim* is said and the traditional *Kaddish* is said. We always remember those who perished at the hands of the Hitlerite murderers.

The *landsmanshaft* also concerned itself with the Ciechanówers in France who pass away. A Jewish cemetery was established, for which the living are responsible. The problem of grave sites is a difficult one, particulary in a world-city such as Paris. For the laast 50 years no separate graves are allowed in Paris. The dead, who while alive did not have the possibility of belonging to an organization that has a cemetery, get buried for only 5 years. After this the remaining bones get burnt. As a result, it is a very serious problem without a Jewish cemetery that is called a *Brider Kever* (Brother Grave),

We have engraved on the monument the names of those who perished and every year the memorial service takes place where we mention as well those who died in Paris.

*

Our annual balls are a true family get-together of all *landsleit* and friends who live in Paris. We also correspond with Ciechanówers who are scattered around the world. Though we are separated from one another by thousands of kilometers, our hearts remain close to one another.

Y. Mlotzker

513

**A monument for the Ciechanówer Jews who perished, erected in the Parisian
"Brother Grave" by their surviving *landsleit***

514

Activities of the Ciechanów Landsmanshaft in Paris in the Light of Announcements in the Local Press

The following announcements that were published in the Parisian Jewish newspapers reflect the activities of the Parisian *landsmanshaftn*.

Society of Ciechanów Landsleit

Because of the situation that has recently arisen on account of the steady influx of our surviving-refugee *landsleit*, it has been decided to form a society in Paris, "Friends of Ciechanów And Its Surroundings," where all *landsleit* will be able to feel at home and will be able to benefit from direction and mutual help. At the last general meeting that took place September 28, in the presence of all Ciechanówers and the surrounding area, such as: Mlava, Proshnitz, Makov, Schegova and Plonsk. After a friendly exchange of ideas the following were elected as a committee: President - Yosl Mlotzker; vice-president - Henekh Perlmutter; secretary -- Laibl Rosenblum; treasurer -- Yitzhak Kleinetz; auditors: Moishe Weinstock, Madame Faige Asherman, and Traister. All those interested in joining our Society can call for information to friend Mlotzker, 14 rue Martel, evenings from 8 to 10.

October 3, 1946

Attention, Ciechanówers!

In order to express our rage at the renewal of racism, particularly the pogroms on Jews in Iraq, and in order to express our desire for peace, we invite all Ciechanówers to participate in a protest meeting today, Monday, in "Mityalita."

Mlotzker
President Of Ciechanów Landsleit 23.11.49

515

The Society "Friends of Ciechanów and Surroundings" And Yiddish Mutual Aid

Bernard Coopershmid

This past Sunday we, "Friends of Ciechanów And surroundings," and "Yiddish Mutual Aid" met in the Jewish cemetery Bania, where a monument was erected on the grave of the young hero, Bernard Coopershmid who, at the age of 20, was shot to death by the Germans on May 25, 1944 in the deportation from Ordesh.

A large crowd responded to both announcements.

First, friend Zilberman spoke as president of the Society "Yiddish Mutual Aid." He was followed by M. Mlotzker, president of the "Society of Ciechanówers and Surroundings." He reminded us of the cause for which the young Bernard had given his life, and called upon those assembled to unite against the new dangers that hang over us.

Finally friend Yitzhak Kleinitz spoke, making a strong appeal, saying that one of the ways of honoring the memory of young Bernard is to provide for the surviving children of deported and murdered Jews.

On the spot there was collected, in the name of both societies, 8,280 francs for the summer camps of the Central Children's Commissiion.

May 6, 1951

Ciechanów and Its Surroundings

Every year in the month of November we recall the destruction of our five thousand families by the Hitler-barbarians. The previous residents as well as new arrivals will come united to this day of curses for all murderers and enemies of the Jewish people.

In order to honor our destroyed ones, we appeal to all *landsleit* to come *Shabbat*, November 8, 9 p.m. to the Lankry Hall for a memorial evening. Our only surviving witness, Jack Kleinitz, will speak of the martyrdom of our dear ones of Ciechanów and surroundings.

Khazan Solomon will make the Azkarah

Nobody should be absent.

November 5, 1952
for the Committee:
President Mlotzker

Society of Friends of Ciechanów

The society "Friends of Ciechanów And Surroundings" appeals to all *landsleit* and friends to come Sunday, November 2, 3 p.m., to the Meri in Drancy in order to honor the tenth *yahrzeit* of the young hero, fallen partisan, Simon Bronstein.

Honor his memory!

All Landsleit of Ciechanów and Surroundings

We are meeting this *Shabbat*, June 12, 9 p.m., in the local of 8 rue Montage for

A Banquet

in honor of the departure of our *landsman* Dovid Shmid to Israel to fight in the ranks of the *Haganah* for the victory of the State of Israel and for the existence of our people.

The Committee

———————

A Festive Gathering of Ciechanówers and the Surroundings

In connection with the election in Paris of the well-known Israeli artist, Yehoshua Grosbard, who spent the youthful years in Ciechanów, and remained dearly beloved by all, we have the pleasure of announcing that we are having a festive gathering with him tomorrow, October 15, 9 p.m. in the "Eden" salon, 36 Bonne Nouvelle Blvd. We invite all our friends. A representative of the "Farband of Jewish Organizations" will be present. Refreshments will be served.

We ask everyone to be punctual

for the Committee
President Mlotzker

———————

We have given the announcements in the style that they were published. For the last three announcements there is no date of their appearance.

(editor's note)

Banquet of Ciechanów *landsleit* **in Paris. Reception for Binyamin Apel in Detroit**

A celebration of Ciechanówers and surroundings

A celebration of Ciechanówers and surroundings

Ciechanów Landsleit in Montreal

In Montreal, Canada, a Ciechanówer *landsmanshaft* has been organized. After the survivors arrived from the German extermination camps, the *landsmanshaft* broadened its activities. One of its main functions was – to help publish the *Yizkor Book* memorial of the perished Ciechanów *Kehillah*.

Ciechanów *landsmanshaft* organization in Montreal.
President -- Dovid Mlovsky, 2nd row from top, 6th one from right

Epilogue

With this Ciechanów book the destroyed holy *Kehillah* of the Polish *shtetl* of Ciechanów near the Lidinia River enters the literary-eternity. We do not use the word *matzaivah* (monument) here as it is usually used for the *Yizkor Books* of destroyed *Kehillot*, because the concept *matzaivah* evokes in our minds a specific earthly place, a heap of earth, over which there is engraved on a stone *"Poh Nikvar"* ("Here lies buried").

The mourners of Ciechanów do not have where to inscribe *"Poh Nikvar."* The German destroyers wiped out the *Kehillah* in such a way that even the bones of the destroyed martyrs did not get their eternal rest in the graves. What did remain, however, were the great deeds of their spiritual ancestral and communal life. The curse of the destroyed ones to those who murdered and hung them and the bright hope of those who died through such agonies, that the truth must have its victory and the murderers will get their punishment.

These non-physical remains that stir the minds of the survivors of the destroyed Ciechanów Kehillah, the exalted historical deeds, recorded in chronicles and old documents, collected and included in this Yizkor Book, give the large picture of the Ciechanów Jewish people who, for hundreds of years, led their lives in sanctity and holiness. The memories of the survivors -- the witnesses and sufferers of the German extermination -- are, in this book -- the great accusation act against the armed military-gangs who tortured and murdered these innocent Jews.

Exalted and holy is the debt that the survivors of the murdered Kehillah took upon themselves to memorialize them in the Yizkor Books. This undertaking is accomplished by a few idealists, true emissaries for us all. Such emissaries are the few Ciechanów Jews who took upon themselves the heavy responsibility of gathering material and documents, to influence the survivors of our Shtetl to write their memoirs.

It is not easy to influence Jews who went through the hell of the German extermination to record their painful experiences. Everyone wants to forget the horrendous past. Therefore, great thanks and recognition are due the idealistic public emissaries who do not let it be forgotten, but demand: Tell, open your wounds, let the world see the wrinkles in your faces. Maybe that will help to remind the world leaders to take precautions that there should never again occur a Nazi fascist extermination of Jews nor others.

The editorial committee of the *Yizkor Book* of the Ciechanów Jewish *Kehillah*.
R to L: Noah Zabludowicz, Zola Apel, Yaacov Rubinstein, editor A. Wolf
Yasni; Moishe Fuchs, Yaacov Bronrot, Riva Gonska-Leshed, Yehoshua
Grosbard, Moishe Kolka

Moishe Leser

Binyamin Apel

The last word has not been said yet about the life and destruction
of Ciechanów Jewry nor of Polish Jewry in general. New writings are

always surfacing about the destroyed Jews who, in their last moments of their tragic lives, remembered to leave for future generations, hidden in the ground, the painful *megillah* of their experiences.

Just recently a diary was found in the Auschwitz extermination lager, half of which was written by a Ciechanówer, Zalman Levental. As this *Yizkor Book* was being finalized, this new-found book had not yet reached us. We simply want to note that such a diary that bears the name, **"Łodz Ghetto"** – was found. The editorial committee of the Ciechanów Jewish *Yizkor Book* will try to bring to its *landsleit* the diary of Zalman Levental, who was painfully put to death in Auschwitz.

A. Wolf Yasni

Paid Announcements Memorializing Families

(Includes names and some photos of Shoah victims)

Please note that the page numbers of the page numbers in the original book.

Name	Page
Atinger	452
Altus	449
Apel	440
Apel	451
Berman	436
Berman	443
Bermson	438
Bronrot	452
Burshtein	445
Dan	441
Eisenberg	448
Fuchs	436
Fuchs	439
Galadzsher	445
Gastamsky	441
Gezuntheit	452
Goldshmit	436
Gonska	446
Greenbaum	452
Groskind	443

Kahane	445
Kalfus	438
Kapota	454
Kirshenbaum	442
Kostsheva (Kesler)	444
Kulka	445
Kviat	449
Listopad	444
Loznik	442
Luxenberg	451
Malina	455
Mandzshok	452
Margolis	454
Mekuver	450
Melotzker	445
Milovsky	455
Mondri	443
Oistriak	448
Parma	456
Pisage	440
Pudolovitz	451
Rosenthal	454
Shablovsky	444

Table of Contents of the Original Yizkor Book

Pictures and Illustrations
Paid announcements memorializing families

INDEX

www.ingramcontent.com/pod-product-compliance
Lightning Source LLC
Chambersburg PA
CBHW082007150426
42814CB00005BA/250